Palgrave Studies in Financial Services Technology

Series Editor
Bernardo Nicoletti, Rome, Roma, Italy

The Palgrave Studies in Financial Services Technology series features original research from leading and emerging scholars on contemporary issues and developments in financial services technology. Falling into 4 broad categories: channels, payments, credit, and governance; topics covered include payments, mobile payments, trading and foreign transactions, big data, risk, compliance, and business intelligence to support consumer and commercial financial services. Covering all topics within the life cycle of financial services, from channels to risk management, from security to advanced applications, from information systems to automation, the series also covers the full range of sectors: retail banking, private banking, corporate banking, custody and brokerage, wholesale banking, and insurance companies. Titles within the series will be of value to both academics and those working in the management of financial services.

Thomas Walker · Elaheh Nikbakht ·
Maher Kooli
Editors

The Fintech Disruption

How Financial Innovation Is Transforming
the Banking Industry

Editors
Thomas Walker
John Molson School of Business
Concordia University
Montreal, QC, Canada

Elaheh Nikbakht
John Molson School of Business
Concordia University
Montreal, QC, Canada

Maher Kooli
Department of Finance, School
of Management (ESG)
University of Quebec at Montreal
Montreal, QC, Canada

ISSN 2662-5083   ISSN 2662-5091   (electronic)
Palgrave Studies in Financial Services Technology
ISBN 978-3-031-23071-4   ISBN 978-3-031-23069-1   (eBook)
https://doi.org/10.1007/978-3-031-23069-1

This Palgrave Macmillan imprint is published by the registered company Springer Nature Switzerland AG
The registered company address is: Gewerbestrasse 11, 6330 Cham, Switzerland

PREFACE

Although banking is a well-known and long-standing concept, the banking industry and its procedures have experienced many changes throughout history. In recent years, financial technologies (fintech) have started to completely transform the banking sector. Thanks to fintech, banks now use more efficient methods to provide their regular services and offer new ones to their clients. Yet, despite these advantages, fintech also brings new challenges to the banking industry. In addition to affecting the regulation and security of banking operations and creating environmental opportunities and challenges, fintech paves the way for new rivals—fintech companies—that offer the same services as traditional banks at a lower cost. As a result, banks experience a significant rise in competition from both other banks and newly emerging fintech firms. This book investigates the effect of fintech on banks and banking procedures and how it revolutionizes the banking sector. Moreover, the book sheds light on the ethical and privacy issues associated with fintech, as well as the new competitors emerging in this market.

The book includes contributions from an international community of scholars and practitioners who work at the interface of fintech, banking, artificial intelligence, and finance. The authors review and critically analyze new developments at the intersection of fintech and banking, and provide different perspectives on its impact on the banking sector. The book features contributions investigating the technical side of fintech, exploring the theory and mechanisms behind these innovations, and examining their applications in the banking context. Moreover, the book includes contributions that explore possible challenges that fintech may pose to the banking industry, and potential policies and solutions to overcome them. The book concludes with contributions highlighting and comparing fintech transformations in the banking sector across different countries and provides tips and lessons learned from these practical cases.

Montreal, Canada   Thomas Walker
                                                       Elaheh Nikbakht
                                                        Maher Kooli

ACKNOWLEDGMENTS

We acknowledge the financial support provided through the Jacques Ménard—BMO Centre for Capital Markets at Concordia University. In addition, we appreciate the excellent copy-editing and editorial assistance we received from Meaghan Landrigan-Buttle, Gabrielle Machnik-Kekesi, Mauran Pavan, Charlotte Frank, Victoria Kelly, Miles Murphy, and Maya Michaeli.

CONTENTS

NOTES ON CONTRIBUTORS

Kaleemullah Abbasi is currently serving as Assistant Professor in the Department of Management Sciences & Technology, the Begum Nusrat Bhutto Women University, Sukkur, Pakistan. He earned his Ph.D. from the University of Salford, UK. His research interests are focused on corporate governance, climate change, fintech, audit committees, and gender diversity. His research work has been published in top-rated journals, namely the *Journal of Business Research, Technological Forecasting and Social Change, Economics Letters,* and *Corporate Governance: The International Journal of Business in Society.* He attained the highest marks in Pakistan for paper F9 (Financial Management) of the Association of Chartered Certified Accountants (ACCA), UK. He obtained his M.A. in Accounting and Finance from the University of Huddersfield, UK, and completed his B.Sc. in Applied Accounting from Oxford Brookes University, UK.

Charles Adjasi is Professor of Development Finance and Economics at Stellenbosch University and Head of Research at Stellenbosch Business School. He is also a visiting professor at ENSEA Cote d'Ivoire and recently an Afreximbank Research Fellow. He previously worked as a visiting professor in the Department of Economics, Econometrics and Finance, University of Groningen. His research focuses on financial markets, firm productivity, and household welfare development in Africa. He has published widely in reputable journals, has co-edited one book, and co-authored another.

Ashraful Alam is a lecturer in accounting and finance at the Salford Business School, University of Salford, UK. He has earned his Ph.D. in the area of R&D investment in emerging economies. His research interest revolves around R&D investment and governance in emerging markets, climate change, fintech, gender diversity, institutions, accounting practices, and accounting changes. He has published articles in *R&D Management*, the *International Journal of Accounting*, *Technological Forecasting & Social Change*, the *Journal of Business Research*, *Business Strategy and the Environment*, *Economics Letters*, the *Annals of Operations Research*, and the *Journal of Applied Accounting Research*.

Andrea Barbon is an assistant professor at the University of St. Gallen and a faculty member of the Swiss Finance Institute. In 2020, he received his Ph.D. in Finance from the University of Lugano, completing the Swiss Finance Institute Ph.D. program. During his Ph.D. studies, he spent the 2018–2019 academic year as a visiting fellow at Harvard Business School. His papers on asset pricing and (unconventional) monetary policy have been published in top-tier journals in finance.

Imtiaz Ali Brohi is Associate Professor in the Department of Information and Communication Technologies at the Begum Nusrat Bhutto Women University, Sukkur, Pakistan, where he is also acting as Director of the Quality Enhancement Cell (QEC). He earned his Ph.D. in Information Technology from International Islamic University Malaysia where he was recognized with a Best Ph.D. Student Award. He has published in various reputable journals. His research interests involve blockchain, fintech, and artificial intelligence.

Noor Ahmed Brohi received his Ph.D. in Management with a dissertation written on the impact of servant leadership on employee psychological safety, psychological capital, and turnover intention at the Putra Business School, Universiti Putra Malaysia (UPM-PBS) in July 2019 with distinction (Best Ph.D. Student Award). His areas of interest are human resources management, leadership, human resource development, human psychology, and organizational behavior. He has authored more than 30 international refereed journal articles, book chapters, and conference papers. He is a trained expert in the usage of various statistical tools such as Structural Equation Modelling (SEM) and Partial Least Squares (PLS-SEM). He has also conducted SEM and Business Research

Methods-related workshops at the Putra Business School, University Putra Malaysia, the International Islamic University Malaysia, and Shaheed Benazir Bhutto University—Sanghar Campus. He is currently serving as Head of the Department of Management Sciences & Technology, Begum Nusrat Bhutto Women University, Sukkur, Pakistan.

Simona Cosma is Associate Professor in Financial Markets and Institutions at the University of Salento, Lecce, Italy, where she teaches risk management in banks and the economics of financial intermediaries. She previously worked as an affiliate professor at the SDA Bocconi School of Management (Banking and Insurance Department), Milan, Italy. Her research activity mainly focuses on risk management, corporate governance, and sustainability. She is the author and co-author of many books and articles in international scholarly journals such as *Business Strategy and the Environment, Corporate Social Responsibility* and *Environmental Management*, and the *Journal of Management & Governance*. She is a board member of a non-listed financial company and a listed non-financial company.

Stefano Cosma is Full Professor of Banking and Finance in the Communication and Economics Department, University of Modena and Reggio Emilia, where he is a member of the Center for Studies in Banking and Finance (CEFIN). He is also a member of the Italian Association of University Teachers in Financial Intermediaries and Markets (Adeimf) and the European Association of University Teachers in Banking and Finance (the Wolpertinger Club). He is a member of the scientific committee of the Banking and Financial Diploma (Italian Banking Association, ABI) and the Foundation for Financial Education and Saving Plans (FEDUF). He is chairman of Sella Personal Credit, Smartika (P2P Lending), and Nephis (Sella Group) and serves as Director of Holostem Advanced Therapies. His recent research topics include consumer credit, retail banking, digital transformation in financial intermediation, customer behavior, and household finance. He is the author of international and national books and articles on these subjects.

Emīls Dārziņš started working at the Bank of Latvia in 2021. Before that, he worked at the Investment and Development Agency of Latvia, where he supported start-ups, including actively participating in the development of fintech companies and innovations. By joining the team of the Bank of Latvia, he actively participates in the development of instant payments and innovative payment infrastructure and services. He received his education at the Faculty of Business, Management and Economics of the University of Latvia. He is now leading the Payment Systems Policy Division at Latvijas Banka.

Dalton Boechat Filho holds an M.B.A. in Finance from the COPPEAD Graduate School of Business of the Federal University of Rio de Janeiro (UFRJ). He is a former senior analyst in economic studies at the Brazilian Association of Financial and Capital Markets Entities (Anbima).

Deniss Filipovs worked at the Bank of Latvia for ten years. He managed the Payment Systems Policy Division of the Payment Systems Department with the responsibility for oversight and development of payment systems and payment instruments in Latvia and Europe. He monitored trends in fintech and analyzed the impact of new technologies on the financial market infrastructure. In February 2022, he joined Tietoevry as a strategic business developer for the payments business line. He is a graduate of Riga Technical University. He holds an M.Sc. in Business Economics and an M.Sc. in Business Informatics (with distinction).

Makhmoor Fiza is currently working as a lecturer (Electrical Technology/Engineering) in the Department of Management Sciences & Technology, Begum Nusrat Bhutto Women University, Sukkur, Pakistan. She previously served as Assistant Director in the Higher Education Commission (HEC), Islamabad. She received her B.E. in Electrical Engineering from Sukkur IBA, Pakistan, in 2015, and her M.Sc. from Abasyn University Islamabad, Pakistan. Her research interests include educational management, machine learning, and deep learning.

Charlotte Frank completed her Bachelor's degree in the Humanities at Carleton University, Ottawa. She holds an M.A. in English Literature and Creative Writing from Concordia University, Montreal, where she is a research associate at the John Molson School of Business. She is currently completing a Ph.D. with a focus on the poet Elizabeth Bishop at McGill University.

Christoph Frei is a professor of mathematical finance at the University of Alberta. After receiving his Ph.D. from ETH Zurich, he was a researcher at École Polytechnique in Paris before joining the University of Alberta. He has collaborated with several financial institutions and companies, including the Alberta Investment Management Corporation (AIMCo), ATB Financial, Canadian Western Bank, and UBS. He was a visiting researcher at the U.S. Federal Reserve Board and currently serves as regional co-director of the Professional Risk Managers' International Association (PRMIA). His research interests are in quantitative finance, mathematical economics, and risk management, including questions related to financial technology.

Calumn Hamilton is a Ph.D. candidate at the University of Groningen and an affiliate of the Groningen Growth and Development Center. His research focuses on development economics at the macroeconomic level, including areas such as structural change, aid effectiveness, the interaction of gender and development, and financial inclusion. He is involved in the construction and maintenance of various publicly available large-scale macroeconomic databases. His first book was co-authored with Charles Adjasi and Robert Lensink and was published by Edward Elgar in the summer of 2022.

Wesley L. Harris is Professor of Technology Management researching in the Department of Aeronautics and Astronautics, Massachusetts Institute of Technology, and at the Leonardo Research Centre, Imperial College London.

Laurenz Heppding is a graduate student of Computer Science and Business Information Systems at the Technical University of Darmstadt, Germany.

Victoria Kelly recently graduated from Concordia University (Montreal) with a B.Sc. in biology with an additional major in Irish Studies. She plans to pursue her studies with an independent master's degree examining the 1832 cholera epidemic and its management on a social, urban, economic, and medical level, drawing parallels to the recent COVID-19 pandemic.

Maher Kooli holds a B.Sc. degree from HEC Carthage, an M.B.A. from Ottawa University, and a Ph.D. in Finance from Université Laval. He is a full professor of finance in the Department of Finance of the School of Management (ESG), Université du Québec à Montréal (UQAM), where he also serves as head of the Finance Department. He is a Caisse de Depot et Placement de Québec (CDPQ) research chair-holder in portfolio management, founder of the trading room at ESG UQAM, and

Autorite des marches financiers (AMF) and Finance Montreal research co-chair-holder in fintech at ESG UQAM. Previously, he worked as a senior research advisor for the Caisse de Depot et Placement de Québec. His research interests include initial public offerings, mergers and acquisitions, venture capital, hedge funds, fintech, portfolio management, and corporate finance. He has published in many prestigious academic journals and has several books on financial management, venture capital, and hedge funds. He is also a member of the editorial board of the *Journal of Asset Management*, the *Journal of Wealth Management*, and *Risk Management*.

Meaghan Landrigan-Buttle holds a Master's degree in History from Concordia University (Montreal), with a focus on Irish Studies. She has experience in project management, conference planning, and tutoring and holds a professional development certificate in professional editing from the University of Waterloo. She has worked as a teaching assistant in the History Department and at the School of Irish Studies at Concordia. Her research interests include the First World War, the uses and misuses of history, the consumption of history via popular culture and commemoration, memory studies, and genealogy. She began her Ph.D. research at Concordia University in the fall of 2022.

Minh T. H. Le is a lecturer in the Department of Marketing at the University of Economics Ho Chi Minh City (UEH), Vietnam. She holds a Ph.D. in Marketing from QUT, Australia. Her research has been published in journals such as *Current Psychology*, the *Spanish Journal of Marketing*, and the *Journal of Marketing Analytics*. Her work has been presented at leading international marketing conferences. Her research focuses on consumer-brand relationships, artificial intelligence in marketing, and scale development.

Robert Lensink is an economist, with specific research interests covering gender studies, impact analyses, and financial inclusion in developing countries. He is a tenured professor of finance at the Faculty of Economics and Business (FEB), University of Groningen (UG), and a "Professor Extraordinary" at the University of Stellenbosch, South Africa. He is currently the vice-dean research at FEB, UG. He is also a resource person for the African Economic Research Consortium (AERC). He has published more than 120 articles in peer-reviewed journals, including economics journals like the *American Economic Review*, the *Economic Journal*, the *Journal of Development Economics*, and the *Journal of Public*

Economics as well as psychology journals like the *British Journal of Social Psychology* and *Frontiers of Psychology*, and multidisciplinary journals like World Development. He has (co-) authored 5 books, edited 4 books, and published more than 30 book chapters.

Luiz Macahyba is a Ph.D. Candidate in Public Policy, Strategies, and Development at the Federal University of Rio de Janeiro (UFRJ). He is the former Superintendent at the Brazilian Association of Financial and Capital Markets Entities (Anbima).

Gabrielle Machnik-Kekesi is a Ph.D. candidate and Hardiman Research Scholar at the Centre for Irish Studies at the National University of Ireland, Galway. She holds an Individualized Program Master's degree from Concordia University, which was funded by both the Social Sciences and Humanities Research Council (SSHRC) and the Fonds de recherche du Québec en Société et Culture (FRQSC), and a Master's in Information Studies from McGill University. Her research interests include modern Irish history, food, domestic space, and cultural heritage.

Norberto Montani Martins is a professor at the Institute of Economics, Federal University of Rio de Janeiro (UFRJ). He holds a Ph.D. in Economics from UFRJ, with a visiting period at the University of Leeds. He is a former senior analyst in regulatory studies at the Brazilian Association of Financial and Capital Markets Entities (Anbima, 2012–2015) and a former research assistant at EBAPE/FGV (2010–2011).

Miles Murphy is a graduate of the School of Irish Studies at Concordia University. He has been a researcher, writer, and editor on a variety of projects and publications. He is a former Professional Test Developer and Standards Manager and was Director of Exam Design and Development with Moody's Analytics. He has experience in areas of adult education, finance, the built environment, mining, energy, health, and public safety.

Shahzad Nasim currently serves as Vice Chancellor of the Begum Nusrat Bhutto Women University, Sukkur, Pakistan. He is also a professor in the Department of Management Sciences & Technology at the Begum Nusrat Bhutto Women University, Sukkur, Pakistan. He possesses both academic and industry experience. He has served as a permanent and visiting faculty member at various institutes and universities in Pakistan for the last seventeen years and has published in various reputable journals. He holds a B.S. (Biomedical Engineering) from Sir Syed University of Engineering and Technology (Pakistan), M.E. (Electronics) from NED University of Engineering & Technology (Pakistan), M.B.A. (Marketing & Finance) from Hamdard University (Pakistan), M.S. (Management Sciences) from the Institute of Business & Technology (IBT) (Pakistan), and a Ph.D. (Economics) from Hamdard University (Pakistan).

Elaheh Nikbakht holds an M.Sc. degree in Finance from the John Molson School of Business, Concordia University. She currently serves as a research assistant in the Department of Finance at Concordia University. In addition, she works as a data and reporting administrator in Global Entity Services at Maples Group. She completed her undergraduate degree and M.B.A. in Iran. She has been awarded several scholarships and awards for her academic performance, including the Arbour Foundation Scholarship and the Bourse D'études D'excellence du Centre Desjardins D'innovation en Financement D'entreprises.

Anna Omarini is a researcher with tenure in financial markets and intermediaries in the Department of Finance at Bocconi University (Italy) where she is also course director for the undergraduate course "FinTech for digital transformation in banking" and for the graduate course "Banks and fintech: Vision and strategy." She is also a Knowledge Group Banking and Insurance faculty member at SDA Bocconi School of Management. Her expertise is in bank strategy and management, digital banking, fintech, open banking and payments, and she has authored articles, papers, and books on these issues. She serves as a reviewer and editorial board member for several journals and is a member of numerous associations, organizations, and scientific committees. She graduated in business administration, with a specialization in banking and financial markets, from Bocconi University. She obtained an ITP (International Teachers Program) degree at the Stern Business School, New York University. She has also been an independent board director in banks and other financial institutions.

Mauran Pavan is an undergraduate student in Computer Science at Concordia University where he specializes on web services and applications. He has previous experience working at a start-up in the entertainment and tourism sector. His interests lie in fintech, sustainability, and emerging new technologies.

Daniela Pennetta is a research fellow in the Marco Biagi Department of Economics, University of Modena and Reggio Emilia. She holds a

Ph.D. in Labour, Development and Innovation from Marco Biagi Foundation, Modena, Italy. Her research interests broadly concern banking and digital transformation in financial intermediation, with a particular focus on fintech, open banking, and banking platforms.

Nadeera Ranabahu is a senior lecturer in entrepreneurship and innovation in the Department of Management, Marketing, and Entrepreneurship at the University of Canterbury, New Zealand. Her research focuses on minority or marginalized groups in entrepreneurship, employment, and innovation in different societies. Currently, she has ongoing research projects focused on women, refugees, youth/students, migrants, and low-income people. In addition, she studies the use of innovative initiatives, such as microfinance and fintech, for entrepreneurship and employment among the marginalized.

Angelo Ranaldo is a full professor of finance and systemic risk at the University of St. Gallen and a Swiss Finance Institute (SFI) senior chair. He has served as a consultant and scientific advisor to international institutions such as the Bank of England, the Bank of International Settlements, Swiss National Bank, and the European Central Bank that awarded him the 2018 Duisenberg Fellowship.

Ramona Rupeika-Apoga is a professor of finance and the head of the Department of Finance and Accounting at the University of Latvia. She holds the positions of visiting professor at the University of Lodz in Poland and affiliate professor at the University of Malta. She has over twenty years of pedagogical experience in Latvian and European higher education institutions, with specialized knowledge in risk management, international finance, fintech, and corporate digital transformation. She has led and participated in a number of international and local studies and research projects.

Paula Marina Sarno is a post-doctoral researcher at the Graduate Program in Economics, Fluminense Federal University (UFF) and worked as an analyst at the Brazilian Securities and Exchange Commission (CVM).

Agnieszka Sikorska has completed her LL.B. (hons.) and her LL.M. in International and Commercial Dispute Resolution at the University of Westminster. She practiced Personal Injury before moving into teaching.

She has taught a range of modules at the University of Law, including mediation and international arbitration.

Malgorzata Sulimierska is a senior lecturer in banking and fintech in the Department of Business and Management at the University of Sussex Business School and is a fellow of the Higher Education Academy. She holds Fintech and Blockchain Qualifications from the University of Oxford and a Ph.D. in Financial Economics from the University of Sussex (UK). She is involved in research and teaching at numerous institutions including Lancaster University (UK), Catholic Leuven University (Belgium), and Loughborough University (UK). Her teaching skills have been valued by several teaching awards including the BMEs Oscar Award for the best seminar tutor, an excellence in teaching award, and a student-led teaching award. Her passion for teaching and discovering new areas of development guides her interests toward fintech, banking digitalization, financial literary, financial inclusion, and political uncertainty.

Thomas Walker is a full professor of finance, the director, and academic lead of the Emerging Risks Information Center (ERIC), the inaugural director for the Jacques Ménard/BMO Center for Capital Markets, and the Concordia University Research Chair in Emerging Risk Management (Tier 1) at Concordia University in Montreal, Canada. He previously served as an associate dean, department chair, and director of Concordia's David O'Brien Centre for Sustainable Enterprise. Prior to his academic career, he worked for firms such as Mercedes Benz, KPMG, and Utility Consultants International. He has published over 70 journal articles and books.

Stefan Wendt is a professor and dean of the Department of Business at Bifröst University in Iceland. Previously, he was an associate professor at Reykjavik University's Department of Business Administration in Iceland and a research and teaching assistant in the Department of Finance at Bamberg University, Germany, where he received his doctoral degree in 2010. He has taught as a visiting lecturer at the École Supérieure de Commerce Montpellier, France, and Baden-Württemberg Cooperative State University (DHBW), Mosbach, Germany. His fields of research include corporate finance and governance, sustainability and ESG, risk management, fintech and digitalization, financial markets and financial intermediation, small and medium-sized enterprises, and behavioral finance.

Axel Wieandt is the former CEO of HRE and Valovis Bank. He currently serves as a full professor of finance at WHU Otto-Beisheim School of Management and as an adjunct professor of finance at the J.L. Kellogg Graduate School of Management, Northwestern University.

Jarunee Wonglimpiyarat is Professor of Technology Management, researching in the Department of Aeronautics and Astronautics, Massachusetts Institute of Technology, and at the Leonardo Research Centre, Imperial College London.

LIST OF FIGURES

LIST OF TABLES

CHAPTER 1

Fintech and Banking: An Overview

Thomas Walker, Elaheh Nikbakht, and Maher Kooli

INTRODUCTION

History records that in ancient Rome, Egypt, and Babylon, wealthy individuals were in the habit of storing their coins and jewels in the basements of temples. Temples, consequently, were able to use this collateral to provide loans to others. This original "bank" later developed into a standalone financial entity in order to be able to provide other types of financial services, like facilitating monetary transactions with foreign countries or investing in a wide variety of assets (Andreau, 2020). Since then, banks have been an inseparable part of the financial services

T. Walker (✉) · E. Nikbakht (✉)
Concordia University, Montreal, QC, Canada
e-mail: thomas.walker@concordia.ca

E. Nikbakht
e-mail: elaheh.nikbakht@concordia.ca

M. Kooli
University of Quebec at Montreal, Montreal, QC, Canada
e-mail: kooli.maher@uqam.ca

1

industry, and although the banking sector has developed gradually since, it is not until very recently that the banking industry has undergone such radical transformations, due, in large part, to emerging technologies (Iman, 2019). New innovations such as artificial intelligence, machine learning, blockchain, cryptocurrencies, and online banking, collectively known as fintech, have revolutionized banking operations and services (Stulz, 2019).

On the one hand, these innovations provide a platform for banks to deliver their existing services faster and more efficiently. For example, by using artificial intelligence, banks can offer chatbots, virtual assistants, and Robo-advisors that establish a direct connection with clients and enable the delivery of multiple services without the need for human intervention (Paul & Singh, 2019). Another example is machine learning, which reduces the risk of human errors when analyzing big datasets, performs highly complex calculations, and develops sophisticated models that ultimately result in better decision-making by banks (Rath et al., 2021). In addition to improving existing services, these technologies can assist banks in offering new services to their clients, such as investing in cryptocurrencies or online banking. Complex technologies like blockchain that make it impossible to change, delete, or destroy information and digital encryption allow customers to operate safely and confidently when using online services to perform financial transactions (Cocco et al., 2017).

On the other hand, fintech technologies also pave the way for other non-bank corporations to provide financial services traditionally offered only by banks (Klus et al., 2019). The creation of the first fintech company occurred in 1866 when Western Union used the Morse code and the telegraph to complete financial transactions. Recent advancements in fintech technologies have allowed companies like Google, Amazon, Microsoft, Apple, and Alibaba to constantly improve the security, availability, and diversity of their financial services (Mohamed & Ali, 2018), to the point where they can now compete directly with banks, by providing easy access to financial services at a lower cost (Arslanian & Fischer, 2019). Bill Gates, the founder of Microsoft, has aptly said that "banking is necessary, banks are not." These new competitors may eventually replace traditional banks altogether.

Though new technologies may reduce entry barriers in the banking sector and offer significant improvements, they bring their own challenges in terms of privacy, security, and regulation (Nuyens, 2019). Advancements such as online payments, digital identity verification methods, traceability of customer interactions, and greater access to personal data bring new security and Information Technology (IT) risks. Regulators and financial institutions are actively working on new rules and strategies to increase the transparency, integrity, and security of fintech innovations. Users are advised to constantly evaluate and assess the ongoing risks and challenges and to update their knowledge and software accordingly (Degerli, 2019).

Thus, fintech innovation is a double-edged sword, helping banks improve and create new services for their users, while at the same time, helping their rivals compete for the same customers. Therefore, it is inevitable that banks will strive to quickly identify these innovations and adopt them in a way that maximizes their benefit. At the same time, banks must understand the new risks and threats caused by implementing these innovations in order to identify and manage them effectively (Temelkov, 2018).

Our book aims to provide both practice-oriented and academic insights into the disruptive power of fintech for the banking industry: (1) whether and how the banking industry can use newly emerging technologies in the financial sphere to its advantage while managing any associated risks, (2) how these technologies affect traditional banking service formats as well as the pricing of these services, and (3) whether the emergence of fintech in the banking industry calls for a rethinking of existing banking regulations such as the Basel Accords, as well as country-specific regulations.

Previous publications in this area typically ignore the interdependent relationships among emerging technologies and overlook the connection between fintech as a whole and the future of the banking industry. Our book aims to address this gap by providing a comprehensive overview of various fintech applications and by analyzing what they mean for the future of banking. By taking both a practitioner-oriented approach and academic approach, featuring insights provided by experts in both finance and technology, we focus on the challenges presented to banking supervisors as they strive to strike a balance between the relative risks and rewards of implementing new financial technology.

Overview of Content

To provide a complete overview of the effects of fintech on the banking sector, the first section of this book is dedicated to describing traditional banking and its challenges. It also investigates different fintech innovations and organizations, and how they are transforming the banking sectors. The following section extensively reviews the opportunities that fintech brings to the banking sector, as well as the unique challenges involved with implementing fintech developments. It also addresses different regulations and policies that could be helpful in order to control and mitigate the risks associated with fintech innovations and organizations. The final section provides real-world case studies from around the globe regarding the subject and offers guidelines to adapt fintech to the banking industry.

PART I: FINANCIAL TECHNOLOGIES AND THEIR EFFECT ON THE BANKING INDUSTRY

The first section looks at the traditional financial system and its challenges and drawbacks. Then, it investigates various innovations under fintech and how they are transforming the banking industry.

The section begins with Chapter 2, *Centralized and Decentralized Finance: Coexistence or Convergence?* a comprehensive study and comparison of centralized and decentralized finance. **Wieandt** and **Heppding** provide an overview of centralized financial institutions (CeFi) like banks that are associated with traditional financial systems and explain their challenges. They next investigate how fintech innovations like blockchain are creating a new form of financial intermediation named decentralized finance (DeFi) and present its advantages and disadvantages compared to CeFi. They also analyze different scenarios about the future paths of CeFi and DeFi and present examples of real-world asset markets to illustrate the subject.

Following this, Chapter 3, *Fintech and the Digital Transformation of the Banking Landscape,* evaluates fintech-based innovations through the lens of systemic innovation to understand how it is transforming the banking landscape. In this chapter, **Harris** and **Wonglimpiyarat** study the development of the systemic innovation model to provide a better understanding of the systemic nature of fintech, as well as the progress and pattern of fintech-based innovation diffusion. They analyze the diffusion of all banking innovations, including fintech-based innovations launched in the last 70 years up to the present, as well as the potential disruption/revolution of the banking landscape due to the global COVID-19 pandemic.

Chapter 4, *The Shifting Paradigm in Banking: A Return to Wide-Banking in Financial Service Formats*, evaluates the approaches by which banks are seeking to retain customer loyalty in a competitive market where fintech and Bigtech companies have developed more innovative financial service formats. In this chapter, **Omarini** highlights the fintech trends impacting banking frameworks and the evolving relationships between banks and fintech companies. She describes upcoming opportunities for all the banking sector players, and the challenges they might face.

Chapter 5, *Competitors and Partners at the Same Time: On the role of Fintech companies in the Latvian financial market*, provides a viewpoint of the new players in the banking sector named fintech companies. As the name suggests, these companies use fintech innovations to offer some banking services to their clients. By following a case study approach, **Rupeika-Apoga**, **Dārziņš**, **Filipovs**, and **Wendt** present a detailed description of fintech companies, their mechanisms, performance, profitability, business, and revenue models, as well as workforce and regulatory challenges. They also discuss how these companies pose new challenges to banks and transform the banking sector.

Chapter 6, *Non-Fungible Tokens*, explores a specific type of fintech innovation named Non-Fungible Tokens (NFT), unique digital assets providing proof of ownership and verification of authenticity held in the blockchain. In Chapter 6, **Barbon** and **Ranaldo** describe NFTs, how they are created, and the different types of them. Then, they discuss deeper how these digital assets could impact financial markets and more specifically banking industry.

PART II: CHALLENGES, OPPORTUNITIES, AND REGULATIONS REGARDING FINTECH IN THE BANKING INDUSTRY

After exploring fintech innovations and companies, their effect on the banking sector, and the necessity to adapt to them, the second section aims to present a deeper insight into the opportunities and challenges that fintech brings to this sector. It also highlights the potential regulations that are required to adjust to this new market.

The section begins with Chapter 7, *Open Banking: Opportunities and Risks*, which describes open banking and presents the risks and challenges it might impose. **Frei** reviews different types of risks associated with open banking including technical, social, economic, and regulatory risks and discusses the mitigation strategies. He also highlights different countries' approaches toward adapting open banking considering their economic, social, and regulatory situation.

Chapter 8, *The Rise of Financial Services Ecosystems: Towards Open Banking Platforms*, looks at the fintech and banking relationship from the perspective of information sharing regulations. **Cosma, Cosma,** and **Pennetta** aim to examine the impact of fintech on the banks' ability to generate value through managing information asymmetry issues and build long-term relationships with their clients and how regulations can be effective in this regard. They investigate a European regulation for electronic payment services (Payment Services Directive 2) and how open banking is a different approach to complying with it.

Chapter 9, *The Crypto-assets Market in the United Kingdom: Regulatory and Legal Challenges,* examines the developments in the crypto-assets market. Using a literature review and case study-guided approach of the UK, **Sulimierska** and **Sikorska** show how the crypto-assets market has changed in the past years and how this is going to affect the banking sector. Next, they extensively investigate this subject from the regulatory perspective and compare different regulatory approaches specifically in the UK market.

Chapter 10, *A Preliminary Comparison of Two Ecosystems: Fintech Opportunities and Challenges for Financial Inclusion*, focuses on the policy, culture, human capital, finance, market, and support domains to identify system-level challenges and opportunities for fintech organizations. **Ranabahu** employs the case study approach of two ecosystems in South Asia to present a comparison between established and emergent systems for fintech organizations. The author investigates the related challenges and regulations in these two ecosystems and how it impacts the banking sector.

The concluding chapter in the section, Chapter 11, *Variables that Increase the Desire and Loyalty to Utilize Fintech After the COVID-19 Lockdown: A New Normal Habit*, studies the bank customers' behavior after the COVID-19 lockdown and how fintech can help banks to acquire the opportunities that this new habit offers. **Le** examines the effect of *COVID-19 lockdown* on bank clients' perceived usefulness of fintech in various aspects including trust, loyalty, data security and privacy, and quality of administrative services.

PART III: EVIDENCE FROM AROUND THE WORLD

The final section of the book, *Evidence from around the world*, takes a case study approach to examine fintech and banking relations from different local perspectives and how these local perspectives could serve as an example for the global landscape.

The first chapter in the section, Chapter 12, *Fintech and Financial Inclusion in Developing Countries*, investigates financial inclusion and provides insights into the current state of fintech in the developing world. By following the case study approach, **Adjasi, Hamilton, and Lensink** provide details on the implications and impacts of different forms of fintech on financial inclusion. They assess the regulatory approaches for instance innovation offices, regulatory sandboxes, and RegTechs in regulating the financial ecosystem.

Following this, Chapter 13, *The Cash Holdings of Fintechs and SMEs: Evidence from OECD Countries*, looks at small and medium enterprises (SMEs) to show how fintech companies are becoming important rivals in the banking industry. By adopting the Generalized Method of Moments and using member countries of the Organisation for Economic Co-operation and Development, **Abbasi, Alam, Noor Brohi, Fiza, Nasim,** and **Brohi** show how fintech companies can facilitate the lending/borrowing money which can lead to a lower rate of cash holdings in SMEs.

The book concludes with Chapter 14, *Fintech Companies in Brazil: Assessing Their Effects on Competition in the Brazilian Financial System from 2018 to 2020*, that analyzes the competitive impacts of fintech companies in the Brazilian financial industry. By using the data from the balance sheets of Brazil's main universal banks and payment fintech companies, **Martins, Sarno, Macahyba,** and **Filho** focus on payment institutions, as regulated by the Central Bank of Brazil (BCB), and evaluate how and through which channels these firms are affecting the profit rate of incumbent banks.

REFERENCES

Andreau, J. (2020). Banking, money-lending, and elite financial life in Rome. *Roman law and economics: Volume II: Exchange, ownership, and disputes* (pp. 81–112). Offord University Press. https://doi.org/10.1093/oso/978 0198787211.003.0015

Arslanian, H., & Fischer, F. (2019). *The future of finance: The impact of Fintech, AI, and crypto on financial services*. Springer. https://doi.org/10.1007/978-3-030-14533-0

Cocco, L., Pinna, A., & Marchesi, M. (2017). Banking on blockchain: Costs savings thanks to the blockchain technology. *Future Internet, 9*(3), 25, 1–20. https://doi.org/10.3390/fi9030025

Degerli, K. (2019). Regulatory challenges and solutions for Fintech in Turkey. *Procedia Computer Science, 158*, 929–937. https://doi.org/10.1016/j.procs.2019.09.133

Iman, N. (2019). Traditional banks against Fintech startups: A field investigation of a regional bank in Indonesia. *Banks and Bank Systems, 14*(3), 20–33. https://doi.org/10.21511/bbs.14(3).2019.03

Klus, M. F., Lohwasser, T. S., Holotiuk, F., & Moormann, J. (2019). Strategic alliances between banks and Fintechs for digital innovation: Motives to collaborate and types of interaction. *The Journal of Entrepreneurial Finance, 21*(1), 1–23. https://digitalcommons.pepperdine.edu/jef/vol21/iss1/1/

Mohamed, H., & Ali, H. (2018). Blockchain, Fintech, and Islamic finance. In Blockchain, Fintech, and Islamic finance. *de Gruyter*. https://doi.org/10.1515/9781547400966.

Nuyens, H. (2019). How disruptive are Fintech and digital for banks and regulators? *Journal of Risk Management in Financial Institutions, 12*(3), 217–222. https://www.ingentaconnect.com/content/hsp/jrmfi/2019/00000012/00000003/art00003

Pal, S. N., & Singh, D. (2019). Chatbots and virtual assistant in Indian banks. *Industrija, 47*(4), 75–101. https://doi.org/10.5937/industrija47-24578

Patnaik, S., Yang, X. S., & Sethi, I. K. (2019). Advances in machine learning and computational intelligence. *Proceedings of ICMLCI*. https://doi.org/10.1007/978-981-15-5243-4

Rath, G. B., Das, D., & Acharya, B. (2021). Modern approach for loan sanctioning in banks using machine learning. In: *Advances in machine learning and computational intelligence* (pp. 179–188). Springer, Singapore. https://doi.org/10.1007/978-981-15-5243-4_15

Stulz, R. M. (2019). Fintech, bigtech, and the future of banks. *Journal of Applied Corporate Finance, 31*(4), 86–97. https://doi.org/10.3386/w26312

Temelkov, Z. (2018). Fintech firms opportunity or threat for banks? *International journal of information, Business and Management, 10*(1), 137–143. https://www.proquest.com/docview/1966054471

PART I

Financial Technologies and Their Effects on the Banking Industry

CHAPTER 2

Centralized and Decentralized Finance: Coexistence or Convergence?

Axel Wieandt and Laurenz Heppding

INTRODUCTION

In the last five years, cryptocurrencies and digital assets have grown explosively. While traditional finance issuers have recently started to experiment with the use of security tokens to manage ownership rights of investments such as stocks, bonds, and mutual funds decentrally on the blockchain, at the same time, the progressive crypto-community has shifted its focus to the development of "decentralized finance" (DeFi) as a means to create

A. Wieandt (✉)
WHU Otto-Beisheim School of Management, Vallendar, Germany
e-mail: axel.wieandt@kellogg.northwestern.edu

Kellogg Graduate School of Management, Northwestern University, Evanston, IL, USA

L. Heppding
Department of Computer Science, Department of Law and Economics, Technical University of Darmstadt, Darmstadt, Germany

© The Author(s), under exclusive license to Springer Nature Switzerland AG 2023
T. Walker et al. (eds.), *The Fintech Disruption*, Palgrave Studies in Financial Services Technology,
https://doi.org/10.1007/978-3-031-23069-1_2

11

and operate decentralized financial service offerings and applications on open-source software platforms. These are developed and deployed using public blockchain systems such as Ethereum, Polygon, or Avalanche.

Fueled by an intense user interest, as well as investments from major venture capital firms such as Andreessen Horowitz or Bain Capital Ventures, DeFi is now one of the fastest growing segments in the burgeoning field of cryptocurrencies. There are already over 1,000 DeFi protocols on various blockchains, and the Ethereum blockchain clearly dominates the space (DeFiLlama, 2022a, 2022b). The economic dimension of DeFi is also impressive, with over USD 200 bn locked up on these protocols as of December 2021 (DeFiLlama, 2022a). DeFi protocols cover a wide range of financial services, ranging from lending and asset management activities and decentralized exchange functionality, to processing derivative and other financial transactions. In the context of DeFi protocols, the crypto asset category of so-called stablecoins, whose value is backed by or pegged to traditional fiat currencies such as the US dollar, must also be mentioned, as it is indispensable in interactions with DeFi protocols.

In essence, DeFi operates as a decentralized financial system, completely without intermediaries such as financial institutions. In centralized finance (CeFi), trust is created by the reputation and guarantees of such intermediaries. In DeFi, this trust is generated by the technical properties of the underlying blockchain technology, such as cryptographic techniques and consensus algorithms, which create transparency and immutability. DeFi's lack of intermediaries also increases operational efficiency and facilitates broader democratic access to financial services, which is why it is frequently associated with the promise of greater financial inclusivity. DeFi also creates a more stable financial system that does not rely on centralized financial institutions or large banks. These centralized institutions were exposed in the 2007–2008 financial crisis as vulnerable, opaque, dominant, and too interconnected to be structurally resolvable without bailouts in the case of failure, and as therefore having an unfair market advantage.

Although DeFi can be seen as a promising alternative to the current CeFi system, the disadvantages and risks associated with DeFi must also be considered. These risks include technical limitations of the underlying blockchain technology, which affect the scaling and further expansion of DeFi, and regulatory loopholes. According to a recent publication of the Financial Stability Board (2022), these and other drawbacks can lead to a rapid escalation of financial stability risks, magnifying the need for policy responses and causing CeFi institutions to avoid DeFi thus far. Going forward, this raises an important set of questions: Will DeFi and CeFi maintain strict separation and merely coexist? Or will they ultimately converge? Furthermore, could DeFi protocols one day fully replace financial intermediaries?

Before attempting to answer these questions, we first review the current state of research into DeFi,[1] building on Schär (2021), Gogel (2021), and Aramonte et al. (2021). However, unlike these authors, we look at DeFi less as an isolated phenomenon and more through the lens of the traditional centralized financial system. We contribute to the existing literature by systematically identifying the main opportunities and risks of DeFi compared to CeFi, and by identifying possible fault lines between these two worlds. Furthermore, we discuss theoretical examples of convergence and coexistence scenarios of DeFi and CeFi, as well as recent real-world attempts of convergence between these two worlds.

The remainder of this paper is structured as follows. After providing a functional view on the traditional financial system and a brief summary of the impact of technological innovation on CeFi, we introduce the key components and architecture of DeFi, centered around a detailed discussion of MakerDAO, one of the oldest and largest DeFi protocols. We then compare DeFi and CeFi to identify their advantages/opportunities as well as their disadvantages/challenges. Using a scenario analysis, we then address whether DeFi and CeFi are more likely to coexist or converge, through a discussion of recent convergence attempts between CeFi and DeFi. We conclude with suggestions for future research.

CENTRALIZED FINANCE (CEFI) AND TECHNOLOGICAL INNOVATION

CeFi—The Architecture of Our Current Financial System

At the macro level, a financial system allocates scarce resources to be used within the business sector in the most productive way. The two fundamental ways in which resources can be allocated are via financial

---

[1] For a systematic review of peer-reviewed DeFi-related publications, see Meyer et al. (2022).

markets or financial intermediaries. The allocation of resources via financial markets, such as equity and debt capital markets, is often referred to as direct finance, while the allocation of funds via financial intermediaries, such as banks, insurance companies, or asset managers, is referred to as indirect finance. The intermediation chain in indirect finance can be long and complex. For example, fund managers, insurance companies, or other non-bank financial intermediaries gather financial resources from the non-financial sectors, i.e., households and corporations, and either deposit them directly with a bank or invest in equity and bonds via centralized exchanges.

For the financial system to work properly, the government must provide a stable legal and regulatory framework. The rule of law protects property rights and allows financial contracts to be enforced. Government regulation and supervision is required to monitor the soundness of individual institutions, as well as of the system overall, to ensure consumer protection and to prevent money laundering and the financing of illicit activities.[2]

Licensed and supervised banks have a special role in our financial system. In fact, most of the money in our financial system is not in the form of cash, but of bank deposits at retail or commercial banks, which provide loans to households and businesses to make investments, pay for expenses and consumption, or repay existing debt.[3] However, banks are surprisingly fragile because most deposit contracts have undefined maturity, which means that depositors can withdraw their deposits immediately.[4] Even financially sound banks with large solvency and liquidity buffers are vulnerable to bank runs if depositors overreact to real or imagined potential threats. Deposit insurance was introduced to protect depositors against complete loss in the event of bank failure, and to stabilize the financial system. As recent history proves, even those two safety nets might not be enough to prevent a melt-down of the financial system. In the 2007–2008 financial crisis, national governments intervened to bail out failing banks and stabilize the financial system. Whether or not

---

[2] For a summary of the role of banks in the financial system, see Wieandt (2017, p. 43).

[3] For this perspective on money creation, see, e.g., McLeay et al. (2014).

[4] See Diamond and Dybvig (1983) for a model of bank runs and the stabilizing effects of deposit insurance.

recently introduced bail-in regulations and orderly resolution regimes will increase global financial stability remains to be seen.

Finance—A Functional View

Merton and Bodie (1995, p. 2) identify six core functions that the financial system performs at the micro-level:

(1) To provide ways of clearing and settling payments to facilitate trade.
(2) To provide a mechanism for the pooling of resources and for the subdividing of shares in various enterprises.
(3) To provide ways to transfer economic resources through time, across borders, and among industries.
(4) To provide ways of managing risk.
(5) To provide price information to help coordinate decentralized decision-making in various sectors of the economy.
(6) To provide ways of dealing with the incentive problems created when one party to a transaction has information that the other party does not or when one party acts as agent for another.

While these finance functions are stable, the institutional setup in which they are performed is not. Reduced trading costs lead to high market volumes and commoditization. Merton and Bodie (1995) note a secular pattern away from opaque institutions and toward transparent institutions as growing trading volumes in new financial products lead to increasing commoditization. Reduced transaction costs ultimately push the boundaries between markets and financial intermediaries toward more markets.

Technological Innovation and CeFi—A 150-Year History

Technological innovation has increased the efficiency of the financial system and enabled new financial products and services, ultimately bringing about institutional change and disintermediation. Technology has been used in finance for over 150 years, as Arner et al. (2015) point out. They distinguish three different phases where the financial sector has been impacted by technological change. The first phase, prompted by the first transatlantic cable of 1866, saw the gradual shift of finance from analog to digital finances. The second started with the advent of automated teller machines in 1967. The third began when widespread internet access enabled online financial transactions and banking. This internet-driven wave includes the emergence of new actors such as fintechs like PayPal or Robinhood, and bigtechs like FAANG,[5] which challenge traditional financial institutions. Fintechs, financed by growing volumes of venture capital, aim to automate and further improve the value creation process of financial services to further increase customer satisfaction and interaction. FAANG are leveraging both their dominant market positions, which has resulted in strong operating cash flows, and their global reach, to move into financial services. Notable examples for bigtechs engaging in financial services are Apple or Google Pay and Amazon Lending. According to the Bank of International Settlements (BIS), there are five overlapping scenarios for how technology might impact banking (Hernández de Cos, 2019). In the first scenario, referred to as "better bank," banks are able to digitize themselves in order to effectively retain the customer relationship and banking services. The other four scenarios imply more drastic changes to the business models of banks. The second scenario, called "new bank," sees incumbent banks replaced by newly established, fully digitized "new" or "neo-banks." The third scenario, called "distributed bank," involves the increasing modularization of financial services. Incumbents can maintain an integrated offering but are forced to integrate plug-and-play offerings of technology companies (e.g., integration of Apple or Android Pay). In the fourth scenario, called "relegated bank," incumbents cede the customer interface to fintechs and bigtechs. Finally, in the fifth scenario, referred to as "disintermediated bank," traditional financial institutions are largely irrelevant because customers prefer to interact directly with new financial service providers.

It is important to ask how new technologies such as biometrics, cloud computing, distributed ledger technology (DLT), and machine learning are going to impact the traditional financial system. In particular, DeFi, with its rapidly growing number of protocols deployed transparently on top of a public permissionless blockchain settlement layer, has the potential to significantly challenge CeFi.

---

[5] FAANG is an abbreviation of the five largest technology companies Facebook (now Meta), Apple, Amazon, Netflix, and Google/Alphabet.

ECONOMICAL AND TECHNICAL INTRODUCTION OF DEFI

DeFi—An Introduction

In decentralized finance (DeFi), financial services and functions are provided via composable building blocks without the involvement of centralized intermediaries. Core components of DeFi include distributed ledger systems and smart contracts, which pose an alternative to the current financial system. Amler et al. (2021, p. 1) define DeFi as "a plethora of traditionally centralized financial instruments [that] are now being deployed and used on distributed blockchain systems". Aramonte et al. (2021, p. 21) consider the core of DeFi to be that it "provides financial services without centralized intermediaries, by operating through automated protocols on blockchains".

From the systemic perspective, Schär (2021, p. 153) sees in DeFi an "alternative financial infrastructure" whose principal purpose is to "replicate existing financial services in a more open, interoperable, and transparent way." Similarly, Gudgeon et al. (2020, p. 1) define DeFi as "a peer-to-peer financial paradigm which leverages blockchain-based smart contracts," which outlines the main technical properties of DeFi. Werner et al. (2021, p. 2) identify four core properties of DeFi, namely (1) non-custodial, (2) permissionless, (3) openly auditable, and (4) composable. Scholars agree that the composability of DeFi products (building blocks) is its most important property (Amler et al., 2021; Harvey et al., 2020; Schär, 2021; Werner et al., 2021). Amler et al. (2021, p. 1) note that "multiple DeFi products can be composed by letting smart contracts interact with each other," while Harvey et al. (2020, p. 16) note that "DeFi seeks to build and combine open-source financial building blocks into sophisticated products."

As these definitions indicate, blockchain technology in conjunction with smart contracts provide the technical basis for DeFi applications. Blockchain technology dates back to 2009, when Satoshi Nakamoto created Bitcoin,[6] a peer-to-peer electronic cash system, using blockchain technology as a medium for recording its transaction data (Nakamoto, 2009). In the case of Bitcoin, the blockchain is the enabler, allowing values to be represented digitally and transferred in a tamper-proof

---

[6] For a comprehensive discussion of Bitcoin and other cryptocurrencies, see Narayanan et al. (2016).

manner without intermediaries. The second major development in blockchain technology is the Ethereum blockchain proposed by Vitalik Buterin in 2013 (Buterin, 2013). The technical attributes of the Ethereum blockchain is suitable to facilitating the execution of so-called smart contracts. The concept of smart contracts was established by Szabo (1997) and describes how contractual clauses can be embedded in hardware and software, to allow for an automatic verification of compliance with contractual terms.[7] In the context of blockchain technology, smart contracts are Turing-complete[8] programs whose source code is stored immutably on the blockchain after its deployment. The code of a smart contract can thus be viewed by anyone, and its functionality is therefore verifiable by a broad user base, with no black box behavior,[9] and with very low vulnerability to errors and manipulation.[10] Both DeFi protocols and their underlying blockchains are mostly open source, which further increases their transparency. On average, approximately 4,000 developers per month further develop the Ethereum blockchain (Shen & Garg, 2022).

The increasing popularity of cryptocurrencies in recent years has also contributed to the strong growth of the application landscape in the DeFi space, such that currently around 1,000 DeFi applications, also referred to as DApps,[11] exist on different blockchains (DefiLlama, 2022b). Most of these DApps run on the Ethereum blockchain followed by

---

[7] Szabo (1997) illustrates the functionality of a smart contract using the example of a vending machine. A vending machine can interact with a user in three automated ways. If the user inserts the appropriate amount of money, the desired product is delivered. If too much money is inserted, the vending machine recognizes this and dispenses change and the desired product accordingly. If not enough money is inserted, no product is dispensed and the inserted money is returned with the message that the inserted amount was not sufficient.

[8] Turing-complete refers to a machine that, given enough time, memory, and the necessary instructions, can solve any computational problem, regardless of its complexity.

[9] We distinguish between transparency and comprehensibility of the source code since technical expertise is needed to understand the logic of the program.

[10] For a detailed introduction to smart contracts, see Antonopoulos and Wood (2018).

[11] DApp differs from DeFi protocols in that DApp encompasses both the functionality of the protocol and the corresponding user interface (UI). However, since the functionality of DeFi is of primary importance, most of the literature refers to protocols without explicitly discussing the UI. For this reason, in this paper we use the terms DApp and DeFi protocol synonymously.

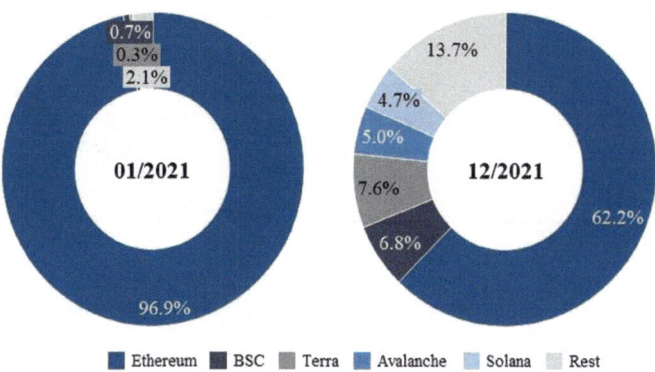

Fig. 2.1 Evolution of market shares of different blockchain types

the Terra and Binance Smart Chain (BSC)[12] blockchains (DefiLlama, 2022b). However, as Fig. 2.1 shows, the relative share of Ethereum drastically decreased from c.97% at the beginning of 2021 (DefiLlama, 2022b), primarily because the Ethereum network is currently operating at its capacity limits. This is reflected in high transaction fees which makes it less attractive for users.

The reason for this problem is the so-called scalability trilemma, according to which only two of the three essential goals of a blockchain, namely scalability, decentralization, and security, can be achieved "if you stick to 'simple' techniques" (Buterin, 2021, p. 1). Traditional blockchains, such as Ethereum, are secure and decentralized, but less able to be scaled, whereas blockchains that can process many transactions per second are scalable and secure, but less decentralized, as they typically operate on a small number of nodes, usually between 10 and 100 (Buterin, 2021). Ethereum's upcoming transition to proof-of-stake (PoS), which will significantly increase throughput, may allow Ethereum to regain lost market shares.

The number of users,[13] measured by unique addresses interacting with DeFi protocols on Ethereum, has steadily increased over the last years

[12] See the Terra (Kereiakes et al., 2019) and Binance Smart Chain (Binance, 2020) whitepapers for further reference.

[13] Since users can have several addresses, the number of unique addresses only approximates the number of users.

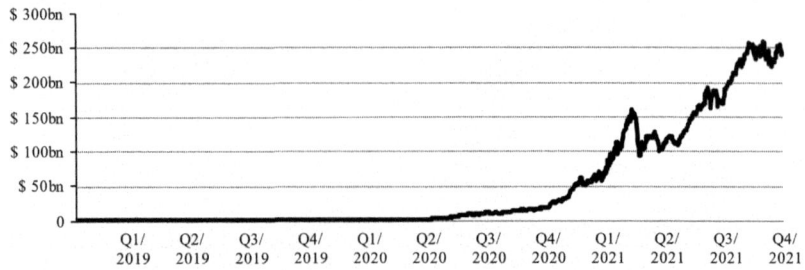

Fig. 2.2 TVL in DeFi protocols across several blockchains (2019–2021)

to currently c.4 m, which is still small compared to the total number of unique addresses on Ethereum (c.180 m) (Dune Analytics, 2022; Etherscan, 2022).

Also, the economic relevance of the DeFi space, measured by the total value locked (TVL), steadily increased between 2019 and 2021, as Fig. 2.2 illustrates (DefiLlama, 2022a). TVL refers to the value of tokens that are stored in DApps and are therefore locked, meaning that these tokens cannot be withdrawn from the protocols easily. For example, when a user wants to lend out USD 100 and deposits this amount on a lending DApp, the TVL of this DApp increases by USD 100.

As such, the TVL of protocols running on several blockchains in 2021 increased from USD c.19 bn to USD c.240 bn between the beginning and the end of the year. However, if we compare these figures with the total value of all financial assets worldwide (USD c.470 trn), it becomes clear that the DeFi space is still in its infancy (Financial Stability Board, 2021). Further, DeFi can be identified as a niche even within the crypto universe whose entire market capitalization is at around USD 2 trn (CoinMarketCap, 2022).

The DeFi Hierarchical Layer Model

For a better overview of DeFi and to consider DeFi in its technological context, the following sections discuss the DeFi layer model generally and the so-called protocol layer, the core of DeFi, more closely.

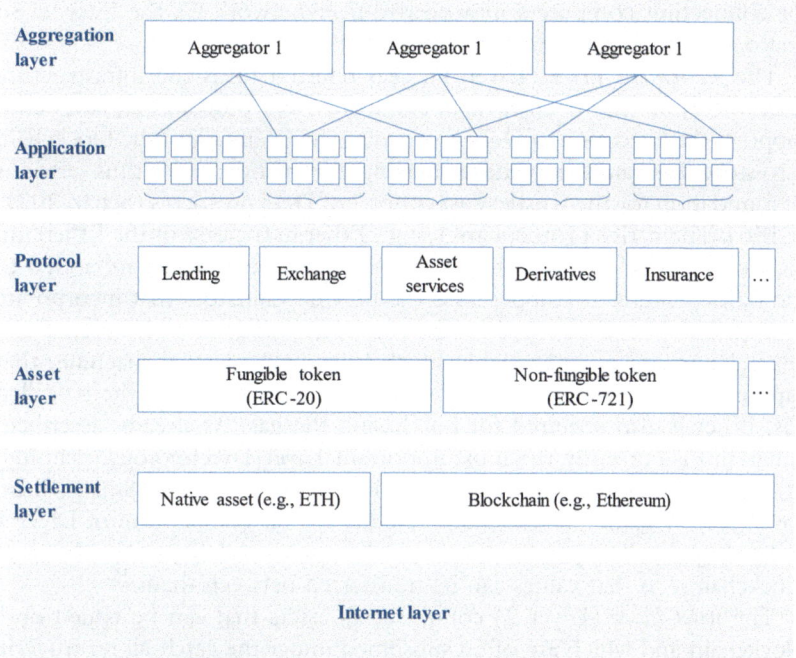

Fig. 2.3 DeFi layer model

The DeFi Layer Model

As proposed by Schär (2021) and Jensen et al. (2021a), among others, DeFi can be described as a hierarchical layer model consisting of five distinct layers.[14] These layers are hierarchical in the sense that an issue at a lower-level layer will impact all layers on top of it. For example, if the blockchain at the lowest layer is compromised, all the layers above it will be insecure (Schär, 2021). Figure 2.3, adapted from Schär (2021, p. 156), visualizes the layer model.

The basis for the layer model is the so-called *internet layer* (Layer 0), which is not a DeFi layer in the narrow sense. Rather, this layer is essential

---

[14] Jensen et al. (2021a) propose a layer system consisting of four layers, in contrast to Schär (2021), combining the protocol and application layer.

for connecting computers in a peer-to-peer network via the internet so that data can be transferred quickly and at a low cost.

The *settlement layer* (Layer 1), also referred to as the infrastructure layer, incorporates the blockchain and its native protocol asset, and hence supports the execution of DeFi protocols. The main task of the blockchain is to store the transaction and ownership information and it thus serves as a "foundation for the trustless execution" of DeFi protocols (Schär, 2021, p. 156). The native protocol asset, e.g., Ether in the case of the Ethereum blockchain, is relevant, on the one hand when new blocks are added to the blockchain, as it compensates the miners/validators that incorporate transactions into a new block. On the other hand, since Ethereum is a general purpose programmable blockchain, i.e., a virtual machine, that supports the execution of smart contracts in exchange for the so-called gas, Ether is also required for purchasing the gas. As already described, Ethereum is currently the most important Layer 1 technology, although other blockchains such as Polygon, Terra, or the Binance Smart Chain have recently gained considerable relevance. This competition of Layer 1 technologies will require and increase the interoperability of the different blockchains, so that values can be transferred between them.[15]

The *asset layer* (Layer 2) comprises all assets that can be issued on a blockchain and which are often subsumed under the catch-all term *token*. In the case of Ethereum, a distinction is made between fungible tokens (ERC-20) and non-fungible tokens[16] (ERC-721).[17] In the context of DeFi, the fungible tokens are of particular interest, as this token standard is used to represent the so-called stablecoins. According to Aramonte et al. (2021, p. 24), stablecoins are "crypto assets that strive to tie their values to fiat currencies, such as the US dollar," which play an important role within DeFi for "facilitating fund transfers across platforms and between users." According to Schär (2021), a major reason for the important role of stablecoins is that many financial contracts require a

---

[15] This transfer between different blockchains through so-called bridges will be addressed in more detail later in a deeper exploration of the protocol layer.

[16] Non-fungible tokens (NFTs) have recently experienced an enormous boom, as they are used, for example, to represent ownership of unique art objects.

[17] Fungible tokens are comparable to, e.g., traditional fiat currencies, non-unique and divisible. Non-fungible tokens, on the other hand, represent unique and indivisible items, e.g., (digital) artworks or flight tickets.

low-volatility asset.[18] Aramonte et al. (2021) also point out that stable-coins enable market participants to convert cryptocurrencies into fiat currencies less frequently, and build an important bridge between the crypto world and the traditional financial system with which they share a common numeraire.

To fulfill the goal of value stability, the value of stablecoins is derived from one or more underlying assets, whereby a differentiation is made between off-chain and on-chain collateralized stablecoins (Berentsen & Schär, 2019). In the case of off-chain collateralized stablecoins, the under-lying assets exist in the real world, independent of the blockchain, possibly deposited physically at a commercial bank. An example of such a stable-coin is Tether, which is backed by US dollars and US dollar-denominated assets held in CeFi bank accounts. In the case of on-chain collateralized stablecoins, in contrast, the underlying assets are digital and locked on the blockchain. An example of an on-chain collateralized stablecoin is the Dai, which aims to provide the same value stability as the US dollar but relies on crypto assets, such as Ether, as underlying assets.

The *protocol layer* (Layer 3) is the heart of DeFi. At its core, the protocol layer describes how the financial logic of the different application areas, e.g., lending or trading, is implemented via smart contracts. This layer is also highly interoperable, in that these protocols can interact with each other and with the end user (Schär, 2021).

The *application layer* (Layer 4) sits directly on top of the protocol layer and is responsible for providing an interaction medium with the protocols and their smart contracts. User interaction with the applications usually takes place via user-friendly interfaces, mainly web-based applications, so that users are not confronted with the underlying technical complexity of the smart contract (Jensen et al., 2021a; Schär, 2021). The combination of the application layer and the protocol layer is often subsumed under the term DApp.

The *aggregation layer* (Layer 5) describes the functionality of so-called aggregators, which are connected to various protocols on their platforms, e.g., to compare and evaluate services or to aggregate information from many sources to make them available to users (Schär, 2021). A prominent example of an aggregator is the yearn.finance platform, which provides

---

[18] For example, in the context of a loan agreement, it is problematic if the interest payments fluctuate significantly due to a highly volatile calculation base, as this results in unfavorable situations for either the lender or the borrower.

users with, among other things, a current comparison of the annual percentage yield (APY) of various lending applications. Furthermore, the user can connect his wallet directly to the platform and deposit funds using one of the applications after considering the comparison.

Deep Dive: Protocol Layer

To date, the three major protocol categories include lending and borrowing protocols, decentralized exchanges (DEXes), and asset service protocols. There are also other protocol categories such as derivatives (e.g., Augur or dYdX), payments (i.e., Connext or StablePay), and insurance (e.g., Bridge Mutual or Nexus Mutual) that show promise, but are not yet relevant in practice.

Current market data shows that *lending and borrowing protocols* is the largest category on Ethereum, with a market share of 44%, followed by DEXes (32%), and asset services (18%) (DeFi Pulse, 2022). The TVL of lending protocols is USD c.42 bn as of December 2021 (DeFi Pulse, 2022). In lending protocols, lending and borrowing agreements, including interest rate determination, are handled automatically via smart contracts. Consequently, smart contracts completely replace financial intermediaries, which, in the case of loans, are usually banks. Since lender and borrower are completely anonymous to each other within these agreements, there are two ways to protect the lender, namely overcollateralization and the possibility of reversing a transaction.. Typically, the loans are overcollateralized, meaning that the value of the collateral deposited by the borrower exceeds the loan amount (Amler et al., 2021; Jensen et al., 2021a; Schär, 2021; Werner et al., 2021). However, there are also loans that do not require the deposit of any collateral, most notably so-called flash loans where the borrowed amount has to be repaid within seconds.[19] Flash loans take advantage of the atomicity characteristic of the blockchain to the extent that the disbursement of the loan amount, the interest and principal payments, and the repayment are all reflected in a single block (Werner et al., 2021). If the borrower fails or is unable to repay, all payments made are reversed and the lender receives his or her original payment (Werner et al., 2021). The best-known examples of DeFi lending platforms are Aave (USD c.11 bn) and Compund (USD c.8

---

[19] Some new projects, such as Goldfinch, also provide unsecured loans for a longer period of time.

bn), in addition to the pioneering MakerDAO with a TVL of USD c.17 bn (Boado, 2020; DeFi Pulse, 2022; MakerDAO Foundation, 2020).

The second most important category of DeFi protocols by value are DEXes, with a TVL of USD c.30 bn on the Ethereum blockchain as of December 2021 (DeFi Pulse, 2022). In DEXes, digital assets are exchanged without an intermediary between buyer and seller.[20] Smart contracts are used to execute the trade and define its logic, i.e., price determination and order matching (Amler et al., 2021; Jensen et al., 2021a; Schär, 2021; Werner et al., 2021). Two common approaches to implementing this trade logic include decentralized order book exchanges and automated market makers (AMMs) (Schär, 2021; Werner et al., 2021). One main type of AMM is the so-called constant function market maker (CFMM), which, based on the idea of so-called liquidity or exchange pools, alleviates the need to maintain an order book. A liquidity pool usually comprises two sides, which are both crypto assets such as Dai and Ethereum, which can be exchanged for each other. Users interacting with liquidity pools can be divided into two categories: liquidity providers and liquidity takers. Liquidity providers deposit pairs of crypto assets into the pool in exchange for a fee and liquidity takers trade one crypto asset for another in exchange for a fee. The determination of the exchange rate between the two crypto assets of a pool essentially follows the so-called constant product function, where the exchange rate is derived from the value ratio of the two deposited cryptocurrencies in the smart contract. This function has a convex profile, which means that the exchange rate automatically adjusts according to the amount of both crypto assets deposited in the smart contract at a given point in time.[21] Practical examples of DEXes are the multichain solutions Curve, with a TVL of USD c.15 bn on Ethereum, Uniswap (USD c.8 bn), and SushiSwap (USD c.2 bn) (Adams et al., 2021; Egorov, 2019, 2021).

The third largest category of DeFi protocols is represented by the collective term *asset services*, which has a TVL of USD c.18 bn as of December 2021 (DeFi Pulse, 2022). The possible applications in the field of asset services range widely from on-chain asset management, to

---

[20] See Chapter 4 for a detailed comparison between a DEX and a traditional (securities) exchange.

[21] For detailed discussions of liquidity pooling and AMMs, see, e.g., Lehar and Parlour (2021), Schär (2021), and Aramonte et al. (2021).

yield-bearing stablecoins, to so-called bridges. On-chain asset management is tightly linked to CeFi-style asset management, but asset manager activities are performed completely without a central authority[22] and the users always have full custody of the deposited assets (Amler et al., 2021; Jensen et al., 2021a; Schär, 2021; Werner et al., 2021). Income from the deposited assets can be generated through a variety of activities, mainly trading, minting,[23] and borrowing. Examples of on-chain asset management applications include yearn.finance's vault functionality and the SetProtocol. Yield-bearing stablecoins combine value stability and yield generation. Users deposit common stablecoins such as Dai or Tether and receive the stablecoins of the respective platform in return, e.g., OUSD from the protocol Origin Dollar. The applications then use the stablecoins received to achieve returns of 10–12% per year, i.e., through lending or liquidity pooling. Examples from this category include Origin Dollar or mStable with TVLs of USD c.281 m and USD c.134 m, respectively (DeFi Pulse, 2022). So-called bridges are used to transfer assets between different blockchains. For example, bridges enable the transfer of Bitcoin to the Ethereum blockchain. Well-known examples of bridges are RenVM and BoringDAO with TVLs of USD c.783 m and USD c.52 m, respectively (DeFi Pulse, 2022).

The largest protocol in asset services is Convex Finance with a TVL of USD c.12 bn, which leverages the governance system of the largest DEX, Curve Finance (DeFi Pulse, 2022). If a user provides liquidity on Curve Finance, he or she receives CRV tokens and a compensation for the provision. By staking these CRV tokens, the user also receives a voting right regarding the fees of the individual liquidity pools, a higher compensation for the liquidity provision, and a revenue share. Users can pool their CRV tokens on the Convex Finance platform, giving Convex Finance influence over governance matters on the Curve Finance platform through the collection of CRV tokens, as well as considerable influence on the fees of the individual liquidity pools and thus also on their liquidity. Convex

---

[22] See Schär (2021) for a discussion of the situation with one or multiple fund managers whose actions are controlled by fixed rules in smart contracts.

[23] In the context of the proof-of-stake consensus mechanism, minting describes the process of validating information and including transactions into a newly created block. To participate in this process, the so-called validators must deposit crypto assets, e.g., Ether, as a security, to ensure their integrity. In return, the validators are compensated in the form of block rewards and transaction fees. Minting is thus the counterpart of the so-called mining, which is used in the proof-of-work consensus mechanism.

Table 2.1 Ten largest DeFi protocols based on TVL on Ethereum

Rank	Protocol	Category	TVL [USD bn]
1	MakerDAO	Lending	16.48
2	Curve Finance	DEX	14.41
3	Convex Finance	Asset Services	11.95
4	Aave	Lending	11.01
5	Uniswap	DEX	8.29
6	Compound	Lending	7.83
7	InstaDApp	Asset Services	6.86
8	yearn.finance	Asset Services	3.84
9	Balancer	DEX	2.19
10	Sushi Swap	DEX	2.17

Finance takes advantage of this position by selling its voting behavior to other protocols that want to increase the liquidity of their tokens on the Curve platform. Thus, in addition to the normal compensation for the liquidity provision on Curve Finance, users who deposit their CRV tokens with Convex Finance receive additional earnings through the mechanism just described, so that it is often referred to as boosted CRV earnings.

Table 2.1 depicts the ten largest protocols in terms of TVL as of December 2021 and includes information about their blockchain and protocol type (DeFi Pulse, 2022).

MakerDAO—A DeFi Protocol Deep Dive

One of the oldest DeFi applications is the lending platform MakerDAO, which runs exclusively on the Ethereum blockchain. Founded in 2015 by Rune Christensen, MakerDAO currently operates as a foundation headquartered in Santa Cruz, CA, USA. Control over the MakerDAO platform is exercised through governance token holders, including in particular early adopters, e.g., founding members and early employees as well as well-known investors such as Andreessen Horowitz and Dragonfly Capital Partners. Currently, the top 100 governance token holders hold a share of c.80 percent of all governance tokens. The technology behind MakerDAO is developed by a team of c.30 developers, with the source code being publicly available on GitHub. To protect the MakerDAO platform against logical errors as well as potential failures of the smart

Fig. 2.4   Historical TVL of MakerDAO (2019–2021)

contract logic, the source code of the platform is audited by special-ized security auditors such as Trail of Bits, PeckShield, and Runtime Verification. Communication and organization within the decentral-ized autonomous organization takes place via the public MakerDAO forum, where, for example, governance and improvement proposals are discussed. Figure 2.4 illustrates the TVL development of MakerDAO between 2019 and 2021 (DeFi Pulse, 2022).

To understand how MakerDao operates, it is essential to understand both the concept of the issued stablecoin, Dai, and the concept of the governance token, MKR. The Dai token is a stablecoin which is pegged to the US dollar through community-based management of supply and demand. Users borrowing through the MakerDAO platform deposit Ether or other supported crypto assets as collateral and receive their loans in newly minted Dai (MakerDAO Foundation, 2020). This procedure is different compared to other lending protocols, such as Compound or Aave, since it does not use liquidity pools containing aggregated capital from multiple lenders against which borrowers can establish their credit positions. What other crypto assets are accepted as collateral, besides Ether, is decided by the governance system of MakerDAO.[24] Loans at MakerDAO are overcollateralized,[25] which means that the loan amount

---

[24] Other collateral assets are, e.g., Basic Attention Token (BAT), USDC, Wrapped Bitcoin (WBTC), and Tether.

[25] MakerDAO requires that, for a loan of 1 Dai, at least a value of 1.5 Dai/USD must be deposited, corresponding to a collateral ratio of 150%. In practice, the collateral ratio is currently (01/2022) c.170%.

is smaller than the value of the collateral. The loaned Dai and an additional stability fee[26] can be paid back at any time in return for the collateral, whereupon the returned Dai are deleted, keeping the circulating supply of Dai elastic. Since the value of crypto assets that are deposited as collateral can be volatile and cause the value of the Dai to erode, if the current collateral-to-debt ratio of a vault falls below a certain liquidation ratio[27] a liquidation of the collateral takes place through so-called collateral auctions. This is the only situation where the borrower loses independent control over collateral assets. This mechanism attracted attention in March 2020 when, through a chain of errors and unforeseen circumstances, users of the MakerDAO platform lost USD c.8 m and USD c.4.5 m DAI were on loan unbacked, meaning that no collateral was deposited for these DAI (Eichholz, 2020). This was triggered by a sharp decline in the Ether price which caused an overload on the Ethereum network, and the skyrocketing of transaction fees (Eichholz, 2020). These high transaction fees caused problems with the functions of so-called oracles, which triggered massive collateral auctions (Eichholz, 2020). Oracles are important because they provide DeFi protocols with real-time exchange rates and other information, and thus significantly influence lending protocols, such as MakerDAO, by directly influencing the loan amount and the current value of the collateral.[28] In the collateral auctions, some users exploited this combination of network congestion and high transaction fees by bidding 0 for the collaterals (Eichholz, 2020). Since these users added high transaction fees to their bids, these bids were prioritized due to the network congestion, eliminating bidding competition for the collaterals, which were auctioned off, for the most part, without any countervalue (Eichholz, 2020).

The governance token MKR serves two purposes on the MakerDAO network. The governance rights conferred by MKR tokens give holders the right to vote on important platform governance decisions, such as which assets are eligible as collateral, liquidation ratios, and stability fees.

---

[26] The stability fee is a compounding interest rate per second, which is used to develop the platform, among other things.

[27] The liquidation ratio is determined for each collateral asset by the governance system of MakerDAO.

[28] For an overview on oracles, see Pasdar et al. (2021), Beniiche (2020), and Liu et al. (2020).

MKR holders also act as buyers of last resort for Dai loans. If the collateral ETH held in the Maker Vaults is insufficient to cover the amount of Dais in circulation, collateral auctions take place. However, if the collateral auction is not able to cover the outstanding debt, a debt auction follows. In this auction, new MKR tokens are created and sold to bidders for Dai, which dilutes the share of existing MKR holders (MakerDAO Foundation, 2020). The threat of debt auctions incentivizes holders to govern the platform responsibly, helping to ensure appropriate liquidation rates and stability fees.

The Technological Future of DeFi

Since DeFi is a highly dynamic and innovative ecosystem, it is important to consider recent innovations and trends, such as fixed rate products, credit delegation and institutional corporate credit (e.g., Maple Finance), as well as risk management innovations such as options, tranched lending, credit default swaps (CDS), and re-insurance.

More important than innovation at the application layer (Layer 3) is innovation at the base blockchain settlement layer (Layer 1), which includes the emergence of alternative base layer protocols such as Binance Smart Chain (BSC), EOS, Solana, and Polygon. Ethereum, the dominant Layer 1 protocol, is undergoing a significant transformation from a proof-of-work (PoW) to a proof-of-stake (PoS) consensus mechanism. This is expected to increase transaction throughput and therefore resolve the scalability issues which have recently driven transaction fees to increase. Additionally, the Ethereum community is working on on-chain scaling solutions such as sharding,[29] and off-chain scaling such as roll-ups,[30] to further limit capacity constraints (Ethereum, 2022a).

---

[29] Sharding is a common concept in the context of database systems as it describes the splitting of a database horizontally to achieve a better distribution of the workload across the nodes (Ethereum, 2022a).

[30] Roll-ups execute transactions outside of the main Ethereum network but post the transaction data back to the Ethereum network, thus ensuring the security provided by the Ethereum protocol (Ethereum, 2022a).

COMPARING DEFI WITH CEFI

A Functional Comparison Along the Value Chain

To illustrate how DeFi works in comparison to CeFi at the functional level, we compare a loan origination and the process of trading on a securities exchange across both systems.[31]

Loan Origination

The first phase of loan origination is the so-called *underwriting phase*. In the traditional CeFi setting, the lender typically evaluates the level of risk of the borrower, including extensive *know your customer* (KYC) and *anti-money laundering* (AML) verification, as the basis for defining the terms and conditions (e.g., duration, interest rate, repayment, and, if necessary, collateral) of the loan agreement. In the DeFi space, the lender cannot evaluate the level of risk because the borrower is typically anonymous. Instead, the key elements of the loan agreement are typically defined by the lender and passed on to the smart contract as parameters. In the DeFi setting, the lack of risk evaluation is typically made up for by overcollateralization.[32] This overcollateralization also buffers the high volatility of crypto assets.

The second phase of loan origination is the *disbursement phase*. This phase refers to when the lender pays out the loan amount to the borrower. In the CeFi setting, the disbursement phase typically takes 1–2 business days. In contrast, in the DeFi setting, the transfer takes place practically immediately and is only limited by network utilization.[33]

In the *servicing and monitoring phase*, the borrower makes payments on interest and principal, while the lender monitors the timeliness and correctness of the payment flows and tracks the residual debt. Depending on the terms of the loan agreement, the lender also adjusts the interest rate and the loan amortization schedule. In the DeFi setting, servicing and monitoring are largely automated because the logic and timing of payment flows are enforced by the underlying smart contract, so assets

---

[31] See also Gogel (2021) for a list of functional differences between DeFi and CeFi.

[32] The lending protocols Aave and Compound currently use a minimum collateral ratio of 120%, which means that someone borrowing USD 100 must deposit at least USD 120 in assets.

[33] In some cases, the current transaction fees are also considered when deciding on the timing of the disbursement to find the most favorable transaction timing.

can be transferred automatically, independent of both parties. Interest rate adjustments are also fully automated because they are also defined in advance, e.g., depending on the current value of the collateral, and enforced automatically during the credit relationship.

In the final *collection phase*, the lender repays the entire or the remainder of the loan amount, including accrued interest. In the DeFi setting, smart contracts ensure that repayment takes place on schedule and in the correct amount without any action required by the borrower. In CeFi, borrower default typically leads to the restructuring and workout of a loan. On the contrary, DeFi relies on overcollateralization and automatic liquidations to avoid loan losses.

Exchange Trading

In CeFi, the starting point for trading securities on an exchange is the submission of a buy or sell order by the respective market participant. The exchange operator records all orders sorted by their type (buy or sell) and their limits in the order book. Buy and sell orders are then matched according to the so-called principle of price-time priority. In DeFi, there are on-chain and off-chain order books. In on-chain order books, all orders are stored on the blockchain, visible to everyone. Such on-chain order books are limited primarily by the transaction speed of the under-lying blockchain (Schär, 2021). Centralized third parties, called *relayers*, maintain off-chain order books and inform the decentralized exchange which orders should be matched, but neither gain control over the funds nor execute the orders themselves (Schär, 2021).

In the clearing phase, we distinguish between decentralized clearing and centralized clearing by clearing houses, which predominate in the CeFi setting. Clearing houses, also referred to as central counterparties (CCPs), are responsible for netting the trading positions of buyers and sellers. As a central counterparty, a clearing house thus acts as a seller for each buyer, and as a buyer for each seller. Since market participants deposit collateral with the CCPs, mutual claims are always secured, even if one contractual party cannot fulfill its obligation. Hence, clearing houses ensure the integrity and stability of the lending markets and minimize risk. The settlement period, immediately following the clearing, involves the conclusion and fulfillment of the transaction. The buyer pays the agreed price, and the seller delivers the securities. Depending on the type of securities transferred, the settlement period typically lasts up to two business days.

In the DeFi setting, clearing and settlement are not as clearly distinguishable as in CeFi, because DeFi mainly takes a decentralized clearing approach, meaning that the trading partners interact directly with each other and no CCP is involved. Furthermore, since the trade is automatically executed by a smart contract in an indivisible transaction, the counterparty credit risk is reduced, and the trading partners remain in exclusive possession of their assets until the transaction is executed, since (a) no collateral must be deposited with a CCP and (b) the settlement period is essentially eliminated because the transaction is executed, in essence, instantly.[34] With regard to the management of the securities transferred, in CeFi the customer's custodian bank is responsible for custody of the transferred securities, and either manages the securities itself or outsources the management to a central securities depository. In DeFi, the trading partners retain exclusive control over the securities, which are typically held in non-custodial wallets.

Defi Advantages and Opportunities

The DeFi community often refers to the technical and user-related advantages and opportunities of DeFi over CeFi as "promises". The main technical advantages resulting from the underlying blockchain respectively distributed ledger technology include high transparency, trustlessness, and immutability.

Transparency, in this context, means that data is stored on public blockchains, so anyone can access or audit the information about DeFi protocol transactions or locked funds (Amler et al., 2021; Meegan & Koens, 2021; Qin et al., 2021; Schär, 2021; Schueffel, 2021). The blocks of a blockchain are connected using cryptographic methods and every manipulation results in a transparent change in the cryptographic signature. The term "pseudo-transparency" is used when the public key of the users is publicly visible while the public key owners remain anonymous (Amler et al., 2021).

In the DeFi setting, *trustlessness* is achieved through distributed ledger technology, which distributes trust across a network instead of relying on one single trust creating entity, such as a bank in the CeFi setting

---

[34] In CeFi, the buyer may pay the agreed purchase price immediately, while the seller delivers the securities at the end of the settlement period. Thus, the buyer's asset position is initially reduced without immediate compensation.

(Amler et al., 2021; Meegan & Koens, 2021; Perez et al., 2020; Schär, 2021; Schueffel, 2021). The system assumes that most network participants are non-malicious and relies on consensus mechanisms to detect and eliminate malicious behavior by a participant.

The blockchain technology underlying the DeFi protocols ensure true *immutability* using cryptographic methods and consensus algorithms, which make it nearly impossible to manipulate data stored on the blockchain. Thus, immutability combines transparency and trustlessness because manipulations are transparent to all, and the network rejects illegitimate changes.

The user-related benefits of DeFi stem from its self-sovereignty approach, permissionless and democratic access to financial products. Self-sovereignty means that DeFi enables users to manage their personal data and funds themselves. Accordingly, users are not dependent on central authorities or intermediaries who can cause them damage through malicious behavior.[35] DeFi also gives everyone permissionless[36] and democratic access to financial products and services at any time. Unlike in the CeFi setting, where barriers to opening a bank account and access to products and services are common, DeFi provides greater financial inclusivity (Amler et al., 2021; Chen & Bellavitis, 2020; Harvey et al., 2020; Meegan & Koens, 2021; Schär, 2021; Schueffel, 2021). In DeFi, financial inclusivity is also increased by lower friction and transaction costs, since no intermediaries such as custodians, escrow agents, or clearing and settlement agents have to be paid, unlike in the CeFi setting.[37] Another important advantage of DeFi over CeFi relates to the interconnectedness and composability of DeFi services. In other words, the fact that different DeFi protocols can be linked together like *LEGO* bricks to provide a wide range of services and functionalities is advantageous for its users (Amler et al., 2021; Gudgeon et al., 2020; Meegan & Koens, 2021; Schär, 2021).

---

[35] The degree of self-sovereignty between a user and a DeFi protocol must be strictly separated from the dependency of a user on a wallet provider. For example, if a user commissions a wallet provider to store his private key, then a dependency relationship exists between the user and the wallet provider. However, this dependency does not explicitly affect the self-sovereignty of a user when dealing with a DeFi protocol.

[36] Even though the basic idea of DeFi is based on permissionless access, permissions can be set, e.g., by using private blockchains or restrictive smart contract configurations.

[37] At times, transaction fees, e.g., on the Ethereum blockchain, have been very volatile, reaching a high of the equivalent of USD 70 in May 2021.

For example, a user may take out a loan via a DeFi protocol and then invest the borrowed amount via a second protocol, which is common in crowdfunding projects. In this case, the lending and investing protocols form a new combined DeFi service.

DeFi Disadvantages and Challenges

DeFi has potential technical, economic, and systemic disadvantages and challenges compared to CeFi. The technical limitations and risks include smart contract vulnerability, limitations regarding the scalability of the underlying blockchain, and privacy concerns. Smart contract vulnerability can be explained based on the theoretical model of "contract complete-ness" proposed by Coase (1937) and Grossman and Hart (1986), who maintain that contracts cannot, per se, account for all contingencies. In the context of DeFi, Aramonte et al. (2021, p. 27) develop this theoret-ical model further, identifying "algorithm incompleteness" in the inability of code, per se, to account for all contingencies. Although such risk can be reduced, for example, by program audits or open-source develop-ment, attackers can exploit bugs and errors in smart contract code, as demonstrated by the failed collateral auction on the MakerDAO platform described above (Amler et al., 2021; Aramonte et al., 2021; Bartoletti et al., 2021; Jensen et al., 2021b; Oosthoek, 2021; Qin et al., 2021; Schueffel, 2021; Werner et al., 2021).

As discussed briefly above, as a result of the scalability trilemma, there are limits to the throughput that Layer 1 technologies can provide,[38] despite techniques to improve throughput, such as side-chains and sharding are currently not used widely in a productive setup (Amler et al., 2021; Harvey et al., 2020; Schär, 2021; Schueffel, 2021). While a core property and advantage of blockchain technology is (pseudo-) trans-parency, it also has potential disadvantages with regard to user privacy,

---

[38] The Ethereum blockchain can currently achieve a throughput of around 15 trans-actions per second, which is expected to increase significantly after the transition to Ethereum 2.0 in early 2022. In comparison, Visa states that their systems are capable of handling more than 65,000 transactions per second and the trading system of NASDAQ currently handles approximately 1,300 transactions per second during a trading day. While such a direct comparison of decentralized and centralized systems is an oversimplification, these figures illustrate that DeFi systems require sufficient throughput volumes to compete with CeFi systems.

such as in financial transactions involving highly sensitive data which users legitimately want to keep confidential (Amler et al., 2021).

From an economic perspective, the main risks and disadvantages of DeFi compared to CeFi relate to oracle dependency, the design of stablecoins, high levels of leverage, impermanent losses in liquidity pools, regulatory uncertainty, and potentially high barriers to entry for less affluent users engaging in lower-value transactions.

The risks relating to oracle dependencies arise from the fact that many DeFi protocols are based on information, e.g., on exchange rates, which is often provided by third-party providers. Thus, DeFi protocols that use such information in their products and services must rely on the reliability, accuracy, and correctness of this information, which may pose a security threat through malicious oracles that have an incentive to provide false information (Amler et al., 2021; Caldarelli & Ellul, 2021; Harvey et al., 2020; Liu et al., 2020; Oosthoek, 2021; Schär, 2021; Werner et al., 2021).

Using stablecoins is essential to many DeFi products and services, but it also involves certain risks and disadvantages (Aramonte et al., 2021; International Monetary Fund, 2021; Li & Mayer, 2021; Liu et al., 2020; Perez et al., 2020; Salami, 2021). Since the value of stablecoins is linked to the value of an underlying asset, e.g., the USD or cryptocurrencies such as Ether, their value depends to a considerable extent on the confidence that stablecoin holders have in the value of the underlying asset (Aramonte et al., 2021). Liquidity mismatches or exposure to market risk can cause fire sales of the underlying assets, which also puts pressure on stablecoins and endangers their intended value stability (Aramonte et al., 2021). For the users of DeFi protocols, the problem in such situations is that they cannot or can only insufficiently react to the possible price decline of the stablecoins with selling/exchanging their stablecoins, since they are often locked in DeFi protocols, e.g., in staking or lending pools.

Since loans on DeFi protocols are mostly overcollateralized, high levels of leverage can be attained by depositing funds borrowed on one protocol as collateral on another protocol (Aramonte et al., 2021; Gudgeon et al., 2020; Werner et al., 2021). These cascading borrowings are particularly dangerous when debt must be reduced, e.g., due to depreciating collateral, which puts further pressure on already eroding prices (Aramonte et al., 2021). Gudgeon et al. (2020) show that, on average, DeFi protocols run the risk of being undercollateralized in about nineteen days after a price crash.

The provision of liquidity via liquidity or exchange pools involves the risk of so-called impermanent losses (Aramonte et al., 2021; Cousaert et al., 2021; Harvey et al., 2020; Jensen et al., 2021a). Impermanent losses occur when there are strong price changes in the deposited assets. For example, if a liquidity provider deposits a pair of crypto assets consisting of Ether and Dai, and the Ether value increases, then liquidity takers have an incentive to withdraw Ether from the pool and deposit Dai. In this case, the liquidity providers cannot benefit from the Ether value increase to the same extent as if they had not provided liquidity. They receive the transaction fee as compensation for providing liquidity, but as soon as this is not sufficient to compensate for the price increase, impermanent losses occur.

The lack of a framework to regulate taxation, KYC/AML requirements, and liability issues in the event of exploits/hacks of protocols, among other issues, create uncertainty and pose economic risks and disadvantages (Amler et al., 2021; Harvey et al., 2020; International Monetary Fund, 2021; Meegan and Koens, 2021; Qin et al., 2021; Salami, 2021; Zetzsche et al., 2020). Zetzsche et al. (2020) recommend a comprehensive, new regulatory approach because CeFi regulation is too limited for the DeFi context. The authors recommend "embedded regulation" aimed to anchor key regulatory objectives such as market integrity, market conduct, and financial stability directly within DeFi protocols, thus creating a form of real-time monitoring.

As democratic access and a higher financial inclusivity were outlined as advantages of DeFi compared to CeFi, this point is valid from a purely theoretical point of view. It is, however, currently inaccurate from a practical point of view. In the case of Ethereum, this is primarily due to the high transaction fees caused by ballooning MEV[39] extraction which particularly affects relatively less wealthy users. Hence, users with higher value transactions are the ones primarily benefitting, as transaction costs

---

[39] Miner extractable value (MEV) describes the maximum value that can be generated from mining a block in addition to the block reward and transaction fees by deciding which transactions are added to a block and in which order. Certain market participants try to take advantage of the MEV by trying to find profitable MEV opportunities, e.g., arbitrage opportunities between different DEXes, and use them for their own benefit by submitting profitable transactions with high transaction fees and thus pushing themselves ahead of other transactions. Such actions are referred to as frontrunning (Ethereum, 2022b). See also Auer et al. (2022) for a comprehensive discussion of MEV and associated risks.

become less impactful when ticket size increases. While Ethereum's transition to PoS may reduce network congestion and thus lower transaction fees, such fixed fees, remain prohibitive for low-value transactions. For example, transaction fees between USD 50 and USD 150 are charged for a transaction on the Uniswap platform, regardless of the value of the transaction, and transaction fees of between USD 100 and 200 are charged for depositing crypto assets using lending protocols such as Aave. Less affluent users may not have sufficient capital to engage in overcollateralized lending and to raise capital via the DeFi system.[40]

Certain design features of DeFi protocols, such as governance tokens, create inherent and systemic risks. Since people holding governance tokens can vote to change the protocol and the platform, attackers may target this governance system to achieve financial gains by exploiting these systems, creating risks and disadvantages for DeFi platform users (Aramonte et al., 2021; International Monetary Fund, 2021; Jensen et al., 2021b; Nadler & Schär, 2020; Oosthoek, 2021; Qin et al., 2021; Werner et al., 2021). For example, Gudgeon et al. (2020) describe how Maker's token supply could be increased by attacking the governance system of MakerDAO.

To illustrate this risk, Table 2.2, based on Nadler and Schär (2020), showing the governance token distribution of selected DeFi platforms, demonstrates that a small group of addresses own a significant portion of governance tokens and thus have great decision-making power, posing a governance risk. On average, the top 500 addresses own around 88 percent of the governance tokens. The Gini coefficient of the top 500 addresses, with a value of 0.79 on average, also indicates a strong unequal distribution of the presented governance tokens. Similarly, in their study of a relatively small sample of DeFi platforms such as Uniswap or Compound, Jensen et al. (2021b) find an unequal distribution of governance tokens indicated by Gini coefficients greater than 0.9. Aramonte et al. (2021) investigate initial token distribution to insiders such as development teams and VC investors, identifying potential governance risks associated with the settlement layer. Their results show that Layer 1 solutions such as Flow and Binance are associated with comparatively high governance risks since they have distributed c.54% and c.50% of their governance tokens to insiders, while other Layer 1 solutions like

---

[40] The same opinion is shared by Aramonte et al. (2022), who also state that access to overcollaterized credits is limited to asset-rich users.

Ethereum, Cardano, and EOS have distributed less than 20% of the tokens to insiders (Aramonte et al., 2021). The sometimes high concentration of governance tokens also creates risks for token holders with smaller stakes, as these tokens are not very liquid and thus cannot be easily converted into stablecoins or fiat currencies. In this context, the turnover ratio of the 30 most valuable governance token in terms of their market capitalization is rather low at c.21 percent. In comparison, World Bank data points out that the global average stock turnover ratio for domestic shares was c.104 percent in 2018 (World Bank, 2022). Additionally, Aramonte et al. (2021) outline a potential governance risk on the settlement layer related to the transition from PoW to PoS on the Ethereum blockchain, which will make it easier for a small number of large validators to change transactions on the blockchain to gain financial advantage.

The composability of DeFi protocols also poses risks, especially since composed DeFi applications are difficult to analyze due to the high degree of interaction between the protocols and are also associated with far-reaching consequences due to the involvement of many different protocols (Amler et al., 2021; Cousaert et al., 2021; Daian et al., 2019; Gudgeon et al., 2020; Jensen et al., 2021a; Kitzler et al., 2021; Qin et al., 2021). Qin et al. (2021) provide an example of such a risk, namely

Table 2.2 Holder concentration of governance tokens of selected DeFi protocols

DApp	Gov. Token	Top 5	Top 10	Top 50	Top 100	Top 500	Gini 500
MakerDAO	MKR	24.4%	36.5%	67.7%	79.5%	93.7%	0.79
Curve Finance	CRV	56.9%	61.1%	73.2%	79.1%	90.3%	0.85
Aave	AAVE	36.7%	43.6%	61.4%	67.4%	80.1%	0.80
Compound	COMP	31.2%	43.8%	86.8%	96.2%	98.9%	0.90
SushiSwap	SUSHI	25.6%	35.3%	58.3%	66.3%	83.8%	0.74
yearn.finance	YFI	11.5%	17.0%	37.3%	48.1%	73.8%	0.58
Balancer	BAL	27.6%	36.7%	77.3%	85.0%	94.9%	0.84
Average		**30.6%**	**39.1%**	**66.0%**	**74.5%**	**87.9%**	**0.79**
Median		**27.6%**	**36.7%**	**67.7%**	**79.1%**	**90.3%**	**0.80**

market manipulation through so-called flash loans,[41] for which no collateral must be deposited.[42] The authors show how arbitrage opportunities can be created by using these flash loans to manipulate exchange rates on different DEXes, leveraging the high complexity of composed protocols (Qin et al., 2021).

DeFi Fault Lines

As with any very new technology that is rapidly deployed at scale, DeFi has some disadvantages and there are challenges to overcome. Since DeFi has been developed, to date, largely independently of CeFi, we identified distinct fault lines between DeFi and CeFi.

Volatility vs. financial stability: Digital assets in the DeFi space have been significantly more volatile than assets in the CeFi setting. For example, Ether, one of the most important cryptocurrencies in the DeFi space, fluctuated c.73% on average between 2018 and 2021, while the S&P 500 only fluctuated c.13% on average in the same period.[43] Central banks are responsible for setting monetary policies to ensure price stability, but no such responsibility is present in DeFi. CeFi balance sheets are increasingly vulnerable to contagion risks as their direct or indirect exposure to crypto assets rises potential threats for financial stability.

Scams/hacks vs. consumer protection: Recent scams and hacks in the DeFi space point to the need for consumer protection. To date, rule compliance in the DeFi space is achieved solely technically, and there is no central supervising authority. In the CeFi space, national and supranational agencies perform supervisory tasks and intervene to ensure consumer protection when necessary. However, scams, such as the Enron and Wirecard scandals, have occurred, nonetheless.

Pseudo-anonymity vs. KYC/AML: As discussed above, users interacting with DeFi protocols are, for the most part, pseudo-anonymous: their actions are publicly observable, but their identity remains hidden

---

[41] For an introduction to flash loans in DeFi, see Wang et al. (2021).

[42] Another popular attack that targets the composability of DeFi protocols is the so-called "frontrunning," described by Daian et al. (2019).

[43] The figures represent the rolling 10-day volatility.

behind a public key. CeFi participants cannot access or interact with financial products and services without establishing and verifying their identity through comprehensive know-your-customer (KYC) and anti-money laundering (AML) processes.

Legal and regulatory uncertainty vs. regulation: In the DeFi space, many legal and regulatory questions remain unanswered, which creates a high degree of uncertainty. As mentioned briefly above, CeFi regulatory approaches cannot be transferred directly to DeFi. The CeFi space has complex regulatory frameworks that have evolved over time and are designed, primarily, to protect investors and creditors, and to reduce liquidity and systemic risks.

Functional view vs. institutional view: In DeFi, there are no institutions or intermediaries in the traditional sense. The financial functionalities implemented with smart contracts to provide financial products and services require no intervention by an institution or an intermediary. In contrast, institutions and intermediaries play an essential role in CeFi, primarily to establish trust and reduce information asymmetries. This difference has important implications for regulators because most regulation is focused on the conduct of institutional actors.

Decentralized vs. single or few points of failure: Fully decentralized technologies without hidden centrality have no centralized vulnerabilities, which dramatically reduces the risk of outages and hacks. Since data on the blockchain is recorded immutably and stored on the many nodes of a network, attacks are more difficult than in the centralized setting. In addition, illicit conduct, or failure on the part of a single actor in a decentralized network, has less far-reaching consequences because it can be offset by other actors more easily.

Inclusive vs. underbanked: A basic principle of DeFi is that anyone with access to the internet can access DeFi financial services and products without restrictions. In contrast, in CeFi, banks and other financial institutions control who can access their financial products and services. Individuals with no or insufficient access are considered underbanked.

DeFi and CeFi—Coexistence or Convergence?

A Scenario Analysis

Most observers assume that the CeFi will continue to exist because of its size and the fact that it is responsible for creating money and setting monetary policy. Given this assumption, in this section, we consider and compare three scenarios for how DeFi and CeFi might develop going forward:

(1) DeFi disappears
(2) DeFi and CeFi coexist separately
(3) DeFi and CeFi converge

There are several reasons why we consider it highly unlikely that DeFi will ultimately disappear. First, investor interest, measured by the TVL, continues to grow steadily and continuously. Second, DeFi is particularly popular among younger users and investors, and benefits from other growing trends among younger people, such as NFTs, the metaverse, Web3, and integration with GameFi. Third, the global transformational wave of digitalization supports greater automation, and DeFi applications demonstrate, at least technically, that large parts of the value chain of many financial services, such as lending and trading, can be automated.

We consider it more likely that DeFi and CeFi will ultimately coexist separately, with minimal linkages between the two sectors. These linkages could be provided by, e.g., dedicated off-ramp service providers, facilitating exchange between fiat currency and cryptocurrencies which would be used to access and interact with DeFi protocols. To minimize the risks of contagion from cryptocurrency price volatility and operational and money laundering risks, CeFi would minimize its direct involvement in DeFi. This is, for the most part, the status quo scenario.

The scenario we consider most likely, however, is that DeFi and CeFi will ultimately converge to leverage synergies and mutual benefits. This scenario is consistent with that of the "distributed bank," which was proposed by Hernández de Cos (2019), and introduced in Sect. 2.2. DeFi will contribute the technical innovation, high growth, agile market environment, and high adaptability of the young customer generation, and CeFi will contribute a well-functioning regulatory system, and a broad and trusting customer base. To support such convergence, from our viewpoint, financial regulators will play a critical role at the fault lines, especially in decreasing regulatory and legal uncertainties, and increasing customer and institutional trust in DeFi (Wieandt, 2021). First, financial regulators should control the gateways in and out of DeFi, ideally including KYC/AML checks to limit illicit activity, and regulate crypto asset service providers such as exchanges, trading venues, and custodians.[44] Second, financial regulators should establish mandatory minimum standards of disclosure, transparency, and cyber-security for DeFi protocols, token issuances, and wallets, to prevent major scams and hacks. Third, they should support international taxation laws and enforcement policies, such as linking public wallet addresses to DeFi tax identification numbers, aided by blockchain transparency. Government supervision would need to shift from focusing on institutions and individuals to monitoring protocol transactions on-chain activities in real-time.[45] Furthermore, technical compatibility between central bank digital currencies (CBDCs) and the DeFi space is key to bridging CeFi and DeFi. Carstens (2022) also sees a DLT-based global network of CBDCs as the foundation for collaboration among DeFi and CeFi players in an innovation-friendly climate without fragmentation or walled gardens. Furthermore, DeFi proponents would need to shift their mindset and give up their anarcho-capitalist opposition to CeFi. From a technical standpoint, the DeFi base layers would need to become more interoperable and much more scalable to handle the significantly larger transaction volumes. The transition to Ethereum 2.0 and the use of proof-of-stake (PoS) consensus mechanism are steps in this direction. To ensure sustainability, the carbon footprint of DeFi must be reduced significantly, which the transition to PoS supports.

Even if, as already mentioned, it is very unlikely that DeFi protocols will completely replace banks, there are nevertheless important implications for banks to generate advantages, especially in competition with other banks. Thereby, it is essential for financial intermediaries to take note of the recent developments in DeFi space, build partnerships, make investments, strengthen the sensitivity and interest of their customers,

---

[44] This thought is also shared by Aramonte et al. (2022), who also claim that more information needs to be collected about, e.g., borrowers in lending protocols, albeit that this decreases the degree of decentralization.

[45] See Zetzsche et al. (2020) for a discussion of a potential regulation approach for DeFi. In addition, Auer et al. (2022) argue that there is a need for new regulatory approaches that are more suitable to deal with potential threats of market manipulation in DeFi (e.g., problems related to MEV).

and, most importantly, participate in the creation of an innovation-friendly regulation of DeFi. The next section of this paper gives an overview of recent examples where DeFi and CeFi have joined forces.

Recent Examples of DeFi–CeFi Convergence

This section discusses several recent DeFi–CeFi convergence initiatives. As an example of convergence efforts initiated by the DeFi World, let us look at the real-world asset (RWA) market that is being built in a collaboration between Aave and Centrifuge.[46] Aave offers decentralized lending protocols whereby users can participate as lenders and borrowers. Aave has over USD 11 bn in TVL as of December 2021, making it a top 5 DeFi protocol, and is currently deployed on Ethereum, Polygon, and Avalanche. Depositors provide liquidity to the market to earn passive income, while borrowers can borrow in an over- or undercollateralized fashion. Until recently, Aave users could only borrow or lend by depositing crypto assets, which tend to be volatile. By opening up to the RWA market, Aave allows its depositors to earn yield against stable, uncorrelated real-world collateral. The Centrifuge network enables users to create on-chain asset funds based on RWAs such as cars or real estate, otherwise known as pools. Each pool issues tokens which represent a share in these pools, and can be used on Aave in exchange for the stablecoin USDC. Hence, users can now borrow from Aave by depositing their stake in a Centrifuge RWA collateral pool. Access to the RWA market will make use of the new permissioned pool feature on Aave called Aave Arc (Aave, 2021). Aave Arc is a simple deployment of a new version of the Aave protocol with an additional layer for whitelisting and KYC to be compliant with AML regulations and US securities rules and regulations. While the protocol itself remains decentralized, centralized intermediaries, such as FireBlocks, handle the onboarding of new users. The pool itself will be publicly readable on Ethereum, but only accessible to users willing to undergo KYC verification. The combination of a whitelisted protocol with RWA asset markets significantly increases the collateral asset and user pool for DeFi protocols. Therefore, Aave Arc highlights the importance of

---

[46] In this context, another interesting example is the cooperation between Aave and RealT which allows user to borrow stablecoins on the Aave platform by using real estate investments made on the RealT platform as collateral.

regulation and compliance in making the full spectrum of DeFi protocols available to a broad user base.

Another initiative coming from the DeFi space is the Goldfinch protocol (Goldfinch, 2022). In essence, this protocol connects liquidity providers from the DeFi space with borrowers outside the DeFi space via lending businesses. In the Goldfinch protocol, liquidity providers, on the one hand, deposit crypto assets into the Goldfinch pool and earn yield. On the other hand, lending businesses can expand their credit lines by withdrawing stablecoins from the pool, without depositing collateral, and lend fiat money to individuals. As soon as an individual makes an interest or principal payment, the lending business returns it to the pool, where it is equally distributed among the liquidity providers.

A convergence initiative coming from the CeFi space is the Société Générale–MakerDao move to refinance tokenized loans. In 2020, Forge, a subsidiary of the French banking group Société Générale, offered to deposit a tokenized bond with a value of USD 40 m in the MakerDAO protocol with 0% interest and maturing in 2025 as collateral for a loan of c.20 m Dai on the Maker platform (MakerDAO Forum, 2021). This pilot transaction demonstrates how using the processing capacity of an underlying blockchain and automating the debt refinancing process using a DeFi protocol can eliminate the need to involve CeFi participants, such as post-trade systems, and hold traditional CeFi negotiations, to thus reduce transaction costs.

Conclusion and Suggestions for Future Research

DeFi has the potential to create a radically new form of financial intermediation, broaden financial inclusion, and increase operational efficiency. This potential stems mainly from the qualities of transparency, immutability, and trustlessness associated with the underlying blockchain technology, and from the nature of the DeFi ecosystem to facilitate composability among highly interoperable protocols implementing financial functions and services, such as lending, borrowing, and exchanges.

However, as with all nascent technologies, there are some drawbacks and risks associated with DeFi. These risks include scalability issues of the underlying blockchain technology, privacy concerns due to the transparency property of blockchains, and legal and regulatory uncertainties, such as the lack of KYC/AML checks. For these reasons, traditional financial institutions have been reluctant to engage in DeFi. There is, however, great potential for synergy and mutual benefits between the two systems, especially in terms of innovation, as well as legal/regulatory compliance.

Assuming the continued existence of the massive, well-established, and systemically vital CeFi space, this paper considers three scenarios of DeFi–CeFi association: (1) DeFi disappears; (2) DeFi and CeFi coexist separately; or (3) DeFi and CeFi converge. We argue that coexistence/strict separation is unlikely, given the growing institutional interest in DeFi and the development of bridging solutions, such as Aave Arc and the RWA market.[47] We propose that these, and other bridging solutions, will pave the way for ultimate CeFi–DeFi convergence, driven by the promise of higher automation, greater access, lower transaction costs, and lower dependence on trusted intermediaries. We anticipate a whitelisting and monitoring layer run by decentrally approved regulated entities and decentralized protocols executing transactions located on public, permissionless blockchains. If successful, these and other bridging solutions between CeFi and DeFi that will no doubt emerge, carry the promise of making finance more efficient.

Future research should quantify and compare the efficiency gains and welfare gains of moving various parts of the CeFi to DeFi protocols. Further, there is an abundance of research possibilities to look at DeFi governance and regulation, particularly when facing various types of systemic stress. From a technological perspective, further research is needed to explore how the scalability of blockchains can be increased without compromises to security and decentralization, and how privacy can be preserved without a loss of transparency.

References

Aave. (2021). *Introducing Aave Arc.* https://aave.mirror.xyz/JcA9DzQHK6o8 YYMmxtH43Vqq5HoHvjrTrFnd_UprKWQ. Accessed on January 24 2022.

Adams, H., Zinsmeister, N., Salem, M., Keefer, R., & Robinson, D. (2021). *Uniswap v3 core.* https://uniswap.org/whitepaper-v3.pdf. Accessed on December 13 2021.

Amler, H., Eckey, L., Faust, S., Kaiser, M., Sandner, P., & Schlosser, B. (2021). DeFi-ning DeFi: Challenges & pathway. https://doi.org/10.48550/arXiv.2101.05589

---

[47] Aramonte et al. (2022) also state that depositing RWAs as collateral in DeFi lending protocols is important to enable bridges between CeFi and DeFi.

Antonopoulos, A. M., & Wood, G. (2018). Mastering Ethereum: Building smart contracts and dapps. O'Reilly.

Aramonte, S., Huang, W., & Schrimpf, A. (2021). DeFi risks and the decentralisation illusion. *BIS Quarterly Review, 25*(4), 21–36

Aramonte, S., Doerr, S., Huang, W., & Schrimpf, A. (2022). *DeFi lending: intermediation without information?* https://www.bis.org/publ/bisbull57.htm. Accessed on June 20 2022.

Arner, D. W., Barberis, J. N., & Buckley, R. P. (2015). The evolution of Fintech: A new post-crisis paradigm? https://doi.org/10.2139/ssrn.2676553

Auer, R., Frost, J., & Pastor, J. M. V. (2022). *Miners as intermediaries: Extractable value and market manipulation in crypto and DeFi.* https://www.bis.org/publ/bisbull58.htm. Accessed on June 20 2022.

Bartoletti, M., Chiang, J. H., & Lluch-Lafuente, A. (2021). Towards a theory of decentralized finance. In M. Bernhard, A. Bracciali, L. Gudgeon, T. Haines, A. Klages-Mundt, S. Matsuo, D. Perez, M. Sala, & S. Werner (Eds.), *Financial cryptography and data security. FC 2021 International Workshops.* Springer.

Beniiche, A. (2020). A study of blockchain oracles. https://doi.org/10.48550/arXiv.2004.07140

Berentsen, A., & Schär, F. (2019). Stablecoins: The quest for a low-volatility cryptocurrency. In A. Fatás (Ed.), *The economics of fintech and digital currencies.* CEPR Press.

Binance. (2020). *Binance smart chain: A parallel binance chain to enable smart contracts.* https://dex-bin.bnbstatic.com/static/Whitepaper_%20Binance%20Smart%20Chain.pdf. Accessed on January 31 2022.

Boado, E. (2020). *Aave protocol whitepaper V1.0.* https://github.com/aave/aave-protocol/blob/master/docs/Aave_Protocol_Whitepaper_v1_0.pdf. Accessed on December 13 2021.

Buterin, V. (2013). *A next-generation smart contract and decentralized application platform.* https://ethereum.org/en/whitepaper/. Accessed on January 12 2022.

Buterin, V. (2021). *Why sharding is great: Demystifying the technical properties.* https://vitalik.ca/general/2021/04/07/sharding.html. Accessed on January 31 2021.

Caldarelli, G., & Ellul, J. (2021). The blockchain oracle problem in decentralized finance—a multivocal approach. *Applied Sciences, 11*(16), 7572. https://doi.org/10.3390/app11167572

Carstens, A. (2022). *Digital currencies and the soul of money.* https://www.bis.org/speeches/sp220118.htm. Accessed on January 23 2022.

Chen, Y., & Bellavitis, C. (2020). Blockchain disruption and decentralized finance: The rise of decentralized business models. *Journal of Business Venturing Insights, 13*(1). https://doi.org/10.1016/j.jbvi.2019.e00151

Coase, R. (1937). The nature of the firm. *Economica, 4*(16), 386–405.
CoinMarketCap. (2022). *Total cryptocurrency market cap.* https://coinmarke
tcap.com/charts/. Accessed on January 10 2022.
Cousaert, S., Xu, J., & Matsui, T. (2021). SoK: Yield aggregators in DeFi.
https://doi.org/10.48550/arXiv.2105.13891
Daian, P., Goldfeder, S., Kell, T., Li, Y., Zhao, X., Bentov, I., Breidenbach, L., &
Juels, A. (2019). Flash boys 2.0: Frontrunning, transaction reordering, and
consensus instability in decentralized exchanges. https://doi.org/10.48550/
arXiv.1904.05234
DefiLlama. (2022a). *Total value locked (USD).* https://defillama.com. Accessed
on January 10 2022.
DefiLlama. (2022b). *Total value locked all chains.* https://defillama.com/chains.
Accessed on January 10 2022.
DeFi Pulse. (2022). Total value locked (USD) in DeFi. https://defipulse.com/.
Accessed on October 12 2022.
Diamond, D. W., & Dybvig, P. H. (1983). Bank runs, deposit insurance, and
liquidity. *The Journal of Political Economy, 91*(3), 401–419.
Dune Analytics. (2022). *Total DeFi users over time.* https://dune.xyz/queries/
2972. Accessed on January 10 2022.
Egorov, M. (2019*). StableSwap—efficient mechanism for Stablecoin liquidity.*
https://curve.fi/files/stableswap-paper.pdf. Accessed on January 12 2022.
Egorov, M. (2021). *Automatic market-making with dynamic Peg.* https://curve.
fi/files/crypto-pools-paper.pdf. Accessed on January 12 2022.
Eichholz, L. (2020). *What really happened to MakerDAO?* https://insights.
glassnode.com/what-really-happened-to-makerdao/. Accessed on January 26
2022.
Ethereum. (2022a). *Scaling.* https://ethereum.org/en/developers/docs/sca
ling/. Accessed on February 1 2022.
Ethereum. (2022b). *Miner extractable value (MEV).* https://ethereum.org/en/
developers/docs/mev/. Accessed on March 3 2022.
Etherscan. (2022). *Ethereum unique addresses chart.* https://etherscan.io/chart/
address. Accessed on January 15 2022.
Financial Stability Board. (2021). *Global monitoring report on non-bank financial intermediation.* https://www.fsb.org/wp-content/uploads/P161221.
pdf. Accessed on January 10 2022.
Financial Stability Board. (2022). *Assessment of risks to financial stability
from crypto-assets.* https://www.fsb.org/wp-content/uploads/P160222.pdf.
Accessed on February 28 2022.
Gogel, D. (2021). *DeFi beyond the hype—the emerging world of decentralized finance.* https://wifpr.wharton.upenn.edu/wp-content/uploads/2021/
05/DeFi-Beyond-the-Hype.pdf. Accessed on January 9 2022.

Goldfinch. (2022). *Bringing crypto loans to the real world.* https://docs.goldfi nch.finance/goldfinch/. Accessed on February 3 2022.

Grossman, S. J., & Hart, O. D. (1986). The costs and benefits of ownership: A theory of vertical and lateral integration. *Journal of Political Economy, 94*(4), 691–719. https://doi.org/10.1086/261404

Gudgeon, L., Perez, D., Harz, D., Livshits, B., & Gervais, A. (2020). The decentralized financial crisis. https://doi.org/10.48550/arXiv.2002.08099

Harvey, C. R., Ramachandran, A., & Santoro, J. (2020). *DeFi and the future of finance.* Hoboken: Wiley.

Hernández de Cos, P. (2019). *Financial technology: The 150-year revolution.* https://www.bis.org/speeches/sp191119.htm. Accessed on January 26 2022.

International Monetary Fund. (2021). *The crypto ecosystem and financial stability challenges.* https://www.elibrary.imf.org/view/books/082/465808-978151 3595603-en/ch002.xml. Accessed on December 13 2021.

Jensen, J. R., von Wachter, V., & Ross, O., (2021a). An introduction to decentralized finance (DeFi). *Complex Systems Informatics and Modeling Quarterly, 7*(1), 46–54. https://doi.org/10.7250/csimq.2021-26.03

Jensen, J. R., von Wachter, V., & Ross, O. (2021b). How decentralized is the governance of blockchain-based finance: Empirical evidence from four governance token distributions. https://doi.org/10.48550/arXiv.2102. 10096

Kereiakes, E., Kwon, D., Di Maggio, M., & Platias, N. (2019). *Terra money: Stability and adoption.* https://assets.website-files.com/611153e7af98147 2d8da199c/618b02d13e938ae1f8ad1e45_Terra_White_paper.pdf. Accessed on January 1 2022.

Kitzler, S., Victor, F., Saggese, P., & Haslhofer, B. (2021). Disentangling decentralized finance (DeFi) compositions. https://doi.org/10.48550/arXiv.2111. 11933

Lehar, A., & Parlour, C. A. (2021). *Dezentralized exchanges.* https://fraconfer ence.com/wp-content/uploads/2021/12/uniswap10_updated.pdf. Accessed on January 12 2022.

Li, Y., & Mayer, S. (2021). Money creation in decentralized finance: A dynamic model of stablecoin and crypto shadow banking. https://doi.org/10.2139/ ssrn.3757083

Liu, B., Szalachowski, P., & Zhou, J. (2020). A first look into DeFi oracles. https://doi.org/10.48550/arXiv.2005.04377

MakerDAO Forum. (2021). [Security Tokens Refinancing] MIP6 Application for OFH tokens. https://forum.makerdao.com/t/security-tokens-refina ncing-mip6-application-for-ofh-tokens/10605. Accessed on January 24 2022.

MakerDAO Foundation. (2020). *The maker protocol: MakerDAO's multi-collateral dai (mcd) system.* https://makerdao.com/whitepaper/White%20P aper%20-The%20Maker%20Protocol_%20MakerDAO%E2%80%99s%20Multi-Collateral%20Dai%20(MCD)%20System-FINAL-%20021720.pdf. Accessed on January 12 2022.

McLeay, M., Radia, A., & Thomas, R. (2014). Money creation in the modern economy. *Bank of England Quarterly Bulletin, 54*(1), 14–27.

Meegan, X., & Koens, T. (2021). *Lessons learned from decentralised finance (DeFi).* https://www.ingwb.com/binaries/content/assets/insights/the mes/distributed-ledger-technology/defi_white_paper_v2.0.pdf. Accessed on December 19 2021.

Merton, R. C., & Bodie, Z. (1995). A framework for analyzing the financial system. In Crane, D. B., Froot, K. A., Mason, S. P., Perold, A. F., Merton, R. C.; Bodie, Z., Sirri, E. R., & Tufano, P. (Eds.), *The global financial system: A functional perspective.* Harvard Business School Press.

Meyer, E., Welpe, I. M., & Sandner, P. G. (2022). Decentralized finance—a systematic literature review and research directions. https://doi.org/10.2139/ssrn.4016497

Nadler, M., & Schär, F. (2020). Decentralized finance, centralized ownership? An iterative mapping process to measure protocol token distribution. https://doi.org/10.48550/arXiv.2012.09306

Nakamoto, S. (2009). Bitcoin: A peer-to-peer electronic cash system. https://bitcoin.org/bitcoin.pdf. Accessed on January 10 2022.

Narayanan, A., Bonneau, J., Felten, E., Miller, A., & Goldfeder, S. (2016). *Bitcoin and cryptocurrency technologies.* Princeton University Press.

Oosthoek, K. (2021). Flash crash for cash: Cyber threats in decentralized finance. https://doi.org/10.48550/arXiv.2106.10740

Pasdar, A., Dong, Z., & Lee, Y. C. (2021). *Blockchain oracle design patterns.* https://arxiv.org/abs/2106.09349

Perez, D., Werner, S. M., Xu, J., & Livshits, B. (2020). Liquidations: DeFi on a knife-edge. https://doi.org/10.48550/arXiv.2009.13235

Popescu, A. (2020). Decentralized finance (DeFi)—The lego of finance. *Social Sciences and Education Research Review, 7*(1), 321–349.

Qin, K., Zhou, L., Afonin, Y., Lazzaretti, L., & Gervais, A. (2021). CeFi vs. DeFi—comparing centralized to decentralized finance. https://doi.org/10.48550/arXiv.2106.08157

Salami, I. (2021). Challenges and approaches to regulating decentralized finance. *American Journal of International Law Unbound, 115*(1), 425–429. https://doi.org/10.1017/aju.2021.66

Schär, F. (2021). Decentralized finance—on blockchain—and smart contract-based financial markets. *Federal Reserve Bank of St. Louis Review, 103*(2), 153–174. https://doi.org/10.20955/r.103.153-74

Schueffel, P. (2021). DeFi: decentralized finance—an introduction and overview. *Journal of Innovation Management, 9*(3), 1–11. https://doi.org/10.24840/2183-0606_009.003_0001

Shen, M., & Garg, A. (2022). Electric Capital Developer Report. (2021). https://github.com/electric-capital/developer-reports/blob/master/dev_report_2021_updated_012622.pdf. Accessed on January 24 2022.

Szabo, N. (1997). Formalizing and securing relationships on public networks. *First Monday, 2*(9). https://doi.org/10.5210/fm.v2i9.548

Wang, D., Wu, S., Lin, Z., Wu, L., Yuan, X., Zhou, Y., Wang, H., & Ren, K. (2021). Towards a first step to understand flash loan and its applications in DeFi ecosystem. https://doi.org/10.48550/arXiv.2010.12252

Werner, S. M., Perez, D., Gudgeon, L., Klages-Mundt, A., Harz, D., & Knottenbelt, W. J. (2021). SoK: Decentralized finance (DeFi). https://doi.org/10.48550/arXiv.2101.08778

Wieandt, A. (2017). Unfinished business: Putting European banking (and Europe) back on track. V&R unipress.

Wieandt, A. (2021). *The future of finance is decentralized—or not?* https://www.law.ox.ac.uk/business-law-blog/blog/2021/06/future-finance-decentralized-or-not. Accessed on March 8 2022.

World Bank. (2022). *Stocks traded, turnover ratio of domestic shares (%).* https://data.worldbank.org/indicator/CM.MKT.TRNR. Accessed on February 3 2022.

Zetzsche, D. A., Arner, D. W., & Buckley, R. P. (2020). Decentralized finance. *Journal of Financial Regulation, 6*(2), 172–203. https://doi.org/10.1093/jfr/fjaa010

CHAPTER 3

Fintech and the Digital Transformation of the Banking Landscape

Wesley L. Harris and Jarunee Wonglimpiyarat

INTRODUCTION

Banking is necessary, banks are not.
Bill Gates, Founder of Microsoft Corporation

This visionary statement made in 1994 by Bill Gates, the Founder of Microsoft Corporation, signaled the shift of a bank-dominated landscape toward the rise of financial technology (or fintech) in the coming decades.

W. L. Harris · J. Wonglimpiyarat (✉)
Department of Aeronautics and Astronautics, Massachusetts Institute of Technology, Cambridge, MA, USA
e-mail: jaruneew@mit.edu; j.wonglimpiyarat@imperial.ac.uk

J. Wonglimpiyarat
Leonardo Research Centre, Imperial College London, South Kensington Campus, London, UK

© The Author(s), under exclusive license to Springer Nature
Switzerland AG 2023
T. Walker et al. (eds.), *The Fintech Disruption*, Palgrave Studies
in Financial Services Technology,
https://doi.org/10.1007/978-3-031-23069-1_3

53

Fintech is seen as one of the technologies that has the ability to revolutionize the banking industry. Fintech has received global attention as the challenging technology (the technology that has potential to revolutionize the banking industry) that would empower firms to compete effectively in the twenty-first century. Governments around the world have paid attention to this challenge and devised policies and regulations to support fintech development. Figure 3.1 depicts global fintech funding from 2016 to 2021. Global fintech funding has seen a significant increase despite the global Corona Virus Disease (COVID-19) pandemic. Fintech funding up to Quarter 3 of 2021 nearly doubled from that in 2020 with a total funding of USD 94.7 billion.

For many decades, banks invested heavily in technology in an attempt to improve the efficiency of the financial innovation system (Barras, 1986, 1990). The banking landscape has witnessed the development of various fintech-based innovations, including, but not limited to, electronic fund transfer at the point-of-sale (EFTPOS), Automated Teller Machines (ATMs), Internet banking, Society for Worldwide Interbank Financial Telecommunication (SWIFT), International electronic fund transfers, Electronic Data Interchange (EDI), mobile banking, Bitcoin banking,

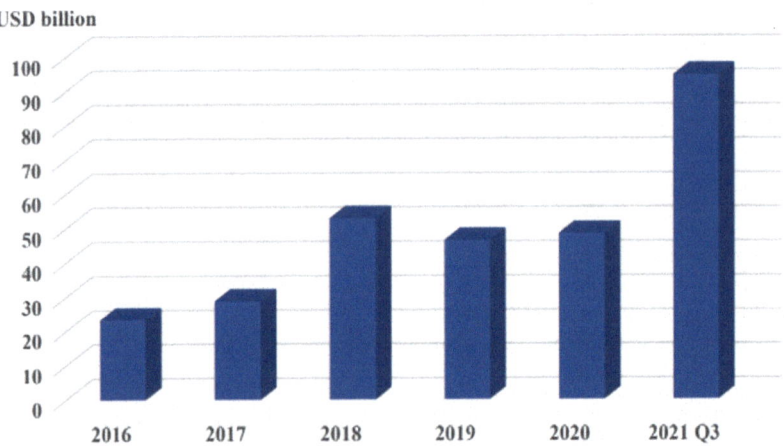

Fig. 3.1 Growth of global fintech funding from 2016 to 2021 (*Source* https://www.businessinsider.com)

Blockchain banking, and crowd funding. This chapter explores the diffusion process of financial technology (fintech) in the financial services industry through the lens of systemic innovation. This study analyzes the extent to which systemic characteristics have influenced the collaborative network solutions and the diffusion of fintech-based innovations.

The structure of this chapter is organized as follows. Section "Theoretical Framework", which follows the introduction, reviews the theoretical framework on innovation, financial innovation, systemic innovation, and technology diffusion process. Section "Systemic Innovation and Digital Transformation of the Banking Landscape" discusses the systemic innovation and digital transformation of the banking landscape. Section "Diffusion of Fintech-Based Innovations and Potential Disruption/Revolution Under the Global Pandemic of COVID-19" analyzes the diffusion of all banking innovations, including fintech-based innovations launched in the last 70 years up to the present, as well as the potential disruption/revolution of the banking landscape as a result of the global COVID-19 pandemic. Section "Research Implications and Conclusions" offers research implications and conclusions.

THEORETICAL FRAMEWORK

Innovation and Financial Innovation

Innovation is a complex process for which many scholars have developed several approaches to define its nature. In the context of technology management, the term "innovation" is defined in several ways. It has been defined as a process to enhance existing technology (Dosi, 1982; Nelson & Winter, 1977, 1982; Rosenberg, 1976, 1982) or as a process of turning opportunities into practical use (Pavitt, 1984; Tidd & Bessant, 2009). In a more comprehensive approach, innovation is defined as an integrated process of enhancing the technology frontier, transforming this into the best commercial opportunities, and delivering the commercialized product/process innovation in a competitive market with widespread use (Daft, 1982; Rothwell & Gardiner, 1985; Schott, 1981).

The banking sector is regarded as a service sector—a tertiary sector where industries involve the transformation of material goods, people, or information (Freeman, 1991; Miles, 1993, 1994, 2003, 2005; Utterback, 1994; Voss, 1994). The financial services industry, specifically banking, is seen as the vanguard sector in the use (not the creation) of information technology (IT) (Barras, 1986, 1990). In recent years, fintech has been seen as one of the technologies that would revolutionize the financial services industry. The term "fintech" encompasses technology-enabled services and solutions with the use of integrated IT. Fintech payment innovations offer new landscape in the digital era of financial industry. Fintech also provides a platform for banks and non-banks to facilitate cross-network transfers and payment services (Luo et al., 2021; Shim & Shin, 2017; Thompson, 2017).

Systemic Innovation

Systemic innovation is a type of innovation which requires a number of complementary systems to realize the value of innovations. It involves information interchange and coordination through a linked system (Chesbrough & Teece, 1996). The concept of systemic innovation emphasizes coordination in terms of the standard setting for an innovation, for example, mobile phones and personal computers (PCs). An allied concept of integration by Lawrence and Lorsch (1986) concerns the required integration among different units in an organization. However, the concept is rather more to do with solving complexity and uncertainty problems in an organization, for example, in the production and delivery process.

The concept of systemic innovation refers to a set of interconnected innovations, whereby an innovative coalition is necessary to achieve market acceptance. The systemic innovation is one where the benefits of an innovation increase disproportionately with the use and diffusion of the innovation among users. Also, the benefits would increase as a result of network externalities (Appleyard & Chesbrough, 2017; Chesbrough, 2003a, 2003b, 2011; Chesbrough & Teece, 1996; Harris & Wonglimpiyarat, 2019; West et al., 2014). In this study, the concept of systemic innovation will build upon these prior studies and help fill the gap in systemic financial innovations.

Technology Diffusion Process

The diffusion theory often deals with the innovation process, which characteristically exhibits an S-pattern. Schumpeter's long-wave theory explains the waves of economic development whereby the shift from an existing business cycle to a new one leads to the growth of industrialization. The Schumpeterian view of creative destruction emphasizes discontinuity of economic development. That is to say, the process of creative destruction brings about the economic growth of which the emergence of new product/process innovations does not grow out of the old ones, but eliminates them (Schumpeter, 1939, 1967).

Table 3.1 summarizes the various concepts of the technology diffusion process. Utterback and Abernathy (1975) articulate the innovation process as S-pattern. Vernon (1966)'s Product Life Cycle (PLC) is a classical model explaining the development as a pattern of product substitution (the S-curve pattern). The phases along the PLC reflect innovation diffusion—the progress of product/process innovations along the stages of introduction, growth, maturity, and decline. Given the competitive environment of the innovation/diffusion process in the industry, Utterback and Abernathy (1975) developed a model of the dynamics of innovation, the innovation life cycle model, to describe the process of innovation and the degree of technological change. The innovation life cycle also provides a basis for technological forecasting. According to the study of the innovation process by Fisher and Pry (1971), when a new innovation reaches about 5% penetration of the potential application market, it provides a reasonable base for forecasting the speed and ultimate penetration achievable.

Systemic Innovation and Digital Transformation of the Banking Landscape

Before analyzing fintech-based innovations through the lens of systemic innovation, it is useful to understand the banking landscape and development of fintech-based innovations. Figure 3.2 portrays the banking landscape in a global context.

The payment innovation of cheques has been used in the banking system since the seventeenth century. The era of fintech-based innovations began with the introduction of the credit card in the 1950s. The credit card, in the form of a Travel and Entertainment (T&E) card, was first launched in 1950 by the Diners Club, followed by the American Express card in 1958. The development of the credit card has been dominated by the systems supported by Visa and MasterCard. Visa and MasterCard have developed standards covering the card design, location and contents of the magnetic stripe tracks, rules for authorization, clearing, and settlement of transactions. Barclays was the first bank in the United Kingdom

Table 3.1   Principal concepts of technology diffusion process

Scholars	Principal concepts of innovation diffusion
Utterback and Abernathy (1975)	The life cycle explains sources and directions of technological change. The life cycle explains the development of technology-related products and processes
Fisher and Pry (1971)	This is a classical model for forecasting innovation diffusion. This study is focused on the diffusion process of product innovations, as well as the substitution rate of technological change
Gort and Klepper (1982)	This study measures and analyzes the diffusion of product innovations. It divides the life cycle of the new product industries into five stages. The study provides a basis for the development of a theory on the evolution of industries
Abernathy et al. (1983)	This study views the innovation process as a process of industrial de-maturity. They argue, from the perspective of evolutionary theory on economic development that technological change may alter the character of innovation and competition and over time affect the structure of the industry
Peres et al. (2010)	This study provides a study of the diffusion processes of new products and services. They view the innovation diffusion as a process of market penetration whereby the launch of new products and services is driven by social influences
Guseo and Guidolin (2015)	This study is focused on the innovation diffusion—the new product life cycle. They propose a multimodal model to the life cycle of the compact cassette format for pre-recorded music in Italy
Vargo et al. (2020)	This study explores the process of diffusion in a wider perspective—service-ecosystems. They analyze technological and market aspects, as well as the roles of different actors/institutions in the service-centered systems

(UK) that made an arrangement with the Bank of America to issue credit cards in 1966.

The fintech-based innovation of the ATM/Cash card was launched by Chemical Bank, headquartered in New York, in the 1970s. The main driving forces for the interconnected ATM networks were the two major

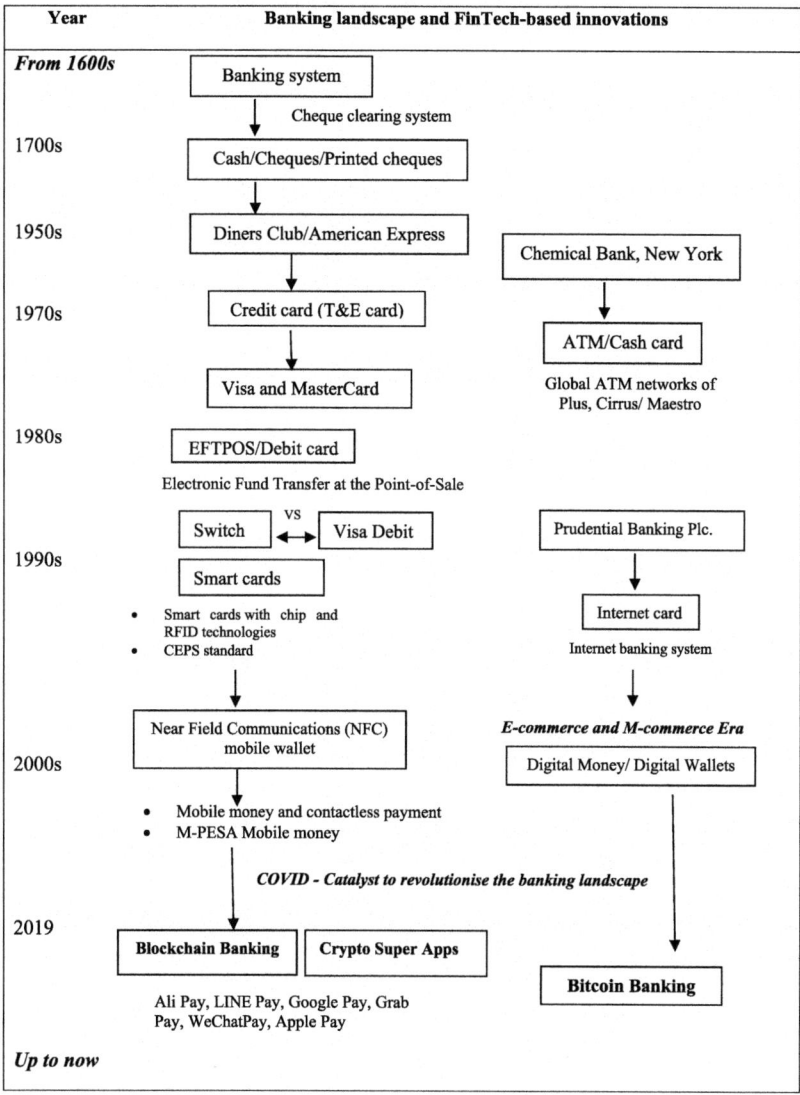

Fig. 3.2   Banking landscape and fintech-based innovations

credit card companies, Visa and Mastercard. In the 1980s, Visa established the Plus ATM network, while MasterCard established the Cirrus ATM network. Visa and MasterCard finally linked up their respective ATM networks in 1991. The electronic fund transfer at the point-of-sale (EFTPOS)/Debit card innovation is another type of electronic money and was introduced in 1985. EFTPOS is a card-based electronic payment system which allows an instant payment to be directly debited from the customer's account by using EFTPOS/Debit cards (Paxson & Wood, 1998). In the UK, there are two major networks of Switch and Visa Debit (Visa Delta). Today, the EFTPOS/Debit card can also be used on the Internet and point-of-sale transactions.

The fintech-based innovation of smart cards using chip technology was launched in 1984. The major payment innovations using smart card technology on electronic cash (e-cash or e-purse) are Visa Cash and Mondex Cards. In 1997, an important pilot project was launched by Visa and MasterCard in the Upper West Side of Manhattan, which offered the prospect of interoperability in the payment system using both Visa Cash and Mondex Cards. The use of smart cards for e-cash application is based on the global CEPS (Common Electronic Purse Specifications) and EMV standards (standards for chip-based debit and credit transactions).

Mobile money is another important fintech-based innovation that allows fund transfers using a cell phone. Mobile money, or electronic money transfer, through cellular networks, was launched in 2007 by the mobile network operator Vodafone. With the power of mobile phone technology, mobile money has opened up mobile commerce (m-commerce) opportunities for banks. Mobile phones also provide a new delivery channel for banks to offer various financial services to their clients.

Bitcoin, an open-source, peer-to-peer digital currency, was introduced by Satoshi Nakamoto in 2009. It is based on the decentralized digital-payment system which provides online payment solutions. The fintech-based innovation of Bitcoin banking allows users to transact directly without needing any payment intermediaries. That is to say, the Bitcoin wallet enables online access to virtual banking. Currently, the outbreak of COVID-19 has acted as a catalyst in digitally transforming the landscape of the banking industry. The adoption of fintech sandboxes by governments around the world has encouraged fintech-based innovations. Currently, the development of crypto super apps such as LINE Pay, GrabPay, and Alipay has further disrupted the banking landscape. These super apps have disintermediated banks from their customers by offering digital financial and non-financial services to meet the growing customers' demands.

Figure 3.3 shows the analytical framework of systemic innovation model. The systemic innovation model provides a basis for analyzing the complexity of fintech-based innovations and the capabilities of innovators in the banking landscape.

The systemic innovation model (Fig. 3.3) provides a dynamic tool to understand the progress and trend of innovation development. The model is helpful in understanding the systemic characteristics of innovation and the pursuit of collaborative strategy in managing fintech-based innovations to achieve a level of diffusion. Further, the model can be applied to the innovations of any industry. The high systemic innovation exhibits most, but not necessarily all, of the following features:

1. The innovation requires interoperability among third parties.
2. The innovation needs necessary investment in assets specific to the system.
3. The innovation comprises extensive software (protocols, procedures) as well as hardware.

	Low systemic nature	High systemic nature
Collaboration used (More than 1 party involved)	Quadrant 1	Quadrant 2
Collaboration not used (More than 1 party not involved)	Quadrant 3	Quadrant 4

Fig. 3.3 Systemic innovation model

According to the systemic innovation model proposed in Fig. 3.3, the types of systemic nature/characteristics can be categorized into 4 quadrants as follows:

Quadrant 1: Low systemic nature and Collaboration used

The categorization of innovations in this quadrant means that all the resources and capabilities required to achieve the level of innovation diffusion are available within a single economic entity or can be bought on a contractual (non-equity, non-participation) basis. However, in actuality, more than one party contributes to the delivery of products or services through commercial use.

Quadrant 2: High systemic nature and Collaboration used

The categorization of innovations in this quadrant means that the core business of innovation requires more than one party for viable diffusion. No obvious innovator has enough of the necessary competencies in-house and there is no third-party market in which they can be acquired on a contract (non-equity) basis. Thus, more than one party is involved in the delivery of products or services for commercial use.

Quadrant 3: Low systemic nature and Collaboration not used

The categorization of innovations in this quadrant means that the core business requires no more than one party for the diffusion of innovation. In other words, the deliverables of product or service innovations are within the capabilities of one firm or third-party contractors who will work on a non-equity basis.

Quadrant 4: High systemic nature and Collaboration not used

The categorization of innovations in this quadrant means that the capabilities for complete or maximum diffusion are required, but the supplementing capabilities are not available from third-party (non-equity) suppliers. If no more than one party in the delivery of products or services for commercial use is involved, then a failed innovation—an innovation that fails to achieve critical mass—is likely.

DIFFUSION OF FINTECH-BASED INNOVATIONS AND POTENTIAL DISRUPTION/REVOLUTION UNDER THE GLOBAL PANDEMIC OF COVID-19

The analyses of fintech-based innovations through the lens of systemic innovation have shown insightful results on the diffusion process. Table 3.2 summarizes the systemic innovation characteristics of all banking innovations including fintech-based innovations launched in the last 70 years up to the present. Electronic fund transfer at the point-of-sale (EFTPOS), smart cards for financial applications (cards which provide payment functionalities such as debits/credits and the smart card e-cash), credit cards, International Electronic Fund Transfer (SWIFT, Eurogiro), travel and entertainment (T&E) cards, and cheque truncation involve high systemic nature (having two or three of the systemic characteristics). Figure 3.4 presents the analyses of systemic characteristics of fintech-based innovations and pattern of technology diffusion in the banking landscape.

Fintech-based innovations with low systemic nature (Quadrant 1 and Quadrant 3 of Fig. 3.4) show that the total potential benefits of the innovation are potentially available to be captured by a single entity (possibly buying missing capability on non-equity sharing purchase arrangements/contracts) and exhibit only one or none of the systemic characteristics. In other words, fintech-based innovations having low

Table 3.2 Systemic characteristics of banking and fintech-based innovations

	ATM/Cash cards	Mobile banking	Bitcoin banking	Proprietary financial electronic data interchange (EDI)	Cheque guarantee cards	Credit cards	Direct debiting
(1) The innovation requires interoperability among third parties						X	
(2) The innovation needs necessary investment in assets specific to the system	X		X	X	X	X	
(3) The innovation comprises extensive software (protocols, procedures) as well as hardware		X	X			X	X

	Telephone banking	Blockchain banking	Retailer cards	Cash management account (CMA)	Internet banking	Cheque truncation	Travel and entertainment (T&E) cards
(1) The innovation requires interoperability among third parties		X				X	X
(2) The innovation needs necessary investment in assets specific to the system	X	X	X			X	X
(3) The innovation comprises extensive software (protocols, procedures) as well as hardware		X		X	X	X	X

(continued)

Table 3.2 (continued)

	Crowd funding	Electronic Fund Transfer at the Point-of-Sale (EFTPOS)	Fixed rate mortgages	Smart cards for financial applications	International Electronic Fund Transfer
(1) The innovation requires interoperability among third parties		X		X	X
(2) The innovation needs necessary investment in assets specific to the system		X		X	X
(3) The innovation comprises extensive software (protocols, procedures) as well as hardware	X	X	X	X	X

Source The authors' design

	Low systemic nature	High systemic nature
Collaboration used (More than 1 party involved)	**Quadrant 1** • ATM/Cash cards • Internet banking • Cheque guarantee cards • Retailer cards • Direct debiting • Cash management account (CMA) • Mobile banking	**Quadrant 2** • Electronic Fund Transfer at the Point of Sale (EFTPOS) • Smart cards for financial applications (cards which provide payment functionalities such as debits/credits, the smart card e-cash) • Credit cards • International Electronic Fund Transfer (SWIFT, Eurogiro) • Travel and entertainment (T&E) cards • Cheque truncation
Collaboration not used (More than 1 party not involved)	**Quadrant 3** • Telephone banking • Proprietary financial electronic data interchange (EDI) • Fixed rate mortgages	**Quadrant 4** Failed innovation

Fig. 3.4 Systemic nature of fintech-based innovations and pattern of technology diffusion

systemic nature do not require collaboration, although for reasons of risk sharing and investment sharing, collaboration may still be evident. An analysis of these research findings has shown that innovations involving low systemic nature whereby banks have pursued collaborative strategy to realize the value of innovations (Quadrant 1 of Fig. 3.4) are ATM/Cash cards, Internet banking, cheque guarantee cards, retailer cards, direct debiting, cash management account (CMA), and mobile banking. The financial technologies that individual banks compete to launch on their own (without pursuing collaborative strategy) are telephone banking, proprietary financial electronic data interchange (EDI), such as that developed by Citibank, and fixed rate mortgages (Quadrant 3 of Fig. 3.4).

While Fig. 3.4 presents the current status of the systemic nature of fintech-based innovations, Fig. 3.5 portrays the dynamics of fintech-based innovations whereby the systemic characteristics change over time.

This study argues that the complexity of fintech-based innovations relative to the capabilities of innovators is the main issue in determining collaborative options. That is to say, innovators who lack appropriate resources in managing the complexity of fintech-based innovations would seek to lower risks of competition or absolute investment by entering into collaboration. The use of collaboration then results in the systemic nature/characteristics of the fintech-based innovations.

Figure 3.5 portrays the dynamics of fintech-based innovations. Although some fintech-based innovations could be provided on an individual basis, innovators see the advantages of collaboration to provide the service on an extended scope basis (external benefits). By pursuing collaborative strategies, banks could extend the scope of service beyond their own internal benefits without having to be involved in high investment costs. Also, the extended scope of usage can be regarded as a great benefit to customers, whose accessibility to banking services would be greatly improved. That is to say, the customer benefits when innovators use technology to facilitate the financial system networks to form interconnected networks (multiple platforms). Interestingly, the empirical analyses have

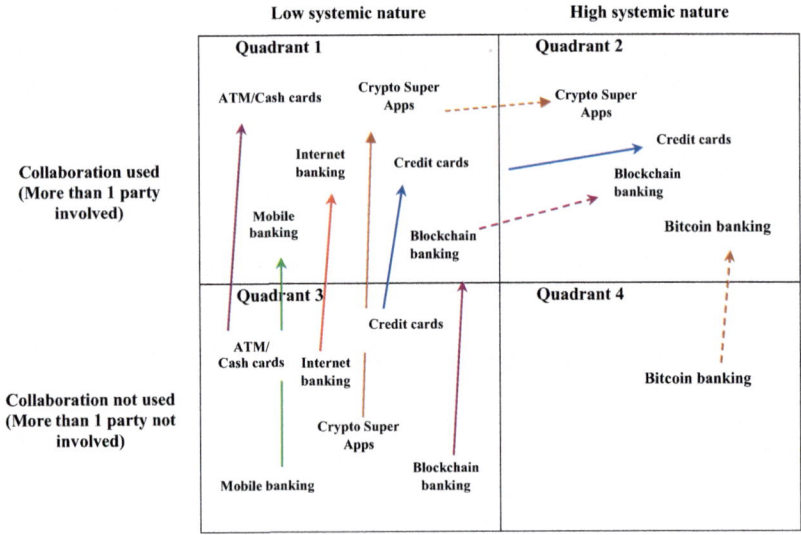

Fig. 3.5   Dynamics of fintech-based innovations

shown that the systemic nature/characteristics of the innovation process are the outcome of interactions between the complexity of the innovation and the capabilities of innovators in managing fintech-based innovations.

Considering the samples of fintech-based innovations shown in Fig. 3.5, banks can compete by launching ATM/Cash cards and Internet and mobile banking on an individual basis (Quadrant 3 of Fig. 3.5). However, banks attempt to overcome obstacles to achieve a level of diffusion by entering a shared network. The fintech-based innovations of ATM/Cash cards, Internet banking, and mobile banking thus progress from Quadrant 3 to Quadrant 1, as banks compete to pursue collaborative strategies in an attempt to expand the bank's network, which would allow it to capture more customers and increase its market shares.

The credit cards show low systemic characteristics (Quadrant 3 of Fig. 3.5). The low systemic characteristics are a result of banks competing to build proprietary networks when the innovation was first launched. Over time, they pursued collaborative strategies to extend network services to improve service quality (Quadrant 1 of Fig. 3.5). The fintech-based innovation of credit cards requires network externalities to complete the core and peripheral functions including issuers, acquirers, merchants, hotels, insurance and car rental companies, etc. The credit card operation under the global payment networks of Visa and MasterCard system has finally determined the high systemic nature/characteristics so as to facilitate the electronic payment (Quadrant 2 of Fig. 3.5).

Blockchain technology has challenged the digital transformation of the banking landscape, particularly during the COVID-19 pandemic (Fig. 3.2). Blockchain banking provides faster, cheaper, and more secure payment transactions. Many banks have already leveraged Blockchain technology to facilitate international and cross-border payments (progressing from Quadrant 3 to Quadrant 1). A transition toward high systemic characteristics (progressing from Quadrant 1 to Quadrant 2) is likely, since high systemic innovations would help reduce the financial barriers. Blockchain banking facilitates fund transfers among different banks when the banking customers visit other countries. Its distributed-ledger architecture offers convenience and security as Blockchain technology helps eliminate the costs of converting currencies.

The fintech-based innovation of Bitcoin banking has not yet achieved large-scale diffusion in the global financial market. The main obstruction to its acceptance is that it is not backed by many governments and is not recognized as a legal tender. The central banks of many countries around the world advise users to be aware of its risks, such as the theft and loss of digital wallets. The competing mining protocol standards, the lack of collaborative solutions, and the problems of insecure computer and Internet infrastructure have hindered Bitcoin's widespread adoption. It will be interesting to see if Bitcoin banking can progress from Quadrant 4 to Quadrant 2 and incorporate high systemic characteristics to achieve wider diffusion.

The analysis of findings shows that the diffusion of fintech-based innovations has different levels of systemic characteristics. According to empirical analysis through the lens of systemic innovation, systemic characteristics influence the need for collaboration and the process of technology diffusion. Considering the future trend of fintech-based innovations in the banking landscape, the study argues that the effectiveness of fintech-based innovations needs high systemic characteristics since the ownership of networks and externalities seems to be an important factor in the diffusion process. During the global COVID-19 crisis, the development of crypto super apps indicated the high systemic requirements involved in offering an effective array of technology-powered financial services. The systemic characteristics of crypto super apps in banking would enable value realization of technology to achieve wide market acceptance. The current situation reflects potential disruption/revolution of the banking landscape under the global pandemic whereby COVID-19 acts as a catalyst toward digital transformation.

RESEARCH IMPLICATIONS AND CONCLUSIONS

This chapter is concerned with the diffusion of financial technology or fintech and digital transformation of the banking landscape. The development of systemic innovation model provides a better understanding of the systemic nature/characteristics, as well as the progress and pattern of fintech-based innovation diffusion. The recent outbreak of the global COVID-19 pandemic has made the banks realize the importance of digital transformation. The strategic implications emanating from this research are that the power of Blockchain technology combined with the scale and infrastructure of the financial innovation system can help deliver superior customer experiences in the digital world. Also, the central banks should offer supervisory tools that encourage an efficient financial innovation system. The pursuit of collaborative strategy can help the financial technologies grow with high systemic characteristics which would support the level of global diffusion. The COVID-19 pandemic crisis has created many opportunities in terms of digital banking innovations during the era of digital transformation. The power of Artificial Intelligence (AI) and Machine Learning offers the new hyper personalization of innovations like crypto super apps—WeChat (China), Alipay (China), GoTo (Indonesia), Grab (Malaysia), Paytm (India), and Kakao (South Korea). The findings of our research suggest that the systemic characteristics of fintech-based innovations are dynamic over time. Innovators might adopt different strategies in exploiting the fintech-based innovations whereby this process in turn determines the systemic characteristics. Interestingly, this research shows that the systemic characteristics may change as coalitions and market sizes change. That is to say that the systemic characteristics of fintech-based innovations seem to vary with the size of the market. As innovators seek to enjoy the external benefits by pursuing collaboration, the pursuit of collaborative strategy may result in the systemic characteristics changing irreversibly. The banking landscape presently faces potential disruption/revolution as COVID-19 acts as a catalyst in transforming the physical banking system into digital banking system leading to bank disintermediation.

References

Abernathy, W. J., Clark, K. B., & Kantrow, A. M. (1983). *Industrial renaissance: Producing a competitive future for America.* Basic Books, Inc.

Appleyard, M. M., & Chesbrough, H. (2017). The dynamics of open strategy: From adoption to reversion. *Long Range Planning, 50*(3), 310–321.

Barras, R. (1986). Towards a theory of innovation in services. *Research Policy, 15,* 161–173.

Barras, R. (1990). Interactive innovation in financial and business services: The vanguard of the service revolution. *Research Policy, 19,* 215–237.

Chesbrough, H. W. (2003a). The era of open innovation. *Sloan Management Review, 44*(3), 35–41.

Chesbrough, H. W. (2003b). *Open innovation: The new imperative for creating and profiting from technology.* Harvard Business School Press.

Chesbrough, H. W. (2011). *Open services innovation: Rethinking your business to grow and compete in a new era.* Jossey Bass.

Chesbrough, H. W., & Teece, D. J. (1996). When is virtual virtuous? *Harvard Business Review, 74*(1), 65–73.

Daft, R. L. (1982). Bureaucratic versus nonbureaucratic structure and the process of innovation and change. *Research in the Sociology of Organisation, 1,* 129–166.

Dosi, G. (1982). Technological paradigms and technological trajectories. *Research Policy, 11,* 146–162.

Fisher, J. C., & Pry, R. H. (1971). A simple substitution model of technological change. *Technological Forecasting and Social Change, 3,* 75–88.

Freeman, C. (1991). Innovation, change of techno-economic paradigm and biological analogies in economics. *Review of Economics, 42*(2), 211–232.

Gort, M., & Klepper, S. (1982). Time paths in the diffusion of product innovations. *The Economic Journal, 92*(367), 630–653.

Guseo, R., & Guidolin, M. (2015). Heterogeneity in diffusion of innovations modelling: A few fundamental types. *Technological Forecasting and Social Change, 90*(PB), 514–524.

Harris, W. L., & Wonglimpiyarat, J. (2019). Blockchain platform and future bank competition. *Foresight Journal, 21*(6), 625–639.

Lawrence, P. R., & Lorsch, J. W. (1986). *Organization and environment: Managing differentiation and integration.* Harvard Business School Press.

Luo, S., Sun, Y., Yang, F., & Zhou, G. (2021). Does fintech innovation promote enterprise transformation? Evidence from China. *Technology in Society, 68,* 1–13.

Miles, I. (1993). Services in the new industrial economy. *Futures, 25*(6), 653–672.

Miles, I. (1994). Innovation in services. In M. Dodgson & R. Rothwell (Eds.), *Handbook of industrial innovations.* Edward Elgar.

Miles, I. (2003). *Knowledge intensive services' suppliers and clients.* Ministry of Trade and Industry Finland Studies and Reports 15/2003.

Miles, I. (2005). Innovation in service. In J. Fagerberg, D. Mowery, & R. Nelson (Eds.), *Oxford handbook of innovation.* Oxford University Press.

Nelson, R., & Winter, S. (1977). In search of a useful theory of innovation. *Research Policy, 6,* 36–76.

Nelson, R., & Winter, S. (1982). *An evolutionary theory of economic change.* Harvard University Press.

Pavitt, K. (1984). Sectoral patterns of technical change: Towards a taxonomy and a theory. *Research Policy, 13*(6), 343–374.

Paxson, D., & Wood, D. (1998). *Encyclopedic dictionary of finance.* Blackwell.

Peres, R., Muller, E., & Mahajan, V. (2010). Innovation diffusion and new product growth models: A critical review and research directions. *International Journal of Research in Marketing, 27*(2), 91–106.

Rosenberg, N. (1976). The directions of technological change: Inducement mechanisms and focusing devices. In N. Rosenberg (Ed.), *Perspectives on technology.* Cambridge University Press.

Rosenberg, N. (1982). Learning by using. In N. Rosenberg (Ed.), *Inside the black box: Technology and economics*. Cambridge University Press.

Rothwell, R., & Gardiner, P. (1985). Invention, innovation, re-innovation and the role of user. *Technovation, 3*, 68–186.

Schott, A. (1981). *Industrial innovation in the United Kingdom, Canada, and the United States*. British-North America Committee.

Schumpeter, J. A. (1939). *Business cycles: A theoretical, historical and statistical analysis of the capitalist process*. McGraw-Hill.

Schumpeter, J. A. (1967). *The theory of economic development*. Oxford University Press.

Shim, Y., & Shin, D. H. (2017). Analyzing China's fintech industry from the perspective of actor–network theory. *Telecommunications Policy, 40*(2–3), 168–181.

Thompson, B. S. (2017). Can financial technology innovate benefit distribution in payments for ecosystem services and REDD+? *Ecological Economics, 139*, 150–157.

Tidd, J., & Bessant, J. (2009). *Managing innovation: Integrating technological, market and organizational change*. Wiley.

Utterback, J. (1994). *Mastering the dynamics of innovation: How companies can seize opportunities in the face of technological change*. Harvard Business School Press.

Utterback, J., & Abernathy, W. (1975). A dynamic model of process and product innovation. *Omega, 3*(6), 639–656.

Vargo, S. L., Akaka, M. A., & Wieland, H. (2020). Rethinking the process of diffusion in innovation: A service-ecosystems and institutional perspective. *Journal of Business Research, 116*, 526–534.

Vernon, R. (1966). International investment and international trade in the product cycle. *Quarterly Journal of Economics, 80*(2), 190–207.

Voss, C. (1994). Significant issues for the future of product innovation. *Journal of Product Innovation, 11*, 460–463.

West, J., Salter, A., Vanhaverbeke, W., & Chesbrough, H. (2014). Open innovation: The next decade. *Research Policy, 43*(5), 805–811.

CHAPTER 4

Shifting Paradigms in Banking: How New Service Concepts and Formats Enhance the Value of Financial Services

Anna Omarini

INTRODUCTION

Digital technologies and their increasing impact on financial services are changing the banking industry. Technological developments impact society widely, changing products and services, as well as the ways in which they are invented, produced, delivered, and consumed. However, the way banking is currently evolving has to do with the fact that in the past, banks were not considered to have been good at differentiating themselves from one another, so that during the last decade customers have come to perceive a high degree of similarity among their strategies, and related offerings. Furthermore, a set of major forces are changing

A. Omarini (✉)
Department of Finance, Bocconi University, Milan, Italy
e-mail: anna.omarini@unibocconi.it

T. Walker et al. (eds.), *The Fintech Disruption*, Palgrave Studies
in Financial Services Technology,
https://doi.org/10.1007/978-3-031-23069-1_4

75

both the paradigm and related boundaries of the banking industry. They are:

- Technology (Balling et al., 2002; Wilson, 2017).
- Regulation.
- New competitors.
- Consumer attitudes and behaviors.

First, technology in banking has always had the power to affect the fundamentals of business, such as information and risk analysis, distribution, monitoring, and processing (Llewellyn, 1999). However, it is useful to make a distinction between technologies of the past and the digital technologies of the present. The latter not only have the power to improve efficiency, and effectiveness in services but have also started to exert increasing influence on banks' products and delivery methods (European Central Bank, 1999). Digitalization also contributes to innovation, leading to further improvements in profitability. Today, the capacity of a company to adapt to technology and exploit its potential depends on its capacity to translate those benefits into products and services, processes and new business models, and to secure and improve its competitiveness. If we take a broader industry perspective, we see that technology is also able to enhance economies of scale, thus changing the proportion of fixed *versus* variable costs and lowering entry barriers. This may increase the contestability of banking markets and invites more agile companies to populate the banking landscape.

The factors listed above are made possible because digital technologies are highly malleable. They open larger domains to new potential functionality (Yoo, 2010; Yoo et al., 2010), disrupting every industry to various degrees. This is because their impacts are spreading also at the societal level (Alijani & Wintjes, 2017), where the borderless extension of financial innovation is experiencing great change, and is also where the new fintech phenomenon has started developing and reshaping the industry's value propositions and related business models (IMF and World Bank, 2019).

In the literature, the term "open innovation" is being used to designate these changes (Chesbrough, 2003, 2006, 2011; Chesbrough et al., 2014; Enkel et al., 2009). Open innovation combines both internal and external resources to create new products, increase the flexibility and timeliness in the way resources respond to market demand, and tailor the services to customers' individual tastes (Schueffel & Vadana, 2015).

The second driving force is regulation. Digital technologies have attracted remarkable attention from legislators. Regulators and authorities, having become aware of the power and magnitude of innovation, have started to invite the financial service industry to embrace new technologies by introducing legal certainty to previously unregulated services. While after the 2008 financial crisis compliance issues and financial stability were the main regulatory concerns, the second EU Payment Services Directive (PSD2) shifted focus to boosting technological innovations and reshaping the industry by introducing an open banking framework with the potential to further evolve toward open finance. In effect, under PSD2 banks are mandated to provide "access to account" and communicate to authorized third parties, their customer, and payment account information. This allows new players to thrive not only in the payments segment, but also in other segments once they have access to account information.

Cortet et al. (2016) maintain that PSD2 goes a step beyond the regulatory scope. The directive is indeed an impressive accelerator of the digitization process that is already affecting banking. It should be noted that this regulation would severely impact revenue streams that were considered sticky by banks.

This phenomenon will, in turn, accelerate the fragmentation of the value chains in the banking sector, as consumers become free to choose services provided by a third party on the basis constituted by the (open) account that they hold within a bank. Those banks, in effect, will not be the only channels through which consumers will be able to access related services, and thus the rather sticky account service relationship could be separated from the related services that banks once sold through that preferential gate. The shift in mindset needed to bring about these changes is making everyone aware of the move from controlling to managing customers' money (Bareisis, 2013; Omarini, 2019).

The move to open banking is already spreading globally, though its actual impact depends largely on the regulatory environment, not only in banking, but also in areas such as open finance and the data economy. Some countries, such as Australia and Singapore, are already undertaking this further evolutionary step while others continue to study the situation.

The third driving force has to do with new competitors. The potential for banks to open a wide array of Application Programming Interfaces

(APIs) and services exceeds the minimum levels mandated by legislation. Open banking enables the development of premium APIs, which, when fully developed, will allow data sharing practices to be effectively applied to a plethora of new sectors. A world without borders is becoming both an opportunity and a challenge for managers and policymakers. It is under these conditions that technology start-ups found a way to enter the financial service industry to offer products and services directly to consumers and businesses. However, incumbents and BigTechs are also catching up with similar projects to keep customers engaged.

Finally, the fourth driving force is the way that consumers' attitudes and behaviors are changing in response to these previously mentioned factors. Open banking and the ways in which it will evolve are both empowering consumers to access not only their accounts, but also their mortgages, credits, student loans, automotive finance, insurances, investments, or pensions and loans. Ultimately, this access allows for the delivery of additional value in the form of saving-related services, identity services, more accurate creditworthiness assessments, or tailored advice and financial support services. However, the success of open finance depends on customers being prepared and educated to engage, and willing to allow third-party providers access to their financial data.

It is worth remembering that consumers are human beings, and what they want and expect from banks can only be partially defined in financial terms. Indeed, "they want their life to be easy and the path to their goals to be a simple one" (Omarini, 2019). At present, the most common set of attitudinal and behavioral characteristics consumers' desire are:

- Convenience, that is, speed and timeliness, due to scarcity of time so that banking is increasingly done in real time and services are available 24/7.
- Product simplicity and ease of use.
- Cost savings as a result of low-income growth.
- Personalized offerings.
- Experiential and functional elements.

The COVID-19 pandemic has further incentivize customers to shift away from traditional branches of banking toward digital channels. The combination of the above factors is fundamentally transforming the industry with intensified competition and shrinking profit margins (KPMG, 2016).

Bank managers can no longer focus solely on costs, product and process quality, or speed and efficiency. They must also strive for new sources of innovation and creativity. These increasingly complex forms of competition force competitors to appeal to customers who hold the power to choose (Omarini, 2015). This new paradigm presents a formidable and constant challenge. Customers are increasingly informed of what options are available to them and are also ever more demanding. These high expectations tend to lower their level of satisfaction. Thus, the paradox of the twenty-first century economy is that consumers have more choices, which yield less satisfaction. Top management, too, has more strategic options that yield less value (Prahalad & Ramaswamy, 2004). These factors combined show that what is increasingly driving this new emerging context is, as usual, the market needs.

This chapter analyzes the above developments by looking at banking evolution in continental Europe. Section "An Outlook on the Future" describes an outlook on the future of banking. Section "The Next Banking" outlines trends in future banking frameworks while taking into consideration what customers want (paragraph 3.1), what open banking may offer to customers (paragraph 3.2) and investigates the next generation of business models (paragraph 3.3). Section "From Disintermediation to Cooperation" describes how the relationships between banks and fintechs have evolved from ones of disintermediation to ones of cooperation, and also considers the evolving need of financial intermediation (paragraph 4.1), the evolution of financial services along with new concepts (paragraph 4.2), as well as some related aspects regarding value chains (paragraph 4.3). Finally, Sect. "Summary and Conclusions: Next Steps Forward" presents a brief conclusion and describes upcoming opportunities and challenges to the banking industry.

An Outlook on the Future

Times have changed, and not even one of banking's main products has remained exclusively in the hands of banks or other conventional financial intermediaries. The banking business is one undergoing major transformations, as many of the boundaries between it and potential competitors have collapsed. New players in the banking industry have different understandings of what customers' value and are more committed to customers than traditional financial service providers. They realized that banks' customer satisfaction was decreasing, that customer inertia is an important market feature, and many of the founders of these new services were former bankers or worked in the industry and thus, were able to depict some of the industry's weaknesses.

The focus of many companies has shifted from the value chain and the company's value proposition (pipeline business models) to value for customers, which requires a change in mindset and pushes companies to develop new solutions for customers. Digital business ecosystems are thus evolving within the market because value is increasingly reliant on networks. This means that new providers and related customized value propositions can be developed in the market where innovation is becoming mandatory for remaining competitive. This phenomenon requires companies to take a more holistic approach to customer knowledge; this means first identifying what knowledge customers have and then using that data to inform new customers, while creating new businesses and developing a wider portfolio of solutions with the goal of measuring customer reaction.

This demonstrates that banking, as a business, is not in search of relevance, but instead has to renew itself and become reactive to customer's behaviors and changes in society, both in developed and developing countries. Banks and non-banks will become even more crucial as individuals are driven to take a more active interest in paying, borrowing, saving, and investing.

In the market, there is a kind of invisible banking that allows the integration of banking products and services with the day-to-day digital touchpoints of customers which also implies that there exists a need for infinite intermediation. As banking will remain a people-focused business, this means that many factors such as trust, distinct professional knowledge, soundness, and a strong culture of fact-based decision-making, will still keep their relevance (Omarini, 2019).

The fact that digital technologies are changing the way individuals do their banking, giving them the perception of being in control, and emphasizing the construct of a service economy (banking-as-a-service, platform-as-a-service, etc.), will concern both banks and new players. Both need to decide to take either a purely transaction-driven business approach—which will allow them to survive under certain circumstances (such as volume, economies of scale.)—or a more relational-driven business approach—which will require them to engage customers with continuous innovation boosted and driven by new ways of data management. However, the new current outlook for the banking industry reveals a nascent ecosystem (Breidbach et al., 2014) approach by independent actors, where the traditional, supply-centered, oligopoly is coupled with fintechs, BigTechs, retailers, etc. Within this new ecosystem lies the disruptive aspect of PSD2 in Europe, and similar trends in other markets. This disruption is key to the unbundling and modularization of banking services which are challenging the financial services landscape. However, all the necessary conditions are already in place for the re-bundling stage. In this latter phase, the core objectives of financial intermediation may remain the same, but the methods and functionaries relating to those objectives change with digital technologies and market developments.

The banking game has changed and is still changing. In this new game, the big challenge is to find a balance between what to keep from the "old" banking system and what to get from the "new" banking system in order to meet customer demand.

As mentioned above, we are currently in the age of an infinite interconnected financial intermediation. As can be seen throughout many historical periods, once money, production, and investment are looked at in an integrated way, banks and non-bank financial intermediaries can be seen as performing complementary functions essential to the economy.

The Next Banking

At present, banking as a business is experiencing an internal struggle as it decides whether to prioritize efficiency or customer's needs, and as financial products and services move onto interconnected platforms (Deutsche Bank, 2017; Smedlund & Faghankhani, 2015). Thus, a new way of serving consumer's needs must be developed, one which provides solutions to customers as they experience important life changes (employment, unemployment, marriage, divorce, child rearing, retirement, etc.). Under these circumstances, customers require help a wide range of problems, which are frequently highly influenced by emotions. Managing this kind of banking entails the use of unfamiliar methods, such as information processing, social responsibility, customer education, self-organization, and even gossip. Awareness of social responsibility and customer education are also included here. Moreover, it is also about caring. Thus, a holistic perspective may be more effective when selling solutions to customers, as such an approach is indeed what customers are looking for. The essence of an integrated consumer banking approach is the notion that in place of traditional savings and loans, customers should be provided with integrated instruments and integrated pricing supported by integrated information (Omarini, 2019). Such an approach gives rise to the following phenomena: embedded finance and contextual banking. The transformation in financial services is ongoing and increasing attention is being paid to customization and personalization of services. This new trend in service perspective finds its roots in the increasing trend of modularity, which lies on the great ability of companies to move toward a product componentization (Accenture, 2021; Tuunanen et al., 2012).

The concept of modularity has been widely adopted in researching a diverse set of services. Important benefits from modularity are customization and personalization, which have been explored by many authors (Bask et al., 2011; de Blok et al., 2014; Moon et al., 2010; Silvestro & Lustrato, 2015).

In particular, notable contributions include:

- Yang and Shan (2009) contend that modular service architecture creates options to reuse, change, standardize, and selectively combine individual modules to develop new service offerings and customized solutions.
- Zhou et al. (2010) mention that the combination of different types of service components creates different attributes of the service package such as variety and changeability to exhibit higher performance.
- Ma et al. (2011) theoretically report on service modularity that can improve the service product innovation and provide more personalized service.
- Rahikka et al. (2011) report on modularity of services that contributes to broaden the services' scope and provides more solutions. Finally, they argue that flexibility in the service offering can create value for the customer.
- Baldwin (2020) shows that technology shapes the ecosystem and helps to create superior digital value as an instrument to solve technical or strategic bottlenecks.

Modularization often changes the service design experienced by the customer. Services differ in their experiential intensity; in transactional services, customer satisfaction focuses on the efficiency and convenience of the service delivery, whereas in experience-centric services, evoking emotional processes in customers is at the core of the service (Voss et al., 2008; Zomerdijk & Voss, 2010).

It has been argued that modularity can be used to increase customization and personalization (cf. Tuunanen et al., 2012). However, unmodularized services may be less standardized, and thus able to accommodate customer requests more flexibly. Thus, it is important for us to increase our understanding of the impact of modularity on the customer experience. While modularity can increase manageable variety, it may also impose restrictions on customers' expectations and habits in a particular service setting when particular configurations are no longer provided. On the other hand, modularization can be used as a means to make the service production more efficient and to enlarge the customer's options. Customers play an essential role in the co-creation of services as they actively participate in the service production process. Customer perceptions are likely to differ between customer segments and depending on the type of service offering (Voss et al., 2008).

Today's traditional banking products are componentized into new micro-products/services that may be sold separately or with their re-bundled versions as can be seen in Fig. 4.1.

This situation enables any other player—a retailer, a BigTech or a neobank—to use these components to create banking experiences or embed financial solutions into their core customer experience. Consider, for instance, how consumer credit is becoming embedded in the shopping experience via buy-now-pay-later services (BNPL) (see Fig. 4.2).

At this point, it must be recognized that providing customers with an active solution means giving them a set of ways to: connect function with experience, and source components flexibly from an ecosystem of partners, all while these solutions evolve dynamically and adapt to customers' needs.

What Customers Want

Customers' attitudes and behaviors are changing, and banks must recognize that social trends shape and reshape customer attitudes. Retail banks' products are cyclical in nature, changing in order to accommodate the specific economic conditions of the people within a banking area. Thus, banking institutions must look continuously to their customers, and allow

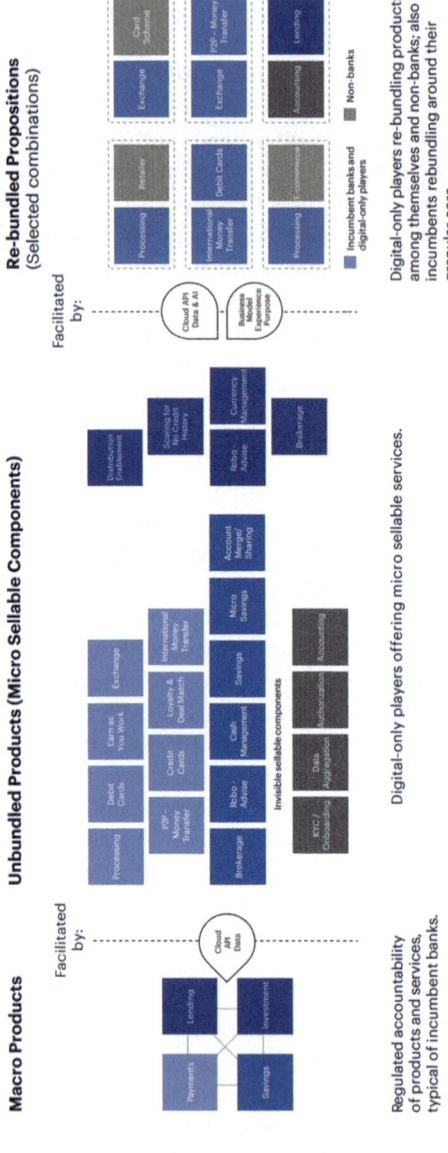

Fig. 4.1 Banks can create further value by re-bundling unbundled product propositions (*Source* Accenture [2021], The Future of Banking. It's time for a change of perspective, p. 19)

> *Consider the business model of Stripe Treasury, which offers Stripe merchant platform customers powerful APIs. This allows the platforms to embed financial products into their services, enabling their customers to easily send, receive and store funds. Shopify is partnering with Stripe and its financial institution partners to build Shopify Balance, the business account designed to help merchants take control of their finances.*
>
> *Stripe, for instance, evolved from a niche payments processor to bundling components from banks and fintechs and providing them to platforms like Shopify.*
>
> *Shopify, in turn, is not only using Stripe's payment processing service to drive Shopify Payments, but also recently embedded an Affirm-powered BNPL offering called Shop Pay Installments into its platform.*

Fig. 4.2 The stripe experience (*Source* Accenture [2021])

customers' behaviors and attitudes to inform which new products and services should be developed and delivered. Nowadays, the most common set of behavioral and attitudinal characteristics showed by consumers include:

1. A demand for convenience, due to time poverty (Oliver Wyman, 2018). Bank convenience used to be a function of the number of physical retail branches that a bank had in a given city, but it is increasingly revolving around the concept of always-on banking (BCG, 2018, 2021), which means that banking is increasingly done 24/7 and in real time (Accenture, 2019, 2021; PwC, 2020);
2. A request for product simplicity and ease of use (PwC, 2020);
3. Attempts at cost savings, driven by low-income growth (Oliver Wyman, 2018);
4. A desire for personalized offerings. Indeed, personalization is quickly becoming a primary mechanism for increasing customer satisfaction (BCG, 2018, 2021) and consequently retention, loyalty, and profitability;
5. A valuation of both experiential and functional elements into one integrated solution. There is no such thing as a good experience if the outcome—price, availability, access—is not useful (Oliver Wyman, 2018);
6. A desire to feel like their bank or any other providers is anticipating their needs, not bombarding them with product offerings;
7. A desire for transparency and no surprise or hidden fees; and

8. A more aware approach to security, due to technology innovations like digital payments and cloud-based applications.

Moreover, what should not be forgotten by banks and new entrants when developing their customer strategies, regardless of current social trends, is that consumers are human beings whose desires and expectations of banks and non-banks can only partially be defined in financial terms. Indeed, they want their life to be easy and the path to their goals to be a simple one (Omarini, 2019). Thus, the financial service provider-customer relationship has shifted. It is now important to understand the solutions customers' desire, rather than how banks, or other financial service providers, should be marketing their services. The solutions, rather than products, they provide are thus what distinguish financial service providers from one another, and the competition between providers revolves around their ability to solve problems rather than sell products.

What Open Banking May Offer to Customers: From Definition to Main Features

Open Banking (OB) can mean a lot of things to different people. For some, OB refers to direct payments; for others it refers to direct transactions with third parties, etc. However, to define it, it is worth outlining regulatory and authority perspectives, and the strategic and managerial ones of the parties involved. Regulators' view of Open Banking is twofold: they look at the increasing opportunity to develop a new competition and its related effects in the market and they have to define new rules to make this new market framework work without or while minimizing any spillover effects. Open Banking is defined by the Bank for International Settlements (BIS, 2019) as "The sharing and leveraging of customer-permissioned data by banks with third party developers and firms to build applications and services, including for example those that provide real-time payments, greater financial transparency options for account holders, marketing, and cross-selling opportunities. Individual jurisdictions may define Open Banking differently." In particular, "(…) a "third-party" is defined as any external legal entity that is not a part of the supervised banking organization. Third parties can be supervised entities (e.g., banks, other regulated financial firms) or non-supervised entities (e.g., financial technology firms, data aggregators, commercial partners, vendors, other non-financial payment firms)."

In OB, third-party financial service providers are given open access to consumer banking, transactions, and eventually also other financial data from banks and non-bank financial institutions, to ensure they are fully compliant. This data exchange is achieved by using APIs that are a way for two or more computer applications to talk to each other over a network using a common language that they both understand.

To facilitate their interactions, technical standards are needed due to the high number of institutions engaged in the market. They oversee how data can be securely shared or openly published through open APIs so as to let third-party apps, such as fintech companies, access users' data through their bank accounts. This allows the connecting of accounts and data across institutions for use by consumers, financial institutions, and third-party service providers. These standards also impose high-level principles on strong customer authentication (SCA) and secure communication.

Usually, technical standards are outlined by many organizations according to the different geographies implementing Open Banking. They are standards from the Berlin Group, UK Open Banking, Czech Standard, Slovak, STET, Polish API, etc., as well as the strict Regulatory Technical Standards (RTS) requirements issued by the European Banking Authority (EBA).

The potential is clear when we think of the benefits of interoperability among heterogeneous technical systems using APIs. However, such possibilities bring about a new question about how open such systems should be. A meaningful way to explore this issue is to consider private versus public or open APIs. Private APIs can either be internal APIs, offered to facilitate integration and operational efficiency across an organization or external APIs that are highly customized and designed specifically for partners who want to interface directly with their suppliers or customers. Private APIs are exclusive to staff and third parties with contractual agreements and are usually unnoticeable otherwise. These private APIs are already commonly used by banks and provide great value to organizations.

Public or open APIs are accessible to almost anyone and available to use with "little or no contractual arrangement" beyond agreeing to the terms and conditions put forward by the API provider. Organizations which provide open APIs can thus create digital economies or business platforms, through which communities of innovators can develop API-consuming applications and pay a fee for using the API. This kind of monetization of APIs is an essential part of the API-economy. However, the implications of open APIs are much more far-reaching and can lead to an entirely new way of doing business and competing in the marketplace (Zachariadis & Oczan, 2017). APIs become the pivotal point between products and distribution. Using APIs to interface products and distribution enables banks to decouple these functions. The combination of decoupling and opening up allows banks and any other financial service providers to play different roles in the different financial value chains with regard to the offering of products and their distribution (EBA, 2017, p. 26).

However, besides the mandatory prescriptions of PSD2, there is a panoply of choices which banks can select in terms of openness and services involved. These choices also have strategic and managerial implications. Based on the above, the notion of Open Banking has become mainstream in relation to open innovation literature to the extent that banks rely on the flow of inside and outside ideas to develop products and services, and innovative processes (Chesbrough, 2003, 2011). Also, existing products and services are provided in new ways and in collaboration with third parties, an additional fact that creates the premises to define an entire ecosystem approach around the concept of OB.

Banks can select the level of openness and the type of value they want to provide according to business and demand, organizational and capital expenditure considerations, and overall, according to their choices in terms of market positioning. In addition, banks can also choose to integrate their offering in the business model of other players. Overall, what matters is the openness of the paradigm, where every player may interact within one or more surrounding ecosystems (Omarini, 2019).

In this sense, the work of Cortet et al. (2016) is relevant as they identify four different strategies available to banks in a PSD2 context:

- Comply: The bank opens information only to the extent it is mandated to do so. There is thus a strong reconsideration of the value proposition. Traditional revenue streams that were deemed as certain are impacted, and third party interfaces disintermediate the bank. Here, banks retain their role as an account service provider and backbone of the system;
- Compete: Banks react, and besides compliance, try to fight for customer proximity which requires banks to rethink their overall business model in terms of value proposition, processes, costs, revenues, and channels;

– Expand: This strategy goes beyond exposing basic account information. Banks can expose open APIs and pursue new revenue streams, especially from providing full account information and specific services, such as data management and identity verification, to third parties. Here, banks become the gate through which third parties can access data and other services; and
– Transform: This is a specific subset of Open Banking where a platform strategy can take its implementation. Here, banks offer a core around which other players can build their offering, in addition to connecting users across different groups, facilitating matchmaking. With this model, there is a radical re-thinking of the business model. Banks indeed also try to monetize APIs as well as competing and profiting from a self-enhanced value proposition to customers, fulfilling shifting market needs.

There are many other contributions highlighting similar schemes of evolution, from the consulting literature overall (Accenture, 2018a, 2018b, 2020; AT Kearney, 2021; Capgemini, 2019, 2020, 2021; Deloitte, 2017, 2020a, 2020b, 2020c; Dratva, 2020; EY, 2017; KPMG, 2020; McKinsey, 2017; Microsoft et al., 2017; PwC, 2016, 2018a, 2018b; Zachariadis & Oczan, 2017).

What has been detailed in this section shows that Open Banking suggests a new vision, where the bank is part of a broader, highly dynamic and interconnected ecosystem, based on relations, platforms, and the sharing of information. Where new business models are required, new actors are becoming more powerful in the market arena (fintechs, BigTechs, incumbents, data providers, etc.), new regulations (PSD2, GDPR, etc.) are spreading, and new business paradigms (not all of them yet experienced) are affecting the market deeply. In this new setting, balancing the opportunities for openness with the need for consumers' protection is fundamental to maintaining trust and security in the market.

To outline some frameworks within which banks and FinTechs may choose to collaborate, compete, or simply interact, I have developed a matrix where two variables (value delivered—low/high—and degree of openness—low/high) are combined. The result is a set of four possible frameworks (Fig. 4.3) where we have outlined:

– The vision the framework may foresee;

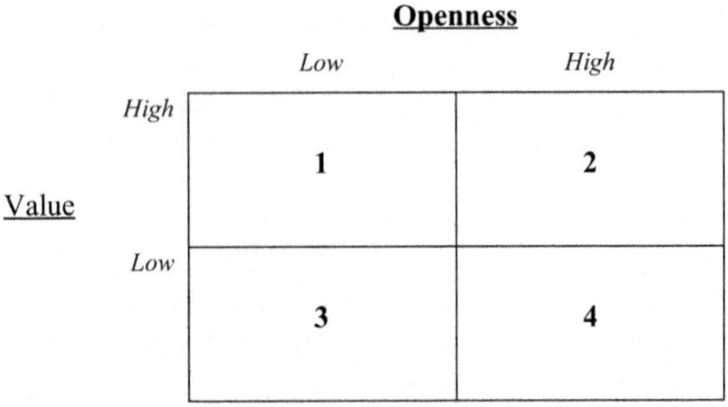

Openness

	Low	High
High	1	2
Low	3	4

Value

Fig. 4.3 Possible scenarios of digital transformation and banks and fintechs collaboration (*Source* Omarini [2022, p. 202])

- The needs and related value propositions; and
- The main features and a selection of possible business models.

In more detail:

- Quadrant 1 (high value, low openness):

  Here, there can be partnerships and collaborative initiatives focused on boosting the banking business by enabling new channels. In particular:
  - Vision: It may regard the development of services incrementally through collaboration.
  - Needs and value proposition: Those of cost and time reduction, as well as risk mitigation, etc.
  - Features and business models: In this quadrant, we can find consortium-partnerships between or among banks and/or focused initiatives close to the existing banking business model.
- Quadrant 2 (high value, high openness):

  Here, there can be platform business models aiming to develop new business ecosystems, in innovative markets with new players. In particular:
  - Vision: It may be that of creating an innovative and data-oriented business ecosystem.

- Needs and value proposition: This might relate to business development, partnership, attractiveness, integration, risk reduction, fly to quality, etc.
- Features and business models: In this quadrant, we may have platform business models, creation of new business ecosystems that position themselves in innovative markets, and networks of value.

– Quadrant 3 (low value, low openness).

Here, technical implementations are minimal as to satisfy regulatory requirements. In particular:
- Vision: It is that of satisfying regulatory requirements.
- Needs and value proposition: They may regard cost and risk reduction.
- Features and business models will only be impacted to follow pure regulatory requirements.

– Quadrant 4 (low value, high openness).

Here, there are multiple situations such as integrating activities in third-party's business models, leveraging on data and business interactions. In particular:
- Vision: It may regard the way to extract value from data sharing.
- Needs and value proposition may look at working for cost reduction, time to market requirements, business development, etc.
- Features and business models may relate to entering into third-party business models to monetize the sale of data and/or leveraging on banking business features.

Together, all this shows a mix of possible combinations under the umbrella name of Open Banking where there are multifaceted situations:
- Banking services are on third parties' platforms
- Third parties' services are on banking platforms
- New platforms may involve different actors and banks, as well as fintechs, may be among them, etc.

These findings point to the fact that banking requires developing a set of new managerial principles to drive its evolution, such as open innovation, sharing economy, open data sharing. This gives us a picture of an interdisciplinary landscape where working on a specific purpose, or a set of purposes, should inspire new visions and missions and their related strategies and business models must face the new market competition.

These observations are consistent with the fact that Open Banking works on a multitude of use cases and financial service providers that help consumers turn their financial behaviors into habits. As an example, Revolut offers users a categorized view of all their spending. While these insights alone do not necessarily contribute to forming better habits, they are useful tools nonetheless to give purpose for consumers.

In the future, banks will no longer be able to control their relationships with customers, thus they must work to increase their interactions. The ways in which banks controlled customers in the past, based on their inertia and industry innovation in the industry, together with an exclusive distribution of banking services, is now changing. The industry is becoming populated with many banking service producers and more and more distributors, both online and offline.

If banks want to keep their customers, they must work at developing new conditions for controlling their customers' money in terms of payments, investments, loans, and risk management tools. This can also be done by leveraging the power of Open Banking data sharing and the adoption of a use case approach. This is the way to reaffirm customers' habits and help marketers better understand how to answer and anticipate customers' wishes by offering them solutions that are immediately relevant and needed. They can also improve their focus on people's needs and decrease consumer exposure to irrelevant ads. All in all, winning in this market means becoming owners of your customers' experiences, such as some providers do by offering buy-now-pay-later services, or budgeting services to direct money toward a recurring saving plan.

This is also possible because an API does not stop at being a source of data for a third party but allows each participant in the system to access and use it and other information, such as that retrieved by social media. The added value is that each bank and/or financial institution can access numerous data sources that generate a large volume of new data and information, that are as valuable as they are unwieldy.

A Next Generation of Business Models: Platforms and Ecosystems for Embedding Financial Services and Develop a Contextual Banking

Today, financial products and services move into interconnected platforms, where collaboration is becoming the new rule in offering integrated consumer banking.

Providing customers with solutions through digital platforms is transforming the banking business into business ecosystems. A business ecosystem is a community of interacting entities. These entities can be organizations, businesses, or individuals, which create value for one another by producing or consuming goods and services which mutually support one another. Digital platforms are able to reduce transaction costs related to the interaction between different entities. In this way, the ecosystem becomes more integrated and agile.

For retail banking in Europe, the advent of digital platforms can be expected to cause a shift away from the traditional universal banking business model toward a new customer-centered universal banking model (integrated consumer banking). In the former, economies of scale and scope dominated strategic thinking, and conflicting interests between business sections arose easily within the same legal entity. In the latter, the unbundling and re-bundling of services and respective business models are chosen for a purpose, such as solving a customer's use case or improving quality and customer experience.

Banking will increasingly focus on customer's needs and not on what banks can and may want to sell. This means organizing around value streams and developing a series of value-adding activities that lead to overall customer satisfaction. The new banking paradigm is supported by open banking and finance frameworks, and as discussed above, by the digital environment and the increasing role banks might play in re-bundling fragmented financial services in the evolving banking landscape.

The concept of ecosystems has become increasingly popular in several streams of the literature (e.g., strategy, organization, innovation, digital models). The notion was first pioneered by Moore (1993), who referred to ecosystems as cross-industry entities. This concept draws from the relevant analogy in biology of "combination of species." In this sense, the ecosystem behaves as a community of players that transform raw inputs into outputs, which satisfy the needs of various participants, within organized relationships. According to Moore's characterization, companies both collaborate and compete to innovate and evolve together, in order to adapt to their environment.

Since its inception, the ecosystem concept has attracted significant interest in the field of strategy. Iansiti and Levien (2004) refer to ecosystems as "loose networks of suppliers, distributors, outsourcing firms, makers of related products or services, technology providers, and a host of other organizations (that) affect, and are affected by, the creation and delivery of a company's own offerings."

These authors underline the idea of interdependence between each single species within the ecosystem. The future of each player is indeed related to that of the others. Ecosystems are characterized by both symbiotic and antagonistic relationships without which each single player would lose its own individual meaning. While the boundaries of an ecosystem may be blurred, companies should try to identify the players on which their success depends (Adner & Kapoor, 2010; Gawer, 2009; Gawer & Cusumano, 2014).

The emergence of the ecosystem phenomenon can be tied to the fact that it ultimately serves the purpose of facilitating innovation and enhancing value proposition to final customers. Adner and Kapoor (2010), for instance, recognize that superior competitive advantages stem from the creation of value and are fostered in turn by innovation. The fostering factor of those ecosystems relies on the advantages that arise from the way most of the players help to co-evolve innovation in the industry and, as a result, this directs each of them toward new, broader ideas of value propositions. Indeed, business ecosystems, like their biological counterparts, thrive when they contain more genetic diversity, and thus have more ways to exploit the opportunities provided by the surrounding and ever-evolving, environment, as well as to adapt to the difficulties it presents (Moore, 1993). According to Brass et al. (2004), motives for inter-organizational ecosystem collaboration include the acquisition of additional assets and resources, reduced costs, and economies of scale and scope. These findings are also in line with what was postulated by Chesbrough (2011), and the achievement of common goals. Again, taking a biological perspective, Iansiti and Levien (2004) define the characteristics of thriving business ecosystems that ultimately justify those constructs: The first is "productivity," meaning that while a biological ecosystem is able to convert inorganic input to living matter, business ecosystems leverage on technology to create new products and foster efficiency. The second is "robustness" wherein an ecosystem is able to be resilient to environmental changes, tempering exogenous shocks and disruption. Third, "niche creation" relates to the diversity of the constituents of the ecosystem and the ability to support diverse modules. Given these characteristics, the big picture for an ecosystem is the aggregation of different actors under different positions where each one collaborates and competes at the same time. Moreover, this approach can be described as that of the ecosystem-as-affiliation, which sees ecosystems as communities of associated actors defined by their networks and platform affiliations. In this perspective, the emphasis is on the breakdown of traditional industry boundaries, the rise of interdependence, and the potential for symbiotic relationships in productive ecosystems, so that the emphasis focuses on governance and community enhancements, with a little insight into the issue of value creation.

The ecosystem also focuses on questions of access and openness, highlighting measures such as number of partners, network density, and actors' centrality in larger networks. In the business context, analyses held at the level of the "healthcare ecosystem," the "Microsoft ecosystem," the "Silicon Valley ecosystem," or the "entrepreneurial ecosystem" fall easily into this category. According to Adner (2017, p. 41), "strategy in the ecosystem-as-affiliation realm tends to focus on increasing the number of actors that link to a focal actor or platform, increasing its centrality and expected power."

In this approach, the focal actor develops its bargaining power by increasing the number and intensity of participants in its ecosystem. It also increases system value through direct and indirect network externalities. In the meantime, the likelihood of serendipitous interactions between partners, which may unlock new interactions and combinations, may increase so that the overall value creation of the system can be produced and widespread.

FROM DISINTERMEDIATION TO COOPERATION

As stated above, nascent ecosystems of independent actors may be the current outlook of the banking industry, so that the traditional supply-centered oligopoly framework has been replaced. Here lies the disruptive aspect of PSD2 which ultimately is a key milestone itself in the unbundling and modularization of banking services. In the second stage of its evolution, we are experiencing a wave of re-bundling of services, which could be developed through a strong integration between infrastructures and business models.

This is possible because ecosystems evolve (Moore, 1993) according to different evolutionary phases (birth, expansion, leadership consolidation, renewal, or death). Within the PSD2 framework, it is clear how the premises of interdependence and modularity, proper of the notion of ecosystem, may also apply to the specific banking case. Firms may co-evolve around a core infrastructure for payments and bank account services. This does not mean that the players will remain the same, or that the core banking infrastructure could not be replaced by another species, becoming marginal (i.e., losing customer interaction and relevance). In fact, literature on the topic has a purely evolutionary view on ecosystems, again based on the biological analogy of the survival of the fittest (Moore, 1993).

As stated above, the emerging business models are responding more effectively and rapidly to changes in the behavior and needs of new digital consumers, where collaboration among traditional banks, pure digital banks, FinTech companies, and other providers may play together. As a result, technological infrastructures have evolved considerably toward an open format and new solutions have been tested in the field reaching an ever-evolving equilibrium.

The outcome for customers is a set of emerging ways to cater to the increasing needs of a market that demands quality, fast response times, transparency, and sustainability while guaranteeing an easy and effective user experience along with integrated, personalized, and secure services.

An important element that encourages banks and non-banks to review their organizational and operating models is the entry of new entities in the sector, the so-called digital natives, which are highly geared toward a tailored customer experience to the new needs of clients.

The Infinitive Financial Intermediation

As banking is a business in deep transformation, it is also worth outlining that whatever banking is doing today is not going to drive its future growth. Banking has evolved from an activity which takes place in a specific location, to one which is part of a customer's everyday life though its digitization. When considering this fact, it means that some banking products are highly contextual. Here are some examples of the context of core retail banking products (King, 2012):

1. Mortgage (at a potential home or with a realtor);
2. Car lease or loan (at a car dealership or when purchasing a car);
3. Credit card (potentially at a mall or any other places devoted to shopping);
4. Travel insurance (when booking a holiday, or at the airport); and
5. Student loan (when enrolling at college or university).

At this point, it is worth highlighting and reinforcing the service dominant perspective in the market (Omarini, 2019). Adopting such a perspective or logic on business directs suppliers' focus in business relationships toward engaging with their customers' business processes. In fact, taking this approach leads to the idea that every customer interaction can be "a generator of service experience and value-in-use" (Ballantyne & Varey, 2006, p. 336). The latter is central to the process of co-creation since it connotes the unique customer value, which is created by using the product in context. This takes banking closer to the context—which is a place or a situation where a customer is ready to buy a product or a service in a bundle where the financial service is included (such as Buy-Now-Pay-Later experiences). All of this shows that some banking products are highly contextual. The role of the supplier in co-creation is to facilitate the creation of value not only through the opportunities their resources and products offer, but also through interactions such as dialogue and additional information that informs the customer about the features and highlights of the product that a customer perceives as significant. This will ultimately create more in-depth experiences for customers as they increase their awareness in terms of quality, service offered, etc. In turn, it is with these co-creation opportunities, when realized, that customer insights can be harnessed, which can lead to strategic opportunities for the firm. Thus, it is important that organizations develop interaction-based platforms that allow dialogue to take place (Alimamy et al., 2018).

The idea of banking as a contextual business is useful for understanding both banks and new competitors in how they manage customer interactions, relationships, and innovation opportunities. For banks, it helps to understand the satisfaction gap between them and their customers. For fintech companies, it helps to highlight where their value propositions stand out in the market. In this regard, both the terms "products" and "services" are used interchangeably to describe the offering of financial service providers—whether they are incumbent or new competitors. The intention here is to describe what a service company should consider best in its strategy overall when technology assumes an important role in delivering value to customers. When it is clear that service is the fundamental basis for exchange, value is always unique and embedded in a values-based process. Innovation is then not defined by what firms produce as output, but how firms can better serve a customer. Again, this is a very different perspective which distinguishes between competing with services and competing through services (Lusch et al., 2007). The latter statement is about more than adding value to "products" it has to do with the entire organization, and with viewing and approaching both itself and the market with a service dominant logic (Vargo & Lusch, 2008, 2014). This approach is based on the understanding of the interwoven fabric of individuals and organizations which are brought together into networks and societies, specializing in and exchanging their respective competences. This logic is grounded in a commitment to collaborative processes with customers, partners, and employees—a wider co-creation process which involves more stakeholders. The more service-centered a company becomes, the more it must be customer-centric and relational, even though it may be argued that some companies and customers seek single transactions rather than relationships. Taking this fact into account, it is important to strengthen the bond between the traditional financial service industry and society. Regaining system stability and public trust has been a core challenge of the financial sector since the financial crisis. This task has been further complicated by the rapid deployment of financial and technological innovation, which have fundamentally changed how a financial service company and the value it delivers are defined. However, the sense of purpose remains relevant, as was also outlined by BlackRock CEO Larry Fink (2018) in his letter to CEOs, where he states that

> Society is demanding that companies, both public and private, serve a social purpose. To prosper over time, every company must not only deliver financial performance, but also show how it makes a positive contribution to society. Companies must benefit all of their stakeholders, including shareholders, employees, customers, and the communities in which they operate. Without a sense of purpose, no company, either public or private, can achieve its full potential. It will ultimately lose the license to operate from key stakeholders. It will succumb to short term pressures to distribute earnings, and, in the process, sacrifice investments in employee development, innovation, and capital expenditures that are necessary for long-term growth. It will remain exposed to activist campaigns that articulate a clearer

goal, even if that goal serves only the shortest and narrowest of objectives. (...) If engagement is to be meaningful and productive – if we collectively are going to focus on benefitting shareholders instead of wasting time and money in proxy fights – then engagement needs to be a year-round conversation about improving long-term value.

These statements convey that a sense of purpose is a key driver in inspiring future strategies for both banks and FinTech companies. This fact is especially true if we consider the present situation, as FinTechs and digital technologies are developing an open net of modular services, which both amplify and integrate the different segments of financial systems. Fintech companies also contribute toward developing economic and financial inclusion, enabling them to become an important engine of the financial system as a whole. By doing so, they are increasing the modularity of services. Modularity can be viewed as one of the key challenges in service design and innovation. In parallel modularity, it is also useful to consider service offerings to be process based and typically dependent on customer input.

However, while there are banking products which are already contextual, there are more which are emerging from the use of context data in a digital space, to target consumers with ads that are highly relevant. For example, bundling services such as those related to budgeting, spending, saving, and investing in one simple app (see Oval Money, Hype, etc.). This is the world of fintech apps and super App that are giving a completely different perspective on how to develop a modern customer relationship, which is more closely related to the ways customers want to use their providers rather than how a single bank, or any other single financial provider markets its services.

New Concepts and Formats of Services: The Case of Account Aggregation Services

The account aggregation service was initially offered by FinTech companies, but following the regulatory input from the PSD2, rapidly spread among banking groups as a lever for monitoring the data of their clients and enabling new revenue streams.

The main characteristics of the customer-centric approach that the digital transformation is undertaking in the market is configurating new concepts and formats of services. In most cases, they usually include the following features:

- Real-time information through push notifications;
- Expense monitoring;
- Personalization;
- Predictive analyses;
- Benchmarking with similar clients; and
- Glocalization as a remote selling factor.

As mentioned above, regulations have kickstarted the development of open innovation frameworks of services, such as so-called account aggregation service. This service can accelerate both the creation of a personalized offer for the client and the enhancing of efficiency of different bank's processes not necessarily linked to the payments area.

Account aggregation services allow the aggregation of, in a single summary view, payment transactions made by a single user on different accounts that are accessible online at different banks. The possibility of aggregating information on several accounts, and the opportunity to get the customer's expenses categorized according to their purposes, the provider, etc., is expanding the possibility of developing personalized multi-bank Personal Financial Management (PFM) services. This is an interesting opportunity to create an integrated picture of the client's spending habits and their related available funds with the goal of developing new business opportunities guided and driven by this new information.

A comprehensive and integrated view of all the information on a client's accounts, besides being useful in all cross-/up-selling activities, also has operational advantages for the bank or any other financial service provider. An important example here is credit rating assessment activities, which are optimized by the possession of additional information capable of providing an even deeper understanding of the client's profile (see Fig. 4.4).

The provision of the account aggregation service requires the design of a specific operating model, in terms of technological infrastructure, processes, and resources within banking and non-banking organizations. In particular, a series of data management tasks (e.g., data cleaning) are

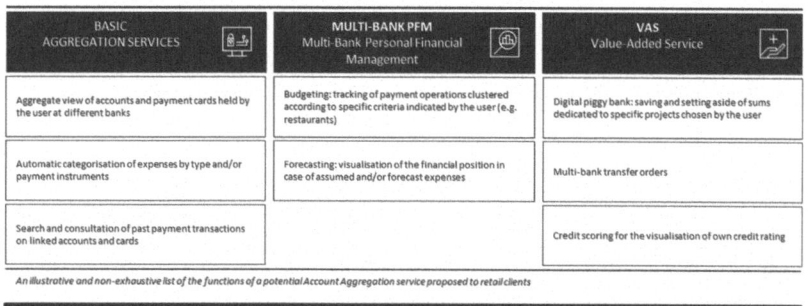

Fig. 4.4 Configuration of an account aggregation service (*Source* ABI Lab and PwC, The new Account Aggregation frontier: a comparison between banks and FinTechs, Report, June 2020)

required to mitigate the complexity arising from the lack of uniformity in data provided by individual payment service providers.

The business models associated with account aggregation services vary in relation to the users of the service—gender, age, education, work experience, etc., and can be associated mainly with forms of indirect revenues (e.g., cross-/up-selling) and direct revenues based on "as-a-service" supply methods. In fact, the direct revenues that can be obtained from the provision of the account aggregation service do not appear to be able to guarantee a sufficient profitability to the service.

A survey conducted by ABI Lab (2020)—which is the Italian Banking Association Innovation Lab devoted to market researches and analysis on market trends—creates a European benchmark, based on their analysis of 25 account aggregation services—selected from the top 10 European banks and 15 FinTechs—according their assets and market relevance, to enable a better understanding of the key factors defining the current market offer.

According to this survey, the account aggregation service is offered by 9 of the top 10 European banking groups for total assets. This service is therefore evolving into a "must have" for Europe's leading banking groups, which in order to bridge the gap with fintechs, have developed a model based on the externalization of one or more phases of the value chain, while maintaining the client's user experience integrated in their channels.

Some 80% of the sample banks use a technological provider to supply the service and in 70% of the cases, the service is integrated in the existing Internet/Mobile channels.

The FinTechs selected in the sample launched the service on average more than 5 years ago, with a total of more than $150 million in capital raised from investors over the years.

Of the FinTechs analyzed, 40% of them adopted a diversified service model that combines the offer of "as-a-service" solutions on the market, in addition to the retail service.

Some 90% of the banks analyzed operate exclusively in their country of origin while 54% of the fintechs analyzed operate in countries other than their country of origin.

The banks cluster focused predominantly on the offer of basic aggregation services. FinTechs, on the other hand, use innovative services as a differentiating aspect with respect to their competitors and almost all the companies in the survey sample (93%) have at least one.

All of the banks analyzed offer the aggregation service free of charge while 46% of the fintechs require memberships or subscriptions to use the service.

The ease of use and intuitive interface are recurrent topics for both clusters with the aim to convey the potential of the new service through an advanced user experience.

Present and Future Developments in Value Chains

To make sense of these developments, there are some observations that should be considered. Banking is becoming increasingly embedded in customers' everyday lives. Therefore, the more banking is embedded in such a way, boosted by an ever-improving user experience, the more it might become invisible to customers. That change will not occur overnight, but its seeds are already sprouting in a number of different areas. For example, banks might offer short-term loans through a given merchant that may encourage customers to buy a given product or service, such as the case of the Buy Now Pay Later (BNPL) service. Customers may believe the loan comes from the retailer, not the bank and the bank may be comfortable with being invisible in that transaction as long as the customer receives a good loan. The worst-case scenario of such a development would be one in which a loan is not suitable for the customer or that he or she is unable to provide enough cash flow to repay it. This risk may require a higher degree of transparency when financial services are embedded in a different value proposition.

Or again, as in the case of the BNPL service that is defined as a payment method enabling consumers to pay for goods in "n," interest-free installments, deferring the financial expense related to the purchase. On the one hand, BNPL can be considered as an Alternative Payment Method (APM) offered to consumers at checkout. On the other hand, BNPL is also a form of credit, in many ways similar to Point-of-sale financing (POS financing). Through the recent COVID-19 pandemic, BNPL services have spread as checkout options available to consumers when purchasing online. Currently, BNPL options are also becoming available at face-to-face instore points of sale to pursue an omnichannel strategy.

Additionally, BNPL models have a dual scope embedded in their value proposition. On the one hand, BNPL services are designed to provide consumers with a seamless purchasing experience while alleviating financial pressure. The use of these services is generally characterized by convenience, transparency, and flexibility. On the other hand, BNPL providers are proposing merchants with a viable tool to increase online sales conversions and order values, reducing user acquisition costs. Currently, the most prominent global BNPL players dominating the market are Klarna, Afterpay, and Affirm.

In addition to the aforementioned global players, the competitive landscape has seen a wide number of new, smaller players as well as large incumbents launching their own BNPL propositions in an attempt to catch up with fast-changing market dynamics and consumer preferences. However, BNPL services not only represent attractive opportunities for banks, but also for payments companies such as PayPal, which launched its BNPL installments plan as well as for network payment processors, namely Mastercard, Visa, and American Express, in June 2020.

In Europe, consumers are looking to use BNPL payment methods mainly for discretionary purchases where merchants have fairly high gross margins and a high customer acquisition cost. These purchases include apparel and footwear, fitness accessories and beauty products, electronics, and more recently, travel. However, global leading BNPL players are starting to integrate new and diverse categories, also through partnerships. This is the case of Afterpay, for instance, who partnered with eBay in Australia to target categories such as vehicle parts and accessories, home and garden products, and electronics. In Australia, BNPL services are also used for healthcare services and are accepted by dentists, optometrists, and veterinarians. Afterpay has also recently expanded its offerings to include concerts and airline tickets. A recent report by Capital Economics (2020) commissioned by Klarna and focused on the UK market has found interesting results on the share of purchase categories for which BNPL payment options are majorly used. The report highlights that many of the respondents reported that they would have not purchased the mentioned items if BNPL was not available at checkout. For instance, since the start of COVID-19, consumers have used BNPL services mainly for purchases in Electrical and Technology (31%) and Fashion (27%) categories.

The fast growth of the BNPL sector is catching the attention of the financial service regulators who are enhancing the regulatory overview on BNPL services and considering raising concerns regarding the lack of ad-hoc rules for POS financing and potential risks to consumers. These risks include late fees and "stacking" risks (for instance, consumers subscribing with too many BNPL providers and taking on too much debt). Regulators across different geographies are increasing their focus on fast growing BNPL platforms, customer debt affordability, consumer protection, and ensuring personal data is used as appropriate. In this regard, several interventions have been made to ensure consumers understand BNPL offers and are not encouraged to use them in an irresponsible way. For instance, in December 2020, the ASA (Advertising Standard Agency) banned some Klarna ads promoted on social media platforms as they were deemed to be irresponsibly encouraging the use of BNPL products during COVID-19 lockdown which could negatively impact users' financial situations.

As stated above, beginning in June 2022 Klarna will share data on whether customers using BNPL services in the United Kingdom paid off their loan to the credit bureaus TransUnion and Experian on time. This information comes as the UK government is looking regulate the BNPL industry by 2023.

Against this oncoming configuration of markets, a focus on control and ownership of resources is giving way to a focus on the importance of accessing and leveraging resources through unique models of collaboration. According to Prahalad and Ramaswamy (2004, p. 197),

Every participant in the experience network collaborates in value creation and competes in value extraction. This results in constant tension in the strategy development process, especially when the various units and individuals in the network must collectively execute that strategy. The key issue is this: how much transparency is needed for effective collaboration for value co-creation versus active competition for co-extracting economic value? The balancing act between collaborating and competing is delicate and crucial.

If co-creation is fundamental to the industry, it must draw on a wider customer perspective. This, in turn, would require introducing the idea of developing ecosystems in which the customer is truly free to move and choose the best deal in more competitive markets. These markets would let consumers make informed decisions that could offset potential market concentrations among market providers. This new configuration of markets represents a new paradigm of competition in which business ecosystems consist of a variety of industries with potentially increasing convergence.

As products and services are increasingly embedded in digital technologies, it is becoming more difficult to disentangle business processes from their underlying IT infrastructures. This trend is likely to continue, which means that banking will become even more dependent on technology, both at an operational and strategic level. Moreover, retail banking will continue to become more modular, flexible, and contextual. Retail customers now expect to be able to integrate e-commerce, social media, and retail payments. As a result, services will become less visible to customers as they are increasingly embedded in and combined with non-financial offers and activities.

The competitive banking game is constantly spiraling into new forms. New innovative concepts of products and services enhance customer engagement. The increased usage of mobile devices enables the onboarding of customers to platforms, where their activities generate data. Data collection and analysis span all areas of business including advertising, financial advice, credit scoring, pricing, claims management, and customer retention. Locking customers into a given platform while granting them seamless switching across platform services generates more data. Supported by artificial intelligence and machine learning, the analysis of the wide array of data streams will allow companies to continuously offer products and services that are increasingly better fit for purpose. Just how much additional value can be generated by knowing customers better seems to be limited only by the ingenuity of the platform company and the actors in the related business ecosystem (Omarini, 2019).

Data-sharing forms are becoming the basis for competitive advantage influencing how services are conceived, produced, delivered, and consumed. Therefore, partnerships with other companies solely for the purpose of data collection can be expected to increase.

As banking moves onto digital platforms, cross-industry interconnections will increase and result in new competitive threats. Providers of banking services will progressively come to see themselves in the role of "enablers" of transactions occurring on digital platforms and within business ecosystems. As the lines between banks and FinTech companies become blurred, traditional definitions of banks, and financial services become obsolete. Every player's goal is to not be perceived as an impersonal service provider, but as the individual customer's personal provider.

Summary and Conclusions: Next Steps Forward

The banking industry is being transformed by a nascent ecosystem of independent actors. Traditional, supply-centered oligopoly as expressed by Gardener et al. has been replaced. These developments demonstrate the disruptive aspect of PSD2 which is ultimately a key milestone in the unbundling and modularization of banking services, prior to the advent of a second wave of re-bundling of services, which could be developed through a strong integration between infrastructures and business models.

Re-bundling is possible because ecosystems evolve (Moore, 1993) according to different evolutionary phases (birth, expansion, leadership consolidation, renewal, or death). Within the PSD2 frame, it is clear how the premises of interdependence and modularity, typical of the notion of ecosystems, may also apply to the specific banking case. Firms may co-evolve around a core infrastructure for payments and bank account services. This does not mean that the players will remain the same, or that the core banking infrastructure could not be replaced by another species, becoming marginal (i.e., losing customer interaction and relevance).

Today, markets are driven by choice, and customers have an abundance of options to choose from to instantly fulfill their desires. It is therefore necessary for companies to adopt a holistic mindset, and realize that, in this digital age, every business is in a permanent state of being in the business of being chosen, whether they are in fashion, finance, food, or any other client-based industry. Choosing from multiple options is always based on differences, implicit or explicit, so that differentiation is needed to give the customer a reason to choose a particular service. Thus, differentiation is one of the most important and challenging features to develop, and at present, it is not discretionary.

From regulation and competition, the opening of data beyond the payments area, but always within the financial service sector—namely from Open Banking and Open Finance—is also introducing business models where the "open" context differs and can vary based on several factors (e.g., types of players, target clients, reference market). The most commonly recognized business models are Banking-as-a-Platform (BaaP) and Banking-as-a-Service (BaaS). They are collaborative models which are not mutually exclusive, but complementary and are both based on the use of APIs as a tool for interacting with financial and non-financial players.

At a global level, there are several firms that adopt the above-mentioned models. Starling Bank, for example, is among the most well-established purely digital banks to have adopted the platform-based business model, which offers a marketplace for partner services. Additionally, Standard Chartered is an important example among the main banks operating at an international level that has developed its own BaaS solution in South-East Asia.

In the above-mentioned survey, ABI Lab (2020, 2021a, 2021b, 2021c) conducted an in-depth analysis on the diffusion of "open" services by focusing mainly on the incremental component of Open Finance (with respect to Open Banking), mainly linked to the sharing of information relative to investments, lending, and insurance. In particular, the services appearing in the developer portals of 54 financial players (traditional banks, pure digital banks, and tech providers) were mapped and then a further in-depth analysis was conducted on the innovative services displayed by a limited sample of 10 players. A significant part of the APIs mapped (roughly 50%) belong to the categories of services enabled by the PSD2 (account/payment information) and thus to the Open Banking context. At the same time, the use of Open Finance has begun to spread. The survey shows that 14% of the total APIs mapped belong to the categories of services based on investment, lending, or insurance data.

Traditional banks have an offer that is more developed on Open Finance. The impact of APIs falling into the investment, lending, or insurance categories is equal to 17% among traditional banks, while it drops to only 4% for purely digital banks and tech providers, since their offer is generally more developed and heterogeneous than traditional players and consequently, they can rely on a larger and different database.

The use cases belonging to the investments category are among the most widespread, followed by services linked to lending. The offer for the insurance segment is still rarely developed and is currently present only in the traditional banks cluster and in a small percentage (6% of the total Open Finance Apis).

Among the most innovative services emerging from the survey are:

- The initialization of pre-approved loans with services such as Santander which allows third parties to verify, through an API call of data displayed by Santander, if a Santander client has a pre-approved loan limit and, if so, to initialize a pre-approved loan;
- The possibility of a point-of-sale loan with services such as Banco Bilbao Vizcaya Argentaria, S.A. (BBVA) which allows for the integration of BBVA credit products, through API technology, which allow for loans to be granted to the end client upon checkout on the basis of the conditions specified by the same (e.g., duration, amount of the loan); and
- The aggregation of investment and lending data with services such as Tink which allows for the collection and aggregation of investment data (e.g., shareholdings, securities) and credit data (e.g., amount of the loan/mortgage), making them visible in aggregate form to the client holding them.

Advances in digitization are increasing opportunities to fundamentally transform businesses and value chains. Major discontinuities in the competitive landscape—ubiquitous connectivity, industry deregulation, technology convergence—are blurring industry boundaries and introducing new concepts and product definitions.

References

ABI Lab. (2020, June). *The new account aggregation frontier: A comparison between banks and fintechs.*

ABI Lab. (2021a, July). *Digital banking: A resilient center of gravity!*

ABI Lab. (2021b, December). *Digitalization and retail banking: The evolution of the bank-client relationship during the pandemic.*

ABI Lab. (2021c, June). *Next step: From open banking to open finance.*

Accenture. (2018a). *The brave new world of open banking* (Report).

Accenture. (2018b). *Competing in the new era* (Report).

Accenture. (2019). *Competing with banking ecosystems* (Report). https://www.accenture.com/_acnmedia/pdf-102/accenture-banking-ecosystem.pdf

Accenture. (2020). *Banking in 2020: New trends to watch* (Report).

Accenture. (2021). *The future of banking* (Report).

Adner, R. (2017). Ecosystem as structure: An actionable construct for strategy. *Journal of Management, 43*(1), 39–58.

Adner, R., & Kapoor, R. (2010). Value creation in innovation ecosystems: How the structure of technological interdependence affects firm performance in new technology generations. *Strategic Management Journal, 31*(3), 306–333.

Alimamy, S., Deans, K. R., & Gnoth, J. (2018). The role of augmented reality in the interactivity of co-creation: A critical review. *International Journal of Technology and Human Interaction (IJTHI), 14*(3), 88–104.

Baldwin, C. Y. (2020). *Design rules, Volume 2: Chapter 6—The value structure of technologies, part 1: Mapping functional components.*

Ballantyne, D., & Varey, R. J. (2006). Creating value-in-use through marketing interaction: The exchange logic of relating, communicating and knowing. *Marketing Theory, 6*(3), 335–348.

Balling, M., Lierman, F., & Mullineux, A. (Eds.). (2002). *Technology and finance: Challenges for financial markets, business strategies and policy makers.* Routledge.

Bank for International Settlements (BIS). (2019). *Report on open banking and application programming interfaces.* https://www.bis.org/bcbs/publ/d486.pdf

Bareisis, Z. (2013). *The rise of the new bank account? The quest for transactional account primacy* (Report).

Bask, A., Lipponen, M., Rajahonka, M., & Tinnilä, M. (2011). Framework for modularity and customization: Service perspective. *Journal of Business & Industrial Marketing, 26*(5), 306–319.

BCG. (Authors: Desmangles, L., Dupas, M., Sachse, H., de T'Serclaes, J. W., Vasy, B., & Walsh, I.). (2018). *Global retail banking 2018: The power of personalization.* https://www.bcg.com/publications/2018/global-retail-banking-2018-power-personalization

BCG. (Authors: Brackert, T., Chen, C., Colado, J., Poddar, B., Dupas, M., Maguire, A., Sachse, H., Stewart, S., Uribe, J., & Wegner, M.). (2021). *Global retail banking 2021: The front-to-back digital retail bank* (Report). https://web-assets.bcg.com/89/ee/054f41d848869dd5e4bb86a82e3e/bcg-global-retail-banking-2021-the-front-to-back-digital-retail-bank-jan-2021.pdf

Brass, D. J., Galaskiewicz, J., Greve, H. R., & Tsai, W. (2004). Taking stock of networks and organizations: A multilevel perspective. *Academy of Management Journal, 47*(6), 795–817.

Breidbach, C. F., Brodie, R., & Hollebeek, L. (2014). Beyond virtuality: From engagement platforms to engagement ecosystems. *Managing Service Quality, 24*(6), 592–611.

Capgemini. (2019). *World retail banking report 2019.* Capgemini. https://www. capgemini.com/news/world-retail-banking-report-2019/

Capgemini. (2020). *World FinTech report.* https://www.capgemini.com/news/ world-fintech-report-2020/

Capgemini. (2021). *World retail banking report 2021.* https://www.capgemini. com/news/press-releases/world-retail-banking-report-2021-to-create-new-value-banks-can-adopt-banking-as-a-service-to-embed-finance-in-consumer-lif estyles/

Chesbrough, H. (2003). *Open innovation: The new imperative for creating and profiting from technology.* Harvard Business Press.

Chesbrough, H. W. (2006). *Open business models: How to thrive in the new innovation landscape.* Harvard Business Press.

Chesbrough, H. (2011). *Open services innovation: Rethinking your business to grow and compete in a new era.* Wiley.

Chesbrough, H., Vanhaverbeke, W., & West, J. (Eds.). (2014). *New frontiers in open innovation.* Oxford University Press.

Cortet, M., Rijks, T., & Nijland, S. (2016). PSD2: The digital transformation accelerator for banks. *Journal of Payments Strategy & Systems, 10*(1), 13–27.

De Blok, C., Meijboom, B., Luijkx, K., Schols, J., & Schroeder, R. (2014). Interfaces in service modularity: A typology developed in modular health care provision. *Journal of Operations Management, 32*(4), 175–189. https://doi. org/10.1016/j.jom.2014.03.001

Deloitte. (2017). *Open banking: How to flourish in an uncertain future* (Report).

Deloitte. (2020a). *Banking and capital markets outlook: Fortifying the core for the next wave of disruption* (Report).

Deloitte. (2020b). *Banking on the future: Vision 2020* (Report).

Deloitte. (2020c). *Open banking around the world: Towards a cross-industry data sharing ecosystem* (Report).

Deutsche Bank. (2017). *Platform replaces pipeline* (Report). https://www.db. com/newsroom_news/2017/ghp/platform-replaces-pipeline-en-11520.htm

Dratva, R. (2020). Is open banking driving the financial industry towards a true electronic market? *Electronic Markets, 30*(1), 65–67.

Enkel, E., Gassmann, O., & Chesbrough, H. (2009). Open R&D and open innovation: Exploring the phenomenon. *R&D Management, 39*(4), 311–316.

European Banking Authority (EBA). (2017, April 25). (Authors: Zetzsche, D. A., Buckley, R. P., Arner, D. W., & Barberis, J. N.).*From FinTech to TechFin—The regulatory challenges of data-driven finance 2017* (Working Paper Series, No. 6).

European Central Bank (ECB). (1999). *The effects of technology on the EU banking systems*. European Central Bank. https://www.ecb.europa.eu/pub/pdf/other/techbnken.pdf

EY. (2017). *Fintech adoption index 2017*. http://www.ey.com/Publication/vwLUAssets/ey-fintech-adoption-index-2017/$FILE/ey-fintech-adoption-index-2017.pdf

Fink, L. (2018). *The sense of purpose*. https://corpgov.law.harvard.edu/2018/01/17/a-sense-of-purpose/

Gawer, A. (2009). Platform dynamics and strategies: From products to services. *Platforms, Markets and Innovation, 45*, 57.

Gawer, A., & Cusumano, M. A. (2014). Industry platforms and ecosystem innovation. *Journal of Product Innovation Management, 31*(3), 417–433.

Iansiti, M., & Levien, R. (2004). Strategy as ecology. *Harvard Business Review, 82*(3), 68–78.

International Monetary Fund (IMF), and World Bank. (2019). *Fintech: The experience so far* (IMF Policy Paper, No.19/024). https://www.imf.org/en/Publications/Policy-Papers/Issues/2019/06/27/Fintech-The-Experience-So-Far-47056

Kearney, A. T. (2021). *Retail banking radar: Change looms in Europe* (Report).

King, B. (2012). *Bank 3.0: Why banking is no longer somewhere you go but something you do*. Wiley.

KPMG. (2016, October). *The profitability of EU banks: Hard work or a lost cause?* (Report). https://assets.kpmg.com/content/dam/kpmg/xx/pdf/2016/10/the-profitability-of-eu-banks.pdf

KPMG. (Author: Ruddenklau, A.). (2020). *Can fintech lead innovation post COVID-19?* (Report). https://home.kpmg/xx/en/blogs/home/posts/2020/05/can-fintech-lead-innovation-post-covid-19.html

Llewellyn, D. T. (1999). *The new economics of banking* (No. 5). SUERF studies.

Lusch, R. F., Vargo, S. L., & O'brien, M. (2007). Competing through service: Insights from service-dominant logic. *Journal of Retailing, 83*(1), 5–18.

Ma, F., Wang, L., & Xu, H. (2011, August). Dynamics mechanism and innovation model of service modularity. In *2011 2nd International Conference on Artificial Intelligence, Management Science and Electronic Commerce (AIMSEC)* (pp. 1077–1080). IEEE.

McKinsey. (2017). *Data sharing and open banking*. https://www.mckinsey.it/sites/default/files/data-sharing-and-open-banking.pdf

Microsoft, Avanade, Accenture. (2017). *PSD2 and open banking: Using regulation to kick-start the transformation of banking* (Report).

Moon, S. K., Shu, J., Simpson, T. W., & Kumara, S. R. (2010). A module-based service model for mass customization: Service family design. *Iie Transactions, 43*(3), 153–163.

Moore, J. F. (1993). Predators and prey: A new ecology of competition. *Harvard Business Review, 71*(3), 75–86.

Oliver Wyman. (Authors: Belinky, M., Rennick, E., & Veitch, A.) (2018). *The Fintech 2.0 paper: rebooting financial services* (Report).

Omarini, A. (2015). *Retail banking: Business transformation and competitive strategies for the future*. Palgrave Macmillan. https://doi.org/10.4172/2223-5833.1000240

Omarini, A. (2019). *Banks and banking: Digital transformation and the hype of Fintech. Business impacts, new frameworks and managerial implications*. McGrawHill.

Omarini, A. (2022). Unbundling and re-bundling the open industry of banking. In K. T. Liaw (Ed.), *The Routledge handbook of fintech*. Routledge.

Prahalad, C. K., & Ramaswamy, V. (2004). *The future of competition: Co-creating unique value with customers*. Harvard Business Press.

PwC. (2016). *Blurred lines: How FinTech is shaping financial services* (Report). https://www.pwc.com/il/en/home/assets/pwc_fintech_global_report.pdf

PwC. (2018a). *Open banking … and so what?* (Report). https://www.pwc.com/it/en/industries/banking/future-open-banking.html

PwC. (2018b). *Five ingredients to catch up open banking* (Report). https://www.pwc.com/it/it/industries/banking-capital-markets/OpenBanking/doc/Five-Ingredients-Banks-Open-Banking-Article.pdf

PwC. (2020). *Retail banking 2020: Evolution or revolution?* (Report). https://www.pwc.com/gx/en/banking-capital-markets/banking-2020/assets/pwc-retail-banking-2020-evolution-or-revolution.pdf

Rahikka, E., Ulkuniemi, P., & Pekkarinen, S. (2011). Developing the value perception of the business customer through service modularity. *Journal of Business & Industrial Marketing, 26*(5), 357–367.

Schueffel, P. E., & Vadana, I. I. (2015). Open innovation in the financial services sector-a global literature review. *Journal of Innovation Management, 3*(1), 25–48. https://www.researchgate.net/publication/275027680_Open_Innovation_in_the_Financial_Services_Sector_-_A_Global_Literature_Review?enrichId=rgreq-20faaa7a608e929520cbd84b0ac73317-XXX&enrichSource=Y29 2ZXJQYWdlOzI3NTAyNzY4MDtBUzoyMTg3ODDk0NTE5NjQ0MTZAMT QyOTE3N

Silvestro, R., & Lustrato, P. (2015). Exploring the "mid office" concept as an enabler of mass customization in services. *International Journal of Operations & Production Management, 35*(6), 866–894.

Smedlund, A., & Faghankhani, H. (2015, January). Platform orchestration for efficiency, development, and innovation. In *2015 48th Hawaii international conference on system sciences* (pp. 1380–1388). IEEE.

Tuunanen, T., Bask, A., & Merisalo-Rantanen, H. (2012). Typology for modular service design: Review of literature. *International Journal of Service Science, Management, Engineering, and Technology (IJSSMET), 3*(3), 99–112.

Vargo, S. L., & Lusch, R. F. (2008). Service-dominant logic: Continuing the evolution. *Journal of the Academy of Marketing Science, 36*(1), 1–10.

Vargo, S. L., & Lusch, R. F. (2014). Evolving to a new dominant logic for marketing. In *The service-dominant logic of marketing* (pp. 21–46). Routledge.

Voss, C., Roth, A. V., & Chase, R. B. (2008). Experience, service operations strategy, and services as destinations: Foundations and exploratory investigation. *Production and Operations Management, 17*(3), 247–266.

Wilson, J. D., Jr. (2017). *Creating strategic value through financial technology.* Wiley.

Wintjes, R. (2017). *Interplay between technological an social innovation* (SIMPACT Working Paper).

Yang, L., & Shan, M. (2009, April). Process analysis of service modularization based on cluster arithmetic. In *2009 First international workshop on database technology and applications* (pp. 263–266). IEEE.

Yoo, Y. (2010). Computing in everyday life: A call for research on experiential computing. *MIS Quarterly, 34*(2), 213–231.

Yoo, Y., Henfridsson, O., & Lyytinen, K. (2010). Research commentary—The new organizing logic of digital innovation: An agenda for information systems research. *Information Systems Research, 21*(4), 724–735.

Zachariadis, M., & Ozcan, P. (2017). *The API economy and digital transformation in financial services: The case of open banking.* https://ssrn.com/abstract=2975199

Zhou, Z., Lin, Y., Ma, S., & Yue, F. (2010, July). Modularity of service design for IT company. In *Proceedings of 2010 IEEE International Conference on Service Operations and Logistics, and Informatics* (pp. 136–141). IEEE.

Zomerdijk, L. G., & Voss, C. A. (2010). Service design for experience-centric services. *Journal of Service Research, 13*(1), 67–82.

CHAPTER 5

Competitors and Partners at the Same Time: On the Role of Fintech Companies in the Latvian Financial Market

Ramona Rupeika-Apoga, Emīls Dārziņš, Deniss Filipovs, and Stefan Wendt

Introduction

Fintech ecosystems are critical to nurturing technological innovation, making financial markets and systems more efficient, and improving the overall customer experience. Moreover, given the scope of financial technology, a vibrant fintech ecosystem can stimulate the entire economy by attracting talented, ambitious people and becoming a locus of creative

---

The opinions expressed in this chapter are those of the author and not of the Bank of Latvia.

R. Rupeika-Apoga (✉)
Faculty of Business, Management and Economics, University of Latvia, Riga, Latvia
e-mail: ramona.rupeika-apoga@lu.lv

115
T. Walker et al. (eds.), *The Fintech Disruption*, Palgrave Studies in Financial Services Technology,
https://doi.org/10.1007/978-3-031-23069-1_5

thinking and business activity. Fintech ecosystems enable growth opportunities for many sectors, including software development, data analytics, payment services, financing, and trading platforms (e.g. peer-to-peer lending, crowdfunding), mobile banking, and algorithmic asset management systems (Oehler et al., 2016, 2021; PwC, 2015). Current trends include, e.g. open banking, open insurance, open data, marketplaces, super-apps, API economy (i.e. business models based on application programming interfaces), embedded finance, and experience banking. These trends are not independent of each other, but rather complement each other, making the financial industry even more open and outward looking (Lochy, 2020).

The purpose of this study is to explore the current development of Latvian fintech companies, their corresponding challenges, and their expected future developments. While the Latvian economy is relatively small on an international scale, our findings provide insight into a small, open economy that has a vibrant financial sector, providing financial services domestically and abroad. In this sense, the implications of our study are not limited to Latvia, but are also of interest for other countries with small economies, such as Malta, Cyprus, Estonia, and Slovenia. Given that fintech development has typically been associated with fintech hubs and financial centres, our study also raises awareness of fintech developments beyond such hubs and centres.

In Latvia, there is no specific legislative framework for fintech companies. Fintech companies are regulated and monitored by the Financial and Capital Markets Commission (FCMC) and/or the Consumer Protection Center (CRPC), depending on which financial services they provide. The main regulator supervising the financial market is FCMC. On the other hand, the CRPC ensures consumer protection, market surveillance, the safety of products and services, etc. Correspondingly, for business activities that need licensing, fintech companies must get the licences from

E. Dārziņš
The Bank of Latvia, Riga, Latvia

D. Filipovs
Tietoevry, Espoo, Finland

S. Wendt
Department of Business, Bifröst University, Bifröst, Iceland

FCMC or CRPC. For instance, such activities requiring licences include deposit-taking, investment management, issuance of financial instruments, payment or electronic money services, insurance, and consumer credit services (Rupeika-Apoga & Wendt, 2021). However, overall fintech development in Latvia is in line with a well-developed financial market infrastructure as well as a highly-skilled labour with relatively high entrepreneurial ability. Additionally, Latvia is highly ranked internationally in the context of information and communications technology (ICT) development, showing strong positions in Internet subscriptions, electricity access and supply quality, and percentage of Internet users among the adult population (World Economic Forum, 2020, 2021).

While there is no official list of fintech companies in Latvia, we applied several criteria, such as the definition of fintech provided by the Bank of Latvia and the entry in the Register of Enterprises of the Republic of Latvia, to identify fintech companies. For the 93 fintech companies that we identified in Latvia, we analysed basic characteristics and performance data. Moreover, we ran a survey among these 93 companies in the summer of 2021. The survey consisted of four main sections: (1) general questions, (2) characteristics of business models, (3) current challenges for fintech companies, and (4) the outlook for the fintech sector. We received 31 responses, which corresponds to a response rate of 33%.

We find that the main financial services provided by fintech companies are digital lending, digital payment, and digital wallets. The majority follow a B2B (business-to-business) business model, providing services to businesses, both in Latvia and abroad. These financial services are potentially disruptive to traditional financial industries because they could replace services that have only been offered by traditional financial service providers so far. The responses to our survey also reveal an interesting new digital finance trend in the Latvian market: B2B2C, i.e. simultaneous fintech aid for small businesses and their customers, with 19% of respondents identifying this as their business model. Commission income from services or products is the main source of income for our survey respondents (61% of respondents), leaving interest income far behind (only 19% of respondents). Fintech companies generally focus on running the daily business and serving existing clients using existing IT support solutions. The main supporting services provided by fintech companies in Latvia are digital identity, data analysis, and RegTech. These services can, in most cases, be considered complementary to traditional financial services, i.e.

having less potential for disruption but new opportunities for collaboration between fintech companies and traditional financial service providers. The survey participants see the largest growth potential in open banking (19 out of 31), digital lending (14 out of 31), and data analysis with instant payments (13 out of 31).

Despite the increasing relevance of fintech in the financial sector, fintech companies in Latvia have been facing a number of challenges when it comes to growth while establishing and maintaining financially sustainable business models. This follows the general pattern in an industry with high levels of innovation and quick pace of development. However, while earlier studies show that regulation was the most urgent problem a few years ago (Rupeika-Apoga & Thalassinos, 2020; Rupeika-Apoga & Wendt, 2021), our survey reveals that fintech companies are now struggling with the lack of availability of qualified personnel and/or experienced managers. This situation also represents a major obstacle for potential expansion into foreign markets and finding new customers.

This chapter is structured as follows. In the next section, we describe the sample selection and data collection based on data from Bureau van Dijk's Orbis database as well as our survey. The subsequent section presents the results, and we provide and discuss conclusions in the last section.

SAMPLE AND SURVEY DESIGN

Sample

The main challenge for our sample selection is the lack of an official list of fintech companies in Latvia. At the international level, the Organisation for Economic Co-operation and Development (OECD) (2018) defines that "fintech involves not only the application of new digital technologies to financial services but also the development of business models and products which rely on these technologies and more generally on digital platforms and processes." Similarly, the Financial Stability Board (2019) defines fintech as "technology-enabled innovation in financial services that could result in new business models, applications, processes or products with an associated material effect on the provision of financial services."

We use the definition of fintech provided by the Bank of Latvia and the FMCM (Bank of Latvia, 2020; FCMC, 2020) that a fintech company is a company that develops and uses new and innovative technologies in the financial services area. This leads to the development of new financial products and services or a significant improvement of the existing ones. We started with companies listed in the article "fintech in Latvia: Status Quo, Current Developments, and Challenges Ahead" (Rupeika-Apoga & Wendt, 2021), then added fintech companies listed in the Swedbank Latvian fintech report 2020 (Swedbank, 2020), and finally double-checked whether these companies fell under our definition. Following a similar procedure, we added fintech companies found from other data sources, namely Latvijas Bankas intelligence (Bank of Latvia, 2021) and the Latvian Startup association Startin.lv Inventio Growth database (Startin, 2021). Moreover, the list of fintech companies was cross-checked against the Register of Enterprises of the Republic of Latvia to ensure that only fintech companies incorporated in Latvia were considered.

In total, we identified 93 companies that meet our criteria. The financial services that they provide can be categorized into:

- *Digital Lending:* Peer-to-peer (P2P) lending, balance sheet lending, invoice trading, leasing, and consumer credit.
- *Digital Capital raising:* equity-based, reward-based, or donation-based crowdfunding, unsecured debt, equity or real-estate crowdfunding, and initial coin offering (ICO) platforms.
- *Digital banking:* fully digital banks, providers of banking as a service (BaaS).
- *Digital Payments:* mobile payments, money transfers, e-money issuers, points of access, and other payment-related services.
- *WealthTech:* robo-advisors, social trading, personal financial management, and financial comparison websites.
- *Digital asset exchange:* trading and brokerage services including different platforms, exchanges, Bitcoin Teller Machines, etc.
- *Digital custody:* digital wallets and key management services.
- *InsurTech:* insurance-related products and services, including digital brokers or agents, peer-to-peer insurance, insurance comparison portals, etc.

  In addition, technology and support services are provided:
- *Credit and data analytics:* credit scoring based on alternative data, solutions based on analysis of biometric and social data.

- *RegTech:* solutions for meeting regulatory requirements, including profiling and due diligence, risk analytics, regulatory reporting, market monitoring, etc.
- *Digital identity:* services related to biometric security, know-your-customer (KYC) services, and fraud prevention.

As the definition of fintech evolves and its interpretation is ambiguous within both regulators and companies, we understand that our list might not include some companies that might consider themselves to be fintech companies. However, we do follow a broader approach than Rupeika-Apoga et al. (2020) who identified only 56 fintech companies in Latvia. Reflecting the different approaches to identify fintech companies, the fintech Latvia Startup Map 2020 report includes 50 fintech companies (Fintech Baltic, 2021) compared to 75 in 2019 and 91 in 2020 identified by Swedbank (Swedbank, 2020).

For the 93 companies that we identified, we collected data on basic characteristics and performance from Bureau van Dijk's Orbis database, the flagship database of the company (a subsidiary of Moody's). Moreover, we sent a survey to the 93 companies in the summer of 2021 via LinkedIn, direct e-mails, and industry associations. We received 31 responses (compared to 21 responses of Rupeika-Apoga et al. [2020]), corresponding to a response rate of 33%, which is satisfactory for this type of survey (Hoque, 2004; Olson & Slater, 2002; Rikhardsson et al., 2020).

Survey Design

The survey questions are based on the World Economic Forum "Global COVID-19 fintech Market Rapid Assessment Study" (World Economic Forum, 2020) and the fintech Report Estonia 2021 (), but they have been modified to assess the development of fintech companies in Latvia. The survey consists of four blocks:

- *General information*: This block includes ten questions. The first two questions relate to identifying information, such as the fintech company's name. The following three questions ask about the maturity of the company, the workforce, and its prediction for the year 2021. Questions 6 and 7 gather information about the 2020 revenue and corresponding prediction for 2021. Question 8 asks about the business model (business-to-business (B2B), business-to-consumer (B2C), business-to-business-to-consumer (B2B2C), or other). Question 9 asks about product delivery channels (application programming interface (API), mobile application, physical connection, web application, instant message, or other). Question 10 asks about the revenue model (interest income, commission income, trading income, licence fee, centralized hosting of business applications, advertising income, data, or other).

- *Characteristics of the company's activity*: This block focuses on the services which are provided by the fintech company and consists of six questions. Beyond clarifying the type of services, the fintech companies provide, these questions focus on their key value proposition to their clients.

- *Current challenges*: This block involves questions asking the participant to rate on a scale from 1 (not pressing) to 7 (extremely pressing) the specific problems their fintech company is facing and the extent to which regulative and regulator-related factors restrict the expansion of the business to foreign markets. An open question follows, asking if there are any other important aspects that the participant would like to mention in this context.

- *Fintech sector outlook*: This part includes questions on how to improve the fintech sector, which activities the respondent sees as having the largest potential for development, and what kind of measures from the government would help better develop this sector. This section also includes two open questions on local and European regulation regarding fintech where respondents are invited to share particular aspects of the regulation, which they would like to change. The final questions focus on collaboration with other market participants (banks, notaries, etc.) and government institutions.

RESULTS

Basic Characteristics and Performance

In this section, we provide an overview of the 93 Latvian fintech companies based on key characteristics and financial performance. The main source of information is Bureau van Dijk's Orbis database. As shown in Table 5.1, 33 out of the 93 companies have their main activity in

Table 5.1 Distribution of fintech companies in Latvia by type of activity in 2021

Main sectors	Number of companies
Computer Software	33
Banking, Insurance and Financial Services	28
Business Services	21
Media and Broadcasting	4
Wholesale	3
Property Services	2
Biotechnology and Life Sciences	1
Business and other management consultancy activities	1
Total	**93**

computer software, followed by 28 companies in banking, insurance, and financial services, and 21 in business services. All other activities, such as media and broadcasting, wholesale, or property services, play a minor role.

When considering the size of the fintech companies, 62% are classified as small companies (total assets less than 2 million euros, number of employees less than 15), 25% as medium-sized companies (total assets from 2 million euros, number of employees from 15), 12% as large companies (total assets from 20 million euros, number of employees from 150), and 1% (total assets from 200 million euros, number of employees from 1000)as very large companies. Additionally, 84% of companies are private limited companies and 16% are public limited companies.

As displayed in Fig. 5.1, the development of fintech companies in Latvia had not really begun to develop until 2014. While the establishment of fintech companies remained at one to four companies per year until 2013, more companies were founded every year since: with five companies in 2014, up to 15 companies in 2019. Two aspects need to be kept in mind here: First, the data only includes companies that still exist, which means that companies that were founded but ceased operations are not included. Second, the number of foundations in 2021 might not reflect all foundations in that year because we might not have been able to identify some of the companies established in 2021 if they were not yet included in the register of enterprises or other lists.

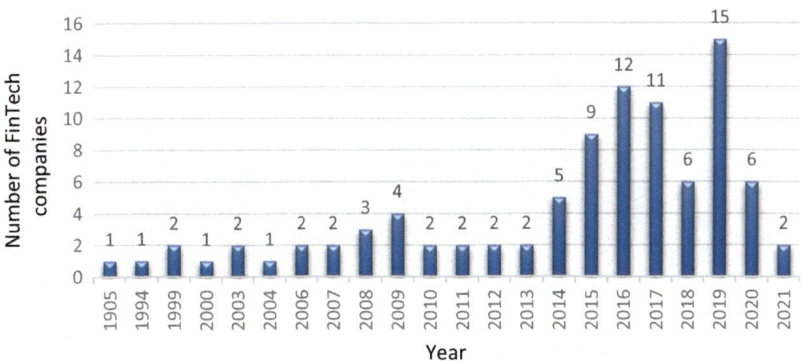

Fig. 5.1   Fintech companies in Latvia by year of foundation

When it comes to the independence of the fintech companies, only one company has no shareholder with more than 25% of direct or total ownership, whereas 17 of the fintech companies have at least one shareholder with ownership between 25 and 50%. 65 of the 93 fintech companies have a majority shareholder with a direct ownership of over 50%, including branches and foreign companies. This means that the fintech companies in Latvia cannot generally be considered very independent due to their dependence on a single block holder, which might be another financial service provider.

Figure 5.2 displays averages for three size measures: number of employees (right axis), total assets, and turnover, while Fig. 5.3 shows the total data for the fintech industry. The average number of employees (Fig. 5.2) ranges from 16 to 35, with a sharp increase from 2012 to 2013, a steady decline until 2017, subsequently stabilizing at 27 to 29 employees by 2020. The total number of employees increases steadily from 2012 to 2019 and only decreases in 2020, which can be explained by the impact of COVID-19 on the labour market.

The development of turnover and total assets is largely in line with the development of the number of employees. Average and industry-wide turnover and total assets increase quite strongly between 2012 and 2013. Subsequently, the turnover fluctuates (with a downward trend in average numbers) and only increases substantially again in 2018. The average total assets drop quite significantly between 2013 and 2016 and largely remain at the 2016 level until 2019. 2020 shows a drop

Fig. 5.2 Average size of Latvian fintech companies

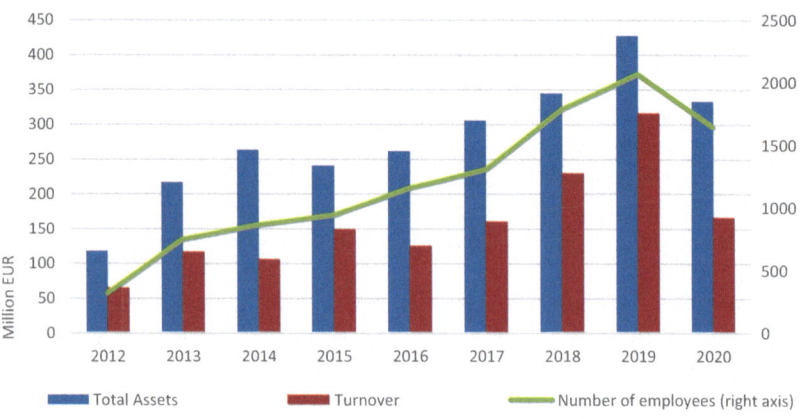

Fig. 5.3 Total size of the Latvian fintech industry

in all metrics. The decline in average turnover and total assets early in the analysed time period can be attributed to several reasons. First, due to increased competition, borrowing interest rates have dropped significantly. While in 2010, the rates of some lending companies reached 400% per annum, maximum rates were about 50% per annum in 2014. Second, due to changes in the legislation to protect clients, several restrictions are imposed on lending companies, including the maximum interest rate, the penalty rate, and the maximum repayment amount. Third, in 2015 two large new players (MINTOS MARKETPLACE AS and TWINO AS) in crowdfunding joined the market, hence, increasing competition for lending companies. Fourth, the Latvian market is small and several large players significantly influence the overall statistics of the development of the fintech industry.

Return on equity (ROE) and return on assets (ROA) are the two most important metrics for assessing how effectively a company's management is doing its job of managing the capital entrusted to it. Figure 5.4 represents the average ROA and ROE across Latvian fintech companies. Most striking is the huge variation in ROE over time, ranging from 86% in 2012 to minus 6% in 2018. However, after a sharp drop in 2013, the ROE has been stabilizing in an upward trend until 2017, again followed by substantial swings. The fintech industry's ROE in 2020, which stood at 19.6%, was significantly higher than the banking industry's ROE for the same year of 7.4% (Statista, 2021).

The ROA variation over the same time period was not as large as the variation of ROE. The ROA ranges from 0.3 in 2015 to 13% in 2012 and was never negative. After a decline until 2015, ROA figures have been showing a positive trend since 2015, though not reaching the 2012/2013 level again. The ROA in the fintech industry is also higher than that of the banking industry with 8.5% versus 0.8% (Statista, 2021). Even though we

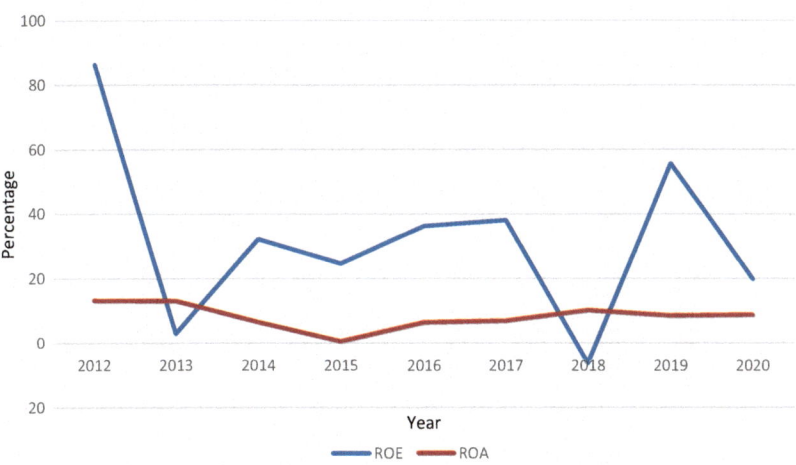

Fig. 5.4 ROE and ROA of Latvian fintechs in percent

would expect a convergence of the indicators of the fintech and the traditional banking sector in the medium to long run, the high fluctuations in the fintech sector do not yet allow such a conclusion.

Figure 5.5 displays two profitability measures, net income after taxes (NIAT), and profit margin, as average across Latvian fintech companies. Figure 5.6 presents these measures for the industry. While NIAT in Fig. 5.6 is cumulated across all companies, the profit margin figures are by definition the same as in Fig. 5.5, but they are again included for comparison purposes. While average and industry-wide NIAT fluctuates substantially, it remains positive across the entire time period. Overall, there is a downward trend in average NIAT, whereas industry-wide NIAT shows an upward trend, except for the sharp drop in 2020.

The profit margin is fluctuating quite substantially around a level of approximately 8%. What is most striking though is not the variation over time, but the variation between companies. Profit margins between different fintech companies vary from as low as negative 67% up to as high as positive 70%.

In 2020, higher positive profit margins were experienced by companies providing computer software services, such as software to help analyse customer payments through the advanced due diligence process, an investment and lending platform, or a white label platform designed to help customers build a payment system business. These companies are mostly small in size and serve B2B. While higher negative profit margins in 2020 were generated by fintechs in Banking, Insurance & Financial Services. However, there is no conclusive evidence that fintechs

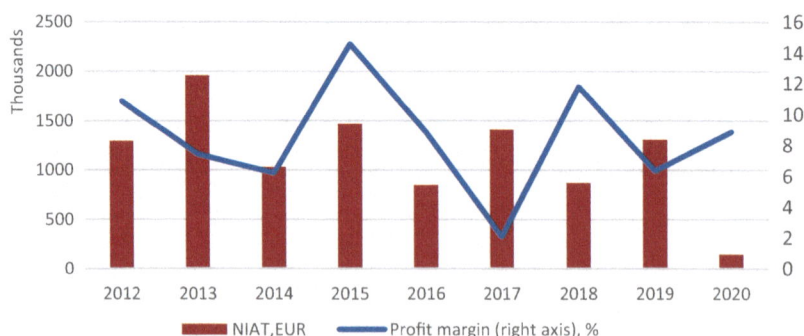

Fig. 5.5   Average profitability of fintech companies

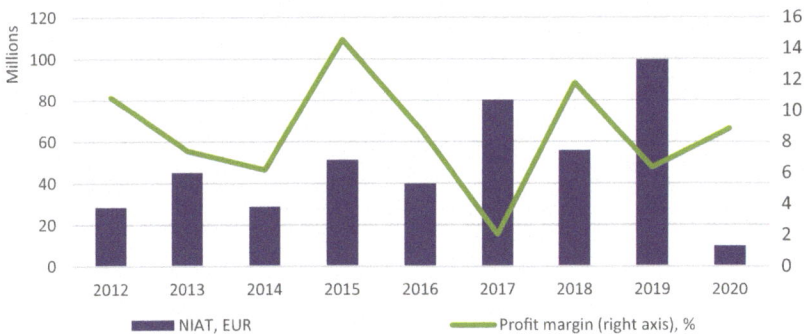

Fig. 5.6 Overall fintech industry profitability

that provide loans perform worse than companies that provide software services. In addition, lending service companies are well-established
companies in the Latvian financial market with a long history, although
they are not as profitable as newcomers providing software services, they
generally have a stable positive profit in the long term. The fluctuations
and variations make the Latvian fintech industry somewhat unstable in the
eyes of creditors and investors. While the average figures indicate relatively
good financial health, investment and debt repayment ability, and growth
potential, the numbers for single companies show that some of them are
far less financially healthy than others.

Figure 5.7 shows the ability of the fintech companies to pay off
short-term liabilities as well as long-term debt and obligations. During
the analysed period, the average current ratio, defined as current assets
divided by current liabilities, ranges from 3 to 5. This means that, on
average, companies have the financial resources to remain solvent in the
short term. The equity ratio is a key metric used to measure a business's
ability to meet its long-term debt obligations and is defined as equity
divided by total assets. It shows how much of a company is funded by
equity instead of debt. The higher the number, the less leverage the
company uses, and in general the less likely the company is to end up
in insolvency due to over-indebtedness. The average equity ratio in our
data set ranges from 25 to 41%, which indicates that a greater portion of
a company's assets are funded by debt, here in the range from 75 to 59%.
This does not indicate financial distress on average. Again, however, the

Fig. 5.7   Liquidity and leverage situation: current ratio and equity ratio

equity ratio varies across companies with some of the fintech companies even having negative equity ratios.

Survey Results

General Characteristics of the Respondents
The majority of the surveyed fintech companies follow the B2B business model providing their services to other businesses (see Fig. 5.8) and focusing on both the Latvian market and international clients. This group is followed by fintech companies providing services to consumers. However, it also becomes obvious that the business model of B2B2C, i.e. simultaneous fintech aid for small businesses and their customers has been established by a number of fintech companies.

Seventeen of the respondents indicated providing financial services themselves and fourteen responded to supporting other companies' financial services, with three respondents being active in both fields.

As displayed in Fig. 5.9, lending services represent the most common type of financial services provided by Latvian fintech companies (29.0%), followed by services related to digital identity (22.6%) and payment services (22.6%). Digital wallets (16.1%), data analysis (12.9%), and digital

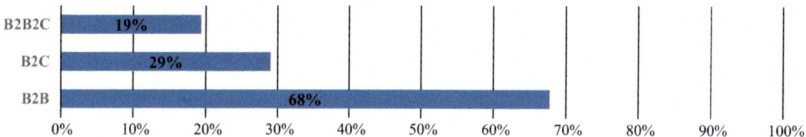

Fig. 5.8 Business model

banking (12.9%) are also relevant business models for these fintech companies, whereas RegTech, raising capital, and other types of services appear to be less of a focus for the surveyed fintech companies.

The participants of the survey report that the main source of revenue is commission income from services and/or products delivered (61.3% of the respondents; see Fig. 5.10). Licence fees, hosting business applications, and interest income also represent quite substantial sources of revenues (about 20 to 25% of the respondents). Other revenue sources, such as gathering and selling data and advertising, appear less relevant.

In terms of the maturity of fintech companies, 18 companies (58% of those surveyed) are already doing business on a daily basis and scaling their business while making a profit. However, nine companies state that they are still in the growth phase as they are trying to get to the break-even point. Finally, four fintech companies are still at the development/preparation phase.

When it comes to current challenges that fintech companies face on a scale from 1 (not pressing) to 7 (extremely pressing), the participants answered as follows, represented in Fig. 5.11. Most pressing are the availability of skilled staff or experienced managers (5), expansion to foreign markets (5), finding customers (5), and regulation (5). Expansion of the product portfolio (4), competition (4), access to finance (4), cost of production or labour (4), building partnerships with established players (4), and product market fit (4) appear to be slightly less pressing.

Figure 5.12 summarizes the barriers faced by fintechs wanting to expand into overseas markets. The most critical issues are readiness of the regulator to consider the proposals of market participants regarding improvement regulations and cooperation and coordination between different regulators, scoring 4 on the scale of 1 to 7.

The physical meeting requirements for initiating client relationships and being able to contact regulators were estimated as less pressing, scoring 3 on the scale of 1 to 7.

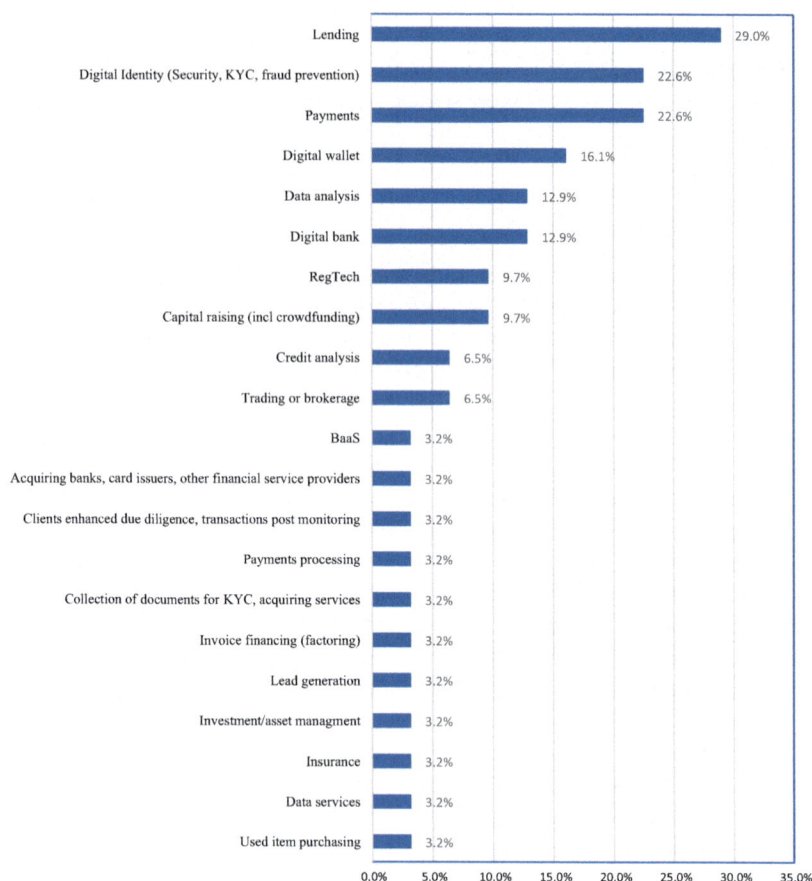

Fig. 5.9 Breakdown by details of the business model

Outlook

Companies expect to grow in the future and 14 of the 31 fintech companies surveyed expect their 2021 revenue to exceed € 1 million. The results of the survey also suggest that the fintech companies expect to substantially grow their workforce (see Fig. 5.13), which is in line with the expected growth of demand for fintech services. Figure 5.13 compares fintech companies' expectations for labour force change in 2020 () with our results for 2021.

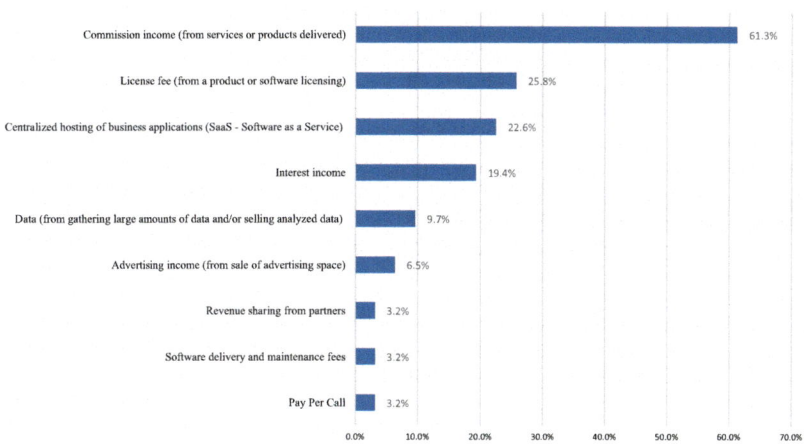

Fig. 5.10   Revenue model

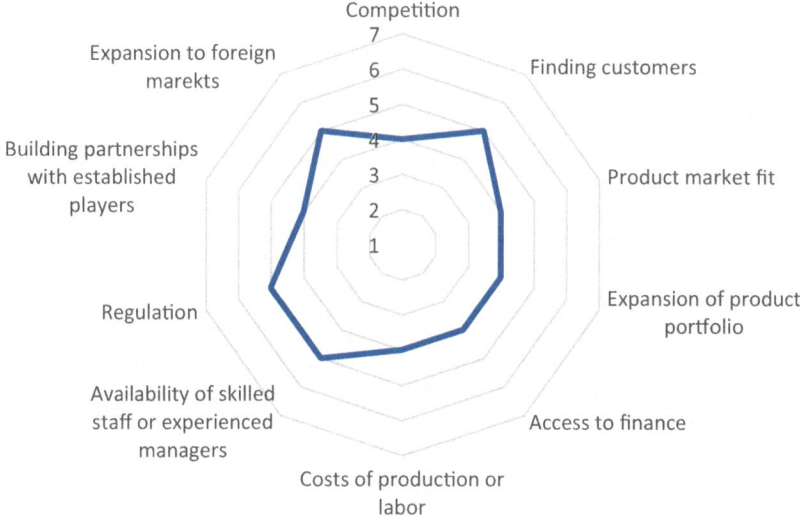

Fig. 5.11   Current problems on the scale from 1 (not pressing) to 7 (extremely pressing), medians

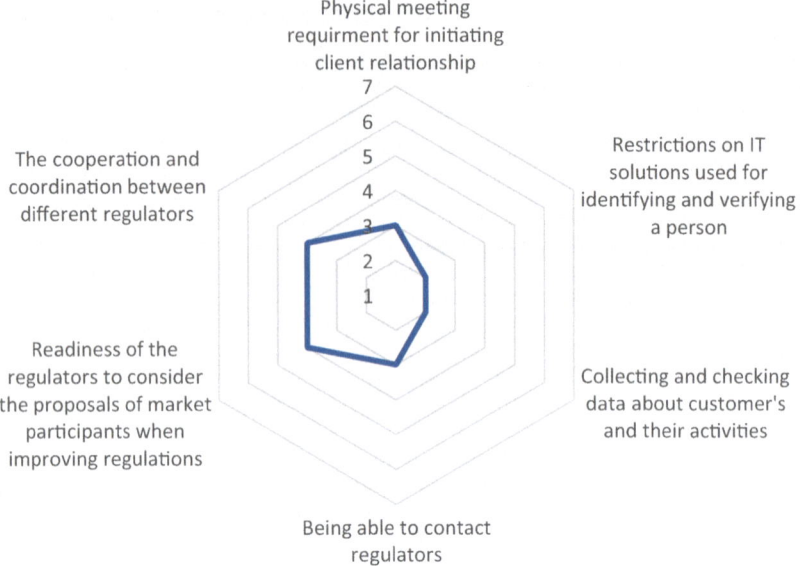

Fig. 5.12 Regulative and regulator-related factors restricting the expansion to foreign markets on the scale from 1 (not pressing) to 7 (extremely pressing), medians

19 of the surveyed fintech companies indicated that the greatest development potential in fintech lies in open banking. Lending was recognized by 14 fintech companies, placing it second, while data analysis and digital currencies were cited as the third most popular trend of the future.

The survey participants also indicated that better cooperation with the regulator could contribute to the development of the fintech sector in Latvia (see Fig. 5.14).

The most important source of funding for the survey respondents in the next three years will be seed capital, named by 58% as their first choice, while only 13% mention equity funding and venture capital as their first choice. Additionally, 58% of fintech companies mentioned venture capital as a second funding option.

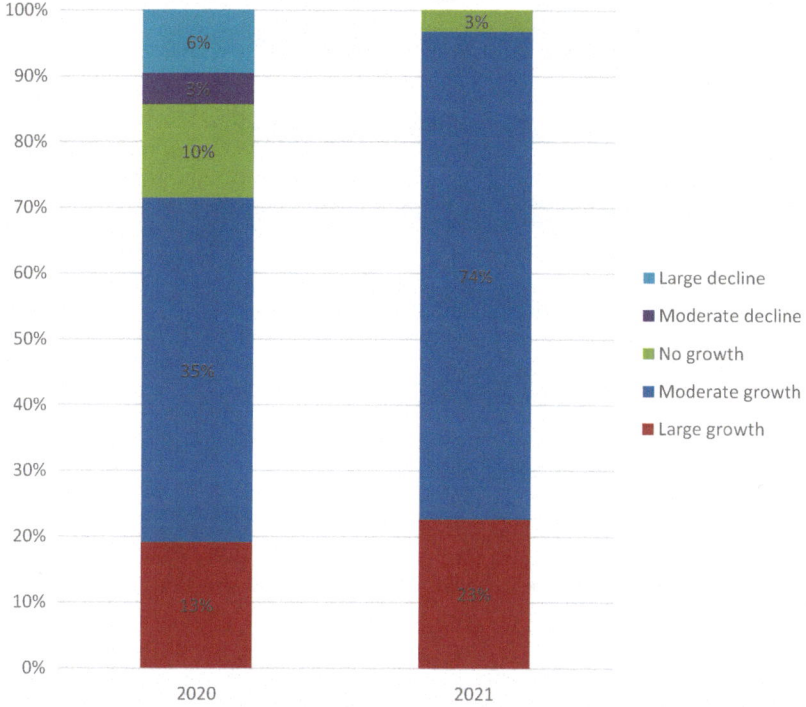

Fig. 5.13 Expected change in the workforce in 2020 and 2021

CONCLUSIONS

Our analysis of the fintech sector in Latvia reveals several insights into the current situation and development of this sector:

- Most of the fintech companies are small and quite young—most of them founded within the last 8 years. While the average size of the companies has been relatively stable since 2015, the size of the sector has increased due to the new market entries. However, 2020 has seen a decrease in size, most likely as a result of the COVID-19 pandemic. (Grima et al., 2020, 2021). Even though the relatively stable average size over time might be interpreted as a positive result, it still also reveals some difficulties with growth.

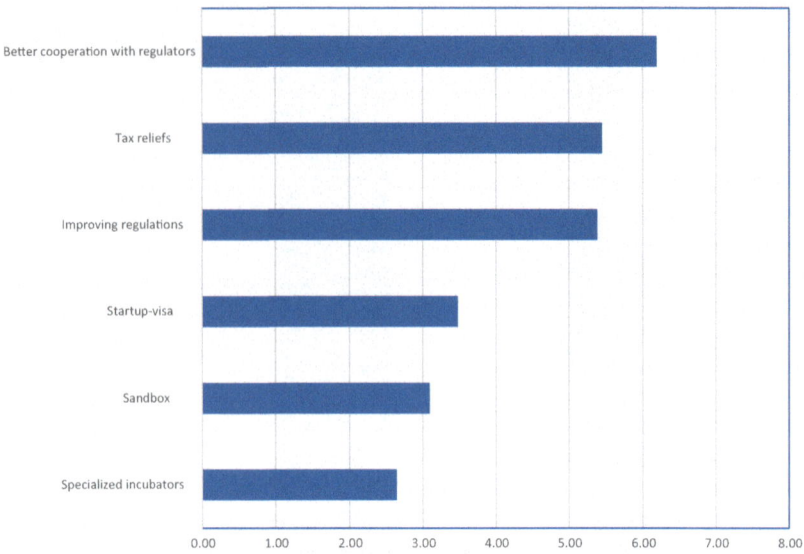

Fig. 5.14 How could the Latvian state contribute to the fintech sector development?

- About two thirds of the fintech companies have a majority shareholder with an ownership share of more than 50%. This means that their level of independence is quite low.
- The financial performance of Latvian fintechs has been fluctuating substantially during the last few years. While average performance has overall, despite the fluctuations, been positive throughout the years, the variation between the companies is substantial. While some companies have very high ROE, ROA, and profit margins, other companies exhibit substantially negative return and margins. This situation reflects some difficulties in establishing and maintaining financially sustainable business models. This corresponds to the general situation in areas with a high degree of innovation and high innovation speed. Business ideas are not always successful, some companies disappear, and others take their place. On average, however, the overall financial health appears relatively stable.
- Most common services that the fintech companies provide include lending services, services related to digital identity, payment services,

digital wallets, data analysis, and digital banking. In line with these finding is also the result that seventeen of the respondents provide financial services themselves, while fourteen support other companies' financial services and three respondents are active in both fields. The main supporting services include digital identity, data analysis, and RegTech. Most revenue is generated as commission income from services and/or products delivered, followed by licence fees, hosting business applications, and interest income. The findings on the services provided by fintech companies in Latvia show that they provide complementary services to traditional financial services, but they also provide services that could potentially replace services provided by traditional financial service providers. Hence, fintech is bringing more competition to the financial services market.

- Fintech companies are not only active in B2B and B2C relationships, but some of them do also provide B2B2C services, which means that they simultaneously provide fintech services for small businesses and their customers. We see some shift in business models compared to earlier findings, where Latvian fintech companies served mostly individual clients (Rupeika-Apoga & Wendt, 2021).

- One of the most pressing challenges for fintech companies is the availability (or lack thereof) of skilled staff or experienced managers, which is why fintech companies advocate startup visas. This is an interesting development, because previously, fintech companies saw regulation as the most pressing problem (Rupeika-Apoga & Wendt, 2021). The expansion to foreign markets, finding customers, and regulation are still also quite pressing. Regulatory aspects, including insufficient collaboration between regulators, are the main challenges when it comes to expansion to foreign markets. These results support earlier findings that the success of fintech development depends on, e.g. access to finance and human resources and the attitude of regulators, in particular with regards to openness to innovation and flexibility (Rupeika-Apoga & Thalassinos, 2020). Also, the risks for potential and actual clients (Horn et al., 2020) and trust in financial services play important roles (Oehler & Wendt, 2018).

- The fintech companies are quite optimistic when it comes to growth opportunities, specifically in the field of open banking, lending, data analysis, and digital currencies. In line with this assessment, they expect to grow their workforce. To support this growth, the fintech companies would like to see primarily better cooperation with the regulator, tax reliefs, and improved regulation. To finance the growth, they consider seed and venture capital as the most important funding options.

At the heart of every developed country is a strong and well-developed financial ecosystem. The Latvian financial market over the past decades has undergone a tremendous transformation from a centralized economy to a free market economy. Latvia is becoming an undeniably famous destination in Europe for fintechs (Z/Yen Group, 2022). Many fintechs were founded relatively recently, mostly between 2016 and 2020, with 2019 being the prime year of creation. Latvia's startup infrastructure consists of more than 400 registered startups, about a third of which are fintech (Swedbank, 2021). Latvia is a place not only for world famous companies such as Mintos, Altero, Creamfinance, 4finance, Nordigen, Bitfury, Twino, Viainvest, Crasula, but also for newcomers. For instance, in the 2021 Financial Times 1000 ranking, Sun Finance was named the fastest-growing European fintech with a revenue increase of 619 times or 61 837.8% (Financial Times, 2022). Latvian fintechs are not geographically limited and are establishing global lending, payments and wealth management businesses in Europe, the USA, Africa, and Asia. This study includes Latvian fintech companies' reflections on their current and future challenges, opportunities, and an overall assessment of the fintech industry situation from a fresh perspective. Thus, these results may be useful to other countries in assessing what needs to be done to help new companies enter the fintech industry and run their business more efficiently.

For future research and discussions in the context of the development of the fintech industry in Latvia, it would be useful to compare Latvia with other small economies.

References

Bank of Latvia. (2020). *FINTECH glossary*. https://www.bank.lv/en/publicati ons-r/other-publications/fintech-glossary

Bank of Latvia. (2021). https://www.bank.lv/en/

FCMC. (2020). *FinTech glossary*. FKTK. https://www.fktk.lv/en/licensing/inn ovation-and-fintech/fintech-glossary/

Financial Stability Board. (2019). *FinTech and market structure in financial services: Market developments and potential financial stability implications— Financial Stability Board. February.*

Fintech Baltic. (2021). *Fintech Latvian Startups*. https://fintechbaltic.com/fin tech-latvia-startups/

Grima, S., Kizilkaya, M., Rupeika-Apoga, R., Romānova, I., Dalli Gonzi, R., & Jakovljevic, M. (2020). A country pandemic risk exposure measurement model. *Risk Management and Healthcare Policy, 13,* 2067–2077. https://doi.org/10.2147/RMHP.S270553

Grima, S., Rupeika-Apoga, R., Kizilkaya, M., Romānova, I., Dalli Gonzi, R., & Jakovljevic, M. (2021). A proactive approach to identify the exposure risk to COVID-19: Validation of the pandemic risk exposure measurement (PREM) model using real-world data. *Risk Management and Healthcare Policy, 14,* 4775–4787. https://doi.org/10.2147/RMHP.S341500

Hoque, Z. (2004). A contingency model of the association between strategy, environmental uncertainty and performance measurement: Impact on organizational performance. *International Business Review, 13*(4), 485–502. https://doi.org/10.1016/j.ibusrev.2004.04.003

Horn, M., Oehler, A., & Wendt, S. (2020). FinTech for consumers and retail investors: Opportunities and risks of digital payment and investment services. In T. Walker, D. Gramlich, M. Bitar, & P. Fardnia (Eds.), *Ecological, Societal, and Technological Risks and the Financial Sector* (pp. 309–327). Springer International Publishing. https://doi.org/10.1007/978-3-030-38858-4_14

Laidroo, L., Koroleva, E., Kliber, A., Rupeika-Apoga, R., & Grigaliuniene, Z. (2021a). Business models of FinTechs—Difference in similarity? *Electronic Commerce Research and Applications, 46,* 101034. https://doi.org/10.1016/j.elerap.2021.101034

Laidroo, L., Tamre, A., Kukk, M.-L., Tasa, E., & Avarmaa, M. (2021b). *FinTech Report Estonia 2021b.* https://doi.org/10.13140/RG.2.2.34303.74408

Lochy, J. (2020, November 16). *Ecosystems—The key to success for all future financial services companies.* Finextra Research. https://www.finextra.com/blogposting/19537/ecosystems---the-key-to-success-for-all-future-financial-services-companies

OECD. (2018). *Financial markets, insurance and private pensions: Digitalisation and finance.* https://www.oecd.org/finance/private-pensions/Financial-markets-insurance-pensions-digital-technologies-and-finance.pdf

Oehler, A., Horn, M., & Wendt, S. (2016). Benefits from social trading? Empirical evidence for certificates on wikifolios. *International Review of Financial Analysis, 46,* 202–210. https://doi.org/10.1016/j.irfa.2016.05.007

Oehler, A., Horn, M., & Wendt, S. (2021). Investor characteristics and their impact on the decision to use a robo-advisor. *Journal of Financial Services Research.* https://doi.org/10.1007/s10693-021-00367-8

Oehler, A., & Wendt, S. (2018). Trust and financial services: The impact of increasing digitalisation and the financial crisis. In T. Olaf Sigurjonsson, D. L. Schwarzkopf, & M. Bryant (Eds.), *The Return of Trust? Institutions and the*

Public after the Icelandic Financial Crisis (pp. 195–211). Emerald Publishing Limited. https://doi.org/10.1108/978-1-78743-347-220181014

Olson, E. M., & Slater, S. F. (2002). The balanced scorecard, competitive strategy, and performance. *Business Horizons, 45*(3), 11–16. https://doi.org/10.1016/S0007-6813(02)00198-2

PwC. (2015). *Developing a FinTech ecosystem in the GCC: Let's get ready for take off*. PwC. https://www.strategyand.pwc.com/m1/en/reports/2015/developing-fintech-ecosystem-gcc.html

Rikhardsson, P., Wendt, S., Arnardóttir, A. A., & Sigurjónsson, T. O. (2020). Is more really better? Performance measure variety and environmental uncertainty. *International Journal of Productivity and Performance Management, 70*(6), 1446–1469. https://doi.org/10.1108/IJPPM-11-2019-0539

Rupeika-Apoga, R., & Thalassinos, E. I. (2020). Ideas for a regulatory definition of FinTech. *International Journal of Economics and Business Administration, VIII*(2), 136–154. https://doi.org/10.35808/ijeba/448

Rupeika-Apoga, R., & Wendt, S. (2021). FinTech in Latvia: Status Quo, current developments, and challenges ahead. *Risks, 9*(10), 181. https://doi.org/10.3390/risks9100181

Startin. (2021). *Latvian Startup database.* Latvian Startup Association "Startin.LV." https://startin.lv/startup-database/

Statista. (2021). *European banks: Return on equity 2020.* https://www.statista.com/statistics/894915/return-on-equity-of-banks-in-european-countries/

Swedbank. (2020). *Latvian Fintech Report 2020* (p. 16). https://www.swedbank.lv/static/pdf/campaign/FinTech_report_2020_ENG.pdf

Swedbank (2021). *Latvian Fintech Report 2021* (p. 20). https://biznesam.swedbank.lv/upload/content/eng_report-2021.pdf

World Economic Forum. (2020). *Global COVID-19 FinTech market rapid assessment study.* World Economic Forum. https://www.weforum.org/reports/63338c21-4a48-4f1b-92d8-8af1d1289c0a/

World Economic Forum. (2021). *Bridging digital and environmental goals: A framework for business action* (p. 27). https://www3.weforum.org/docs/WEF_Bridging_Digital_and_Environmental_Goals_2021.pdf

Z/Yen Group. (2022). *The Global Financial Centres Index 31* (p. 63). file:///C:/Users/BVEF/Favorites/Downloads/GFCI_31_Report_2022.03.24_v1.0.pdf

CHAPTER 6

Non-Fungible Tokens

Andrea Barbon and Angelo Ranaldo

DEFINITION AND BASIC CONCEPTS

A non-fungible token (NFT) is a unique digital asset such as an image, video, or another file that has proof of ownership and verification of authenticity held in the blockchain. In essence, there are three crucial concepts that define any NFT: blockchain, token, and non-fungible.

First, NFTs operate through the blockchain that supports the creation and exchange of these digital assets. The creation of an NFT is recorded in a block of the blockchain ledger. Then, when one exchanges the digital asset for cryptocurrencies such as Ether, the transaction is verified in

We thank Kirill Kazakov, Luc-Vincent Lauper, and Esteban Rivera for their comments and research assistance.

A. Barbon · A. Ranaldo (✉)
University of St. Gallen and Swiss Finance Institute, St. Gallen, Switzerland
e-mail: angelo.ranaldo@unisg.ch

A. Barbon
e-mail: andrea.barbon@unisg.ch

T. Walker et al. (eds.), *The Fintech Disruption*, Palgrave Studies in Financial Services Technology,
https://doi.org/10.1007/978-3-031-23069-1_6

another block of the chain. After the block is filled and the transaction is confirmed, the block of transactions is appended to the previously verified block iterating this process. So, the blockchain of a cryptocurrency is a list of all transactions of that currency, going all the way back to its origination. For an NFT, the blockchain enables to trace the proof of provenance from its origination through the following ownership.

Second, a cryptographic token is the generic term for a digital unit of value that operates on the blockchain. Tokens are built on an existing blockchain, using smart contracts, whereas cryptocurrencies that are coins, such as Bitcoin, Litecoin, Dogecoin, and Ethereum, have their own respective blockchains. Instead, NFTs are tokens utilizing another coin's blockchain, which is the Ethereum blockchain predominantly although more recently other blockchains have been introduced.

Third, non-fungible means unique. This refers to the underlying digital asset of an NFT that has its own identity that distinguishes itself from others. Being unique by design, there is no one NFT that is exactly like another. When cryptocurrency coins and tokens are created, they are minted. Minting an NFT means transforming digital data into a digital asset crypto collection recorded on the blockchain. For a given cryptocurrency, many coins or tokens are generally minted. Each NFT token functions in a way similar to a cryptocurrency token, the main difference being that an NFT is created and supplied as a single one.[1] There exist also semi-fungible tokens, whose supply is not unitary but limited to a small number of units.

Let us have a look at two representative examples of NFTs. Figure 6.1 shows the image titled "Beeple's collage, Everydays: The First 5000 Days." It is a collage of 5,000 digital images created by Mike Winkelmann, a well-known digital artist. On May 11, 2021, the NFT of his artwork was sold for $69 million in a Christie's auction.[2] The purchaser of this NFT was Vignesh Sundaresan, a Singapore-based programmer and cryptocurrency investor. As stated in the smart contract, rather than the copyright, Mr. Sundaresan received rights to display the artwork, which he did in a digital museum within "the metaverse" (Kastrenakes, 2021).

---

[1] How to create NFT is explained in detail in Sect. 4.6.

[2] In addition to bespoke private sales, Christie's is a world-leading company running live and online art auctions.

Fig. 6.1 NFT titled "Beeple's collage, Everydays: The First 5000 Days"

A second example is related to a physical product. Distillers William Grant and Son sold 15 bottles of 46-year-old Glenfiddich whisky for $18,000 apiece. An individual NFT artistic image was associated to each bottle. In addition to artistic expression, whether you may like it or not, this NFT acts as a counterfeit-proof certificate of ownership (Marr, 2021).

Sources of Value

It is not easy to tell what determines the value of an NFT. It sounds simple but if you dig deeper, it becomes more complicated. If you look at it as a financial security, an investor will consider an NFT as a simple security since it does not generate future cash in—and out-flows such as dividend payments, rents, or bond coupon payments. Also, being digital, it does not imply inventory, maintenance, or storage costs except for very limited ones. Like financial securities, it is negotiable and therefore, depending on how its price evolves on the secondary market, the owner of an NFT may benefit from a capital gain or suffer a loss. From this perspective, expectations about net cash flows play a minor role while the expected resalable price of an NFT might matter.

NFTs as Financial Assets

The main difference between an NFT and a common financial security is that the former is non-fungible while the latter is. Therefore, what essentially determines its value is the uniqueness of every NFT and the perceived value attributed to the NFT's exclusive characteristics by its current and prospective owners.

Since it is not fungible, it is in the nature of an NFT to be illiquid. It cannot be interchanged with other equivalent tokens and its idiosyncratic characteristics make it more detached from common valuations. This issue arguably generates higher (idiosyncratic) volatility of its price and commands a liquidity premium.

In addition, NFTs have not been accepted as collateral, at least until recently. Only lately, some dApps such as NFTfi (nftfi.com), PawnFi (pawnfi.com), and TrustNFT (trustnft.org) allow investors to borrow and lend using NFTs as collateral. If this practice becomes more widespread, it is to be expected that the NFT's ability to act as collateral will become an additional pricing factor for NFTs. As with traditional financial securities, the higher this ability, the higher the market value of the underlying NFT will be (e.g., Gârleanu & Pedersen, 2011). Another relevant issue is whether or not an NFT generates intangible benefits, such as a highly symbolic image or a widely known and appreciated name of a website. As an intangible asset such as patents, logos, franchises, and trademarks, it can provide a future pecuniary benefit to the owner and to the creator. As we will discuss below, this may be the case for a digital artist who will continue to earn royalties, if so, defined in the smart contract.

Academic research on NFT asset pricing is in its infancy. There is no clear evidence that there is a connection between NFT and cryptocurrency values.[3] Future research should highlight what the systematic pricing factors are that explain the time-series and cross-sectional variation of NFT prices.

---

[3] Dowling (2022a) shows weak correlation between the market value of NFTs with that of cryptocurrencies while Pinto-Gutiérrez et al. (2022) find that Bitcoin and Ether returns lead the attention to NFTs.

Unique Benefits of NFTs

Aside from the general considerations listed above, NFTs confer other specific benefits. When one creates an NFT, she receives a token or proof of ownership that is held on the blockchain, which makes it easily verifiable by anyone who looks it up. In some cases, such as artworks, this allows an artist to seal the authorship of the work, thereby receiving royalties and capitalizing from future sales of the artwork. Thus, NFTs provide a record of authenticity and ownership which is held and verifiable on the blockchain.

Another advantage is that the NFT's reliance on (smart) contracts improves efficiency by streamlining processes and getting rid of intermediaries. A smart contract is a piece of a computer program to formalize and execute a contractual agreement between two parties. The last advantage we want to emphasize is the innovation represented by NFTs. Because they are new, they can create new products and services that were previously unthinkable, making the market more complete in the sense that there is the possibility to create a good or service and then exchange it whenever a utility is attributed to it.[4] For example, NFTs can be used to give real-world perks such as tailor-made access to high-end events, groups, associations, or usage digital forms of art and the claim of property in the metaverse. Seen as financial securities, NFTs can therefore provide diversification benefits in portfolio holdings of traditional assets.

TYPES OF NFTS

An NFT can be any digital asset. Below we present the broad existing categories and conclude with the most recent uses.

Digital Art

Digital art currently represents the most extensive use of NFTs. Although it has been around for several decades, digital art has witnessed a recent boom thanks to NFTs. Compared to the traditional fine art world, NFTs

---

[4] From an academic perspective and in an Arrow-Debreu sense, a market is complete when it satisfies two conditions: there is a price for every asset in every possible state of the world; the market is frictionless in terms of negligible transaction costs and perfect information.

can improve many issues including authentication, efficiency, and fairness in attributing royalties. Every NFT's smart contract has a 42-character Ethereum address. Therefore, anyone can go to a block explorer, enter an NFT's address into the search bar, and easily find the NFT's smart contract. All of this tremendously facilitates tasks related to establishing the provenance, documentation, and verification of a specific piece of artwork. As a result, this will prevent counterfeiting and misappropriation.

The artistic expression can be in the form of digital art or digital collectibles, which are similar to digital art but with have the intent to remain in digital format and have a specific popular theme. Digital art or collectible NFTs can take on one of the following forms: images, videos, Gifs, audio, 3D models, or simply a digital file containing a text related to a book and prose.

Many NFTs are simple images, such as the famous CryptoPunks, CyberKongz, or Beeple creations. An image can be either raster images or a (scalable) vector graphic. One advantage of raster images is the granularity of the colors, which can be a suitable feature for photographs. Videos are also widespread in digital art. Often the video is a.gif file repeated in a loop. The NFT can also be an audio file typically as.wav or.mp3 format.

Play-to-Earn Video Games

NFTs are spreading out worldwide among video gamers. The reason for this increasing popularity is that some game developers are creating NFTs of in-game items for popular games. These include weapons, equipment, accessories, or resources that video gamers buy. The exchange market for such in-game items has also begun to flourish as players who have previously purchased in-game items want to sell them to buy new ones or to buy other games. Further, some people living in relatively poor countries started relying on play-to-earn games as their main source of income. Indeed, the monetary value that can be generated by playing certain blockchain-based games (e.g., Axie Infinity) is driven by the global aggregate demand and, thus, much more attractive for people with lower incomes.

Digital Real Estate and Other Applications

NFTs can also be used as digital real estate assets in online environments such as Decentraland[5] and Sandbox that essentially let people interact through their avatars, which are tailored digital representations of the user. For instance, on Sandbox, all assets and land are NFT-based. Other uses of NFTs are domain names. Top-level domains with extensions (e.g.,.com,.net,.org,.tv) are administered by dedicated authorities such as the Internet Corporation for Assigned Names and Numbers (ICANN). Another way to manage Internet domain names that is gaining momentum is through the blockchain using NFTs.

The innovations and flexibility inherent in the NFT concept enable innumerable applications. Here, we mention only four of them. First, NFTs can be used for event tickets. The process is pretty simple: After receiving the payment, the smart contract processes an NFT ticket to be sent to the buyer from the ticketing company's database. Depending on how the exchange is organized, ticket owners can also resell NFT tickets on a NFT marketplace. Compared to the traditional system, NFT tickets can provide several advantages including a more efficient and rapid process, preventing the creation and business of fake tickets, and scams, as well as new and possibly perpetual revenue opportunities. Second, NFTs can be backed by real-world assets of any kind and the smart contract can define warranties, insurance, and legal enforceability to create trust in trade. Examples of real-world assets are *physical* real estate, paintings, jewelry, or vehicles. Third, the NFT is useful and effective when one wants to capitalize the singularity of a physical or juridical person or of what distinguishes it, such as its identity, DNA, and domain names. Fourth, NFTs are effective in tracking and reconstructing the information flow about users, owners, and others involved in the NFT production participated in a given process and how they did it. Some of the natural applications concern the logistics industry, products, and services for which quality or temporal sequences are crucial (e.g., luxury industry, patents, and pollution rights).

---

[5] Dowling (2022b) analyze Decentraland LAND and finds no empirical evidence for price efficiency.

NFT Creation and Smart Contracts

Ethereum-based NFTs rely on smart contracts, which are pieces of programming code written in Solidity[6] and deployed on the Ethereum blockchain. While fungible tokens rely on the ERC20 standard, there are two widely used standards for NFTs: ERC 721 for non-fungible tokens and ERC 1155 for semi-fungible ones. For ERC20 tokens, the smart contract contains basic information like name, symbol, maximum supply, deployer, and keeps track of ownership.

Moreover, the smart contract is used to *mint* one or multiple tokens by executing the corresponding function. Often, minting is expensive: the minter must attach a value to the transaction, equal to the price of the NFT (chosen by the creator of the contract), multiplied by the number of tokens to be minted, plus the gas fees.[7]

NFT Collections

NFTs are often released in the form of *collections*, that is, a set of NFTs created by the same artist and/or related to the same artistic concept or technique. It is important to note that a collection is usually identified by a specific smart contract, containing the basic information about the collection including the name, the author, the maximum supply (if limited), the mint price, the release date, etc. A dedicated function of the smart contract—the *mint* or *purchase* function—allows the author or external actors to bring the single elements of the collection to life, by registering the issuance of the corresponding NFT token on the smart contract—and thus on the blockchain.[8] Hence, multiple NFT tokens are often backed by a single smart contract, which keeps track of the ownership of a specific set of NFTs.

---

[6] Solidity is an object-oriented programming, devised specifically for smart contracts. Created by former Ethereum core developers, it is used for smart contracts on the Ethereum blockchain, but also for different blockchain platforms, for instance, the Binance Smart Chain.

[7] NFT gas is the fee that one needs to pay to execute any transactions on the blockchain. It compensates miners for the computing energy and resources used to validate transactions and to include them in the blockchain. The gas fee varies depending on the activity and level of congestion. It is calculated by multiplying the Gas Limit and the Gas Price.

[8] A detailed explanation of the minting process will be provided in Sect. 4.5.

In some marketplaces, for instance, on OpenSea or LooksRare, NFTs are organized and displayed in collections. Apart from the fact that collections (versus single NFTs) are advertised on the homepage, the platforms report statistics at the collection-level on the total volume traded and average transaction prices, in real time. Another collection-level statistic is the so-called *floor-price*, which represents the lowest price at which one can immediately buy an NFT belonging to the collection. This quantity can be thought of as the equivalent of the *ask price* in the equity market, but it can also be seen as a proxy for the price at which one can sell an NFT of that collection in a reasonable amount of time (similar to the *bid price*).

Some other platforms, like SuperRare.co, are organized in their backend as if they were a single (or a limited number of) collections. In this case, all NFTs created and traded on the platform are backed by the same smart contract, initially deployed by the platform itself.

Non-Fungible vs Semi-Fungible

As noted above, strictly non-fungible tokens rely on the ERC 721 standard. Every NFT token minted on these kinds of contracts is uniquely identified (within the contract) by a *token_id*. To identify the asset on the blockchain on which the contract is deployed, one needs both the contract address (a 42-character hexadecimal string) and the *token_id*. Collections based on this contract are made exclusively of unique NFTs. This means that each minted token has unitary maximum supply. Therefore, it is a unique asset.

There exist also semi-fungible tokens, relying on the more sophisticated ERC 1155 standard. In these contracts, individual tokens are not forced to have unitary supply but, rather, can enjoy a limited supply (declared in the contract) that can be heterogeneous across token_ids. It is important to stress that, even though the supply can be greater than one, each token is linked to the same digital asset (image, video, etc.). Hence, in the case of visual art, for instance, the same picture can have multiple *incarnations* and be sold multiple times. In that situation, the buyers are aware that they don't own a unique artwork but a copy of one available in limited supply.

Note that the ERC 721 can be seen as a special case of the ERC 1155 contract, where the supply of all tokens is unitary. Even though tokens based on ERC 1155 are not strictly non-fungible, they are usually referred

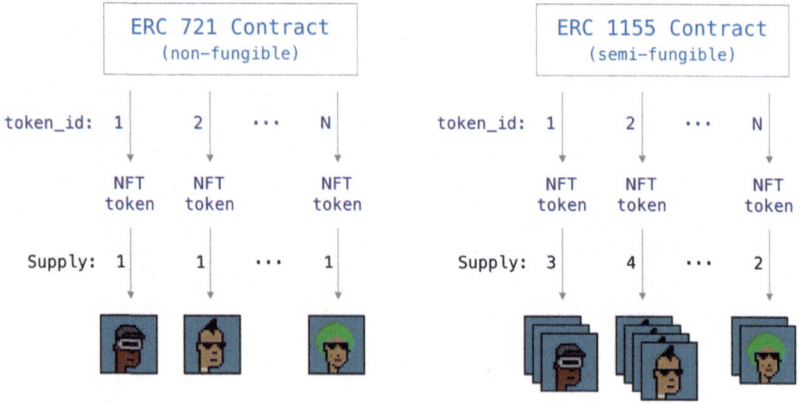

Fig. 6.2 Structure arising from these two different types of contracts

to as NFTs. However, one should not confuse the maximum token supply, i.e., the maximum number of tokens that can be minted from the contract with the supplies of individual tokens.

Figure 6.2 depicts the structure arising from these two different types of contracts. Most of the exchange platforms support NFTs based on both standards but display semi-fungible tokens differently from purely non-fungible ones.

Deployment of an NFT Collection

Assuming the media files have been created, deploying them as a collection of NFTs can be achieved in two ways: (i) deploying a dedicated smart contract or (ii) leveraging on the web-interface provided by an exchange platform.

The first option involves a number of steps. First, the media files linked to the collection are uploaded on a publicly accessible server or using IPFS.[9] Second, a *metadata* file (usually in *JSON* format) is compiled and uploaded to the same hosting service. The metadata file is basically a mapping between token_ids and the relevant information describing the corresponding token, including its name, a textual description, the

---

[9] A definition and discussion of IPFS-based hosting services will be given in Sect. 4.7.

URL of the linked media file, the attributes,[10] and—for semi-fungible tokens—the limited supply. Third, a smart contract is coded and deployed to the relevant blockchain. The smart contract contains basic information about the collection (as discussed above) and a link to the metadata file.[11] The contract also contains the address of the *proxy registry address* which allows different platforms to track the newly deployed collections. Hence, once the contract is deployed on chain, these platforms will automatically react by creating a web-page displaying the corresponding collection.

The second option requires less technical skills since one is not required to write a smart contract in Solidity (or another programming language specific to the blockchain platform of interest). Moreover, the platform allows the creator to upload the media files to the servers run by the platform itself and, thus, the creator does not have to spend time and money finding a hosting service.

The main advantage of the second option is the ease-of-use and accessibility to individuals with no prior knowledge of smart contract programming and hosting services. The main drawbacks are that the creator is forced to manually specify the attributes and upload the media for a number of items equal to the supply of the collection, which can be a significant burdensome and error-prone process in the case of large collections.[12] Moreover, this method does not allow the author of the collection to deviate from the standard ERC721 or ERC1155 contracts, thus, making it impossible to add unique features to the NFTs or introducing a different minting process.

Metadata and Attributes

Every NFT token is linked to a specific media file (image, audio, video, etc.) through the collection's smart contract. More precisely, the token is linked to a metadata file, which contains the URL of the media file and a variable number of attributes associated to the token and/or the media file. An example of a metadata file is reported below:

---

[10] A brief description of the concept of the *attributes* of NFTs are provided in Sect. 4.4.

[11] More information about this linkage is provided in Sect. 4.4.

[12] Famous collections like *Cryptopunks* or *Bored Apes Yatch Club* have supply of 10,000 NFTs and, obviously, were created using custom smart contracts.

```
{
"description": "Fashion Attractor in a neighbourhood of the point
(-0.74452860, -0.14808387), on the surface of the Mandelbrot
set",
"external_url": "https://mandelbrot.fractalnft.art",
"image": "https://mandelbrot.fractalnft.art/items/
1398_ec78e3e82a773f6246da.png",
"name": "#1398 - Surface Fashion Attractor",
"attributes":
[
{"trait_type": "Point", "value": "Attractor"},
{"trait_type": "Color", "value": "Fashion"},
{"trait_type": "Location", "value": "Surface"},
{"trait_type": "Zoom", "value": "200"},
{"trait_type": "Cycles", "value": "2"},
{"trait_type": "Shrinkage", "value": "100 bps"}
]
}
```

Specifically, this link is provided by the *BaseTokenUri* and the *tokenURI* functions. A code snippet for a basic implementation in Solidity is provided below:

```
function baseTokenURI() override public pure returns (string
memory) {
return "https://mandelbrot.fractalnft.art/item?token_id=";
}
function tokenURI(uint256 tokenId) override public pure returns
(string memory) {
return                string(abi.encodePacked(baseTokenURI(),
Strings.toString(tokenId)));
}
```

The first function contains the initial part of the URL, which is shared by all tokens of the contract. The second function takes as input a *token_id* and returns an extended version of the common part of the URL, by adding the *token_id* at the end. For instance, the above metadata file is obtained by calling the *tokenURL* function with the *token_id* equal to *1398*, thus obtaining the following URL:

https://mandelbrot.fractalnft.art/item?token_id=1398

The main attributes of the NFT contained in the metadata file are used by the exchange platform to display the item (*name*, *description*, *image*), while the additional ones (in this example *Point*, *Color*, *Location*, etc.) can be used as filters to browse the collection and assign a *rarity score* to each individual NFT. If the attributes of an NFT of the collection are rare (meaning that there are few pieces in the collection with that attribute), the NFT has a high *rarity score*, and it is usually traded at a premium with respect to less rare items.

Minting and Unveiling

Minting refers to the process of creating a new *token* from a smart contract representing a NFT collection. Initially, after the contract is deployed, the number of minted NFTs equal zero. The author or external actors can use the so-called *minting function* of the contract to mint one or multiple NFTs from the collection. Usually, the caller of the minting function receives the newly minted NFTs to his/her wallet used to call the function.

The minting function can be called manually from the contract page on etherscan.io or through a script by using *web3*. In addition, the authors of the NFT collection often create a dedicated website that allows people to mint in a more user-friendly fashion. Such a website, implemented using *web3* libraries, connects to the user's non-custodial wallet (like Meta-Mask) and provides the user with a simple interface to choose the number of NFTs to be minted and execute the transaction. Usually, the user must pay a predefined amount of ETH (or other cryptocurrencies) for each minted NFT. Additionally, the minter must cover the gas costs of the transaction, which vary depending on the complexity of the minting function.

Often, the attributes and the media file connected to each individual NFT are hidden during the minting period. People know what the subject of the collection is, but they don't know which specific NFT they will get by minting. As such, the artworks of the collection and the corresponding rarities are assigned randomly during the mining process. At this point, trading on the secondary market (OpenSea, etc.,) is already possible. Only after the collection is sold-out (the number of minted items equals the maximum supply) or after a pre-determined amount of time, the collection is unveiled and the identity of each NFT is revealed. Thus, there is a *bet* component to the minting process, as people pay the same price for each hidden NFTs, but lucky minters who get the rarest pieces may experience significant capital gains after unveiling.

The following code snipped provides an example of a basic minting function (written in Solidity), in which the unveiling is handled externally.

```
function purchase(uint256 fractals) external payable {
require(_active, "Inactive");
require(block.timestamp  >=  _activeTime  +  PRESALE_TIME,
"Purchasing not active");
require(fractals <= remaining() && fractals <= MAX_QUANTITY,
"Too many fractals requested");
require(msg.value == fractals*PRICE, "Invalid purchase amount
sent");
for (uint i = 0; i < fractals; i++) {
mintTo(msg.sender);
}
give_to_community(fractals);
}
```

The input parameter *fractals* refers to the number of NFT the user is minting/purchasing. Notice that the function requires that this number multiply by the *PRICE* (defined as a constant in the contract) equals *msg.value*, that is, the amount of ETH sent by the caller attached to the transaction. The rest of the logic is contained inside the *mintTo* function, not reported here. The full contract underlying this example can be browsed here: https://etherscan.io/address/0x6E96Fb1f6D8cb1463E0 18A2Cc6E09C64eD474deA#code.

Media Storage

The NFT collections created using on the web interfaces of exchanges like OpenSea or SuperRare are linked to metadata files which are automatically generated by the platform and are hosted by the platform's server, together with the corresponding media files.

If an NFT collection is deployed with a custom smart contract, the linked media and the associated metadata file can be stored on a privately owned web server, a cloud service, or in IPFS. The latter stands for Inter-Planetary File System, which is a peer-to-peer network for storing data in a distributed file system. The IPFS storage is the most decentralized storage solution available to NFT creators and it is used by the most famous and valuable NFT collections (e.g., *Bored Ape Yacht Club*). The main advantages of IPFS are that (i) multiple copies of the files are saved on different servers of the network, thus reducing risks related to a central point of failure and (ii) the files cannot be modified nor deleted by the creator. Despite these advantages, a majority of the collections that exist so far do not rely on IPFS storage. In fact, it is more common to store the media on third-party servers or on one's own websites, which represents a significant risk for the buyers (e.g., data breaches).

Alternative Blockchains and Additional Features

Currently, the Ethereum blockchain is by far the most popular blockchain for NFTs. The Ethereum platform is very flexible. However, due to trans-action costs related to high gas prices, it limits the features and the utility of the Ethereum-based NFTs. Below, we briefly describe alterna-tive Blockchains hosting NFT assets and more exotic NFT features and applications.

Alternative Blockchains

Among the most prominent alternative blockchains are the World Asset eXchange (WAX) and Flow. For instance, some top brands such as Topps, Capcom, Atari, Funko, and Lionsgate based their NFT collections on WAX. Flow was created more recently with the intent to avoid congestion, thereby supporting a larger number of users in decentralized apps.

One of the major companies using WAX for NFTs is Topps, which has licenses for the collectible rights (both physical and digital) for a number of sports leagues, including Major League Baseball (MLB). The other NFT blockchains, FLOW, features the National Baseketball Association (NBA) Top Shots NFTs and the Binance Smart Chain.

Among more recent blockchains, Solana is one that deserves special consideration. It supports decentralized and scalable applications such as smart contracts and the SOL cryptocurrency. Compared to the Ethereum blockchain, it provides two main advantages: a much faster transaction speed and lower trading costs.

Additional Features

In addition to allowing NFTs on the Ethereum blockchain to be owned and transferable, the standards discussed earlier allow NFTs to contain the following aspects embedded in the smart contract.u

First, the name of the NFT, which can be unique or slightly adapted from existing names by adding an edition number at the end of the name of a digital artwork.

Second, the main NFT's content that can be in any file format. For image-based files, it can be a GIF, video, or 3D model, while for a domain name, in addition to the domain name itself, it can also include some distinguishing images and traits associated with that particular domain name. For digital land, the main content should specify the coordinate of the land within a given virtual world. Although in principle, there would be a lot of freedom in defining the NFT content, the marketplace where NFT is created and traded often imposes limits, for instance, in terms of file format and size. If the NFT is not an image, there is a possibility to offer an image-based preview. For instance, one can associate an evocative image as preview content to an audio file.

Third, an NFT includes a description and information about the unlockable content, copyright, or trademark notice, and mentions other perks (e.g., live or digital networking events or meetups). This section is particularly important because it not only summarizes the characteristics of the NFT, but also sets out its rights and conditions. If the NFT is tied to a physical asset, this is where one can state how to take possession of it or how to redeem the NFT in order to receive a physical item. Similarly, for in-game NFTs, the creator can specify the attributes in terms of properties, powers, or advantages.

Fourth, an NFT may contain unlockable content that only the owner of the NFT can access. The unlockable content can provide confidential information such as login credentials, game activation keys, or specific information on how to exercise ownership or redemption rights. This offers a unique and privileged role to the owner, creating a certain asymmetry of information and potentially added value.

Fifth, the NFT can involve royalties set by the creator. This is an important innovation implying that each time the NFT will be sold, a pre-established part of the price will automatically be paid by the buyer to the originator's wallet. The degree of transparency about royalties can vary across NFTs and marketplaces; for instance, OpenSea does not disclose the exact amount of the ongoing royalty to buyers.

Finally, an NFT defines the quantity for whom it is offered. The minimum is one and often that is the quantity that makes it unique. But sometimes, an NFT is released in different editions with a number that distinguishes them or as multiple NFTs which obviously reduces its scarcity and potentially its market value.

MARKETPLACES

In the last two or three years, the number of places where one can trade NFTs has increased tremendously. Here, we describe the most common ones. Let us start with marketplaces focusing on digital art. The historical hub for digital artists is Larva Labs/CryptoPunks (larvalabs.com), whose history goes all the way back to 2017. Their crypto art projects are well known as CryptoPunks and Autoglyphs and were initially distributed for free.

Table 6.1 provides a summary of a selection among the largest NFT exchanges by volume, as of March 2022. For each trading venue, we report the total exchange volume in USD, the percentage of fees charged by the exchange, the date of inception, whether or not it is open to the public or restricted to invited individuals, the available sale options, and the defining features. We remark that the trading volume includes wash-trading, that is, fictitious transactions executed by NFT creators to inflate the real trading volume. This issue is highly relevant in open-access platforms. In particular, for LooksRare, only about 20% of the volume is estimated to be real.

OpenSea (Opensea.io) is the largest NFT marketplace for digital art. However, its portfolio goes beyond digital art. Currently, it includes almost 30 million NFTs. OpenSea is essentially based on the Ethereum blockchain, even if it has recently expanded to Polygon and Klaytn. The positive aspects of this platform include the ease with which it is possible to create, sell, and buy NFTs. It offers a wide variety of NFTs, which can be an added value for collectors, and wide set of NFT categories: art, collectibles, music, photography, domain names, sports, utility, and

Table 6.1   Descriptive information for largest NFT exchanges by volume

Exchange Name	OpenSea	SupeRare	LooksRare	Foundation	Rarible
Total Volume (USD)	15,567,131,505	243,000,000	19,382,067,819	139,000,000	292,850,000
Percentage Fees	2.5%	3%	2%	15%	2.5%
Launch Date	November 2017	May 2018	January 2022	February 2021	Early 2020
Open Access	Yes	No	Yes	No	Yes
Sales options	Fixed price, auctions, bids	Fixed price, auctions, bids	Fixed price, bids	Fixed price, auctions, bids	Fixed price, auctions, bids
Defining Feature	First and largest NFT marketplace	Native token and widespread social media presence	Native token providing incentives to trade on the platform	Very selective: accessible only by private invitation	Messenger system, Native token

virtual worlds. It is also possible to purchase and sell NFTs only using cryptocurrency.

A similar marketplace is Rarible (rarible.com). It is also user-friendly in terms of origination and exchange of NFTs, as well as navigation of the platform. It features the Ethereum, Tezos, and Flow blockchains. As a proof-of-stake blockchains, Tezos and Flow reduce gas fees and energy consumption. Furthermore, Rarible is designed to facilitate to follow or contact NFT creators and to accommodate some social media elements. Another distinguishing feature is that the native governance token they have created called the RARI token.

Figure 6.3 presents the time-series evolution of the cumulative trading volume (in million US dollars) of OpenSea and SuperRare, in logarithmic scale.dollars) of OpenSea and SuperRare, in logarithmic scale.

Nifty Gateway (Niftygateway.com) is the marketplace for well-established digital artists, celebrities, and brands. Only top artists and brands who have applied and successfully passed an inspection process are listed on Nifty Gateway. Here, NFTs are categorized as curated and

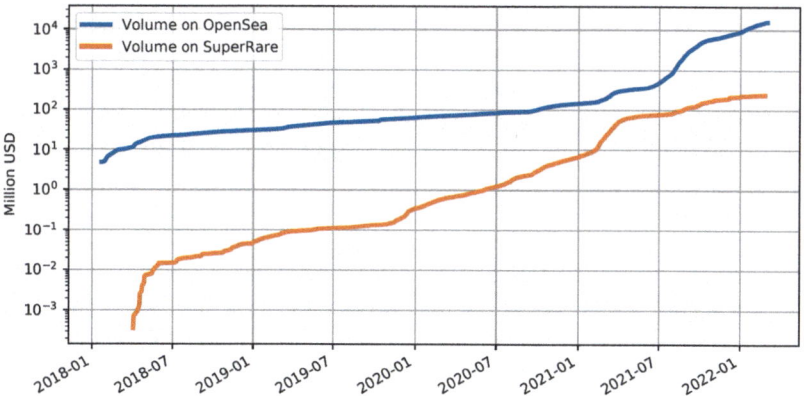

Fig. 6.3 Time-series evolution of the cumulative trading volume

verified and can be purchased in ETH and US dollars with credit or debit cards.

Foundation (Foundation.app) built a network in which NFT creators of digital art and collectors support each other. Anyone can sign up, but the incoming member needs to be approved by existing community members. Also based on the Ethereum blockchain, it shares the same pros and cons of the other marketplaces that are based on ETH.

Another platform for top artists is SuperRare (Superrare.co). The peculiarity of SuperRare is that it sells only single-edition and exclusive NFTs. This means that they cannot be purchased anywhere else. Additionally, the fee for a primary sale is relatively high, i.e., 15%. This platform aims to establish a strong base for its community by organizing (virtual) exhibitions and events.

There are other interesting marketplaces for digital art such as Known Origin (Knownorigin.io), Mintable (https://mintable.app/), Makers-Place (makersplace.com), or Zora (zora.co) that for the sake of space, we do not discuss in detail.

We now turn to other marketplaces that offer NFTs beyond the art world or that merit discussion for technical or institutional issues, such the reliance on blockchains other than Ethereum.

Atomic Hub (Wax.atomichub.io) is based on the WAX blockchain, which is different than, and disconnected from, the Ethereum (ETH) blockchain. The advantages of WAX are low transaction fees and the use of proof-of-stake validation, which reduces the environmental impact. Another advantage is that the user fee is relatively small. Atomic Hub is notorious for offering packs of NFTs in which one does not know exactly what will be inside it. This implies that the buyer will not know if they possess something common or rare until they purchased and open their NFT package.

NBA Top Shot (NBAtopshot.com) was designed by Dapper Labs, the creator of CryptoKitties. As the name suggests, NBA Top Shot refers to the National Basketball Association (NBA) and Women's National Basketball Association (WNBA). It is a marketplace for historical NBA moments immortalized by NFT videos. Like Atomic Hub, this platform points to rarities associated with famous individuals. Furthermore, it relies on the FLOW blockchain, which uses proof-of-stake validation, like WAX. Also related to sports, Sorare (sorare.com) is a marketplace associated with football and football players.

VeVe (Veve.me) is a mobile app, downloadable from the App Store and Google Play Store, selling only 3D image NFTs of major brands such as Spiderman, Back to the Future, and Star Trek: The Next Generation. The purchaser can customize the 3D images from the NFTs by changing the size and angle which can be placed in other apps and shared on social media.

Axie Marketplace is an online shop for the video game Axie Infinity, while Myth Market (Myth.market) focuses on trading card NFTs. It is a hub for the following markets: (i) GPK.Market, offering digital Garbage Pail Kids Trading Cards, (ii) GoPepe.Market, offering trading cards featuring the Pepe meme, (iii) Heroes.Market, featuring blockchain heroes trading cards; (iv) KOGS.Market, KOGS trading cards, and (v) Shatner.Market, for trading cards featuring William Shatner. Similar to Atomic Hub, Myth Market relies on the WAX blockchain.

In regard to NFT videos, it is worth mentioning Theta Drop, which features a decentralized peer-to-peer network that delivers streams efficiently globally. It provides the distribution of online videos and TV, and who wants to exchange in it needs to purchase Theta Token.

Finally, Valuables (v.cent.co) allow for the trading of tweets while, Zeptagram (zeptagram.com) is used for trading music and has issued Zeptacoin to trade music rights.

It is important to underline that NFTs can also represent real-world assets, such as physical artwork, real estate, vehicles, loans, financial securities, and more.

On the Economics of NFTs

Now that we have a better understanding of what NFTs are, we want to briefly discuss how they can contribute to economic efficiency and the welfare of society.

In economics, several sources of inefficiency or "frictions" have been theorized. Here, we concisely discuss how NFTs could help alleviate some of these sources of inefficiency. First, when the markets are incomplete, in the sense that not all products or services requested are offered, the economy does not reach an optimal equilibrium and the resources allocation are constrained (Hart, 1975). The smart contract, together with other technological innovations of NFTs, gives the possibility to complete more of the market in a flexible and consistent way to meet the needs of its agents. This can be done by revisiting existing products, such as art. But the plethora of new products and services is innumerable. As we mentioned above, NFTs have recently been introduced to address environmental issues, or more specifically, to tokenize carbon credits. Or, in response to the Russian invasion of Ukraine, the creation of an NFT has been used to raise funds to finance the Ukrainian resistance.

Second, NFTs allow for the lowering of many production and intermediation costs when compared to traditional methods. For instance, we have seen that NFTs allow digital artists to reach a global audience and present their work both effectively and quickly. Although the costs associated with the Ethereum blockchain are still relatively high, new solutions and lower cost blockchains are emerging.

A third possible source of inefficiency is intermediation. For example, intermediaries may exercise their market or negotiating power in their favor, thus distorting incentives, and preventing a fair resource allocation. Or there may be a conflict in priorities between a person, for instance the artist, and the representative authorized to act on their behalf, for instance the artist's agent, i.e., the so-called principal-agent problem (Ross, 1973). One sector of the economy in which intermediaries have traditionally played a predominant role and where the author has not fully capitalized on his creative work is within the art market. As we discussed, NFTs enable artists to protect the authenticity and provenance of the original creation. It also allows for fair compensation, as it is a standard that royalties are to be paid to those who created the work.

A fourth source of economic inefficiency is the lack of information or asymmetry of information that can be to the detriment of those who are less informed making adverse selection problems and poor decisions (Akerlof, 1970). The transparency and richness of information offered by the blockchain combined with the clarity and precision with which an NFT can be designed allow for a reduction in the opacity and fragmentation of information. Obviously, a certain learning process is necessary since we are dealing with new technologies. But the increased transparency and accessibility offered by NFT is unquestionable.

Often, the reduction of the above-mentioned inefficiencies leads to more liquid markets and products, i.e., it is easier for everyone to create and promptly trade at relatively low cost obtaining the fair price, i.e., a market price aligned with product's intrinsic value.

However, NFTs can also reflect inefficiencies if actors in this market act irrationally, fraudulently, or need time to learn about them. Economic theory demonstrates that irrational behaviors, and even rational agents making decisions based on limited information, can give rise to inflated prices or even speculative bubbles. This is also due to unavoidable learning processes, as has already happened in the past with major institutional or technological changes, such as the advent of the Internet (Pástor & Veronesi, 2009). The extraordinary increase in the market value of NFTs has prompted many to wonder whether a speculative bubble has been created and is now showing signs of cracking (e.g., Financial Kauflin, 2022; Times, 2022).

Furthermore, uncertainty is inherent in every novelty. This is evident in the legal and contractual aspects of NFTs and the controversies of how they can be interpreted. Purchasers of NFTs typically acquire neither a physical object nor the copyright to a digital one. Also, "smart contracts" are self-executing transaction protocols that cannot fully replace traditional legal frameworks governing ownership and authorship (Rizzo, 2022). Even if the NFT allows the identity of the authors to be carved in the blockchain, it does not mean that the risk of plagiarism is not removed. On the contrary, plagiarism and fraud have been an issue since the NFT market has taken off in 2021 (Harrison, 2022). Checking the authorship of the work is difficult especially in a new and booming market. Additionally, lack of oversight and central authorities limits the ability to protect authors and consumers. Some new tools have been introduced and some marketplaces attempt to address this issue, but the problem remains serious and unsolved for the moment.[13]

Finally, the inattention of individuals to consider the negative externalities could be to the detriment of the common good, such as in terms of energy consumption and environmental impact.

Conclusion

In this paper, we introduced what a non-fungible token (NFT) is—that is—a unique token stored on a blockchain. We explained its main features: (i) it represents a unique or non-fungible digital asset; (ii) the blockchain provides proof of its ownership and verification of authenticity; (iii) it is governed by a smart contract, which is a piece of a computer program that determines and executes the underlying contractual agreement. Then, we overviewed the current wide variety of applications, including digital art, video games, and real estate assets, some important technical aspects, and the characteristics of the markets in which NFTs are issued and traded.

The combination of these three aforesaid elements, i.e., uniqueness, blockchain, and smart contract, have enormous innovative potential that is already transforming some industries from (digital) art to sports and fashion. An important question for this article is how NFTs will impact the banking sector.

Essentially, a commercial bank provides transactional, savings, and money market accounts and accepts time deposits. An investment bank assists individuals, corporations, and governments in raising capital by underwriting and/or acting as the client's agent in the issuance of securities. In addition, an investment bank performs market making and trading of a variety of financial assets (e.g., derivatives, fixed income instruments, foreign exchange, commodities, and equity securities) on behalf of its customers or on its own (i.e., proprietary trading).

The smart contract embedded in an NFT allows banks for a very high degree of customization of their service and product. For instance, a commercial bank can use NFTs for providing tailor-made documentary and standby letter of credit, guarantees, performance bonds, securities

---

[13] For instance, DeviantArt introduced Protect, an image recognition tool, to notify users of copyright infringement on NFT marketplaces, leading to a flood of matches. Rarible struggles with plagiarism by implementing a human-moderated verification system.

underwriting commitments, and other forms of off-balance sheet exposures. The blockchain technology enables to trace the proof of provenance from its origination through the following users by enhancing the reliability and inviolability of information. In fact, the on-chain data encoded into an NFT cannot be altered, counterfeited or accessed by anyone who does not have the cryptographic keys.

For a commercial bank, the easiest way is to consider an NFT as an alternative financial instrument that offers a great risk diversification benefit since by its nature it is very different from traditional assets. But the intrinsic benefits of an NFT go far beyond that. With their proliferation and exchange, NFTs may increasingly be used as collateral assets. More in general, an NFT can be an efficient way of meeting the customers' needs, for example, by designing a bank contract that exactly matches the customer's requirements, risk profile, as well as the time-varying market conditions as agreed upon by the parties.

What matters most is whether banks see the new financial technology including NFTs as a threat or an opportunity. The NFT represents something new, and like any novelty it must be understood with knowledge and a critical spirit. In all likelihood, the euphoria of recent months has led to the formation of some irrational behaviors and speculative bubbles. But as was the case with the Internet, the bursting of the speculative bubble in 2000 did not take away all the good that the Internet represented. So banks should see NFTs as a gateway to access new technologies to cater more efficiently to their customers and to modernize given that in the near future, the ability to operate in the metaverse could be a competitive advantage if not a necessity.

References

Akerlof, G. A. (1970). The market for 'Lemons': Quality uncertainty and the market mechanism. *Quarterly Journal of Economics, 84*(3), 488–500. https://doi.org/10.2307/1879431

Dowling, M. (2022a). Is non-fungible token pricing driven by cryptocurrencies? *Finance Research Letters, 44*, 1–6. https://doi.org/10.1016/j.frl.2021.102097

Dowling, M. (2022b). Fertile LAND: Pricing non-fungible tokens. *Finance Research Letters, 44*, 1–5. https://doi.org/10.1016/j.frl.2021.102096

Financial Times (2022). The great NFT sell-off: has the digital collectibles craze hit its peak? Article published on March 11, 2022.

Gârleanu, N., & Pedersen, L. H. (2011). Margin-based asset pricing and deviations from the law of one price. *Review of Financial Studies, 24*(6), 1980–2022. https://doi.org/10.1093/rfs/hhr027

Harrison J. (2022). The counterfeit NFT problem is only getting worse: So artists are joining together to fight back. *The Verge*. Published online on Feb. 8, 2022. Available at https://www.theverge.com/22905295/counterfeit-nft-artist-ripoffs-opensea-deviantart

Hart, O. D. (1975). On the optimality of equilibrium when the market structure is incomplete. *Journal of Economic Theory, 11*(3), 418–443. https://doi.org/10.1016/0022-0531(75)90028-9

Kastrenakes, J. (2021). Beeple sold an NFT for $69 million. *The Verge*. Published online on May 11, 2021. Available https://www.theverge.com/2021/3/11/22325054/beeple-christies-nft-sale-cost-everydays-69-million

Kauflin, J. (2022). Why Jack Dorsey's first-tweet NFT plummeted 99% in value in a year. Forbes, Apr 14, 2022. Available at https://www.forbes.com/sites/jeffkauflin/2022/04/14/why-jack-dorseys-first-tweet-nft-plummeted-99-in-value-in-a-year/?sh=33c1e3265cba

Marr, B. (2021). Glenfiddich Sells $18,000 Super-Rare Whisky As NFTs – Here's What That Means. Blog's post released on Nov. 9, 2021. Available at https://bernardmarr.com/glenfiddich-sells-18000-super-rare-whisky-as-nfts-heres-what-that-means/

Pástor, L., & Veronesi, P. (2009). Technological Revolutions and Stock Prices. *American Economic Review, 99*(4), 1451–1483. https://doi.org/10.1257/aer.99.4.1451

Pinto-Gutiérrez, C., Gaitán, S., Jaramillo, D., & Velasquez, S. (2022). The NFT Hype: What Draws Attention to Non-Fungible Tokens? *Mathematics, 10*(3), 1–13. https://doi.org/10.3390/math10030335

Rizzo J. (2022). The Dune NFT Fiasco Is the Least of Crypto's Legal Worries. *The Verge*. Published online on Jan. 19, 2022. Available at https://www.wired.com/story/nft-cryptocurrency-art-regulation-law/

Ross, S. A. (1973). The economic theory of agency: The principal's problem. *American Economic Review, 63*(2), 134–139.

Challenges, Opportunities, and Regulations Regarding Fintech in the Banking Industry

CHAPTER 7

Open Banking: Opportunities and Risks

Christoph Frei

WHAT IS OPEN BANKING?

Many people in the financial and technology sectors consider data to be the gold of the twenty-first century. Indeed, technological advancements have led to considerable improvements in collecting, processing, and profitably using data in all areas of our lives. An important source and user of data is the banking sector as data stored through banking transactions and holdings contain essential customer information. As was the case during the gold rushes one-and-a-half centuries ago, the increasing importance of banking data gives rise to questions about accessibility and ownership. Unlike gold, however, data are nonrival goods, which can be accessed by different people and companies at the same time. This property of sharing is at the heart of open banking. In traditional banking, only the directly involved bank and its customer can access the customer's banking data. By contrast, under open banking, the customer can allow

C. Frei (✉)
Department of Mathematical and Statistical Sciences, University of Alberta, Edmonton, AB, Canada
e-mail: cfrei@ualberta.ca

© The Author(s), under exclusive license to Springer Nature Switzerland AG 2023
T. Walker et al. (eds.), *The Fintech Disruption*, Palgrave Studies in Financial Services Technology,
https://doi.org/10.1007/978-3-031-23069-1_7

third-party providers to access and potentially modify financial transaction data and customer information. Third-party providers include other banks and financial technology (fintech) companies offering innovative financial products.

Open banking transmits data through an application programming interface (API), a method that securely communicates data between the bank and the third-party provider upon the customer's approval. APIs allow customers to maintain control over which data the third-party provider receives, and customers can withdraw their consent at any time. APIs are popular in the digital economy beyond open banking; for example, many online businesses use the Google Maps API to embed maps into their websites and overlay them with map-specific information. For a discussion of various aspects and technical details of APIs related to open banking, I refer to Bahri and Lobo (2020) and Farrow (2020a, b). Legal aspects of APIs in open banking are discussed in Zukowsky (2019).

Often, we can distinguish between two levels of open banking: read access and write access. Read access allows third-party providers to receive a customer's financial data and use it for data processing, but they may not edit it. Services based on read access include building a financial dashboard summarizing the customer's different accounts or customer-specific mortgage offerings. By contrast, write access allows third-party providers to modify a customer's financial data, for example, by initiating a payment, opening/closing an account, or changing personal information.

Open banking may fundamentally change the customer-bank relationship and potentially alter the financial sector and the broader economy. Open banking raises important economic policy questions related to innovation, banking services accessibility, privacy, competition, and the structure of the financial sector.

The structure of the remainder of the chapter is as follows: Sect. 7.2 discusses the advantages of open banking for a banking customer, then for the financial industry, and finally, from a broader economic and social perspective. At the same time, open banking brings risks, which I present in Sect. 7.3, along with potential mitigation strategies. Section 7.4 gives a global view of the current status and planned implementations of open banking. Section 7.5 concludes.

OPPORTUNITIES

For a banking customer, a probable candidate for the most significant advantage of open banking is secure and easy access to innovative financial products. A customer may be interested in a financial product offered by another company that is not offered at their home bank. However, there are hurdles to overcome to access such a financial product. Switching financial institutions is cumbersome and time-consuming, while establishing multiple banking relationships means undertaking additional commitments and may make the financial situation confusing. Open banking reduces this hurdle by allowing the customer to stay with their bank while using one or more financial products offered by a third party. This advantage is particularly important, as many financial innovations are driven by fintech companies that may not have classical banking relationships with customers. Indeed, Koeppl & Kronick (2020) see the primary purpose of open banking in generating value for consumers.

A related advantage is that there are no good alternatives to open banking. As previously mentioned, many consumers are interested in sharing their banking data. Without open banking, this often happens through screen scraping, a process through which consumers share their banking login credentials with third-party service providers, thereby putting their personal data and information at risk. For example, a survey conducted in March 2021 in Canada estimates that more than four million Canadians, or 12% of the adult population, use screen scraping (Leger, 2021). In contrast to the APIs that open banking uses, screen scraping takes away the customer's control over their financial data. Figure 1 illustrates the differences between screen scraping and open banking through APIs. We can compare these differences to a customer who gives their partner access to their bank account: the customer simply providing their partner with the login credentials is easier, but comes with substantial risk for the customer, as they lose control and violate the bank's terms of use. By contrast, if the customer issues a bank authorization for their partner to secure their own login credentials, the process is more complicated but safer for the customer, who can then modify or withdraw the authorization and remain compliant with the terms of use. Typically, banks' terms of use do not allow customers to share their login information, so screen scraping likely violates such conditions. For these reasons, open banking can effectively reduce security and liability risks. Due to the related risks, many banks introduced measures to block

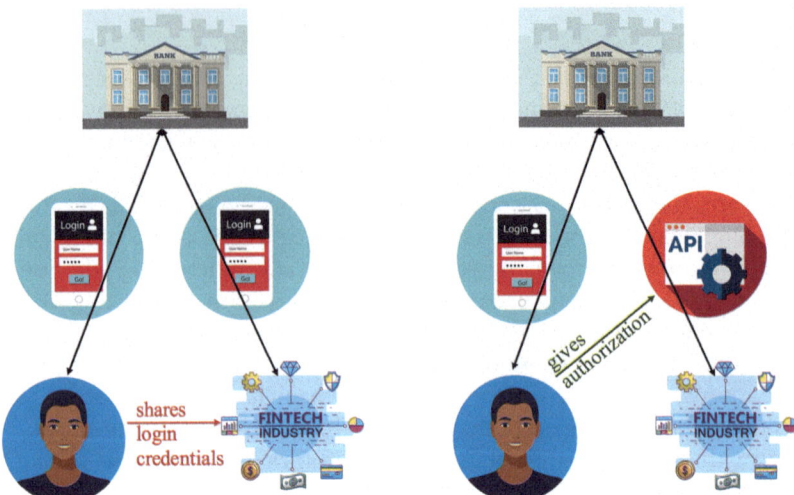

Fig. 7.1 Screen Scraping vs. Open Banking. *Note* Comparison of screen scraping (left), where the customer shares their login credentials with third-party providers, and open banking (right), where the customer gives third-party providers authorization to access banking data through an API

screen scraping, demonstrating the urgent need for reliable open banking platforms (Fig. 7.1).

In addition to open banking via an API and screen scraping, another possibility is to ask the customer to download their banking data from their online bank account and then upload it to an account at a third-party provider. The generation of a CSV[1] file might achieve this and means that unlike screen scraping, the user does not need to share login credentials. However, it requires the customer to manually complete multiple steps, which is inconvenient for the customer. It is not dynamic and requires the customer to perform the download and upload functions repeatedly to ensure that the third-party provider has current and accurate data. For example, Wesabe was a fintech company in the United States that used a download-upload approach: their customers would download information from their banks in a CSV file, upload it to Wesabe's website

---

[1] CSV stands for comma-separated values, which is a format frequently used when storing data in plain text.

for analysis, and then receive financial planning advice. Wesabe started offering its service in November 2006 and shut down in December 2010, largely because people preferred other, easier-to-use services, as the former Wesabe CEO Marc Hedlund wrote in a blog entry (Hedlund, 2010).

From an industry perspective, open banking allows fintech companies and financial institutions to offer new services and products to a broader customer base. In open banking, banks may take a new role as share points of financial services and "custodians of personal data" (van Zeeland & Pierson, 2021). As previously mentioned, changing one's banking relationship is cumbersome, hence few people do it; this is the main reason why there is limited competition among banks in many markets globally. Open banking effectively reduces the costs to access financial products from third-party providers, thus increasing the competition in the financial sector.

Open banking can also have a transformative influence on society, as it provides people with the possibility to connect their financial data. Moreover, a larger part of the population, including geographically isolated people and marginalized groups, would benefit from open banking, as it opens access to financial services including budgeting and savings tools, enabling them to manage their finances more efficiently. For instance, del Carpio Ponce (2018) reports that people living in rural areas of Peru need on average 1.5 hours to reach a financial institution, a financial agent, or an automated teller machine. For many of these people, the costs (transportation cost to the next bank, opportunity costs for the travel time, and bank charges) of maintaining a bank account are prohibitively high, which explains why they currently do not have a bank account. Open banking could give these underbanked people access to financial services. Even in countries where most people have a bank account, broad segments of the population could benefit from applications based on open banking. Indeed, financial planning tools that were previously restricted to wealthy people may become accessible to everyone thanks to open banking and technological progress.

Risks and Mitigation Strategies

The risks of open banking can be identified by the four following aspects: technical, social, economic, and regulatory.

Technical Risks

The technical risks include exposure to data breaches and hacker attacks. Establishing a robust platform for open banking and a solid accreditation system for companies participating in open banking can reduce these risks. Regulators play an essential role in creating a reliable accreditation system and establishing standards. In the next section, I discuss different regulatory approaches in a regional comparison.

Social Risks

Risks also come from the fear of potential discrimination in offering financial services. This concern refers specifically to customer-specific mortgage offerings and underwriting insurance policies, where open banking may lead to potentially discriminatory offerings and coverage. Indeed, open banking makes customer-specific pricing more exact, as third-party providers can use the information on individual income and spending patterns. Low-risk customers will pay less on a mortgage or an insurance policy while those with higher risk will pay more. The latter are typically the poorer and socially disadvantaged people. Moreover, since the pricing is based on customer information, it is an imperfect measure and can amplify unconscious biases. Such risks are mitigatable by denying insurance underwriters participation in open banking and enforcing strong privacy and data protection, as van Zeeland and Pierson (2021) highlight. Discrimination issues may also arise because many rural and remote communities lack reliable access to the internet, which would need to be addressed by heavy investment in broadband internet infrastructure, as the Senate of Canada (2019) and the Consultative Group to Assist the Poor (Plaitakis & Staschen, 2020) note. An additional social aspect refers to financial and technological education. Open banking relies on customers giving their consent to a third party to accessing their banking data. Customers can make an informed decision only if they understand the benefits and risks of open banking. To make an informed decision for or against the use of open banking, customers need to be financially and technologically literate, which will require mass education of the public on these topics.

Economic Risks

As a result of open banking, customers may become more flexible in where they place their savings and investments, which could lead to more volatility in account balances and potentially harm the stability of the financial system. If many customers use the same automatic service, they may behave similarly and make the same type of (dis)investments, potentially leading to systemic risk for the financial system. Koeppl and Kronick (2020) also mention that open banking may make it more difficult for financial institutions to bundle their products to reduce risk and subsidize their less profitable services from the more profitable ones. This could result in higher prices for some banking services and lower prices for others. As this may better reflect effective risks and costs, it could result in positive change but could also affect population segments in different ways. He et al. (2020) show, in a model of credit market competition, that sharing customer data with banks could make all customers who are borrowers on the lending market worse off while making the entire financial industry better off. Low-risk borrowers face pressure to share their information, while high-risk borrowers suffer from the improved screening ability on the lending market. He et al. (2020)'s results show that the increased competitiveness of fintech companies, thanks to data shared with them by banks, may backfire for the borrowers, depending on the screening ability of banks and fintech companies.

Regulatory Risks

Other risks are of a regulatory nature, i.e., when the regulation between participating companies in open banking is not consistent. For example, banks need to satisfy many jurisdictions' different regulations, not solely those of fintech companies. If all these companies have equal access to open banking while simultaneously being subjected to different regulation, it can lead to regulatory arbitrage in the sense that the less regulated companies have a strategic benefit over the higher regulated companies. At the same time, it may not be meaningful to impose the same regulations on fintech companies as on banks because the risk to their customers and the financial system is different. Indeed, banks are among the most regulated companies because a default of a bank can have enormous impacts: not only for its customers, but also for financial markets and the wider economy. To satisfy these regulations and ensure their stability, banks have large compliance and risk departments, which are neither feasible nor necessary for a small fintech company, whose investors are willing to take higher risk and whose failure would not have a large economic impact. However, third-party providers may not only be typical fintech start-ups, but could also be subsidiaries of one of the large tech companies, such as Alphabet (Google), Amazon, or Meta (Facebook). Therefore, the impression that open banking levels the playing field between large banks and small start-up companies may not be accurate. This is not a statement against open banking, but rather one arguing that regulation should be designed to protect legitimate customer, social, and economic interests, instead of targeting a specific type of company. Additional issues may arise when different levels of government, for example, state or provincial vs. federal levels, regulate financial institutions and fintech companies. Open banking may also expand the markets of banks and fintech companies geographically so that state or provincial regulations need to be reconsidered.

Open Banking in Global View

In this section, I provide a global overview of various open banking initiatives. The level of, and approach to, open banking vary greatly from country to country; they depend on the structure of the banking system and the regulatory and legal framework, which are country-specific. The Basel Committee on Banking Supervision (2019) and Deloitte (2019) offer an overview of open banking developments in different jurisdictions. While those reports are only a few years old, the scope and regulation of open banking have significantly developed since then. In this section, I provide an overview of these developments as they pertain to the current open banking environment. Figure 7.2 shows the number of open banking APIs, which serves as an indicator of global open banking activity. In the following, the extent of the coverage of the different countries depends on how advanced open banking is in each country as well as the country's economic importance.

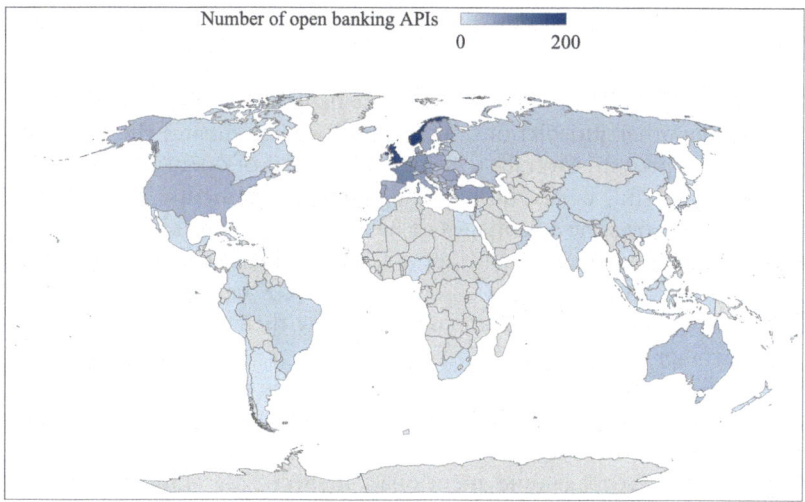

Fig. 7.2 Number of open banking APIs per country around the world (*Note* Data source www.openbankingtracker.com [as of March 5, 2022], illustration created using Microsoft Bing)

Europe

I begin this discussion with the situation in Europe, as the regulation for open banking initiatives began in the United Kingdom (UK) and the European Union (EU).

United Kingdom

The UK is a pioneer in open banking. In August 2016, the UK Competition & Markets Authority issued a report (UK Competition & Markets Authority, 2016) that found insufficient competition and high entry barriers in the UK retail banking market. To remedy these problems, the UK Competition & Markets Authority issued a directive, effective January 2018, requiring the nine banks with the largest UK market share (HSBC, Barclays, Royal Bank of Scotland, Santander, Bank of Ireland, Allied Irish Bank, Danske Bank, Lloyds, and Nationwide) to allow licensed fintech companies access to customer data upon approval by the customer. These nine banks had to set up a non-profit entity, Open Banking Implementation Entity (n.d.) with the trading name Open Banking Limited, to ensure common standards and rules. For a detailed description of the history of open banking in the UK, I refer to Littlejohn et al. (2022).

Since the UK is a trailblazer in open banking, it often serves as an example for other jurisdictions, and it is worth discussing the reception of the UK approach. Overall, the implementation of open banking in the UK was successful, while still requiring some adjustments. The UK case study clearly shows the advantages of API-based open banking over screen scraping and download-upload approaches, as I discuss in the previous section. Before introducing open banking, the UK had an initiative called Midata, which encouraged companies to allow their customers to download customer data in a CSV file and share it with other companies (UK Government, 2011). However, Midata was not successful, mainly because of low standardization among the data providers and inconvenient usage for customers, who would need to handle downloaded files, like in the Wesabe example mentioned in Sect. 7.2 (Littlejohn et al., 2022). By contrast, the non-profit entity Open Banking Limited ensures that common standards form the basis of open banking in the UK. In the beginning, the nine participating banks interpreted the specifications differently, so the banks' APIs were not consistent. This made it difficult for fintech companies to connect via the APIs to the customers' data and caused inconvenience to customers. The UK Competition & Markets Authority addressed this issue by requiring the nine participating banks to use the so-called Financial Grade API standard (OpenID, n.d.), which provides consistency among banks' APIs and thus improves customer experience. It substantially reduces the implementation times for fintech companies accessing customer data through the banks' APIs. The fact that only nine banks are participating in the UK open banking initiative made implementing regulation standards easier. This standardization proved to be an essential component for the success of open banking in the UK, making it different from other jurisdictions, as I discuss later in this section. Other key factors for the success of open banking in the UK are the services that Open Banking Limited provides, namely, a trust framework, a developer portal, and sandboxes for fintech companies to test in the Financial Grade API standard.

Possible improvements in UK open banking relate to restrictions regarding both participating banks and customer data. While the restriction to the nine biggest banks facilitates the implementation of open banking in the UK, it also means that customers of smaller banks cannot benefit from it. Similarly, the scope of open banking could expand to include a broader range of financial products. Additional outstanding issues are that the liability framework is not perfectly aligned with practical use and that solid customer authentication hinders fintech companies from frequently updating customer data (Littlejohn et al., 2022). The problem is related to the authentication process. Under open banking, the customer authorizes a fintech company to access the customer's banking data. However, some services and tools of fintech companies need frequent access to the data. Such access requests become inconvenient for the customer when they repeatedly require customer authentication.

Overall, the UK follows a standard-based approach in open banking, where the regulator plays an important role. The main lessons learned in establishing open banking relate to the importance of consumer rights, standardization, and market oversight. A single-standard approach ensures consistency among service providers while potentially hindering innovation and technological competition in the long term. Given the different structures and country-specific regulations of the banking sector, there is no unique approach to open banking. Still, the UK provides an excellent example of how open banking can work, serving as a case study for many other markets.

European Union

The UK openbanking initiative started when the UK was still part of the EU,[2] which provided a broader regulatory framework of open banking. In the EU, the Revised Payment Services Directive (PSD2) became effective in September 2019, but its discussion started several years earlier. PSD2's main objectives were to harmonize payment products in the EU, make them safer, and increase competition. PSD2 is also the legal basis for open banking in the EU, as it requires banks to give third-party providers access to customer accounts, but it does not require it through APIs; this is because PSD2 was designed to be technologically neutral, which means that it does not impose the use of a specific technology. Moreover, at the time of its drafting, screen scraping was still the dominant method. EU member states are responsible for incorporating PSD2 into their national laws. The adaptation of open banking greatly varies across EU member

---

[2] As a consequence of the UK's withdrawal from the EU, the UK had to adjust the requirements for certificates of UK service providers, which were no longer recognized by the European Banking Authority (Crown, 2020).

states, which Fig. 7.3 reflects, showing how many open banking APIs and third-party providers exist in each EU member state. France (FR), Germany (DE), and Sweden (SE) have more than 25 regulated third-party providers each, while Malta (MT) and Portugal (PT) have none. A challenge of open banking in the EU is the lack of standardization,

as different national organizations define and oversee standards, rules, and the accreditation of third-party providers (Woods, 2021). As I discussed above, the introduction of the Financial Grade API standard fixed the issue of standardization in the UK, while it is up to the EU member states and their regulatory authorities to take steps in this direction. The structure of the EU and the way it reaches decisions can explain much of the fragmentation of the open banking framework in the union. Since the initiation of the Digital Finance Strategy in 2020, the EU is attempting to address some of the issues related to the fragmentation of the digital finance market.

As Arner et al. (2022) explain, we should seePSD2 in connection with the General Data Protection Regulation (GDPR) and the regulation on electronic Identification, Authentication, and Trust Services (eIDAS). GDPR gives people protection in the processing of their personal data. It

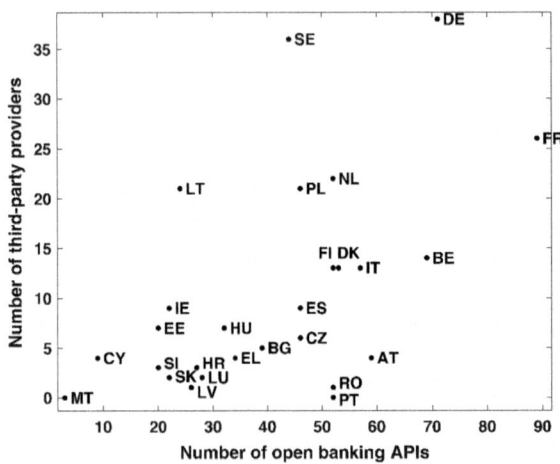

Fig. 7.3 Numbers of open banking APIs and third-party providers in the EU member states (*Note* Data source www.openbankingtracker.com [as of March 5, 2022])

also provides people with ownership and control rights over their personal data. As such, GDPR can be seen as a step toward open data, a generalization of open banking in all aspects of life. While GDPR is an EU regulation, it impacts on a worldwide scale; other jurisdictions around the globe also introduced similar legislation. The eIDAS Regulation aims to harmonize the digital identities in the EU. It ensures that digital identities that different EU member states issue are mutually accepted. Digital identities are important for open banking: they increase convenience for customers because people can use one personal digital identity rather than an abundance of different usernames and passwords. They also help businesses onboard new customers with greater ease. Thus, digital identities are an important consideration when discussing open banking. In summary, open banking in the EU is fragmented while its related regulation with PSD2, GDPR, and eIDAS has helped build an important legal framework for digital services beyond open banking.

Asia

Progress toward open banking varies depending on the jurisdiction. At the forefront of open banking in Asia are Hong Kong, India, and Singapore, whose approaches I survey in this section. I also briefly discuss open banking in China and Japan, given the importance of their financial markets and economies.

Hong Kong

In recent years, Hong Kong made substantial progress toward open banking. The Hong Kong Monetary Authority introduced open banking in four phases (Hong Kong Monetary Authority, 2022):

1. Product information: January 2019
2. Customer information: October 2019
3. Account information: progressively starting in December 2021
4. Transaction information: progressively starting in December 2021.

Most of the 28 participating banks in Hong Kong started introducing phases 3 and 4 for retail and corporate customers during the second quarter of 2022. Compared to the situation in the UK, open banking in Hong Kong is less standardized and is driven by the banks, rather than forced by regulation. Indeed, Hong Kong imposes less detailed regulation on banks to implement open banking, and more banks participate in open banking (28 participating banks in Hong Kong compared to the nine banks participating in UK's Open Banking Limited). The lower level of standardization makes it more difficult for fintech companies to implement tools under open banking. Despite the challenging environment for third-party providers, several fintech companies in Hong Kong (e.g., GoBear, Planto.io, and MoneyHero) are making progress in offering their services using open banking.

India

India chose a hybrid approach to open banking, where fintech companies partner with traditional banks. The infrastructure behind India's open banking is called the India Stack (n.d.), which is a much broader initiative that aims to advance digitalization and promote financial inclusion based on open API. The India Stack consists of several features, including a universal digital ID and a payment system. Unlike the approaches in the EU and UK, the India Stack brings fintech companies and banks together, as opposed to giving fintech companies unilateral access to banking data through an API and customer consent. Since inception, India Stack saw enormous growth in its user numbers and increased potential for reaching underbanked parts of society, as well as countries beyond India.

When comparing India Stack with the open banking approaches in the EU and UK, we need to consider that the goals and starting points were different: India created the India Stack to have a centralized database and increase digitalization. By contrast, the main purposes of the UK's and EU's open banking approaches were to give consumers ownership over their banking data and increase competition in the financial industry. On the one hand, the growth in India Stack shows that it fosters innovation and could serve as a model for industries other than the financial sector and countries other than India. On the other hand, the EU's GDPR constitutes an exemplary data protection law for open banking. By contrast, the India Stack is based on user consent rather than compliance, which might raise privacy concerns and limit its acceptance among consumers if such a framework were introduced elsewhere. I refer to Carriere-Swallow et al. (2021) and Jenkins (2022) for a more detailed description of India's approach to open banking and its comparison with the EU and UK.

Singapore

Singapore is also a pioneer in open banking and is often seen as a leader of open banking in Asia. A key driver behind Singapore's open banking framework is the Monetary Authority of Singapore, which helped introduce API (Exchange), supporting open API and financial innovation. Similar to the Hong Kong Monetary Authority, the Monetary Authority of Singapore takes a phased approach in collaboration with the banking industry. While not required, many banks in Singapore participate in API development or partnering with fintech companies. The Monetary Authority of Singapore initiated API Exchange, which is a collaboration platform for financial institutions and fintech companies to connect (Monetary Authority of Singapore, 2018). Interestingly and differently from other countries, API Exchange is a cross-border platform and its participants are not restricted to a single jurisdiction; for example, Abu Dhabi Global Market is a member of API Exchange.

Japan

As in Singapore, participation in open banking is not mandatory for banks in Japan. Several leading Japanese banks, as well as fintech companies, are moving toward open banking. Japan's Financial Services Agency, which oversees the financial industry, supports this development. The relatively high share of cash transactions in the Japanese economy is often seen as the reason for the slower adaptation of open banking compared to elsewhere in the world, but also shows the high potential for efficiency gains related to digitalization in general and open banking specifically. Several Japanese banks have taken initiatives toward open banking by building joint payment systems: Mitsubishi UFJ Financial Group, Sumitomo Mitsui Financial Group, and Mizuho Financial Group are building a joint payment infrastructure, and Resona Bank, the Bank of Fukuoka, and the Bank of Yokohama are collaborating in another payment system (Lashuk, 2021).

China

The developments toward open banking in China are relatively slow. A regulatory push toward open banking is largely missing. Nonetheless, several banks in China are building infrastructure to use API and partner with fintech companies to offer innovative financial services. Given that there are approximately 225 million adults in China without a bank account (Demirgüç-Kunt et al., 2017), there is enormous potential for open banking, but a suitable framework for open banking would be necessary to make better use of this potential. As the experience in other countries such as the UK and India showed, open banking can be successful in different frameworks; what is suitable for a country depends on its economic, social, and regulatory environment.

Australia

Australia chose a phased approach to open banking and introduced it in the following steps:

- July 1, 2020: banking transaction data available for open banking of Australia's biggest four banks (Westpac, NAB, Commonwealth Bank, and ANZ)
- November 1, 2020: loan data available for open banking of Australia's biggest four banks
- July 1, 2021: all banks in Australia participate in open banking.

The Consumer Data Right—a legal framework introduced by the Australian Government in 2018—forms the basis of open banking in Australia. Consumer Data Right gives Australian consumers data sharing rights beyond banking data. Industry sectors implement it sequentially, starting with the banking sector, followed by the energy and telecommunications sectors (Australian Government, 2019). Australia's approach to open banking follows the UK example in regard to the high degree of standardization and the required involvement of the biggest banks. Major differences are the later introduction in Australia and the restriction to read access in Australia as opposed to the write access in the UK. On the one hand, Australia's approach means fewer risks for consumers, the financial industry, and regulators, as Australia introduced open banking step by step, benefitting from the experience with open banking in the UK. On the other hand, it meant fewer opportunities for financial innovation for some time, compared to the earlier adopters of open banking.

Americas

Overall, the development of open banking in North and Latin America lacks the scope and breadth of that in the UK and in several of the aforementioned countries. Nonetheless, several American countries took important steps toward open banking, which the following paragraphs outline.

United States

Unlike the standard-driven approach in the UK, the United States (US) followed a market-based approach. Section 1033 of the Dodd-Frank Wall Street Reform and Consumer Protection Act (United States, 2010), enacted in July 2010 in response to the financial crisis 2007–2010, gives customers the right to access their banking data. Section 1033 also requires banks to make this information available in a usable format upon request by the customer. However, it does not mention the right to transfer the data to a third-party provider through an API.

The US Consumer Financial Protection Bureau (2017) issued a set of non-binding principles, which allowed consumers to give informed consent to data access of third-party providers without sharing their login credentials. Therefore, these principles put into action the very idea that the creation of open banking was born from. While some US banks introduced APIs allowing customers to give third-party providers access to their banking data securely, many US customers still provide fintech companies with access through screen scraping. In July 2021, an Executive Order (White House, 2021) by US President Joe Biden requested the following:

> The Director of the Consumer Financial Protection Bureau, consistent with the pro-competition objectives stated in section 1021 of the Dodd-Frank Act, is encouraged to consider: commencing or continuing a rulemaking under section 1033 of the Dodd-Frank Act to facilitate the portability of consumer financial transaction data so consumers can more easily switch financial institutions and use new, innovative financial products (Sec. 5t(i)).

This Executive Order may be a step toward open banking in the US, but the country's approach remains underdeveloped, particularly compared to the approaches in the EU and the UK. The slow progress toward open banking in the US may hinder financial innovation and also imposes risks on consumers who give fintech companies access to their data through screen scraping.

Canada

As in the US, Canada lacks a coherent regulatory framework for open banking, but discussion on the topic is progressing. After a three-year consultation process, the Department of Finance Canada released the final report of its Advisory Committee on Open Banking in August 2021 (Government of Canada, 2021). The key recommendations in the report were to appoint an open banking lead and implement open banking quickly, with the system becoming operational by January 2023. The Government of Canada named Abraham Tachjian as the open banking lead on March 22, 2022, which constitutes an important step in following the report's recommendations. Nonetheless, it remains questionable that open banking in Canada will be operational in January 2023, given the regulatory and technical changes required. Part of Canada's slow progress toward open banking is related to its close economic ties with the US, where open banking is advancing only slowly.

Latin America

Open banking has great potential in Latin America because banks do not adequately serve a substantial part of the population; more than 50% of Latin America's population lacks access to banks by a report by the World Bank (Demirgüç-Kunt & Klapper, 2012). Currently, the most advanced countries in Latin America with respect to open banking are Brazil and Mexico, while other Latin American countries are in the process of creating legislation for open banking. In March 2018, Mexico was the first Latin American country to introduce a legal framework for data sharing as part of its Law to Regulate Financial Technology Institutions. Despite the early start, the implementation of open banking in Mexico is slow, and the data sharing of banking transactions through APIs is yet to be introduced across the financial industry. By contrast, Brazil initiated open banking somewhat later but it is quickly catching up. The Central Bank of Brazil started its open banking initiative in 2018, and it is gaining momentum in 2022. Brazil's National Monetary Council officially launched its open finance project in 2022, extending the previous open banking initiative. Mercado Page, a fintech company, became in 2022 the first payment initiator in Brazil (The Payers, 2022). While there is still a long way to go to reach large parts of the population, these are encouraging signs of the progress of open banking in Latin America.

Africa

Several African countries introduced data protection laws based on the example of the EU's GDPR; an example of this includes South Africa's 2013 Protection of Personal Information Act. In Nigeria, the non-profit organization Open Technology Foundation (n.d.) promotes open banking and develops common APIs for Nigerian banks. Nonetheless, open banking is not widely adopted across Africa. Open banking would offer particularly high potential benefits in developing countries with less access to financial services (White et al., 2021). Indeed, in countries with a large population without bank accounts, open banking could increase access to the financial system thanks to its lower costs compared to the establishment of physical branches of financial institutions. Consequently, open banking would not only allow for increased opportunities for existing banking customers but could also give unbanked segments of the population access to financial services.

CONCLUSION

Open banking brings ample opportunities to customers by providing them with control over their banking data. However, its implementation requires a suitable framework on the technological side with appropriate standards from a legal and regulatory perspective to ensure privacy and consumer protection and mitigate liability risks. Open banking takes various forms, depending on the legal, regulatory, economic, and social environment. While the detailed regulations and structures for open banking are still in the works in many countries, further developments of open banking are underway: open finance, which expands open banking to all financial aspects, including insurance and pension products (UK Financial Conduct Authority, 2021), and even open data, which gives customers ownership and sharing rights of data from all life circumstances. This chapter discussed how different countries chose various approaches to open banking depending on their economic, social, and regulatory situation. While we may see a convergence of the underlying technology, I expect that country-specific differences in the implementation and regulation of open banking will remain or even deepen, as they reflect each country's particularities. On a country level, open banking can give people new financial opportunities and make access to financial services more equitable if it is well implemented. However, given the regional differences, it is unlikely that open banking will lead to globally equal access to financial services.

Acknowledgements I would like to thank Meaghan Landrigan-Buttle, Elaheh Nikbakht, and an anonymous reviewer for valuable comments and helpful suggestions. Financial support by the Social Sciences and Humanities Research Council of Canada through Insight Grant 435-2018-0049 is gratefully acknowledged.

Bibliography

Arner, D. W., Buckley, R. P., & Zetzsche, D. A. (2022). Open banking, open data, and open finance: lessons from the European Union. In L. Jeng (Ed.), *Open Banking* (pp. 147–172). Oxford University Press. https://doi.org/10.1093/oso/9780197582879.003.0009

Australian Government (2019, October). *Government response: Inquiry into impacts on local businesses in Australia from global internet-based competition—Recommendation 6.* https://www.industry.gov.au/data-and-publicati ons/government-response-inquiry-into-impacts-on-local-businesses-in-austra lia-from-global-internet-based-competition/recommendation-6

Bahri, G., & Lobo, T. (2020). The seven highly effective strategies to survive in the open banking world. *Journal of Digital Banking, 5*(2), 102–109. https://hstalks.com/article/5918/the-seven-highly-effective-strategies-to-survive-i/?business

Basel Committee on Banking Supervision. (2019). *Report on open banking and application programming interfaces.* https://www.bis.org/bcbs/publ/d486.htm

Carriere-Swallow, Y., Haksar, V., & Patnam, M. (2021). India's approach to open banking: some implications for financial inclusion. *International Monetary Fund Working Papers, 52.* https://www.imf.org/en/Publications/WP/Issues/2021/02/26/Indias-Approach-to-Open-Banking-Some-Implic ations-for-Financial-Inclusion-50049

Crown, S. (2020, November 20). *Open banking and eIDAS certificates: The impact of Brexit.* https://www.cliffordchance.com/insights/resources/hubs-and-toolkits/talking-tech/en/articles/2020/11/open-banking-and-eidas-cer tificates--brexit-impact.html

Deloitte. (2019). *Creating an open banking framework for Canada: Considerations and implications of key design choices.* https://www2.deloitte.com/ca/en/pages/financial-services/articles/creating-open-banking-framework-can ada.html

del Carpio Ponce, P.E. (2018). Modelo Peru: A mobile money platform offering interoperability towards financial inclusion. *EMCompass, 54. International Finance Corporation.* https://openknowledge.worldbank.org/handle/10986/30380

Demirgüç-Kunt, A., & Klapper, L. (2012, May 18). *Latin America: Most still keep their money under the mattress.* https://blogs.worldbank.org/latinamer ica/latin-america-most-still-keep-their-money-under-the-mattress

Demirgüç-Kunt, A., Klapper, L., Signer, D., Ansar, S., & Hess, J. (2017). *The global findex database: Measuring financial inclusion and the FinTech revolution.* https://globalfindex.worldbank.org/#GF-ReportChapters

Farrow, G. S. (2020a). An application programming interface model for open banking ecosystems. *Journal of Payments Strategy & Systems, 14*(1), 75–91. https://www.ingentaconnect.com/contentone/hsp/jpss/2020a/000 00014/00000001/art00010

Farrow, G. S. (2020b). Open banking: The rise of the cloud platform. *Journal of Payments Strategy & Systems, 14*(2), 128–146. https://www.ingentaconnect. com/contentone/hsp/jpss/2020b/00000014/00000002/art00006

Government of Canada. (2021). *Final report: Advisory committee on open banking.* https://www.canada.ca/en/department-finance/programs/consul tations/2021/final-report-advisory-committee-open-banking.html

He, Z., Huang, J., & Zhou, J. (2020). *Open banking: Credit market competition when borrowers own the data.* (Becker Friedman Institute for Economics Working Paper No. 2020–168). University of Chicago. https://bfi.uchicago.edu/working-paper/open-banking-credit-mar ket-competition-when-borrowers-own-the-data/

Hedlund, M. (2010, Oct 1). *Why Wesabe lost to Mint.* http://blog.precipice. org/why-wesabe-lost-to-mint/

Hong Kong Monetary Authority (2022, May 17). *Phased approach: The four phases of open API.* https://www.hkma.gov.hk/eng/key-functions/internati onal-financial-centre/fintech/open-application-programming-interface-api-for-the-banking-sector/phase-approach/

India Stack (n.d.). *India Stack is a collection of open API empowering people and businesses.* Retrieved June 21, 2022, from https://indiastack.org

Jenkins, M. (2022, January 6). *India Stack vs open banking.* https://fintechac rossthepond.substack.com/p/open-banking-vs-upi

Koeppl, T. V., & Kronick, J. (2020). *Open banking in Canada—The path to implementation.* C.D. HOWE Institute. Commentary No. 579. https://www. cdhowe.org/sites/default/files/2021-12/Commentary_579.pdf

Lashuk, A. (2021, March 8). *The many faces of open banking: Australia, the U.K., and Japan.* https://readwrite.com/the-many-faces-of-open-banking-australia-the-u-k-and-japan/

Leger. (2021). *Online survey on financial data sharing and financial data security.* Prepared for the Government of Canada. https://publications.gc.ca/ site/eng/9.898562/publication.html

Littlejohn, G., Boskovich, G., & Prior, R. (2022). United Kingdom: The butterfly effect. In L. Jeng (Ed.), *Open Banking* (pp. 173–200). Oxford University Press. https://doi.org/10.1093/oso/9780197582879.003.0010

Monetary Authority of Singapore (2018, September 18). *World's first cross-border, open-architecture platform to improve financial inclusion.* https:// www.mas.gov.sg/news/media-releases/2018/worlds-first-cross-border-open-architecture-platform-to-improve-financial-inclusion

Open Banking Implementation Entity (n.d.). *About the Open Banking Implementation Entity.* Retrieved June 21, 2022, from https://www.openbanking.org. uk/about-us/

Open Technology Foundation (n.d.). *Open API standards for banking in Nigeria.* Retrieved June 21, 2022, from https://openbanking.ng

OpenID (n.d.). *Open banking.* Retrieved June 21, 2022, from https://fapi.ope nid.net

Plaitakis, A., & Staschen, S. (2020, October). *Open banking: How to design for financial inclusion.* Consultative Group to Assist the Poor. Working paper. https://www.cgap.org/research/publication/open-banking-how-design-financial-inclusion

Senate of Canada. (2019). *Open banking: What it means for you.* Standing Senate Committee on Banking, Trade, and Commerce. https://sencanada.ca/en/ info-page/parl-42-1/banc-open-banking/

The Payers. (2022, February 21). *Mercado Pago to become payments initiator.* https://thepaypers.com/online-payments/mercado-pago-to-become-pay ments-initiator--1254709

UK Competition & Markets Authority. (2016). *Retail banking market investigation—final report.* https://www.gov.uk/cma-cases/review-of-banking-for-small-and-medium-sized-businesses-smes-in-the-uk

UK Financial Conduct Authority. (2021). *Open finance—feedback statement.* https://www.fca.org.uk/publications/feedback-statements/fs21-7-open-fin ance-feedback-statement

UK Government (2011, November 3). *The Midata vision of consumer empowerment*. https://www.gov.uk/government/news/the-midata-vision-of-consumer-empowerment

US Consumer Financial Protection Bureau (2017, October 18). *Consumer protection principles: consumer-authorized financial data sharing and aggregation*. https://files.consumerfinance.gov/f/documents/cfpb_consumer-protection-principles_data-aggregation.pdf

United States (2010). *Dodd-Frank Wall Street Reform and Consumer Protection Act*. https://www.govinfo.gov/content/pkg/PLAW-111publ203/pdf/PLAW-111publ203.pdf

van Zeeland, I., & Pierson, J. (2021). *In banks we trust: Banks as custodians of personal data in open banking ecosystems*. Preprint available at SSRN: https://ssrn.com/abstract=3896405.

White, O., Madgavkar, A., Townsend, Z., Manyika, J., Olanrewaju, T., Sibanda, T., & Kaufman, S. (2021). *Financial data unbound: For individuals and institutions*. McKinsey Global Institute. https://www.mckinsey.com/industries/financial-services/our-insights/financial-data-unbound-the-value-of-open-data-for-individuals-and-institutions

White House (2021, July 9). *Executive Order on promoting competition in the American economy*. https://www.whitehouse.gov/briefing-room/presidential-actions/2021/07/09/executive-order-on-promoting-competition-in-the-american-economy/

Woods, M. (2021). Two years of PSD2 open banking. How far have we come? In O. Ifrim (Ed.), *Open Banking Report 2021—Open Finance and the Race for Relevance and New Business Models in Banking* (pp. 10–16). The Paypers. https://thepaypers.com/reports/open-banking-report-2021/r1251959

Zukowsky, R. (2019). *Open banking, APIs, and liability issues*. https://www.dwt.com/blogs/financial-services-law-advisor/2019/12/open-banking-api-liability

CHAPTER 8

The Rise of Financial Services Ecosystems: Towards Open Banking Platforms

Simona Cosma◉, Stefano Cosma◉, and Daniela Pennetta◉

Introduction: Origin and Definition of the Open Banking Phenomenon

Payment Services Directive 2 (PSD2) is a European regulation for electronic payment services, applied by EU State Members starting from 13 January 2018, who were obliged to become fully compliant within 14 September 2019. PSD2, although limited to the payment services

S. Cosma (✉)
Department of Management, University of Bologna, Bologna, Italy
e-mail: simona.cosma@unisalento.it

S. Cosma · D. Pennetta
Marco Biagi Department of Economics, University of Modena and Reggio Emilia, Modena, Italy
e-mail: stefano.cosma@unimore.it

D. Pennetta
e-mail: daniela.pennetta@unimore.it

T. Walker et al. (eds.), *The Fintech Disruption*, Palgrave Studies in Financial Services Technology,
https://doi.org/10.1007/978-3-031-23069-1_8

191

segment, promotes a greater level of competition and efficiency within the European financial market, reducing entry barriers to the financial services market, and at the same time, strengthening the confidence of consumers, who can rely on a harmonized payments market, higher transparency, security, as well as a better quality and convenience of services (Romānova et al., 2018; Zachariadis & Ozcan, 2017).

Through PSD2, the European legislature has renewed the regulatory framework for payment services, making it more appropriate for the large number of innovations introduced in the market and the emergence of new players, such as FinTech and TechFin companies.

These newcomers, leveraging on digital channels and automation of processes, are generating new opportunities and risks for customers and the entire financial system (Rabitti & Sciarrone Alibrandi, 2019). FinTechs usually follow a specialization rather than a diversification strategy (Tanda & Schena, 2019): their offering has limited scope and their business model is the opposite of universal banking (Navaretti et al., 2018). New entrants create niche products and compete with incumbents for the few products they have on offer, contributing to the unbundling of financial services (Basole & Patel, 2018; Gomber et al., 2018), and the exposition of banks to a high risk of disintermediation (Rabitti & Sciarrone Alibrandi, 2019).

The changes occurring in the way customers access financial services, and in the competitive environment in general, are fostered by PSD2, that explicitly empowers online payment account holders with the authority to share data, removing the financial institution's role as gatekeeper. PSD2 includes FinTechs within the regulatory perimeter (also referred to Third Party Providers or TPPs), with the aim to promote and boost their activity to the benefit of the efficiency and competition of the market (Brodsky & Oakes, 2017). Therefore, the intellectual property of payment data is shifted from the bank to customers (Omarini, 2018), who have the power to authorize TPPs to access, collect and process such data for the purpose of developing and offering its own payment services (Brodsky & Oakes, 2017; Romānova et al., 2018).

The opening up of information assets to authorized TPPs is also known in the literature as "Open Banking". Here, Open Banking is often defined as a customer-oriented model in which banking data, services and applications are shared through Application Programming Interfaces (APIs) with partners, internal and external developers, and customers in a secure and controlled way (Brodsky & Oakes, 2017; Evans & Basole, 2016; Premchand & Choudhry, 2018).

APIs are scalable interfaces based on a set of codes and protocols allowing different software and applications to communicate and interact with one another according to a predetermined scope and level of access (Omarini, 2020). Therefore, the APIs represent a point of contact between the three subjects that participate in the Open Banking model (Open Data Institute, 2016):

i. banks, that hold customer payment data, which are provided to authorized TPPs
ii. TPPs, which ask for permission to access, receive and process customer payment data held at banks
iii. customers, who hold their payment information at banks and who, at their own discretion, make it available to TPPs, which can offer them value-added products and services.

Whenbanks actively comply with PSD2 (Fratini Passi, 2018), i.e. by enlarging the ways data is exchanged, the type of data exchanged and the purposes for which they are exchanged (Cosma et al., 2020), they can go beyond the willingness to fully control the whole value chain and the customer experience and new credit and financial ecosystems and Open Banking platforms can arise, in which, according to different rules, traditional financial intermediaries, banks and TPPs can cooperate. This enables banks and TPPs to develop new financial products and services that better meet customer needs.

The obligation to share information about the payment transactions of customers with other market participants, under certain conditions, may upset one of the fundamentals of banks' existence: the ability to produce confidential and qualified information, and to overcome the problems and risks arising from the existence of information asymmetries in financial exchanges (Bhattacharya & Thakor, 1993). Obtaining information on the financial flows that characterize the bank-customer relationship means, on the one hand, obtaining credible customer information (Campbell & Kracaw, 1980; Millon & Thakor, 1985; Ramakrishnan & Thakor, 1984), and on the other, obtaining the bank's assessments of customer quality and creditworthiness (Boyd-Prescott, 1986; Diamond, 1989; Fama, 1985).

Now, customers can authorize other financial intermediaries to acquire and use all the relational information generated by the (long) customer-bank relationships, regardless of whether or not the bank at which they hold their payment accounts participates in Open Banking platforms. The new regulatory framework undermines the exclusive ownership banks have traditionally held of such data. Now, other financial services providers can also access banks' confidential and qualified information assets, by acquiring the ability to assess the riskiness and opportunism that characterize individual customers. This is carried out by integrating new types of information available through innovative channels, such as digital footprints (Addo et al., 2018; Berg et al., 2020; Onay & Öztürk, 2018; Wei et al., 2016).

In any case, relational behaviours, implicit contracts, mutual commitment, and trust that the customer-bank relationship has generated cannot be acquired solely with access to the existing financial data on customer accounts. These assets and customer relationships remain into the bank, thus potentially reducing the customer's contestability.

PSD2 creates the conditions for sharing customer information, but does information sharing, although limited by regulation, reduce banks' ability to generate value through the management of information asymmetry issues and their ability to build long-term relationships? This is our research question.

We argue that banks' ability to generate value can be negatively affected to the extent that banks decide to preserve their status quo, thus the way in which banks decide to comply to PSD2 is the crucial factor to consider. However, to comprehensively answer our research question, it is important to analyse and discuss some issues arising from the new regulatory framework. In particular, in Sect. 8.2, we explore who TPPs are, and what limits exist within which they should carry out their activities, particularly in terms of data access, usage and storing. In Sect. 8.3, we examine how banks can comply with the obligation to share data with authorized TPPs, with a specific focus on the implementation and functioning of API-infrastructures. In Sect. 8.4, we present the undergoing changes within the competitive environment and intermediation models, while the possible reactions and responses of incumbent banks are discussed in Sect. 8.5. In Sect. 8.6, we focus on the risks and challenges of the Open Banking phenomenon, and, finally, in Sect. 8.7, we conclude and answer to our research question.

New Actors in the Financial Services Market: Identifying TPPs and Their Activities

All entities providing payment services that, in line with PSD2, are authorized to access the bank's payment data can assume the role of TPP. These entities include newcomers in the financial services market, particularly FinTech and TechFin companies, other traditional banks, and financial intermediaries. In Article 4 of Directive, 2015/2366, three types of TPPs are identified:

i. Payment Initiation Service Provider (PISP) which lies between the customer and the bank and holds the customer's payment account, also called Account Servicing Payment Service Providers (ASPSP), and which initializes payment transactions

ii. Account Information Service Provider (AISP) that offers an information aggregation service to customers who hold payment accounts with several ASPSPs

iii. Card Issuer Service Provider (CISP) which offers a fund checking service, i.e. it checks the availability of a certain amount of money in a payment account before the customer pays by all cards linked to his or her payment accounts.

A representation of the activity of TPPs is shown in Fig. 8.1. It is important to underline that the access, collection and usage of ASPSPs' customers payment data is also regulated in accordance with the General Data Protection Regulation (GDPR), introduced in 2016, and the Commission Delegated Regulation (EU) 389 of 2018, which integrates and completes the PSD2 with Regulatory Technical Standards (RTSs). In accordance with GDPR, PSD2 states that TPPs should comply with the principles of transparency, purpose limitation, minimization, accuracy, storage limitation, integrity and confidentiality. The access to payment data held at ASPSPs should be requested by TPPs only after explicit consent is given by the customer. The subsequent data flow should be accomplished through safe and efficient channels to ensure that customers' credentials cannot be accessed by entities other than the customer and the involved TPP and ASPSP. ASPSPs cannot deny authorized access to such information unless there are justified and substantiated reasons relating to fraudulent or unauthorized access to the payment account by such TPPs, or if the customer decides to stop using TPPs' services, thus withdrawing the consent to access to his or her payment information.

Furthermore, PISPs cannot hold the customer's funds and cannot (Directive, 2015/2366, Article 66):

i. collect information unnecessary for the payment arrangement
ii. collect, use, store and access information for purposes other than the payment arrangement
iii. collect and store sensitive information about the payment arrangements
iv. modify the amount the payee or any other feature of the transaction.

AISPs, on the other hand, (Directive, 2015/2366, Article 67):

i. can access information on customer's accounts and related payment operations without asking for sensitive information about the payment arrangements
ii. cannot collect and use data for purposes other than aggregation information services.

As concernsCISPs, the information acquired from the customer's ASPSP consists of confirmation or denial of the availability of a certain amount of funds, as they do not have access customers' account balance or other qualitative or quantitative information. The "yes" or "no" answer shall not be stored or used for purposes other than for the execution of the card-based payment transaction (Directive, 2015/2366, Article 65). Finally, in line with RTSs, consumers should re-authorize their ASPSPs to release their data to TPPs every 90 days. Additionally, TPPs (AISPs in particular) can only access a customer's data 4 times per day.

The above requirements clearly pose limitations for the activity of TPPs, since data flow is not continuous and can be interrupted if customers do not execute the quarterly authentication process.

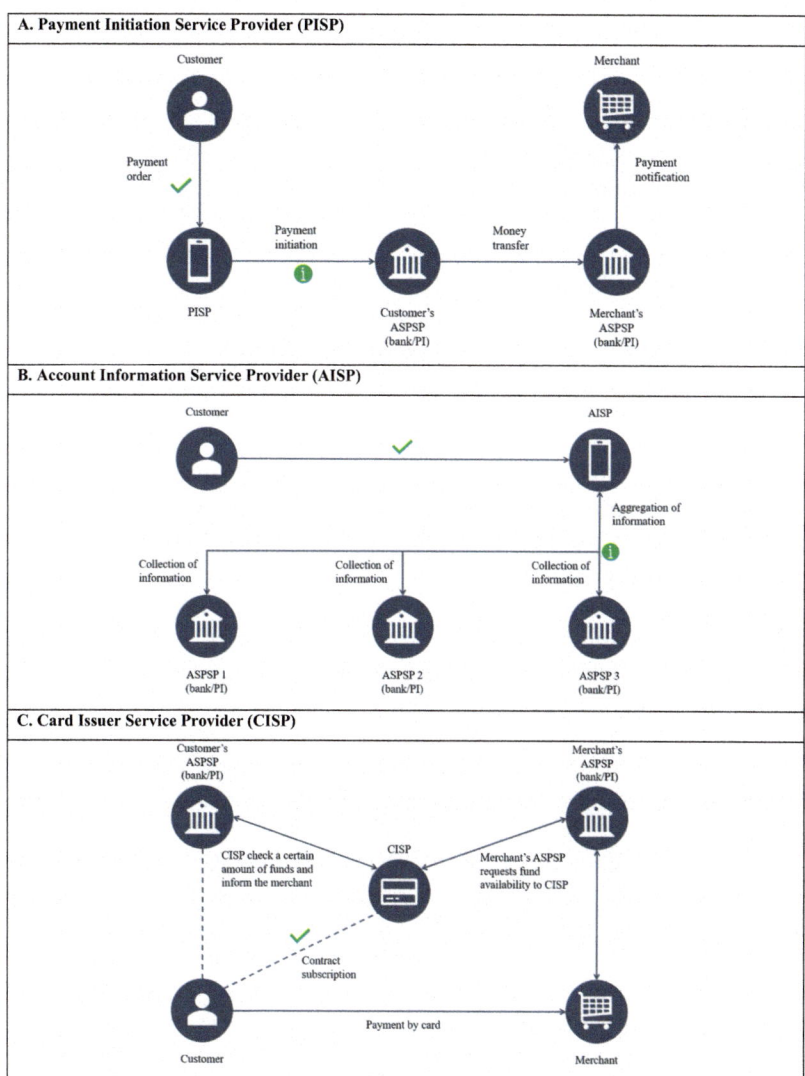

Fig. 8.1 The activity of TPPs. In all cases, customers should give their consent to the access, collection and process of personal data

Application Programming Interfaces (Apis) as a Technological Tool of Open Banking

ThroughRTSs, regulators state that ASPSPs offering customers online payment accounts shall have an interface in which TPPs can identify themselves. Through this interface:

i. PISPs must be able to communicate securely to initiate a payment order from the payer's payment account and receive all information on the initiation of the payment transaction and all related execution information accessible to the ASPSPs

ii. AISPs must be able to communicate securely to request and receive information on one or more designated payment accounts and associated payment transactions

iii. CISPs must be able to securely communicate to check the availability of funds on a customers' payment account, while the transmission of personalized security credentials should ensure integrity and confidentiality.

Also, ASPSPs must provide the documentation of communication interfaces that specify routines, protocols and tools needed by TPPs "for allowing their software and applications to interoperate with the systems of the ASPSPs", and must make a testing facility available that enables TPPs "to test their software and applications used for offering a payment service to users" (Commission Delegated Regulation, 2018/389, Article 30).

In order to foster innovation, the legislator does not impose specific techniques for the implementation of communication interfaces (principle of technological neutrality) but leaves ASPSPs to choose the most suitable solution. Nevertheless, to fulfil the requirements of open standards of communication with the implementation of APIs, a technological solution that enables organizations to share data, services and applications with partners and internal and external developers in a secure and controlled way should be considered (Premchand & Choudhry, 2018). APIs are scalable interfaces based on a set of codes and protocols allowing different software and applications to communicate and interact with one another according to a predetermined scope and level of access (Omarini, 2020).

More specifically, we can distinguish private APIs from open (or public) APIs (Zachariadis & Ozcan, 2017). Private APIs are already commonly used by banks. Here, we classify APIs that can be accessed only within the organization (internal APIs), which are implemented to improve the operational efficiency of the organization, and APIs that are specifically designed to communicate with strategic partners and customers based on bilateral agreements (external APIs). In contrast, open APIs can be accessed by almost anyone through little or no contractual arrangement, after accepting terms and conditions stated by the API provider, and after some form of basic registration for identification and authentication purposes.

The enactmentof PSD2 and the underlying obligation for payment service providers to share payment data with external TPPs are clearly influencing them to shift from private to open APIs. Indeed, PSD2-compliant APIs fall into the open APIs category, since all TPPs authorized or registered in accordance with the regulation are allowed to access to banks' informative assets independently, on the basis of a bilateral contractual agreement between them.

It is worth noting that APIs allow banks and TPPs to communicate automatically and without any human intervention. For each software or application, APIs specify the connection mechanism, the available data and functionalities, and the rules and standards for the interaction. In this regard, neither the PSD2 nor the RTSs specify the language that open communication interfaces should adopt. For this reason, and to enhance efficient and effective data-sharing, some Open Banking standards have been proposed to provide a uniform infrastructure and improve access to APIs and data. Such standards avoid TPPs to develop as many interfaces as the multitude of languages that ASPSPs can potentially use. Open Banking standards usually include technical standards concerning protocols for data transmission and a standard format for exchanged data. They identify who gets access to what data and how this occurs,[1] and they

---

[1] There are two possible access rights depending on data types: i) read access, a permission that is granted to a TPP that can read but not modify files or data (e.g. AISP), and ii) write access, a permission that is granted to a TPP to modify or execute files or data (e.g. PISP).

introduce an architectural style of APIs, the latter intended as a common language[2] (Euro Banking Association, 2016).

AN INCREASING COMPETITION: HOW IS THE ACCESS TO FINANCIAL SERVICES CHANGING?

PSD2 is effectively increasing competition and efficiency within the financial services market. Indeed, there is evidence that PSD2 has positively influenced the establishment of new TPPs in the early years of its introduction (Polasik et al., 2020), notably FinTech companies. FinTechs carry out numerous activities that range from payments services to financing and investment and insurance services, usually following a specialization rather than a diversification strategy. This means that their offering has limited scope and their business model is the opposite of universal banking (Navaretti et al., 2018). New entrants create niche products that target very specific groups of customers based on specific characteristics, thus competing with incumbents for the few products they have on offer, contributing to the unbundling of financial services (Basole & Patel, 2018; Gomber et al., 2018) and the exposition of banks to a high risk of disintermediation (Rabitti & Sciarrone Alibrandi, 2019).

Depending on the legal framework of the country in which FinTech firms operate, the disaggregation of incumbents' value chain allows these firms to position themselves in operational segments which escape regulatory and supervision requirements, thus reducing compliance costs (e.g. licences and capital and liquidity requirements). Also, FinTechs are able to enter in market segments where traditional financial institutions cannot effectively meet customers' needs (Tanda & Schena, 2019), i.e. underserved, excluded and unsatisfied segments, such as vulnerable households, MSMEs (Micro and Small-Medium Enterprises) and digital natives (Arner et al., 2020; Salampasis & Mention, 2018).

In other words, the new regulatory framework is fostering the activity of FinTech companies. FinTechs are gaining ever larger market shares thanks to their ability to meet the profound changes occurring in the purchase and consumption habits of customers, whose main choice motivators are personalization, convenience, accessibility and ease of use

---

[2] Examples of standardisation initiatives are the Open Banking Standards (UK Open Banking Working Group), NextGenPSD2 (Berlin Group), Controlled Access to Payment Services (CAPS) and Banking Industry Architecture Network (BIAN).

(Ernst & Young, 2019), which have strong benefits in terms of market completeness and competitiveness.

The unbundling of banking activities is transforming the way in which customers access and use financial services (Fig. 8.2). Instead of satisfying all financial needs by relying on a single bank based on an average benefit/cost analysis, customers can access single, preferred financial services offered by different financial firms (banks, other financial institutions and FinTech and TechFin companies), usually after a re-bundling of financial services is made possible through aggregation and comparison platforms (Colombari and Borgogno & Colangelo, 2020; Tedeschi, 2019). Unbundled services offered by several financial firms are selected and combined according to customers' needs and offered as "new" financial products. This leads to the shift from a traditional universal banking model to a modular banking model with a strong customer-centric orientation (Euro Banking Association, 2016).

A DIFFERENT APPROACH TO COMPLYING WITH PSD2: TOWARDS OPEN BANKING PLATFORMS

The profound changes occurring in the competitive scenario due to the new regulatory framework are increasing banks' efforts in trying to reduce the risk of disintermediation and stay relevant to the customers. Banks' managers are increasingly aware that the alignment with PSD2 can be accomplished not only through the literal adaptation to the dictates of the regulation, but also through an interpretation of regulatory obligations able to seize the opportunities arising from information sharing and to improve the product governance. Thanks to a different approach to doing business and competing within the market, the concept of Open Banking can take a broader and more valuable meaning (Fratini Passi, 2018).

More specifically, it is important that we distinguish between banks that passively or actively comply with PSD2. What separates these two possible avenues is the different approach to implementing open APIs, that is, how data is exchanged, the type of data exchanged, and the purposes for which they are exchanged (Cosma et al., 2020). Using a passive approach, banks comply with the minimum requirements requested by regulation, allowing authorized TPPs to access customer data through a forced collaboration model in which the exchange of data is unidirectional (from bank to TPPs), limited to the type and quantity of data for which authorization is given by the customer, and aimed exclusively at

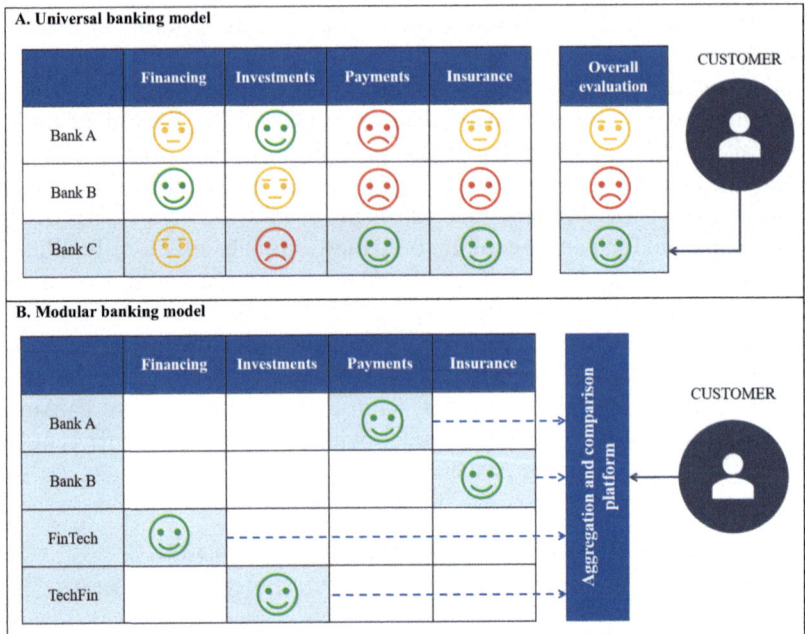

Fig. 8.2 Universal banking model vs modular banking model. Adapted from Colombari and Tedeschi (2019)

providing the latter with the service offered by the TPPs. Then, TPPs can eventually exploit the data within the limits imposed by PSD2 and the GDPR to improve the financial products and services they offer. In contrast, through an active approach to regulation compliance, a model of voluntary collaboration is established, according to which the exchange of data is bidirectional (from bank to TPPs and vice versa). It may concern a wider set of information for which the customer gives authorization and which is finalized through collaborations in the different stages of development, production and distribution of financial services, to improve the processes and overall offering of financial products and services of both the banks and the TPPs. Such collaborations are strongly, but not solely, based on the Bank-as-a-Service (BaaS) concept: an end-to-end process that connects TPPs to banks' systems directly through use of open APIs, which helps to build up banks' and TPPs offerings (Omarini, 2020; Zachariadis & Ozcan, 2017).

Through an active approach, insofar as this involves the use of open APIs at their maximum level of openness, banks can go beyond the willingness to fully control the whole value chain and the customer experience (or to do so at most by relying on a few partnerships with external parties). New credit and financial ecosystems and Open Banking platforms can arise, in which, according to different rules, traditional financial intermediaries, banks, and TPPs can cooperate. Within Open Banking platforms, the role of banks will depend on the distribution and production agreements established between participants, and can also contemplate the possibility for banks to leave their active role in financial intermediation (a role also known as Bank-as-a-Platform [BaaP]). Through the BaaP role, banks continue to operate in the background as re-intermediaries by providing online tools and systems that offer valuable services and trust to the participants of the platform (Parker et al., 2016; Zachariadis & Ozcan, 2017; Gozman et al., 2018). This means that banks neither produce nor distribute financial products, but offer different capabilities to TPPs, such as the matching of parties, security, Know Your Customer (KYC) and Anti Money Laundering (AML) competences and open APIs infrastructures. These services allow TPPs to set up strategic alliances to scale up their business and benefit from direct and indirect network effects, as usually occurs in platform environments (Evans & Schmalensee, 2016). Through an "embedded finance" logic, Open Banking platforms may also include non-financial companies, which aim to offer integrated and comprehensive user experiences and are able to provide quick and easy access to goods and services through the integration of financial services into their core offering (Sella Insights, 2022). This, for example, is already occurring in utilities and telecom companies. Certainly, platform curation is important to nurture positive network effects by applying filters, controlling and limiting the access of users to the platform, and avoiding poor quality services (Zachariadis & Ozcan, 2017; Parker et al., 2016).

Therefore, PSD2 gives regulatory concreteness to a phenomenon already underway in the banking system that sees some actors, such as banks, TPPs, non-financial institutions, and technology providers, share information and technologies to improve innovation capacity, to better serve their customers, and at most, share their customers to offer more innovative services and to enhance their competitive advantage.

Open Banking platforms not only bring benefits to participating financial services providers but also represent a valuable solution to the complexities faced by customers arising from the shift to a modular banking model, as explained in the previous paragraph. Indeed, the underlying process of the re-bundling of financial services and establishment of relationships with multiple financial institutions exposes the customer to greater risks of information asymmetry and higher transaction costs, especially they rely on online comparators and have to evaluate several financial products. This is a cumbersome process that takes time and effort to find the provider best suited to their needs. Therefore, the Open Banking platform can act as a single point of contact for the customer, becoming a one-stop-shop (Mensah & Muroura, 2017), offering best-in-class digital financial products and services, more in line with the new features of market demand that are the result of collaborations between the participants of the platform.

Risks and Challenges of the Open Banking Phenomenon

PSD2 intends to develop an integrated market for payment services, providing TPPs with access to customer data held at credit institutions. At the same time, PSD2 also aims to ensure a high level of consumer protection, payment security and protection against fraud (Wolters & Jacobs, 2019). Open Banking platforms introduce a series of challenges that banks must face, including security, customer control, and stability.

The first category of risks associated with the PSD2 concerns technological and infrastructural components. The implementation of the new Aggregation Information Service (AIS) and Payment Initiation Service (PIS) strategies increases the so-called attack surface and therefore the cyber risk as any service accessible via the internet has the possibility of being attacked by cybercriminals. This risk can have several implications, including the possible loss of personal data in cases of privacy violation (Wolters & Jacobs, 2019).

Banks invest heavily to increase data security and protection, representing sources of reputational risk (Romānova et al., 2018) and legal risk. However, the interposition of the TPP between customers and banks generates the risk of a possible weakening of anti-fraud procedures (Gabudeanu et al., 2021). Third-party applications may not pay the same attention to data security, protection and confidentiality, whose ultimate responsibility is attributed to banks by PSD2. Therefore, banks will have to find a way to ensure secure access to data and increased permission management (Noctor, 2018).

The presence of numerous authentications constitutes another source of risk, and encryption keys with life cycles are required to be adequately managed to ensure the security of the communication channels and at the same time, the correct identification of the subjects involved. The lifecycle of data held by an application is essentially the duration of time that the app will have access to that data. Suppose the third-party app provider will be able to access such data at any time. In that case, even if the user is not logged into the app, banks will need to provide customers with ways to manage their data, including when and what data is accessed, as well as providing information on the subjects who accessed the account, when they last accessed that account, and which data they accessed, and allow customers to block such access (Noctor, 2018).

Another category of risk is attributable to legal risks and concerns the protection of customer data. The data acquired from the customer for the offer of services can be used for purposes other than those related to payment services and can sometimes be transferred to third parties. In these cases, it is necessary for the intermediary to rigorously acquire the consent of the end customer, distinguishing between:

i. Consents necessary to allow access to customer data by the person offering the PIS/AIS services, according to PSD2
ii. Consents necessary for the possible transfer of data to other subjects and for the subsequent re-processing for purposes other than those related to payment services, as per the GDPR (the privacy legislation).

The complexity of Open Banking increases with the presence of TPPs residing outside the European Union, which put customer data at even greater risk and which, if previously stored in the data centres of European operators, can now also be stored outside the EU territory.

From this point of view, the risks associated with mobile payment or account information services are innumerable for those who use them. However, various forms of guarantees have already been introduced to protect customers. Currently, AISPs and PISPs[3] must document the possession of appropriate civil liability insurance policies for any damage caused in the exercise of their business. Additionally, they must prove that their calculation methods comply with the EBA Guidelines on the criteria for establishing the minimum amount of insurance for professional indemnity or similar guarantee according to Article 5, paragraph 4 of EU Directive, 2015/2366.

In addition to the risks relating to digital intrusions, illicit use of data and privacy issues that can impact the financial intermediary's reputation poses a strategic risk. This risk is related to the partial disintermediation of banks, due to the difficulty of maintaining a direct relationship with the customer if the latter prefers to purchase financial products and services from other TPPs and intermediaries participating in the Open Banking platform. However, the risks related to customer retention and their choice of services depend on the quality of the individual bank's offer (Cosma et al., 2020). FinTech firms, with the development of innovative products and services, have already created strong pressure on banks' margins, sometimes leading to a loss of market share in some services, such as payments (Romānova et al., 2018). Traditional credit institutions, therefore, bear the additional burden of protecting their market shares through the ability to change and adapt to customer demand, and to innovate by developing new technologies and new customer retention techniques.

Another category of risk generated by Open Banking is related to stability. From an income statement perspective, there is a risk of underperformance in terms of Return on Equity (ROE) due to the contraction in profits generated by the increase in costs incurred for investments in the internal IT infrastructures of banks (Romānova et al., 2018) to limit operational risks. Banks need to develop robust APIs and effectively install security management measures with inevitable cost increases. In the literature, however, there is still no empirical evidence on the effects of Open Banking platforms on participants' business and financial performance, so the reflections relating to the possible advantages and risks for banks

---

[3] Some examples of European FinTechs who obtained AISP or PISP licence are Olinda SAS (a French company that developed Qonto, a banking app dedicated to professionals and MSMEs), Billie GmbH (a German company offering Buy Now, Pay Later (BNPL) services) and Hype S.p.A (an Italian company that offers innovative banking services to individuals and professionals through the eponymous app).

appear to be of a theoretical and hypothetical nature due to the embryonic phase that characterizes the phenomenon of Open Banking (Vives, 2018).

The increased competition in the market can also undermine financial stability to the extent that banks fail to interpret and undertake change, while maintaining their status quo. Although competition is often a factor capable of determining greater efficiency in the market, when linked to the presence of new players and services, can compromise stability. The rise of new operators, who perform many of the functions of traditional banks through big data, complex algorithms of artificial intelligence, and machine learning to make near-instant decisions, exacerbates competition. In 2017, the Financial Stability Board considered the so-called aggregators (service providers that use technology to facilitate the transfer of money between institutions) capable of increasing the volatility induced by investors who are particularly sensitive to market news, highlighting a risk to stability and the "worsening" of systemic risk.

Conclusive Remarks

To conclude, we answer the question posed at the beginning of the chapter: does information sharing, although limited by regulation, reduce banks' ability to generate value through the management of information asymmetry issues and their ability to build long-term relationships?

We have identified who TPPs are and the limits within which they should carry out their activities, and we have followed the depiction of the different possible uses of API-infrastructures and the responses of banks faced with profound changes in the competitive environment and consumers' habits. Now, we can conclude that the new regulatory framework affects, and can reduce, the ability of banks to generate value from their ability to overcome information asymmetry issues, to the extent that banks decide to preserve their status quo.

The choice to passively align to PSD2 can negatively affect banks' value generation in two ways. First, even if banks still benefit from exclusivity in deposit-taking activities and continuous and complete availability of customers' data, they are no longer the only entities able to evaluate customers and manage the risks arising from information asymmetries. New entrants, although with some limits in terms of data access, usage and storing, can obtain bank information and leverage the advantages allowed by the implementation of new technologies. In this regard,

FinTechs can rely on a better collection, management and analysis of data, carried out by also considering non-traditional and unstructured data (Berg et al., 2020), such as those retrieved from social media, user behaviour when using apps and websites, e-commerce platforms, geo-localization and telecom companies (also known as *digital footprints*). This can lead to a better understanding of each customer's financial position, potentially reducing information asymmetries.

Second, customers are increasingly informed of new digital financial products introduced in the market by TPPs and are increasingly prone to evaluate and buy them. This sometimes displaces the capacity of banks to satisfy a more demanding and digitally aware clientele, with a negative impact on banks' value proposition.

As can be understood from the above arguments, a conservative strategy towards PSD2 partially shifts the benefits of the ability to generate value through the overcoming of information asymmetry from banks to new entrants (TPPs). From the banks' perspective, this value transfer can be equally- or over-compensated through an active approach in aligning with the new regulation, thus establishing a model of voluntary collaboration based on a bidirectional exchange of data to enhance the relational dimensions existing in the customer-bank relationship together with the innovative proposal of newcomers.

It is important to underline that banks, like TPPs, can take advantage of the possibility of aggregating and enriching customer information with that held by other TPPs (Brodsky & Oakes, 2017; Euro Banking Association, 2016), which, in turn, act as PISPs and AISPs. This means that also banks can access to TPPs' informative assets as outlined in the PSD2. The bidirectional exchange of data, especially in Open Banking platform contexts, can help banks enhance their innovation capacity, develop and improve their offering, and reduce the mismatch between the typical features of traditional financial services and those expected and deemed most valuable by customers. Therefore, the shift from a forced collaboration to a voluntary collaboration also extends to financial services other than payment services and may represent an opportunity for banks to better serve their clients with innovative and highly differentiating customer experiences while finding new revenue streams (Guibaud, 2016) and enabling the combination of unconventional teamwork, competition and open models (Sella Insights, 2022).

Certainly, the active approach in aligning with the new regulatory framework may depend on the actual cultural and structural factors characterizing banks, which, consequently, also affect the formation of Open Banking platforms. From a cultural point of view, bank managers may not be keen to collaborate actively with TPPs because of something known as NIH (Not Invented Here) syndrome, thus refusing to accept/share ideas and solutions and technologies from/with external parties. This attitude-based bias in decision-making may result in the irrational tendency of devaluating external knowledge, even if it might be valuable from the perspective of the organization (Antons & Piller, 2015). Beyond the crucial initial decision of whether or not to open up the boundaries to external TPPs, there are other structural factors that may affect banks' attitudes towards collaboration. More specifically, larger banks that usually own all the necessary structures and strategic resources and competences to internally develop and distribute financial products and services may be associated with a reluctant attitude to partnership in Open Banking platform contexts (Grant & Baden-Fuller, 1995; Madhok & Tallman, 1998; Gulati, 1999; Dyer and Singh, 2002). To quickly innovate themselves, larger banks may also consider the possibility to acquire or merge TPPs, thus carrying external tangible and intangible assets within the banking group perimeter. Accordingly, smaller banks, with lower risk capacity (lacking funds) and pursuing a diversification strategy, could be more inclined to source development or distribution activities to TPPs to overcome size, financial and competences constraints (Cosma et al., 2020). Also, from a strategic point of view, outsourcing decisions could target saturating and exploiting production capacity, thus generating scale and scope economies (Cosma et al., 2020; Mariti & Smiley, 1983; Varadarajan & Cunningham, 1995).

However, the recent development of the Open Banking phenomenon still makes unclear what the effect of PSD2 will be in terms of the evolution of the structures of the financial services market and of the activity of the actors operating within it (Zachariadis & Ozcan, 2017). Open Banking ecosystems and platforms are at the forefront of their development, and the related theorized opportunities and risks are not yet visible. What is certain is that the digital transformation process of the financial market is deeply changing the interpretation of the concept of competition and the key factors that should be considered in the formulation of competitive strategies.

REFERENCES

Addo, P. M., Guegan, D., & Hassani, B. (2018). Credit risk analysis using machine and deep learning models. *Risks, 6*(2), 38. https://doi.org/10. 3390/risks6020038

Antons, D., & Piller, F. T. (2015). Opening the black box of "Not Invented Here": Attitudes, decision biases, and behavioral consequences. *Academy of Management Perspectives, 29*(2), 193–217. https://doi.org/10.5465/amp. 2013.0091

Arner, D. W., Buckley, R. P., Zetzsche, D. A., & Robin, V. (2020). Sustainability, fintech and financial inclusion. *European Business Organization Law Review, 21*(1), 7–35. https://doi.org/10.1007/s40804-020-00183-y

Basole, R. C., & Patel, S. S. (2018). Transformation through unbundling: Visualizing the global FinTech ecosystem. *Service Science, 10*(4), 379–396. https://doi.org/10.1287/serv.2018.0210

Berg, T., Burg, V., Gombović, A., & Puri, M. (2020). On the rise of fintechs: Credit scoring using digital footprints. *The Review of Financial Studies, 33*(7), 2845–2897. https://doi.org/10.1093/rfs/hhz099

Bhattacharya, S., & Thakor, A. (1993). Contemporary banking theory. *Journal of Financial Intermediation, 3*(1), 2–50. https://doi.org/10.1006/jfin.1993. 1001

Borgogno, O., & Colangelo, G. (2020). Data, innovation and competition in finance: The case of the access to account rule. *European Business Law Review, 31*(4), 573–610. https://doi.org/10.2139/ssrn.3251584

Boyd, J., & Prescott, E. C. (1986). Financial intermediary coalitions. *Journal of Economic Theory, 38*(2), 211–232. https://doi.org/10.1016/0022-053 1(86)90115-8

Brodsky, L., & Oakes, L. (2017). *Data sharing and open banking.* McKinsey & Company.

Campbell, T. S., & Kracaw, W. A. (1980). Information production, market signaling and the theory of financial intermediation. *Journal of Finance, 35*(4), 863–882. https://doi.org/10.2307/2327206

Colombari, E., & Tedeschi, R. (2019). *Regolamentazione e apertura volontaria: breve guida all'open banking in Italia e all'estero.* Prometeia.

Commission Delegated Regulation 2018/389. *Regulatory technical standards for strong customer authentication and common and secure open standards of communication.* European Parliament, Council of the European Union. http://data.europa.eu/eli/reg_del/2018/389/oj

Cosma, S., Pattarin, F., & Pennetta, D. (2020). Banks, business models and Open Banking: Which interpretation of Psd2. *Bancaria, 11*, 36–46.

Diamond, D. (1989). Reputation acquisition in debt market. *Journal of Political Economy, 97*(4), 828–862. https://doi.org/10.1086/261630

Directive 2015/2366. *Payment services in the internal market.* European Parliament, Council of the European Union. http://data.europa.eu/eli/dir/2015/2366/oj

Dyer, J. H., & Singh, H. (1998). The relational view: Cooperative strategy and sources of interorganizational competitive advantage. *Academy of Management Review, 23*(4), 660–679. https://doi.org/10.5465/amr.1998.1255632

Ernst&Young. (2019). *Global FinTech Adoption Index 2019.*

Euro Banking Association. (2016). *Understanding the business relevance of Open APIs and Open Banking for banks.*

Evans, D. S., & Schmalensee, R. (2016). *Matchmakers: The new economics of multisided platforms.* Harvard Business Review Press.

Evans, P. C., & Basole, R. C. (2016). Revealing the API ecosystem and enterprise strategy via visual analytics. *Communications of the ACM, 59*(2), 26–28. https://doi.org/10.1145/2856447

Fama, E. (1985). What's different about banks. *Journal of Monetary Economics, 15*(1), 29–39. https://doi.org/10.1016/0304-3932(85)90051-0

Fratini Passi, L. (2018). An open banking ecosystem to survive the revised Payment Services Directive: Connecting international banks and FinTechs with the CBI Globe platform. *Journal of Payments Strategy & Systems, 12*(4), 335–345.

Gabudeanu, L., Brici, I., Mare, C., Mihai, I. C., & Scheau, M. C. (2021). Privacy intrusiveness in financial-banking fraud detection. *Risks, 9*(6), 104. https://doi.org/10.3390/risks9060104

Gomber, P., Kauffman, R. J., Parker, C., & Weber, B. W. (2018). On the fintech revolution: Interpreting the forces of innovation, disruption, and transformation in financial services. *Journal of Management Information Systems, 35*(1), 220–265. https://doi.org/10.1080/07421222.2018.1440766

Gozman, D., Hedman, J., & Sylvest, K. (2018). Open Banking: Emergent roles, risks & opportunities. In *ECIS 2018 Proceedings Association for Information Systems.* AIS Electronic Library (AISeL). Proceedings of the European Conference on Information Systems

Grant, R. M., & Baden-Fuller, C. (August). A knowledge-based theory of inter-firm collaboration. In *Academy of management proceedings, 55*(1), 17–21. https://doi.org/10.5465/ambpp.1995.17536229

Guibaud, S. (2016). How to develop a profitable, customer-focused digital banking strategy: Open banking services and developer-friendly APIs. *Journal of Digital Banking, 1*(1), 6–12.

Gulati, R. (1999). Network location and learning: The influence of network resources and firm capabilities on alliance formation. *Strategic Management Journal, 20*(5), 397–420. https://doi.org/10.1002/(SICI)1097-0266(199905)20:5%3C397::AID-SMJ35%3E3.0.CO;2-K

Madhok, A., & Tallman, S. B. (1998). Resources, transactions and rents: Managing value through interfirm collaborative relationships. *Organization Science, 9*(3), 326–339. https://doi.org/10.1287/orsc.9.3.326

Mariti, P., & Smiley, R. H. (1983). Co-operative agreements and the organization of industry. *The Journal of Industrial Economics, 437–451,*. https://doi.org/10.2307/2098340

Mensah B., & Muroura M. (2017). Sustaining networks in the new age: Turning Open Banking into a sustainable competitive advantage. *Africa Expansion Project 2017.*

Millon, M., & Thakor, A. (1985). Moral hazard and information sharing: A model of financial information gathering agencies. *The Journal of Finance, 40*(5), 1403–1422. https://doi.org/10.1111/j.1540-6261.1985.tb02391.x

Navaretti, G. B., Calzolari, G., Mansilla-Fernandez, J. M., & Pozzolo, A. F. (2018). Fintech and banking. Friends or foes?. *European Economy – Banks. Regulation, and the Real Sector, 2*, 9–30. https://doi.org/10.2139/ssrn.3099337

Noctor, M. (2018). PSD2: Is the banking industry prepared? *Computer Fraud and Security, 2018*(6), 9–11. https://doi.org/10.1016/S1361-3723(18)30053-8

Omarini, A. (2020). FinTech: A new hedge for a financial re-intermediation. Strategy and risk perspectives. *Frontiers in Artificial Intelligence, 3*, 63. https://doi.org/10.3389/frai.2020.00063

Omarini, A. E. (2018). Banks and Fintechs: How to develop a digital Open Banking approach for the bank's future. *International Business Research, 11*(9), 23–36. http://dx.doi.org/https://doi.org/10.5539%2Fibr.v11n9p23

Onay, C., & Öztürk, E. (2018). A review of credit scoring research in the age of Big Data. *Journal of Financial Regulation and Compliance, 26*(3), 382–405. https://doi.org/10.1108/JFRC-06-2017-0054

Open Data Institute. (2016). *Open banking standard.* UK Open Banking Working Group.

Parker, G. G., Van Alstyne, M. W., & Choudary, S. P. (2016). *Platform revolution: How networked markets are transforming the economy? and how to make them work for you.* WW Norton & Company.

Polasik, M., Huterska, A., Iftikhar, R., & Mikula, Š. (2020). The impact of payment services directive 2 on the PayTech sector development in Europe. *Journal of Economic Behavior & Organization, 178*, 385–401. https://doi.org/10.1016/j.jebo.2020.07.010

Premchand, A., & Choudhry, A. (2018, February). Open Banking & APIs for transformation in banking. In *2018 International Conference on Communication, Computing and Internet of Things (IC3IoT)*, 25–29, IEEE. https://doi.org/10.1109/IC3IoT.2018.8668107

Rabitti, M., & Sciarrone Alibrandi, A. (2019). *Dalla PSD alla PSD2: Open Banking e servizi di pagamento.* Università Cattolica del Sacro Cuore.

Ramakrishnan, R., & Thakor, A. (1984). Information reliability and the theory of financial intermediation. *Review of Economic Studies, 51*(3), 415–432. https://doi.org/10.2307/2297431

Regulation 2016/679. *Protection of natural persons with regard to the processing of personal data and on the free movement of such data and repealing Directive 95/46/EC (General Data Protection Regulation).* European Parliament, Council of the European Union. http://data.europa.eu/eli/reg/2016/679/oj

Romānova, I., Grima, S., Spiteri, J., & Kudinska, M. (2018). The payment services directive 2 and competitiveness: The perspective of European Fintech companies. *European Research Studies Journal, 21*(2), 3–22. https://doi.org/10.35808/ersj/981

Salampasis, D., & Mention, A. L. (2018). FinTech: Harnessing innovation for financial inclusion. In *Handbook of blockchain, digital finance, and inclusion, Volume 2,* 451–461. Academic Press. https://doi.org/10.1016/B978-0-12-812282-2.00018-8

Sella Insights (2022, February 1). *The 'Open' paradigm and the evolution of financial ecosystems.* https://sellainsights.it/-/the-open-paradigm-and-the-evolution-of-financial-ecosystems

Tanda, A., & Schena, C. M. (2019). *FinTech, BigTech and banks: Digitalisation and its impact on banking business models.* Springer. https://doi.org/10.1007/978-3-030-22426-4_1

Varadarajan, P. R., & Cunningham, M. H. (1995). Strategic alliances: A synthesis of conceptual foundations. *Journal of the Academy of Marketing Science, 23*(4), 282. https://doi.org/10.1177/009207039502300408

Vives, X. (2018). Competition and stability in modern banking: A post-crisis perspective. *International Journal of Industrial Organization, 64*(C), 55–69. https://doi.org/10.1016/j.ijindorg.2018.08.011

Wei, Y., Yildirim, P., Van den Bulte, C., & Dellarocas, C. (2016). Credit scoring with social network data. *Marketing Science, 35*(2), 234–258. https://doi.org/10.1287/mksc.2015.0949

Wolters, P. T. J., & Jacobs, B. P. F. (2019). The security of access to accounts under the PSD2. *Computer Law and Security Review, 35*(1), 29–41. https://doi.org/10.1016/j.clsr.2018.10.005

Zachariadis, M., & Ozcan, P. (2017, June). *The API economy and digital transformation in financial services: The case of open banking* (SWIFT Institute Working Paper No. 2016–001). https://doi.org/10.2139/ssrn.2975199

CHAPTER 9

The Cryptoassets Market in the United Kingdom: Regulatory and Legal Challenges

Malgorzata Sulimierska and Agnieszka Sikorska

Introduction

We live in a world surrounded by technology and the way we do our banking has changed dramatically over the last two to three decades. One of these changes is cryptoassets, a term which for some means new opportunities while for others it brings about a degree of controversy. Let us imagine a secure type of technology that records payments made by one user to another who owns a digital currency, and where there is no need for a middleman, no state-controlled currency. This may sound very futuristic but in a sense, cryptoassets are a way of banking without a traditional bank involved. In its current state, it is very private and (at least in theory)

M. Sulimierska (✉)
University of Sussex, Brighton, UK
e-mail: ms70@sussex.ac.uk

A. Sikorska
University of Law, London, UK

© The Author(s), under exclusive license to Springer Nature Switzerland AG 2023
T. Walker et al. (eds.), *The Fintech Disruption*, Palgrave Studies in Financial Services Technology,
https://doi.org/10.1007/978-3-031-23069-1_9

secure. This appears very innovative, but it tells us what cryptoassets are in a simple form.

Cryptoassets operate through both blockchain technology and a larger Distributed Ledger Technology (DLT). Blockchain is a form of DLT platform on which cryptoassets were developed. Blockchains work as a peer-to-peer system via a network of computers. There is no central server but rather each computer receives information from the other computers in the network. Structured this way, the aim of blockchains and other DLTs is decentralization. One of the many things that can be stored on a blockchain is so-called smart contracts, which are types of digital contracts that allow for automatic execution when the terms and conditions of the smart contract are met. Smart contracts do not require a middleman and the automatic execution takes place through a code.

The popularity of digital cash has grown over the past decade. After the global financial crisis of 2008–2009, investors began looking into new potential investment opportunities. Many of them found success with cryptoassets. In the UK, the 2018 Cryptoassets Taskforce Report highlights that there exist significant risks related to innovation arising from cryptoassets, and governments and authorities are especially aware of this and are taking actions to address them. The Taskforce emphasizes in its report that it '*will take action to mitigate the risks that cryptoassets pose to consumers and market integrity; to prevent the use of cryptoassets for illicit activity; to guard against threats to financial stability that could emerge in the future; and to encourage responsible development of legitimate DLT and cryptoasset-related activity in the UK*' (Cryptoassets Taskforce Report, 2018). This chapter focuses on the illustration of the market development in the UK by first providing a historical background of the cryptoassets market and its current state. The discussion will then focus on considering difficulties with applying financial regulation to the cryptoassets and some of the legal challenges created by the use of cryptoassets, such as data protection or cybercrimes. Recent development to the regulatory regime in the UK and EU will also be discussed.

The development of the cryptoassets has caused significant worry of financial institutions such as banks due to the potential use of these assets as a medium for money laundering activities. It is certain that policy-makers are looking at the prospect of these new digital assets being used to clean the 'dirty' money acquired by means of criminal activities. Moreover, they are analyzing how these processes can be stopped or even controlled. As a 2022 analysis by Chainalysis points out, cybercriminals using cryptocurrencies have increased by 30% compared to 2020. Given this statistic, it seems that this activity is continuing to increase annually. Therefore, the aim of this research is to weigh up the speculative investments in cryptocurrency and consumer protection, focus on wider public interest, and analyze the regulatory regime of cryptoassets in the UK and whether they can be self-regulated.

Furthermore, the expansion of the cryptocurrency market provides new methods available for banking operations through developments of new banking products such as crypto-loans or better diversification of investment portfolios. However, there is a certain risk related to new banking businesses, which without proper regulation might lead to instability in the banking sector.

In this chapter, we will first analyze the development of this market by looking at the aspects of regulations. Secondly, we will investigate the problems cybercrimes pose to this market, especially regarding money laundering and other legal challenges in the UK, such as issues relating to data protection. Thirdly, we will look at the possible impact of cryptocurrency development on the banking sector, in the context of potential channels of this impact and risk related to banking services for consumers.

The Developments in the Cryptoassets Market

The cryptocurrency market began with Bitcoin at the beginning of 2009, and then gradually rose the of more than 100 different cryptocurrencies (Bratspies, 2018). In 2021, this market was worth USD 1.6 billion and is estimated to grow up to 2.2 billion by 2026, at a Compound Annual Growth Rate (CAGR) of 7.1 (Markets and Markets, 2022).

Nowadays, more than 500 cryptoasset trading platforms are operating, which allows trading crypto intermediates such as cryptoassets and cryptocurrencies. As previously mentioned, the most well-known trading platform is Bitcoin, and it is also worth noting that, as a medium of exchange, it is therefore arguable whether it could be a currency. Other examples of cryptocurrencies are Ethereum, Libra Coin, and Dogecoin, to name a few. Many of these cryptocurrencies have the following properties: no physical form, no legal tender, and are not currently backed by any government or legal entity (US congressional research service, 2021).

As the cryptocurrency market grew, a CME Bitcoin and CME Ether were developed. Both of these contacts are futures contact, where USD cash-settled is contracted on the Bitcoin or Ether reference rate. The

Cboe Options Exchange offered the first bitcoin futures contract in 2017. The Cboe Option is one of the largest US equity market operator on any given day. These contracts have a cash settlement on the Chicago Mercantile Exchange (CME), which means there is no need to have a Bitcoin wallet to cash this contract. In the other words, it is not necessary to have digital wallet to transfer Bitcoin into cash (Cboe Global Markets, 2017).

The one feature that is clearly visible for cryptocurrencies is that they can be volatile, which means that investing in them can be risky. For instance, the volatility of Bitcoin against the dollar on a Bitcoin exchange is about five to seven times the volatility of traditional foreign exchange trading (PwC, 2015). The analysis of the Bloomberg Galaxy Bitcoin Index (BTC index),[1] ETH index,[2] and Bloomberg Galaxy Crypto Index (BGCI Index)[3] confirms that these securities and assets are more volatile than the stock prices index (S&P 500 index) as presents in Fig. 9.1.

The global economy has drastically been affected by the COVID-19 pandemic due to the closing of numerous companies and the increased level of systematic risk in the economy. Nevertheless, the uncertainty raised by the COVID-19 pandemic has allowed cryptocurrencies to garner significant attention from investors and financial institutions.

An analysis of the correlation between the S&P 500 index and BGCI represented in Fig. 9.2 shows a significant increase in cryptocurrency demand, which is measured by the increase of prices in the Crypto Index. This increase was not only potential diversification of their investment portfolio but also a potential way of development for banks. Banks started creating own blockchain-based systems, in order to absorb more which enabled business-to-business (B2B) cryptocurrency payments operations between banks' customers (Markets and Markets, 2022). Moreover, in 2021, we noticed a significant increase in investors' interest as the exchange-traded fund (ETF) started to trade its first Bitcoin ETF. The ETF works as funds that trade on exchanges and mainly tracks a specific index. In other words, they operate similar to a mutual fund but they will track only certain indexes, sectors, or commodity or cryptocurrencies.

---

[1] Bloomberg Galaxy Bitcoin Index (BTC Index) is designed to measure the performance of Bitcoin trade in USD.

[2] The Bloomberg Galaxy Ethereum Index ('Index') is designed to measure the performance of Ethereum traded in USD.

[3] Bloomberg Galaxy Crypto Index (BCGI Index) is designed to measure the performance of the largest cryptocurrencies traded in USD.

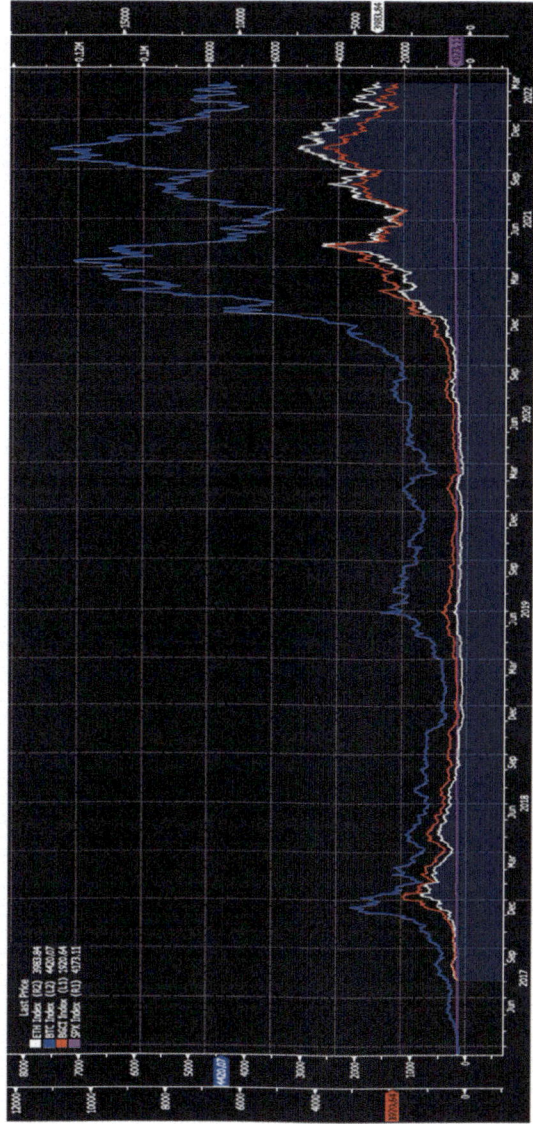

Fig. 9.1 S&P 500, BTC index, ETH index, and BGCI index performance over 5 years (*Note* SPX Index-S&P 500 Index, BGCI Index—Bloomberg Galaxy Crypto Index. *Source* Bloomberg)

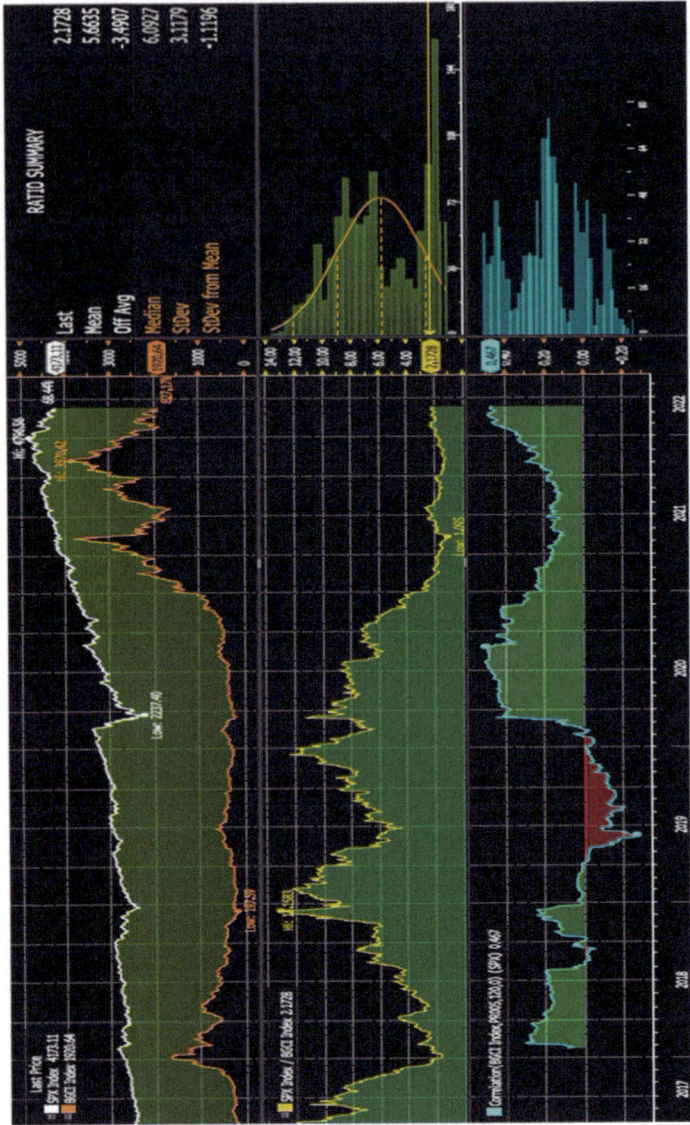

Fig. 9.2 The ratio between S&P 500 Index and BGCI over last 5 years (*Note* SPX index-S&P 500 index, BGCI index—Bloomberg Galaxy Crypto Index and SPX index/BGCI index. *Source* Bloomberg)

There is intense debate about why investors are using cryptoassets. According to the FCA's consumer research (2020), the main motivating reason for investing in cryptoassets is speculative. Their research shows 47% of UK cryptoasset consumers bought cryptocurrencies '*as a gamble*' and expected high returns, while 89% understood that there is not enough regulation in place to protect their investments. As the cryptoassets market is still in its infancy of development, it is not yet clear how this market will evolve but its growth appears to be rapid.

The element of decentralization in DLT means that there is no middleman such as a central bank, meaning there is no third party gathering a user's personal data. The DLT is based on public-key cryptography, meaning that communication with third parties is secure. One of the main developments of cryptocurrencies is the creation of smart contracts, which use a computer code that facilitates the exchange of cryptoassets on the blockchain. A smart contract enforces the relationship with cryptographic code compared to a standard contract, outlining a legal relationship's terms. This also means that if someone forgets their password to their digital wallet, access to their digital wallet account and its cryptoassets would unfortunately also be lost. What can therefore be observed is that if something goes wrong, the consumer cannot be offered protection by the FCA (FSCS, 2021; Rodgers, 2022).

It can likewise be observed that the regulatory regime around businesses dealing with cryptocurrency is tightening. Without a doubt, this trend intends to protect consumers and investors. However, it also questionable as to how the dynamic of businesses dealing with cryptocurrency-related services is changing and where they are heading. There are numerous discussions about whether this market self-regulate if regulations need to be imposed by FCA. Another important concern which we will discuss later in this chapter is that this crypto-system can also be exploited by criminals as a medium for money laundering. Moreover, we will look at what is the impact of cryptocurrency development on the banking industry and exposure to cryptocurrency risk.

The Regulation Landscape of the Cryptoassets Market

The Reasons for the Regulations

Authorities around the globe are looking into how they can control the cryptoassets market and are facing challenges in achieving this. One of the key questions being asked is how effective these regulations can be and on what level they can be implemented.

Currently, national authorities—such as HM Treasury, the Bank of England, and FCA—can make decisions about fiscal, monetary, and foreign exchange policies that affect the integrity of currencies. However, it is not possible for these authorities to control the cryptocurrencies of many crypto markets, as they are more decentralized than conventional trust-based intermediary systems.

There are several reasons why authorities want to implement regulations on crypto markets, including fighting money laundering, combating the financing of terrorism, ensuring investor and consumer protections, and combating tax evasion. Cryptocurrencies can also be highly volatile posing a risk for consumers. It is, therefore, important for authorities to catch up with the challenges and changes of this market, for instance, the development of new services such as stablecoins. Stablecoins are pegged to national currencies which provides stability and can enhance the use of cryptocurrencies in the certain markets. To this end, the UK government currently plans to legislate stablecoins with a view to '(..) make UK a global cryptoassets technology hub' (gov.uk).

In March 2018 the UK's Financial Policy Committee (FPC) Statement it was emphasized that 'the existing cryptoassets (...) do not currently pose a material risk to UK financial stability.' However, in the same statement by FPC it was also mentioned that cryptoassets can nevertheless raise 'public policy concerns' as they do not provide protection to these investing in them and can be used for criminal activities such as 'money laundering or terrorism financing.' This meant that the decisions could not be made at the central level and required a network of stakeholders to achieve consensus. Due to the risks linked with the use of cryptoassets, the Cryptoassets Taskforce was created in March 2018 with the aim to 'maintains the UK's international reputation as a safe and transparent place to do business in financial services; ensures high regulatory standards *in financial markets; protects consumers; guards against threats to finan-cial stability that could emerge in the future; and allows those innovators in the financial sector that play by the rules to thrive'* (Cryptoassets Taskforce Report, 2018).

What Regulations Exist Thus Far?

In the UK, the Cryptoassets Taskforce Report (2018) aimed to set out regulatory challenges in relation to cryptoassets. In so doing, three categories of cryptoassets were identified:

1. Exchange Tokens—used as a means of exchange and for investment (i.e., Bitcoin or another cryptocurrency).
2. Security Tokens—used as a capital-raising tool and for investments. They are considered as 'specified investments' in the Financial Services and Markets Act 2000 (FSMA) Regulated Activities Order 2001 (RAO) and provide for certain rights (i.e., bonds, warranties, or shares in a property).
3. Utility Tokens—as with Security Tokens, these are used as a capital-raising tool and for investments, but Utility Tokens can also be exchanged for access to a service or a product (i.e., to use the software).

When writing this chapter, the UK had yet to enact any legislation specifically designed to regulate cryptocurrency, although there are currently plans to legislate stablecoins. As such, the legislative measures which are currently applied to financial services and financial markets are also applied to cryptocurrency. The FCA is a key player as a supervisor of the conduct of financial service providers. For example, security tokens fall under FSMA RAO and may also fall under the second Markets in Financial Instruments Directive (MiFID II); E-money tokens fall under the Electronic Money Regulations 2011. However, since there is no cryptocurrency-specific legislation at the time this chapter is written, the currently applied measures are predominantly focused on combating money laundering. Undoubtedly, in its attempt to eliminate criminal activities and money laundering, the current regulation applied to financial services and financial markets (which is also being applied to cryptoassets) does offer protection to both consumers and investors.

However, consumer who has invested in cryptoassets which are not security tokens or e-money (therefore classed as unregulated cryptoassets) can be left with little or no possibility of redress if they lose their money.

Interestingly, although there is no specific legislation dealing with cryptocurrency, there has been some development through case law recognizing the status of cryptoassets (i.e., through acknowledging that cryptocurrency could be a form of property to seek injunction, case *AA v. Persons Unknown* [2019]).

What Is Regulated and What Is Unregulated?

The financial market operation falls under already mentioned FSMA RAO and MiFID II. FSMA simply defines regulated activity as that which is 'of the specified kind which is carried on by way of business and—(a) relates to an investment of a specified kind; or (b) in the case of an activity of a kind which is also specified for the purposes of this paragraph, is carried on in relation to property of any kind' (Financial Services and Markets Act, 2000).

When considering cryptocurrencies, the FCA's position is that utility tokens and exchange tokens are unregulated, while security tokens are regulated. That means that cryptocurrencies do not fall within FSMA's definition of specific investment. Despite that, the FCA decided to curb the cryptocurrency business. In 2018, it indicated that cryptocurrency derivatives (including futures, options, and contracts for difference referring to cryptocurrencies) do fall within the meaning of financial instruments under MiFID II. The FCA's decision means that the business needs to register (and obtain authorization under FSMA) any business providing or dealing with cryptocurrency derivatives or related services. Moreover, in 2019, the FCA published policy statement PS19/22, entitled Guidance on Cryptoassets: Feedback and Final Guidance to CP 19/3. This guidance describes three core categories of tokens: (1) e-money tokens, (2) security tokens, and (3) unregulated tokens. Within this guidance, the FCA also published a warning list of known firms running scams in an effort to warn consumers about cryptoasset scams. Furthermore, the Fifth Anti-Money Laundering Directive (5AMLD) discusses custodian wallet providers and cryptoasset exchange providers in the context of anti-money laundering and counter-terrorist financing regulation. In 2021, the FCA banned the sale, marketing, and distribution of derivatives and exchange-traded notes that reference unregulated, and transferable cryptoassets.

It cannot be denied that there is significant progress being made in regard to the regulation of the cryptoasset market. However, it will take time to observe the effectiveness of these regulations as this market is extremely dynamic.

Regulatory and Some Legal Challenges

Given that cryptocurrency is relatively new to the financial markets, it has met with several legal and regulatory challenges. Here, we discuss issues of data protection, intellectual property law, legal jurisdiction, and cybercrimes.

Concerning data protection, storing data on a blockchain raises many questions, such as who is responsible for protecting that data and complying with the UK General Data Protection Regulation (UK GDPR). Blockchain transactions are transparent by nature and any transaction entered onto a blockchain identifies every user by a so-called public key. Although personal data is not included in the public key, the transaction itself can be viewed by the public key. There is, therefore, no obvious data controller to ensure that data is in compliance with the regulation. In the usual GDPR context, there is either a commercial or public controller of the personal data. This does not apply to information stored in the blockchain system as this information is only limited to public key and distributed across the whole network of given cryptocurrency, providing each user with equal access to the available information.

Another challenge facing cryptocurrency relates to the intellectual property (IP) law. Although using a blockchain is secure, especially in terms of user's anonymity, and is often used as a tool for IP protection, the legal status of data stored on blockchains has not been firmly defined at this point. The main concerns are currently raised about the content encrypted and distributed with the use of blockchains. A typical question would be whether each node holding the entire copy of the blockchain is legally responsible for the content of the blockchain. If blockchain is used for IP infringement, does it make all nodes complacent in facilitating this infringement?

Furthermore, there have also been challenges in relation to jurisdictional issues due to the decentralized nature of cryptocurrency, as well as questions about the legal status of decentralized autonomous organizations (DAO) that are used to record the activity on a blockchain and to execute smart contracts.

The biggest concern and most substantial challenge to cryptoassets, however, are cybercrimes and money laundering.

As previously mentioned, cybercriminals using cryptocurrencies have increased by 30% in comparison with 2020, a rate that continues to increase (Chainalysis, 2022). This might be due to the anonymity cryptocurrency provides for cybercriminals. Moreover, as most crypto exchanges and virtual asset service providers currently operate under less regulated norms and allow for faster transfers across borders, these attributes may encourage cybercriminals. However, this also begs the question, as to whether the current regulatory regime in the UK is sufficient to protect the public interest.

Cybercrimes and Cryptosystems: What Is the Definition of Money Laundering?

In the UK, it is illegal to process or clean 'dirty' money, which is any money generated from criminal activities, such as drug trafficking, terrorist funding, or other illegal activities, and by injecting them into the legitimate financial system. The main concern here is the source of the 'dirty' money, and to remain undetected, criminals find ways to circumvent the system by using a series of financial transactions and bookkeeping tricks to make this money legitimate.[4]

Money laundering is done in various ways, from smurfing electronic forms to the use of cryptocurrencies. Traditionally, smurfing was used to divide large chunks of money into small deposits which were then spread between different accounts, often by using currency exchanges and cash smugglers to move this money across borders and into banks abroad. With advancements in technology, especially the growth of the internet, new electronic methods to 'clean' money now exist through the use of proxy servers, online auctions, and virtual gambling.

The newest form of money laundering happens using cryptocurrencies. Like cash-based money laundering, the process of money laundering

---

[4] The financial transactions are followed by smurfing, invoices frauds, offshore accounts, carrying small sums of cash abroad, and aborted transactions.

via the use of cryptocurrency has three stages: placement, layering, and integration.

In the first stage, the 'dirty' money is put into the financial system, using cryptocurrencies. In the second stage, they use structured transactions to make it difficult to decode the actual source of the funds. This is known as layering and often involves the use of an Initial Coin Offering (ICO). The third stage is integration, which is when the illegal money is transferred as 'clean' money. Here, criminals use over-the-counter brokers who are responsible for the medium of exchange between buyers and sellers of cryptocurrencies. In the next section, we discuss the ways in which cryptocurrencies are being used for money laundering.

The Cryptocurrency Methods of Money Laundering

These are four identifiable techniques being used to legitimize 'dirty' money through cryptocurrency transactions: (1) crypto mixing (tumblers), (2) P2P crypto networks, (3) crypto ATMs, and (4) online gambling. As these methods are based on the use of the crypto exchanges and virtual asset service providers operating with significantly less regulatory scrutiny and therefore allow for them to easily circumvent international borders compared to the traditional methods of money laundering.

Crypto tumblers are a technique used to conduct mixed transactions of different cryptocurrencies between two clients using different IP addresses or crypto wallets, resulting in 'clean' cryptocurrency.

Secondly, P2P networks are also used. A P2P network is a decentralized network that allows the transmission of money from one location to another, where the use of crypto exchanges is legal for the use of exchanging funds.

The third technique is the use of crypto ATMs. Using these machines, clients can trade digital currencies using credit and debit cards, with the option to deposit cash.

Lastly, online gambling is the fourth technique used to launder money. Some online gambling platforms allow clients to use cryptocurrency to purchase chips and exchange them for money.

Money Laundering Regulations in the UK

In December 2021, the FCA announced an amendment to the current Money Laundering Regulations, first introduced on 10 January 2020. This new amendment provides two key updates: the first relates to the existing cryptoassets market in the UK. As of January 2020, every cryptoasset business must be compliant with the Money Laundering, Terrorist Financial, and Transfer of Funds Regulations of 2017. The second change is linked to new businesses in the cryptoassets market, requiring each of them to be registered with the FCA before beginning or conducting new business. The FCA has also created a Temporary Registration Regime (TRR) for existing cryptoasset businesses up to 31 March 2022. If a business is on this TRR list, it implies that this business meets the requirements of Money Laundering Regulations.

Importantly, this regulation defines the scope of cryptoassets activities which must be analyzed in respect to the money laundering activities. Therefore, in essence, this regulation mainly exists to provide transparency of cryptoasset transfers and to conduct their business by using these new digital currencies.

In 2021, the FCA banned the sale, marketing, and distribution of derivatives and exchange-traded notes that reference unregulated, and transferable cryptoassets.

Scope of Cryptoasset Activities

Cryptoasset businesses are divided in two groups: cryptoasset exchange providers and Custodian Wallet Providers. The first group includes cryptoasset ATMs, P2P providers, businesses issuing new cryptoassets such as Initial Coin Offering (ICO) and Initial Exchange Offering. The second group includes firms or sole practitioners who carry out business on behalf of cryptoasset customers and provide private cryptographic keys to store and transfer cryptoassets (FCA, 2019).

The EU Perspective on Regulating Cryptoassets

The EU is on track to regulate cryptoassets and thus attempt to harmonize the market. The EU's parliament has recently agreed on the Markets in Crypto-Assets (MiCA) law which will come into effect in 2023. MiCA is a first European wide regulation for cryptoassets and will contain provisions focusing on consumers protection and the providers of cryptoassets services will be liable if '*if they loose investors' cryptoassets*' (Consilium. europa.eu, Digital finance agreement reached on European cryptoassets regulation mica 2022). MiCA comes as a response to tackle what has been referred to as a '*Wild West of cryptoassets*' by Berger (Euronews, July 2022). To that extend, the UK's new Financial Services Bill is following the EU's footsteps to regulate cryptoassets.

The Cryptocurrency Impact on the UK Banking Sector

In the last decade, the increase and phenomenal growth of cryptocurrencies raise important questions about their footprint on the banking sector. Even though the crypto market grows at an incredible pace, the exposure to cryptocurrencies was less than 0.02% of the banks' total risk-weighted assets, on average with the maximum exposure at about 0.05% according to BIS standards in 2021 (Auer, Farag, et al., 2022).

However, as the BIS data shows there are five main headquartered centers around the world in regard to cryptocurrency exposure, located in Canada, France, South Korea, the UK, and the United States (Auer, Holti, et al., 2022). The UK is one of the main leading centers, which includes banks that would appear well positioned to leverage on existing infrastructure and governance structures to establish a robust custodial network to facilitate trading in cryptocurrencies Fig. 9.3.

According to the Crypto Market Sizing Report (2022), global crypto owners are 300 million and by the end of 2022, it might be 1 billion. The banks see a huge potential in this market, and it is visible, UK high-street banks are integrating crypto solutions into their systems, and we can see a trend in crypto-friendly banks (see Table 9.1 for the year 2021). Most high-street banks in the UK have opened up transactions in cryptocurrency apart from HSBC and TSB banks. It appears most of the restrictions were imposed mainly to allow clients to purchase cryptoassets directly from cryptocurrency trading platforms, such as Binance, Kraken, Kucoin, and Coinbase.

However, in the middle of 2021, the FCA reported that around £60 million was lost due to social media investment scams 2020. Partly in relation to this, a ban was against Binance Markets Ltd which had operated as a cryptocurrency trading platform. And as a result, UK banks

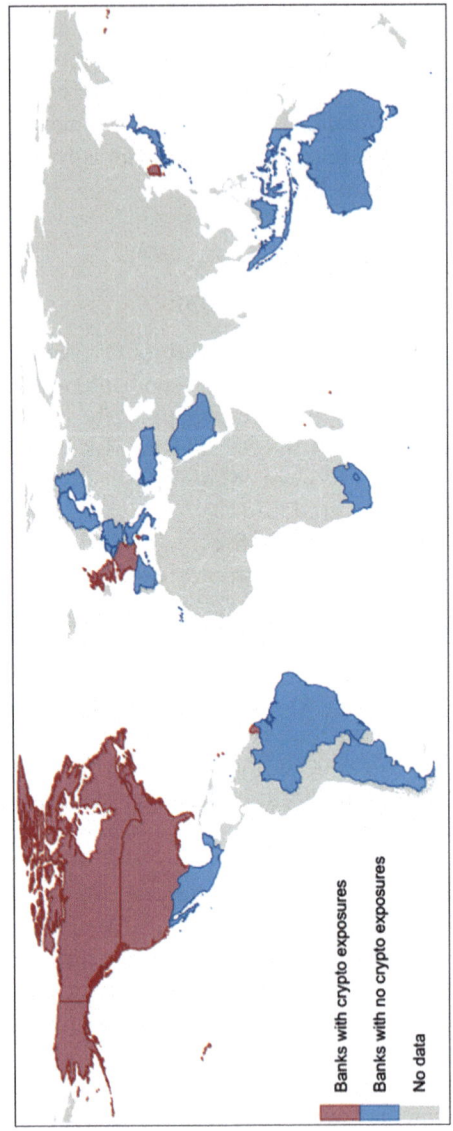

Fig. 9.3 Cryptocurrencies' exposure in the banking sector (*Note* The use of this map does not constitute, and should not be construed as constituting, an expression of a position by the BIS regarding the legal status of, or sovereignty to authorities, to the delimitation of international frontiers and boundaries, and/or to the name and designation of any territory, city, or area. Countries where banks reported having cryptocurrency exposures (red) or having no or only minimal exposures (blue) for the combined end-2018, end-2019, and end-2020 collection periods. Banks in BCBS jurisdictions that did not participate in the data-collection exercise on cryptocurrencies and non-BCBS jurisdictions are highlighted in gray. *Source* Auer, Farag, et al. [2022, p. 12])

have decided to stop customers from making payments to crypto trading platforms (Bank of England, 2022a, 2022b). Tables 9.1 and 9.2 present a comparison of two years showing the changes in bank cryptocurrency operations. Now, bank account holders are advised to invest in cryptocurrency by eToro. which is a regulated cryptocurrency exchange by the FCA in the UK (Bank of England, 2022a, 2022b).

As it can be seen the cryptocurrency development exposure to the banking sector through direct and indirect channels. Table 9.3 presents a possible interlinkage with the traditional banking sector.

The exposure to the cryptocurrency ecosystem uses a multitude of direct channels in its interlinkage to the traditional banking sector.

The first channel is related to payment and exchange. Banks can be involved in delivering currency-trading services or/and crypto-enabled digital payments and transactions; furthermore, banks can allow account owners to use credit and debit cards that they have issued without restrictions for trading in crypto. Usually, exchanges generally accept a wide range of payments and can be administrator-affiliated, non-affiliated, or a third-party provider.

Table 9.1 UK Banks and their cryptocurrency exposure in July 2021

	Debit purchases	Credit purchases	Transaction/Exchange	Coinbase collaboration
Barclays	Always	Always	Not always	Not always
HSBC	Prohibited	Prohibited	Prohibited	Prohibited
Royal Bank of Scotland (RBS)	Always	Always	Always	Always
Nationwide	Always	Prohibited	Always	Always
Lloyds Bank	Prohibited	Not Always	Not Always	Prohibited
NatWest	Prohibited	Prohibited	Always	Always
Santander	Always	Always	Not always	Not always
TSB	Prohibited	Prohibited	Prohibited	Prohibited
Standard Chartered Bank	Not always	Not always	Always	Prohibited
The Co-operative Bank	Always	Always	Always	Always

Notes Always: There are not any major issues with making crypto-related transactions, Not always: There are a number of issues making crypto-related transactions with this bank, Prohibited: No crypto-related transactions allow

Source My own analysis based on cryptobuyersclub.co.uk, https://www.indieinvestor.co.uk, Binance. com, Circle.com, Bitcoin.com

Table 9.2   UK Banks and their cryptocurrency exposure in July 2022

	Debit purchases	*Credit purchases*	*Transaction/Exchange*	*Coinbase collaboration*
Barclays	Always	Always	Not always	Under Review
HSBC	Prohibited	Prohibited	Prohibited	Prohibited
Royal Bank of Scotland (RBS)	Always	Always	Always	Prohibited
Nationwide	Always	Prohibited	Always	Under Review
Lloyds Bank	Prohibited	Not Always	Not Always	Under Review
NatWest	Prohibited	Prohibited	Always	Under Review
Santander	Always	Always	Not always	Prohibited
TSB	Prohibited	Prohibited	Prohibited	Prohibited
Standard Chartered Bank	Prohibited	Prohibited	Always	Prohibited
The Co-operative Bank	Always	Always	Always	Prohibited

Notes Always: There are not any major issues with making crypto-related transactions, Not always: There are a number of issues making crypto-related transactions with this bank, Prohibited: No crypto-related transactions allow
Source My own analysis based on cryptobuyersclub.co.uk, https://www.indieinvestor.co.uk, Binance. com, Circle.com, Bitcoin.com

Table 9.3   The pattern of direct and indirect channels of crypto-system in the banking industry

Direct channel	*Indirect channel*
Payments and exchange Investment, deposits, and trading Lending	Cryptoassets operators Wallet providers Crypto custodial Competitions: Crypto banks, P2P lenders, MPLs, crypto lending platforms Crypto decentralization Cryptocurrency technology (Blockchain, Smart Contracts) Impact on real economy balance sheets

Source My own analysis based on LeBlanc (2016), Bank of England (2020), BCG White&Case (2020), Panetta (2021a, 2021b), Cong and Mayer (2021), Auer, Holti, et al. (2022), Auer, Farag, et al. (2022), KPMG (2020a, 2020b)

According to Auer, Holti, et al. (2022), Bank of England (2021), and Panetta (2021a, 2021b), there are three types of exchanges:

1. Central-bank digital currencies (CBDCs) issued by national financial authorities
2. Private blockchain-based currencies from a bank/company
3. Network-issued currencies with a public blockchain, such as Bitcoin or Litecoin.

Many central banks such as the Bank of England and ECB are looking into the creation of central bank digital currencies; however, so far there are no real implementations (Bank of England, 2021; Panetta, 2021a). One of these examples of a private blockchain-based currency is Onyx JP Morgan Coin in 2019. It is a digital currency set against the dollar, run on the structure of a blockchain called Quorum. It is an internal system, which is similar to the public blockchain currency network (Crosman, 2022). Another case is Ripple connect which allows for the synchronized movement of two different currencies across two different real-time gross settlement systems that are linked to 100 banks.[5] 38% of the world's top 100 banks was linked to Ripple (Bank of England, 2022b; S&P Global Market Intelligence, 2019). To process these network-issued currency transactions, traditional banks have collaborated with cryptocurrency-trading platforms, such as Binance, Kraken, Kucoin, and Coinbase. As the table above has pointed out, there are several crypto-ready banks in the UK. One of these banks is Barclays, one of the oldest and largest banks in the UK so-called crypto-friendly banks. For instance, Barclays has an official banking partner for Coinbase; however, in August 2019, this collaboration was ended due to the lack of the right systems being in place to prevent money laundering (Reuters, 2019).

To continue the cryptocurrency transaction one solution was to create cryptocurrency custodians (Custody) for traditional banks. The crypto-custodian's main job is to protect the private key used to access the cryptocurrencies and make certain that investors are able to gain access to their funds held in crypto wallets (CoinDesk, 2022; KPMG, 2020a, 2020b). Figure 9.4 explains the process of the crypto-custodian.

---

[5] More information regarding Ripple network is available https://www.xrparcade.com/world-top-100-banks/.

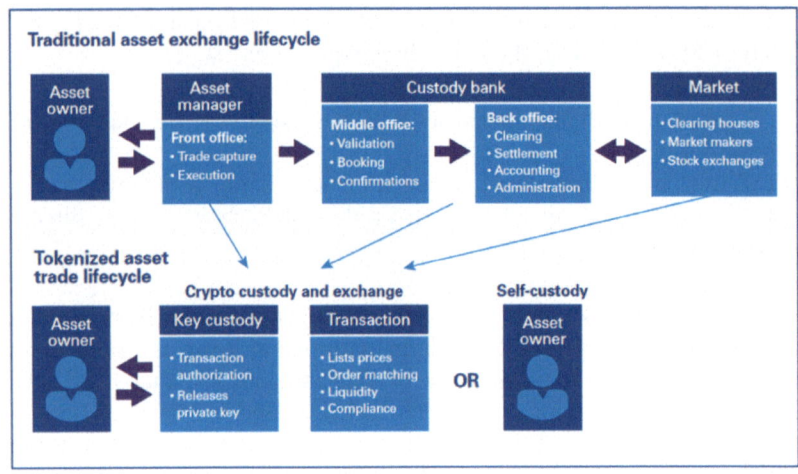

Fig. 9.4   The process of the crypto-custodian (*Source* KPMG [2020b, p. 5])

In 2020, the investment arm of Standard Chartered Bank which is Standard Chartered Ventures (SCV) creates a custodial service called Zodia. It is officially partnered with Northern Trust. This service allows for the provision of investments and transactions in Bitcoin, Ethereum, Bitcoin Cash, Litecoin, and Ripple (Wilfred, 2020).

The second direct channel Investment, Deposits, and Trading is strictly linked to crypto custody which allows for investment in cryptocurrencies. Apart from investing in cryptocurrencies, there are more variety of assets, such as cryptoassets derivatives, cryptoassets exchange-traded funds, and stable coins. Another option is to invest in the initial coin offering (ICOs) for large retail banks to get involved in.

The third direct channel is lending through crypto-collateralized loans. In April 2022, Goldman Sachs had a partnership with Coinbase to create bitcoin-backed loans. These loans allowed Bitcoin holders to borrow fiat currency such as dollars against Bitcoin as collateral to the bank. These crypto-collateralized loans are not only delivered by financial institutions, such as Goldman Sachs but also to crypto lending platforms, such as BlockFi, Nexo, and Celsius. These crypto users can pledge against the other fiat currencies (Dollars or Euros) or other stablecoins (USDT, USDC) on these platforms (Bloomberg UK, 2022).

The Leading is another indirect channel of the cryptocurrency ecosystem's impact on the banking sector. The development of cryptocurrencies creates a new lending ecosystem that includes P2P lenders and Marketplace lenders (MPLs), wallet providers, crypto banks, cryptoasset operators, and cryptocurrency lending platforms. These new lending and finance providers bring new methods of delivering various new lending products. Ended up in the creation of crypto banks, such as Kraken, Avanti, and Custodia. These banks include cryptocurrency banking and investment applications. These applications also allow bank account users to gain unlimited access to process transactions through the usage of digital assets, compared cryptocurrency wallets and crypto banks usually have federally insured bank accounts and use prepaid debit cards in addition to their cryptocurrency wallets. As these new players appear in the cryptocurrency ecosystem, they provide additional competition in the banking sector and can affect the real-time balance sheet position of the banks (Bank of England, 2022a, 2022b).

The last important indirect impact on traditional banks is the utilization of technology behind cryptocurrencies, such as DLT, blockchain, and smart contracts. The deploying DLTs and blockchain can be done from either front or back-office operations, making banking transactions more reliable. Blockchain technologies can also be used to set up smart-contract offerings, with automated time stamps, updates, and verification of milestones (KPMG, 2020a, b; LeBlanc, 2016).

The significant and rapid progress of the cryptocurrency ecosystem in the banking and financial sector shows that there are significant crypto-risks. These risks are listed in Table 9.4.

According to BCG, White&Case (2020), these are the following possible solutions in practicing due diligence for these risks, banks can mainly rely on three types of solutions:

– Know your transaction (KYT)
– Structured regulatory compliance (SRC)
– Custodian services.

Figure 9.5 explains each of these solutions in detail.

Table 9.4   Cryptocurrency risk and banking industry

Type of risk	Descriptions of the risk and its impact on the banking sector
Cryptos' volatility	The cryptocurrencies price is unstable in the medium and long term. In this case, the underlying volatility of cryptocurrencies can make crypto-collateralized loans risky When the price of cryptocurrencies declines significantly, the borrower may be required to increase their collateral which can be transferred into liquidity problems
Cryptos' decentralization	Decentralizing cryptocurrencies and cryptoassets seem to undermine the central banks' authority The lack of supervision over the cryptocurrency ecosystem can lead to the flow of investors with a low credit score which can destabilize the system in the future and affect the position of the real economy lenience sheets of financial institutions. Also, it is not easy to implement Know Your Customer (KYC) regulations. This could lead to coins' transactions that could be used in scams and illegal activities, illicit trade, tax evasion, financing terrorist activities, and money laundering
Increase in illegal activities: – Wash trading – Dead coins	As Cong and Mayer (2021) have pointed out the problems of 'wash trading.' According to the research on average, 70% of the reported volumes on unregulated crypto exchanges are to simultaneously trade the same financial cryptocurrencies used to inflate volumes and prices Also, there is the case of 'dead coins,[6]' it is at around 2,000 cryptocurrencies according to Coinopsy

Source My analysis based on BCG, While&Case (2020), Panetta (2021a, 2021b), Cong and Mayer (2021), Bank of England (2022a, 2022b), Auer, Holti, et al. (2022), Auer, Farag, et al. (2022), KPMG (2020b)

CONCLUSION

The development of cryptoassets has happened at a lightning pace in the past decade, moving from the simple digital medium of exchange to being implemented as a form of payment in official banking systems. However,

---

[6] The 'dead coins' is defined as cryptocurrencies that have been abandoned, are used as scam, whose website is down, have no nodes, have wallet issues, do not have social updates, have low volume, or whose developers have walked away from the project.

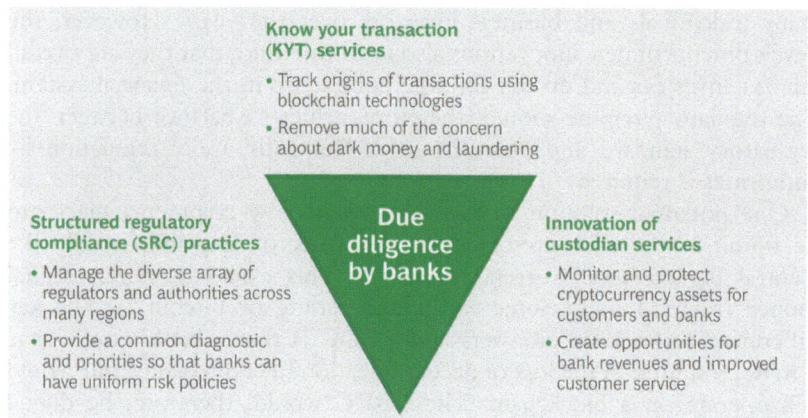

Fig. 9.5 Possible solutions in practicing due diligence for Cryptocurrency risk (*Source* BCG, While&Case [2020, p. 9])

this new digital investing provides a new environment for developing cybercrimes and the abuse of the existing system.

The regulatory regime in the UK is mainly administered through the FCA. Although the regime has clearly been tightened, including registration requirements for cryptoassets firms, it appears that cybercrime is still on the rise (Chainalysis, 2022). It is, therefore, difficult to predict where the development of cryptocurrency is heading (Joint Statement from UK financial regulatory authorities on sanctions and cryptoassets sector, 2022).

When trying to answer the question as to whether self-regulation is possible by looking at the UK's experience, several aspects need to be addressed. As a starting point, we should ascertain what self-regulation is. M. Finck (2019, p. 169) concludes that 'self-regulation ... refers to a situation in which regulation is devised through the collaboration of private actors with no or little involvement from the state.' It is difficult to imagine this would be possible when considering the UK's perspective. Given the volatile nature of the cryptocurrency market, the lack of protection for the consumer involved in cryptocurrency transactions, as well as overall challenges from various legal aspects and general public interest, it is doubtful that self-regulation would be sufficient. Cryptoassets are a type of innovation that have been widely discussed and one which has attracted many individuals and business investors over the years. However, the developments of new innovations also need to ensure that they are overall safe for investors and do not infringe confidence in the financial system. The regulatory regime should, therefore, achieve a balance between the regulatory standard and potential risks. Currently, more regulation by authorities is required.

One potential solution to problems created by cryptocurrencies can be found in the idea presented by the Bank of England, mainly the Central Bank Digital Currency (CBDC). This would be purely digital money (referred to by some as 'digital sterling or Bitcoin'[7]). The key difference between cryptoassets and CBDC is that a bank would issue CBDC, resulting in the loss of decentralization of cryptoassets, but would still operate on a blockchain. The CBDC would, therefore, be digital money issued by the Bank of England in the UK which would keep the element of innovation and offer protection to the consumers. It would also allow for more efficiency in terms of making payments (Bank of England, 2022a, 2022b) and meet the demands of consumers in digital age. Another possibility to help with the issues surrounding cryptoassets is the introduction of Financial Services Bill by the UK government in order to 'enhance competitiveness of the financial services sector' (gov.uk). The Bill is being introduced to the parliament at the time of writing this article and includes provisions on safe use of cryptoassets to promote stability of the use of stablecoins. This solution can help reduce the crypto-risk for the banking sector, which now is quite a significant for banks that use Coinbase transactions.

REFERENCES

BOOKS

Armstrong, D., Hyde, D., & Thomas, S. (2019). *Blockchain and cryptocurrency: International legal and regulatory challenges*. Bloomsbury Professional Ltd.
Finck, M. (2019). *Blockchain regulation and governance in Europe*. Cambridge University Press.

---

[7] UK central bank digital currency at https://www.bankofengland.co.uk/research/dig ital-currencies.

Articles/Papers/Blogs

Auer, R., Farag, M., Lewrick, U., Orazem, L., & Zoss, M. (2022, May). *Banking in the shadow of Bitcoin? The institutional adoption of cryptocurrencies Monetary and Economic Department* (BIS Working Papers, No. 1013).

Auer, R., Holti, B., Yaa Boakye-Adjei, N., Faragallah, A., Frost, J., Natarajan, H., & Prenio, J. (2022). *Central bank digital currencies: A new tool in the financial inclusion toolkit?* (FSI Insights on Policy Implementation, No. 41).

Bank of England. (2020). *Central bank digital currency opportunities, challenges and design.* https://www.bankofengland.co.uk/-/media/boe/files/paper/2020/central-bank-digital-currencyopportunities-challenges-and-design.pdf

Bank of England. (2021). *UK central bank digital currency.* https://www.bankofengland.co.uk/research/digital-currencies

Bank of England. (2022a). *Financial stability in Focus crypto assets and decentralized finance, Financial Policy Committee.* https://www.bankofengland.co.uk/financial-stability-in-focus/2022/march-2022

Bank of England. (2022b). *Fintech Accelerator Proof of Concept. Ripple-exploring the synchronized settlements of payments using the Interledger Protocol.* https://www.bankofengland.co.uk/research/fintech/proofs-of-concept/ripple

BCG, White&Case. (2020). *How banks can succeed with cryptocurrency.* https://web-assets.bcg.com/e4/ee/793e01364af79789bf26c5690b36/bcg-how-banks-can-succeed-with-cryptocurrency-nov-2020.pdf

Bloomberg UK. (2022). *Goldman offered its first Bitcoin-backed loan in crypto Push.* https://www.bloomberg.com/news/articles/2022-04-28/goldman-offers-its-first-bitcoin-backed-loan-in-crypto-push#xj4y7vzkg

Bratspies, R. M. (2018, March). *Cryptocurrencies and the myth of the trustless transaction.* https://ssrn.com/abstract=3141605

CBoe Global Markets. (2017). *Cboe plans December 10 launch of bitcoin futures trading.* https://ir.cboe.com/news-andevents/2017/12-04-2017/cboe-plans-december-10-launch-bitcoin-futures-trading

Central Bank Digital Currencies, Bank of England. https://www.bankofengland.co.uk/research/digital-currencies

Chainalysis. (2022). *Crime and NFTs: Chainalysis detects significant wash trading and some money laundering in this emerging asset class.* https://blog.chainalysis.com/reports/2022-crypto-crime-report-preview-nft-wash-trading-money-laundering/

CoinDesk. (2022). *What is crypto custody?* https://www.coindesk.com/learn/what-is-crypto-custody/

Cong, L. W., & Mayer, S. (2021). *The coming battle of digital currencies.* First Draft: December 2021; Current Draft: February 2022.

CPMI. (2015, November). *Digital currencies.* https://www.bis.org/cpmi/publ/d137.pdf

Crosman, P. (2022). How JPMorgan is developing an internet of money. *American Banker*. https://www.americanbanker.com/news/how-jpmorgan-is-developing-an-internet-of-money

Cryptoassets Taskforce Report. (2018, October). https://assets.publishing.service.gov.uk/government/uploads/system/uploads/attachment_data/file/752070/cryptoassets_taskforce_final_report_final_web.pdf

Crypto Market Sizing Report. (2022). crypto.com. https://crypto.com/research/2021-crypto-market-sizing-report-2022-forecast

Douglas, L., & Clifford Chance. (2021). The virtual currency regulation review: United Kingdom. *The Law Review*. https://thelawreviews.co.uk/title/the-virtual-currency-regulation-review/united-kingdom#footnote-009-backlink

Elliott and De Lima. (2018). https://www.oliverwyman.com/our-expertise/insights/2018/oct/crypto-assets.html

Euronews. (2022, July). *EU agrees on landmark crypto regulation in wake of Terra meltdown and Bitcoin plunge*. Retrieved from EU agrees on landmark crypto regulation in wake of Terra meltdown and Bitcoin plunge | Euronews.

European Council, Council of the EU. (2022, June). *Digital finance: Agreement reached on European crypto-assets regulation (MiCA)*. Retrieved from Digital finance: Agreement reached on European crypto-assets regulation (MiCA)—Consilium (europa.eu).

FCA. (2019). *Cryptoassets: AML/CTF regime*. https://www.fca.org.uk/firms/financial-crime/cryptoassets-aml-ctf-regime

Financial Committee Policy Statement. (2018, March 16). https://www.bankofengland.co.uk/-/media/boe/files/statement/fpc/2018/financial-policy-committee-statement-march-2018.pdf?la=en&hash=61059A79F4453B2EFA6BA88A598739DD67FC0CD7

Financial Services Bill to unlock growth and investment in the UK. https://www.gov.uk/government/news/financial-services-bill-to-unlock-growth-and-investment-across-the-uk

FSCS. (2021). *Five things to consider about cryptoassets*. https://www.fscs.org.uk/news/protection/cryptocurrencies-risk-cover/

Guide to the UK General Data Protection Regulation (GDPR). Information Commissioner's Office. https://ico.org.uk/for-organisations/guide-to-data-protection/guide-to-the-general-data-protection-regulation-gdpr/

Government sets out plan to make UK a global cryptoasset technology hub. https://www.gov.uk/government/news/government-sets-out-plan-to-make-uk-a-global-cryptoasset-technology-hub

Joint Statement from UK financial regulatory authorities on sanctions and cryptoassets sector. (2022). *Financial Conduct Authority*. www.gca.org.uk/news/statements/uk-financial-regulatory-authorities-sanctions-cryptoasset-sector

KPMG. (2020a). *Institutionalization of crypto assets. Crypto assets have arrived. Are you ready for institutionalization.* https://assets.kpmg/content/dam/ kpmg/us/pdf/2018/11/institutionalization-cryptoassets.pdf

KPMG. (2020b). *Cracking crypto custody.* https://advisory.kpmg.us/articles/ 2020b/cracking-crypto-custody.html

LeBlanc, G. (2016). *The effects of cryptocurrencies on the banking industry and monetary policy.* https://core.ac.uk/download/pdf/268097027.pdf

Mandeng, O. J. (2019, 4th draft). *Basic Principles for regulating Cryptoassets.* London School of Economics. https://www.lse.ac.uk/iga/assets/docume nts/research-and-publications/Cryptocurrencies-and-monetary-and-financial-regulation-4.pdf

Markets and Markets. (2022). *Market research report.* https://www.marketsan dmarkets.com/Market-Reports/cryptocurrency-market-158061641.html

Panetta, F. (2021a, November 5). *Central bank digital currencies: A monetary anchor for digital innovation.* Speech at the Elcano Royal Institute.

Panetta, F. (2021b, February). *Evolution or revolution? The impact of a digital euro on the financial system.* Speech at a Breugel online seminar; Bank for International Settlements (2021).

Publication of the Cryptoassets Taskforce Report. (2018). https://www.bankof england.co.uk/report/2018/publication-of-the-hmt-fca-boe-cryptoasset-tas kforce-report

PwC. (2015). *Money is no object—Understanding the evolving cryptocurrency market.* https://www.pwc-cryptocurrency-evolution.pdf

Reuters. (2019). *Barclays ends partnership with cryptocurrency exchange Coinbase: Sources.* https://www.reuters.com/article/us-barclays-coinbase/barclays-ends-partnership-with-cryptocurrency-exchange-coinbase-sources-idUSKC N1V40ZV

Roders, T. (2022). How does cryptocurrency work? *The Times.* https://www. thetimes.co.uk/money-mentor/article/how-cryptocurrency-works/

S&P Global Market Intelligence. (2019). *The worlds 100 largest banks.* https:// www.spglobal.com/marketintelligence/en/news-insights/trending/t-38wta5 twjgrrqccf4_ca2

US congressional research service. (2021). *Digital assets and SEC regulation.* https://crsreports.congress.gov/product/pdf/R/R46208

Wilfred, M. (2020). *Standard Chartered Partners Northern Trust to Launch London-based Crypto Custodia.* https://bitcourier.co.uk/news/standard-cha rtered-northern-trust-zodia-custody

World Bank Group (Natarajan, H., Krause, S., & Gradstein, S.). (2017). *Distributed Ledger Technology (DLT) and blockchain* (FinTech Note, No.

1). http://documents.worldbank.org/curated/en/177911513714062215/pdf/122140-WP-PUBLIC-DistributedLedger-Technology-and-Blockchain-Fintech-Notes.pdf

Legislation and Case Law

AA v. Persons Unknown [2019] EWHC 3556 (Comm). Bailii.org. https://www.bailii.org/ew/cases/EWHC/Comm/2019/3556.html

Financial Services and Markets Act 2000. Legislation.gov.uk. https://www.legislation.gov.uk/ukpga/2000/8/section/19

A Preliminary Comparison of Two Ecosystems: Fintech Opportunities and Challenges for Financial Inclusion

Nadeera Ranabahu

INTRODUCTION

In developing countries, entrepreneurial solutions are required to promote financial inclusion and incorporate disadvantaged, low-income, and marginalized populations into the mainstream financial system (Dev, 2006; Ozili, 2018). Such entrepreneurial solutions, which aim to enhance effectiveness, transparency, security, and efficiency in service delivery, often rely on financial technology (i.e., fintech) that uses innovations, such as peer-to-peer lending, crowdfunding, mobile money, and blockchain technology (Liu et al., 2020; Murthy & Faz, 2021; Palmié et al., 2020). However, pro-poor fintech organizations face ecosystem challenges in service delivery as a result of under-developed financial

N. Ranabahu (✉)
UC Business School, University of Canterbury, Christchurch, New Zealand
e-mail: nadeera.ranabahu@canterbury.ac.nz

© The Author(s), under exclusive license to Springer Nature Switzerland AG 2023
T. Walker et al. (eds.), *The Fintech Disruption*, Palgrave Studies in Financial Services Technology,
https://doi.org/10.1007/978-3-031-23069-1_10

243

and technological infrastructure, limited number of formal institutions, predominance of cash in their targeted demographics, security and fraud concerns associated with online banking/digital money, or hacking and other forms of negative exposure (Agwu, 2021; Aziz & Naima, 2021; Jones, 2018). At the same time, the ecosystem also provides opportunities for pursuing financial inclusion missions, including the ability to connect the poor with banks, employers, suppliers, and new markets in a more affordable manner (Klapper, 2017). Nevertheless, these challenges and opportunities faced by fintech organizations have not been given much attention in relation to poverty (Lagna & Ravishankar, 2021). This is surprising, as fintech-led pro-poor entrepreneurial solutions require the support of and are "built on the actions of stakeholders such as business partners, customers, governments, civil society organizations and philanthropic foundations in the broader environment" (Lagna & Ravishankar, 2021, p. 11). In other words, the ecosystem shapes the way fintech organizations address the pro-poor mission; hence, understanding the entrepreneurial ecosystem will facilitate achieving financial inclusion.

Addressing the need to better understand fintech ecosystems, this chapter explores policy, culture, human capital, finance, markets, and support domains (Isenberg, 2016) of two fintech ecosystems in South Asia. The aim is to identify ecosystem opportunities and challenges faced by fintech organizations in order to achieve financial inclusion. The chapter uses Isenberg's (2016) entrepreneurial ecosystem as the theoretical foundation, and the findings describe how the ecosystem shapes fintech operations. Considering institutional and stakeholder realities, this chapter also outlines opportunities and challenges through which fintech organizations embed their operations in the entrepreneurial ecosystem.

The remainder of the chapter is arranged as follows. The next section first explains the theory related to entrepreneurial ecosystems, followed by the methods of data collection and analysis in section "Method". Then, the chapter presents its findings in section "Findings" and offers a discussion of findings in the section "Discussion of Research Results". Finally, section "Conclusion" presents a summary of key findings and a conclusion.

THEORY: ENTREPRENEURIAL ECOSYSTEMS

Aligning with the ecological ecosystem metaphor, Isenberg (2016) describes entrepreneurial ecosystems as systems with visible geographical concentration. The ecosystems include different agents and interactions, evolve naturally, and largely self-organize its components and interactions. Isenberg (2016) establishes six domains (i.e., policy, finance, culture, support, human capital, and markets) to explain entrepreneurial ecosystems comprehensively (see Table 10.1).

Spigel (2017) also identifies components, similar to the ones listed in Table 10.1, in an entrepreneurial ecosystem. However, these components are named as attributes and categorized as cultural, social, and material. These components of an ecosystem are not isolated and interact with each other (Spigel, 2017). These interactions lead to multiple configurations

Table 10.1   Domains: Entrepreneurial ecosystem

Domain	Dimensions	Selected examples
Policy	Leadership	Social legitimacy, strategy, handling crisis, and challenges
	Government	Regulatory framework research institutions, investment support
Finance	Financial capital	Loans, investments, debt
Culture	Success stores	Visible successes, international reputation, wealth generation for founders
	Societal norms	Tolerance of risk, innovation, social status of the entrepreneur
Support	Infrastructure	Telecommunication, transport and logistics, entrepreneurial zones or incubators
	Support professions	Legal, accounting, investment bankers, technical experts
	Non-government institutions	Business plan contests, conferences, entrepreneurship promotion in non-profits
Human capital	Labor	Skilled and unskilled, serial entrepreneurs
	Educational institutions	General degrees, specific entrepreneurial training
Market	Networks	Entrepreneur's networks, diaspora networks, multinational corporations
	Early customers	Early adopters for proof-of-concept, reference customer, first review

Adapted from Isenberg (2016)

between the components of an ecosystem and provide resources to new ventures (Spigel, 2017). Hence, entrepreneurial ecosystems evolve and transform with time.

Fintech literature has already adopted the concept of entrepreneurial ecosystems to illustrate the different types of processes and practices, types of agents (e.g., digital/online information providers, finance institutions, ICT providers) and their complex interactions, and transformation processes within a system over time (Muthukannan et al., 2020; Roundy et al., 2018). For example, political uncertainties and imminent institutional changes trigger alterations in an ecosystem and prompt responses by agents (Sohns & W'ojcik, 2020). Similarly, entrepreneurial actors, resource providers, connectors, and entrepreneurial culture shape fintech ecosystems (Alaassar et al., 2021). Specifically, institutional voids such as the lack of regulations for blockchain and cryptocurrencies have given rise to new business models and even the formation of new ecosystems (Alaassar et al., 2021). Hence, as Harris (2021) points out, ecological metaphors, commonly used in entrepreneurial ecosystem literature where ecosystems gradually evolve over time, cannot be used to explain a fintech ecosystem. This is because the ecosystem transformation process is not serendipitous but is deliberate and led by actors, such as policymakers, technology companies, or investors. Therefore, a better understanding of the fintech ecosystem is required in terms of the actions of agents, sociocultural characteristics, organizational and regulatory practices, and the relationships between systems and institutions within and sometimes across geographical boundaries (Harris, 2021; Muthukannan et al., 2020). This chapter aims to achieve this objective by providing a preliminary analysis of two ecosystems and explaining the implications of these two ecosystems in achieving the pro-poor mission. The chapter also outlines how organizations manage opportunities and challenges in these two ecosystems.

METHOD

This study uses a case study methodology and focuses on pro-poor fintech practitioners and how they view the ecosystem where they operate. This study's focus is on fintech organizations and practitioner associations.

Two case countries[1] are selected from South Asia for data collection. This region was selected for multiple reasons. First, the South Asian region, as a whole, has high mobile phone penetration in comparison to number of people, with around 85 per 100 people having a mobile phone subscription (The World Bank, 2021). At the same time, South Asia accounts for around 29% of the estimated 736 million extreme poor worldwide, with India and Bangladesh having the highest low-income demographics (The World Bank, 2020). However, variations across countries exist. For example, in Bangladesh, low-income individuals cannot afford smartphones, and many do not have bank accounts (Deloitte, 2020). In India, although a significant percentage of the population is poor, with the recent removal of large banknotes from circulation, the use of digital banking has increased rapidly (Deloitte, 2020). Similar trends are visible in other South Asian countries, such as Sri Lanka and Pakistan. In this study, with the careful selection of the two case countries, this chapter aims to capture some of the variations in the region.

The study uses a subset of primary data from an ongoing project which studies innovations for financial inclusion in South Asia. The ongoing project collects data from fintech organizations and stakeholders that support financial inclusion in India, Bangladesh, Sri Lanka, Nepal, and Pakistan. The case organizations in this study are from only two countries. These two countries are selected due to the level of maturity of the fintech industry. Using the case data of the two countries, this chapter presents a preliminary assessment of the two ecosystems.

The ongoing project collects primary data by interviewing fintech organizations. A total of six interviews, three per country, were used for the preliminary analysis here. Out of these interviews, five were conducted with pro-poor fintech organizations, while the remaining interview was conducted with a fintech network organization operating in the country. These selected organizations have typical characteristics of a pro-poor fintech, such as targeting the under-served, having systems and procedures to accommodate the poor, and having a mission to promote entrepreneurial activities that boost rural economies. Hence, these organizations reflect a typical pro-poor fintech. Table 10.2 provides a brief overview of the interviewed organizations. Secondary data was also collected in order to verify the claims made by these organizations. This

---

[1] Case countries are anonymized as otherwise fintech organizations could be identified by associating with the country.

secondary data includes industry level reports, or reports by the Central Bank of each country.

The data analysis software, NVivo, was used to organize and analyze the data. First, open codes were made according to the six domains of the entrepreneurial ecosystem. Then open codes in each of the ecosystem domains were further analyzed to develop key themes. These key themes were then verified by looking at each country's industry reports and secondary data. The interrelations and dependencies between themes

Table 10.2 Summary of case organizations

Organization[a]	Target population	Core products and services	Core business purpose
MoMoney	• Unbanked poor • Micro-merchants	• Digital financial services	Fulfilling the daily financial needs of the unbanked
DigiVenture	• Micro and small businesses	• B2B [business to business] product sourcing services • Last mile delivery • Digital-embedded credit	Using technology to build, manage and grow micro and small businesses
FinAgro	• Agri-business owners • Rural farmers	• Financial services • Input and advisory • Access to buyers	Enhancing smallholder farmers and agri-business owners' business profit
EMicro	• Micro-merchants • Small businesses	• Trade finance	Providing technology enabled financial services to bridge the finance gap
ITradie	• Micro-businesses • Urban poor	• Trade finance • Consumer finance	P2P [person to person] finance to manage income fluctuations
BusiNet	• Fintech practitioners • Technology enthusiasts	• Providing education, capacity building, and networking opportunities	A network organization, providing fintech organizations a place for collective action and lobbying

[a]Pseudonyms are given to organizations

were also identified during this analysis process. These themes are used to gain insights and identify implications.

FINDINGS

The findings reveal that these two countries reflect polar opposites in relation to fintech operations. That is, one selected case country has more established fintech organizations, while the other has more emergent fintech organizations. The organizations MoMoney, DigiVenture, and FinAgro are operating in the country with a mature fintech ecosystem. In contrast, organizations EMicro, ITradie, and BusiNet are operating in an emergent fintech ecosystem. Hence, the organizational views on ecosystem challenges and opportunities also differ.

An Ecosystem with Established Fintech Organizations

Fintech organizations in the first case country focused on operational level challenges and their conversion to opportunities (see Fig. 10.1). Although these organizations highlighted issues they faced during their start-up, having a mature ecosystem with pre-existing fintechs created a unique set of challenges and opportunities.

Policy: As Fig. 10.1 illustrates, policy challenges relate to national directives, strategies, and regulations. For example, both organizations MoMoney and DigiVenture highlight that innovation friendly regulations are required to promote novel ways of servicing customers. Similarly, the lack of a clear strategy and coordination between government agencies also pose problems. In addition, organization DigiVenture contends that the mindset of government agencies needs to change. DigiVenture organization experienced this when they supported the government to formulate a financial inclusion strategy:

> [...] we had helped the government to formulate the national financial inclusion strategy. [...]. To this took about two and half years to develop [...]. So the total thing, this the mindset of the government needs to be changed. (DigiVenture)

As explained by DigiVenture, financial inclusion strategy/policy is an urgent need as the lack of a clear policy affects business direction. Hence, the government's slow approach does not suit with the rate of growth

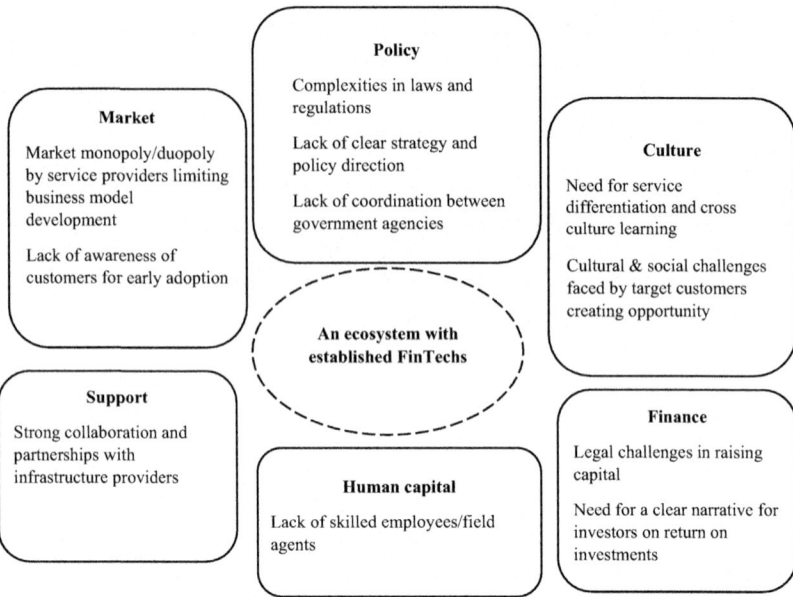

Fig. 10.1 Challenges and opportunities in an ecosystem with established fintechs

of the industry. DigiVenture organization further explains that, although a strategy had been developed, it had not yet been communicated or widely circulated. Hence, the strategy might require revisions, delaying implementation further.

Having a clear strategy would also facilitate establishing a cohesive narrative and coordination between government agencies. The DigiVenture organization highlights that government agencies conduct activities to advance the industry; but, they work in silos:

> [...] there are many good things that they are ministries, Minister of finance trying to set up. There are many things that central bank is trying to execute. There are many good things that the ICT ministry is trying get approval from the other departments of the government, but there is no cohesion or collaboration between all the parties, so there is no basically a roadmap to cater to these customers. (DigiVenture)

As organization DigiVenture explains, such cohesion would also strengthen inter-departmental collaborations and policy efforts.

Culture: The cultural domain of the ecosystem shapes fintech organizational learning and the way all three case organizations develop product/service solutions for target customers. For example, organization MoMoney highlights that following a strategy similar to that of their competitors was ineffective. Therefore, MoMoney focuses on product/service differentiation:

> From a competition perspective you're going to be doing the same thing that the competition is doing because you know, they have done it, mastered it [that will affect the business]. You have to do things differently for the consumer and also against the competition. (MoMoney)

In order to do things differently, MoMoney requires a culture of innovation; this is seen as their strategy to maintain the competitive advantage. An emphasis on innovation led to business model developments and learning within the organization MoMoney.

At the same time, familiarity and in-depth knowledge of the culture, society, and behaviors of the target customers lead the organizations to be more empathetic and cater to the needs of the customers. For example, organization FinAgro mentions that their target customers, farmers, and agri-business owners have very limited knowledge of the use of mobile apps. FinAgro also mentions that promoting the use of mobile applications takes time as families usually only had one phone. Such understanding of the culture and social environment shaped the product and service development process in organization FinAgro.

Similarly, organization DigiVenture mentioned that women did not go to banks, without a male member of the family. Explaining this further, DigiVenture elaborates that women in the family do not make financial decisions without men:

> And the female applicant is afraid of this process and they feel shy to go to the bank and discuss about is financial needs without the intervention of the males in the family. (DigiVenture)

Therefore, organization DigiVenture eliminated the requirement for women to go to banks and used alternative ways to assess creditworthiness and grant loans. The main mechanism they used was assessing Facebook pages of F-commerce merchants for lending. According to organization DigiVenture, data extracted from Facebook pages (e.g., messages, profile information, etc.) provided adequate information to assess a client's creditworthiness with approximately 80% accuracy.

Finance: Out of the three organizations, only organization FinAgro specifically mentioned funding and finance-related challenges in the ecosystem. This could be because FinAgro raised money using a P2P platform, and they often experienced challenges when obtaining funds. Even in FinAgro, at the time of its start-up, the co-founders relied on personal funding. But, soon they realized they needed a lot more than they had:

> [...] the co-founders, they decided that they do not want to go to banks for any form of loans. So they did their own investments, personal investment but you know they definitely need a lot more seed money to make this work, because it is very expensive. (FinAgro)

Then, when the FinAgro organization started raising money, it identified legal challenges in relation to cross-border funding. Although FinAgro had the avenues for cross-border funding, they had realized that it was easier to raise money within the country.

However, convincing local funders to invest was also challenging without first developing authenticity and a convincing brand. The FinAgro organization found that convincing investors or funders and asking them to wait for healthy return, but not been able to tell exact return on investment FinAgro could offer, limited investments. FinAgro mentions that:

> Funding that's a bigger challenge. I will say, because you, for example, are investing money before seeing your return. (FinAgro)

Those who took the risk and went ahead with the investments first time came back again because of their 'healthy' returns.

Human capital: One of the main challenges for fintech organizations is a lack of skilled employees or field agents who can carry out tasks. All of the interviewed organizations in the first case country found it difficult to find skilled workers. Hence, they were required to spend time and money to train and develop the capacity of the staff. Organization MoMoney relied on field level agents, but also conducted capacity building programs for the organization's agent network. This was required as MoMoney's agents were small boutique owners in rural areas and they were not familiar with using a mobile app:

> The first thing you had to do was you had to teach the retailers how to do a digital KYC [know your customer] registration and these are people who have been using USSD [Unstructured Supplementary Service Data for mobile communications] and it's very difficult for them to suddenly start using an app. (MoMoney)

On top of a lack of skilled staff, fintech organizations face difficulties in finding staff whom, on one the hand, are trustworthy, and on the other hand, communities accept. This was particularly important for organization FinAgro as they relied heavily on their field staff and handled cash on behalf of their customers:

> Oh, one of the biggest challenges we have is finding the right field officers, because they're handling a lot of cash. They're handling an obscene amount of cash really. So, you know, being able to trust traceability, we are working very, very hard and every day, we're thinking on how to increase the traceability of our field facilitators. (FinAgro)

Hence, organization FinAgro constantly improved their traceability systems.

Similarly, organization MoMoney developed systems to reduce the dependence on people for data verification. For example, MoMoney used to verify data (e.g., national identity card, photo) manually:

> So that was again a huge challenge because you know, it was people dependent. I could think that, these two person pretty much look the same and there was always the possibility of error. (MoMoney)

As illustrated by the above quote, MoMoney quickly realized that the probability of error was high in manual processing and replaced the manual system with an automated data extraction process.

Support: Fintech organizations developed collaborations and partnerships with infrastructure providers. These organizational partnerships varied with their business model. For example, organization FinAgro formed collaborations with seed or fertilizer suppliers and crop or animal husbandry insurance providers as they operated in the agriculture sector. In contrast, organization MoMoney, whose main focus was mobile cash transfers, partnered with telecommunication providers to easily manage the operations:

> Third thing we did was we tied up with [telecommunication] operators through to an agreement where if as an individual, I did not have a mobile financial account and I wanted one, all I needed to do was, press the desired code for the company [....] and set my PIN and that's all. We would fix the data from the operator. We would verify that data from the operator. (MoMoney)

Organization DigiVenture formed partnerships and collaborations with banks and with a fast-moving consumer goods (FMCG) company. These partnerships with banks were essential as DigiVenture is an intermediary financial solution provider and could not directly provide loans:

> We are also working with XXX Bank. We are also working with Citibank Limited and also there are 2 NBFIs where there is advanced level discussion and implementation process is going on. (DigiVenture)

However, the challenge for organization DigiVenture was system integration, as the banking system was not compatible with the system used by them. Hence, DigiVenture was working with banks and banking regulators to develop a more compatible system.

The partnership with the FMCG company was beneficial for all parties involved (i.e., retailers, FMCG distributors, bank, and customers). The FMCG company ensured that retailers were not getting cash and they were able to sell more consumer goods. For example, DigiVenture argues that:

> The retailer's initially, they had not been able to get a loan from the market which we are ensuring that at this moment. And this has also been a very motivational thing for Unilever and the distributors, because in the POC [proof of concept], we have already done POC with 20 retailer shops, where we have seen that average lifting has been increased by 200%. (DigiVenture)

The bank benefited because the loan money was used for business purposes and ensuring loan repayment, while retailers were able to expand their business and address the needs of customers.

Market: As MoMoney, DigiVenture, and FinAgro operate in a mature market, all struggle with the competition. This is because established fintech organizations have resources to maintain their existing market share; this limits new innovative players entering the market. In particular, when establishing themselves as a key player in the market, MoMoney struggled as a result of the existing duopoly of fintechs in the country:

> We are operating at about 14 percent of the market. [...] it's extremely difficult because it's used to be two player market where about 85 percent was controlled by one and 15 percent was controlled by another and that had been the case for the last seven years. Many, there has been many attempts to break into the market but that has never happened. (MoMoney)

Explaining this further, MoMoney mentions that this stifled the emergence of innovative business models.

Another consequence of few players dominating the market is that it takes some time for new entrants to develop trust within the community, and for target customers to get familiar with the business model. FinAgro explains this situation further:

> Then you go to the field level selecting the farmers is very hard. How do we go up to the farmers and say, Hi. I'm a new company, why don't you take money from me. And you return it back to me after this time, and it's a new model. It's not a regular model. So, you know, farmers cannot really relate to it. (FinAgro)

An Ecosystem with Emergent Fintech Organizations

The data collected demonstrates that the second case country has an emergent fintech ecosystem. Hence, the opportunities and challenges fintech organizations encounter are different compared to the first case country. Figure 10.2 summarizes the key findings.

Policy: As Fig. 10.2 illustrates, case country two has a regulatory sandbox initiated by the Central Bank. This is a major difference from the case country one. The objective of the fintech sandbox is to provide organizations opportunities to trial things:

> They [the Central Bank] have recently started a fintech sandbox. That means, say we are the start-up and if you have come up with [a new idea],

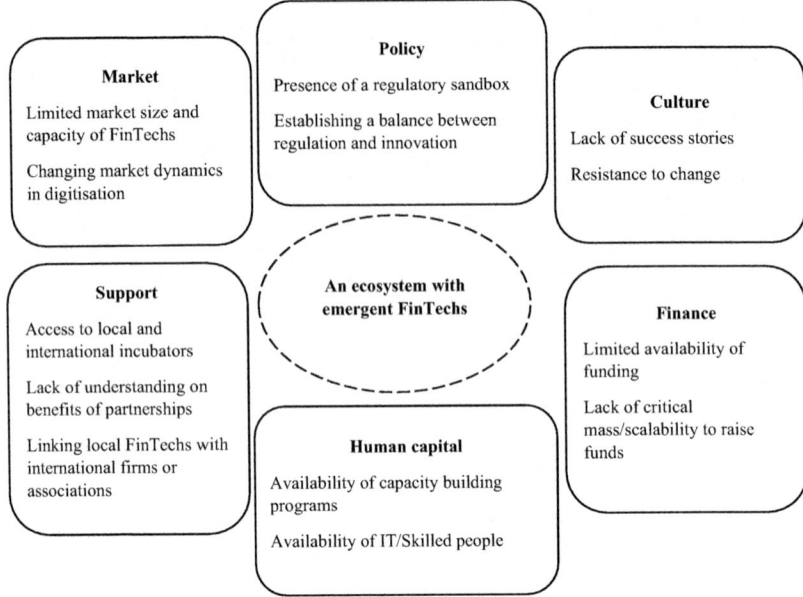

Fig. 10.2 Challenges and opportunities in an ecosystem with emergent FinTechs

you can join in the fintech sandbox and you can work with one, one bank or something in a unit across customers in a limited way. (BusiNet)

According to BusiNet, this was beneficial as emergent business models could be tested with the regulator's supervision. Explaining this further, BusiNet mentions that "although market disruption is good, the tasks of a Central Bank is to ensure financial stability." Hence, having a regulatory sandbox helped in managing that:

So they [The Central Bank] don't want some fintech companies coming all of a sudden, we are going to disrupt [the market], the central bank is going to allow [organizations to conduct operations] such a way. The disruption is good, but you know, it's not at the expense of the existing bank stability or the financial stability. (BusiNet)

Another benefit of the regulatory sandbox was having a specific contact person who liaised between fintechs and the regulator. Organization ITradie explains that this was one of the concerns the organization had before the establishment of the regulatory sandbox:

> Some of the challenges we faced in the past was, you know, getting connectivity to the regulators because what we do is currently within the legal framework of XXX [the country name], but this is a sort of like a grey area. (ITradie)

Although all three organizations welcomed the regulatory sandbox, they were also cautious as the country had a tendency to over-regulate. Taking an example from regulations in Asia, organization EMicro explains that the expectation for the sandbox was to have a practical environment where innovations could flourish:

> We need to have a pretty good and a pretty practicality based sandbox environment. [...] I think that's one of the best sandbox environments in the world where like the Monetary Authority of Singapore lets you kind of play around the system and be innovative and disruptive. But if you kind of try to do like something illegal, they'd obviously intervene but they let you play around and they also like, kind of keeping an eye on you. But they don't over-regulate. (EMicro)

Culture: Due to the nascent nature of the ecosystem, in the second case country there are no clear success stories, especially in the fintech area. Organization EMicro saw this as a challenge as there were no clear role models or stories to which fintech organizations could relate:

> I think what AAA [the country name] lacks as ecosystem is that one big break. We have had one big break with this company called BBB. [...] They were into supply chain, it's a supply chain management software which was developed for the garment industry. And they are one of the few success stories for a start-up. (EMicro)

The resistance to change is also high within the country. Although organization EMicro cannot pin point or explain the reasons for resistance, EMicro expressed that it could be because of the culture:

> I think that's cultural as well. I feel like AAA [the country name], being an island and what-not, I don't know, maybe we have resistance to change. (EMicro)

Explaining instances of such resistance, organization EMicro mentions that retailers do not use bank accounts. Hence, transactions are not properly recorded. A similar behavioral challenge, which the fintechs struggle with, is the predominance of cash. That is, people living in rural areas still largely prefer traditional banking and rely heavily on cash:

> The people in AAA [the country name], they choose the bricks and mortar, I mean everything in a traditional way. So you can't suddenly change few people in CCC [the name of the capital city], very tech savvy people, for us fintech okay maybe and that's a lot but for our rural person, he prefers always the traditional way of handling money. (BusiNet)

In organizational settings, it was not always the resistance to change, but the system complexity that made it hard for existing institutions to change. Taking the example of the banks, organization BusiNet elaborates this further:

> So they [banks] also trying to innovate. But suddenly they can't change it because they are come up with the setup for a long time, so they can't easily change. It's not like small fintech companies, suddenly they can change. (BusiNet)

Finance: One of the main challenges for emergent fintechs was the lack of finance options. This is different from the case country one. Both organizations EMicro and BusiNet mention that finance and/or investments are a major concern. There are only very limited opportunities for investments in the country. For example, both organizations EMicro and ITradie started their operations with a mix of funding strategies, such as bootstrapping, entering into pitching competitions, and the use of their own money. One reason for this is that existing banks are not coming onboard with fintechs. The organization EMicro first developed the concept, tested, and validated the business model in an incubator setting. With this proof-of-concept, EMicro approached investors. Even with the proof-of-concept, EMicro's growth was difficult due to funding limitations and banking requirements:

The other challenge was getting banks on board because banks are saying, okay, when we first started lending out, we have to keep bank guarantees and lend against them. (EMicro)

Explaining the situation further, EMicro organization mentions that investors are interested only if there is a critical mass. Thus, EMicro emphasizes that the country gets overlooked by investors as there is no critical mass for fintechs. This is because the country's size of population is relatively low compared to other countries in the region. In addition, the country in which fintech is registered makes a difference in seeking investment. The organization EMicro mentions that most fintechs in the region, upon reaching a critical mass, set up a holding company in countries like Singapore:

But most start-ups in South and Southeast Asia, once they reach a critical mass, they go to Singapore and they set up a holding company where your IP would sit in Singapore. The reason is you get better valuations there. You have a better like the investor sentiment towards coming to Singaporean companies, more comfortable. (EMicro)

Organization EMicro suspects they might also have to adopt the same strategy to raise money.

Human capital: In the second case country, although the fintech ecosystem is nascent, organizations express no concerns in terms of finding reliable employees. This is a difference in comparison with the first case country. This could be because there are so few employment opportunities in the second case country; hence, the fintech organizations can easily recruit skilled workers. There were also a number of capacity building sessions, awareness programs, and discussion sessions conducted by the fintech association. In particular, the fintech association in the country ran face-to-face forums (now mostly conducted online due to COVID-19) and summits:

We usually have workshops, fintech workshop, the Hong Kong's fintech courses there, so based on their presentation, online presentation, we used to have a session in CCC [the capital city] and I used to do the presentation. (BusiNet)

Organization EMicro's founder also conducted mentoring sessions and engaged in developing emerging technology innovators. Hence, the concern for the organizations was that skilled people are leaving the country due to lack of opportunities:

> We should have more traction because otherwise, what will happen is most people either going to leave the country, like especially the capable ones because there are no opportunities. (BusiNet)

Support: All organizations in the second case country report that having access to a local incubator facilitated their business innovation and the development of new fintech ideas. In fact, both organizations EMicro and ITradie are winners of a local innovation challenge competition, and their businesses began as a result:

> So we actually pitched this for 2017 BBB innovation challenge, me and my co-founder and once we were shortlisted and, we are winners of that challenge, we decided to carry on with this idea. (ITradie)

The incubator setting and participation in the innovation challenge allowed both EMicro and ITradie organizations to test their ideas, get feedback, and develop these further. This experience also gave them more opportunities to pitch their ideas internationally. In fact, the local fintech association recognizes that their task was mainly to connect organizations with other fintechs and regional organizations:

> The only thing is we should connect these people. So that's what I am doing. I am connecting with all these regional, all these fintech events, fintech summits to our people also. I'm connecting my network around the world. (BusiNet)

However, organization EMicro explains that although international experiences, more specifically participating in regional level incubators, was good for them personally, the local accelerator setup provided country-level insights and a more local 'flavor' in developing ideas and business models:

> It was good and what I've realized is some of these international incubators are good at a generic sense but when it comes to understanding of, you know, market you're active in, you might need some local flavour to it. (EMicro)

Due to the emergent nature of the ecosystem, establishing partnerships is a challenge for organizations. On the one hand, fintech organizations understand that they are intermediaries for the mainstream banking system in the country and they are not there to replace the existing banking system:

> As a start-up, a fintech start-up, what we would love to do is like create more partnerships, because we are not here to replace the banking system obviously. We are here to support it. (ITradie)

At the same time, as organizations BusiNet explains, fintechs are reluctant to rely too heavily upon, and collaborate with, existing banks due to system incompatibilities and the time required to make any changes.

Furthermore, partnerships with other types of stakeholders also take time due to the mindset of the existing stakeholders. Organization EMicro experienced this when developing a partnership with a FMCG company:

> They were like, why are we doing this, they were like, you're a startup. I mean, I've been running FMCG for 20 years. This won't work. You know, da de da de da de. So getting people to change their mindset from a legacy based thinking or traditional thinking to, like, you know what you can actually do this, that took a considerable amount of time. (EMicro)

Hence, significant efforts are needed to change the mindset of people to form partnerships.

Market: One reason fintech products and services are not widespread in the second case country is also due to having only a few players in the market. According to the organization BusiNet, there are few start-ups and only few people enthusiastic about the fintech ecosystem. It is also partly due to the size and income level of the market; hence, the country gets overlooked in fintech developments and investments:

> It's like we are not an extremely poor country and we're not like a rich country. We're like that in between countries where people tend to overlook. (EMicro)

However, organization EMicro mentions that the "country is an interesting space to be in right now," as regulatory changes are taking place, creating new opportunities for fintechs:

So it's a very interesting space to be in XXX [the country name] and we feel like the whole digital transformation in commercial activity, even the central bank has endorsed QR payments. They are actively pursuing it. That would enable a lot of people who are not traditionally represented in the financial markets or the financial system to get into the financial system and benefit from financial products. (EMicro)

At the same time, organization BusiNet points to the fact that existing fintech start-ups are not yet at a stage to take advantage of the opportunities in the market. According to organization BusiNet, capacity, skills and knowledge, and awareness of the latest developments in the fintech global environment are some areas in which the country's fintechs are lagging.

DISCUSSION OF RESEARCH RESULTS

This study provides a preliminary analysis of the fintech ecosystem in two countries in South Asia. The findings from these two countries illustrate that one country has established fintech organizations, while the other has emergent fintech organizations. Hence, there are differences between the two countries, and two ecosystems, as well as how organizations manage opportunities and challenges aligning with the level of maturity of their ecosystem.

The findings show that in the first country, where fintech organizations are already established, regulators and policymakers seem to be in 'catch-up' mode. There are established partnerships, funding flows, and an established market for fintechs. Hence, policymakers seem to be unable to keep up with the industry's maturity and growth. At the same time, the challenges faced by fintechs are similar to the struggles of any organization operating in a mature industry. Consequently, fintechs must find ways to constantly innovate to keep up with their competition and maintain their market share.

In contrast, the second case country has few fintechs, but does have a regulatory sandbox. Although this allows fintech organizations to trial and test ideas, the concern is whether or not these will promote or hinder innovation. Another main concern for fintech organizations is the lack of understanding of the stakeholders due to a lack of success stories, role models, or significant market shares. There seems to be slow momentum for fintech organizations here. Therefore, the opportunities and challenges of the second country are a result of the emergent nature of the industry.

These findings also highlight that addressing the needs of impoverished citizens is challenging as organizations need to balance multiple dimensions within the ecosystem. Both Isenberg (2016) and Spigel (2017) provide a theoretical foundation to explore these issues and interrelations from an ecosystem perspective. The findings demonstrate that pro-poor institutions in ecosystems with established fintech organizations (in this case MoMoney, DigiVenture, and FinAgro), face challenges in relation to policy, market, finance, and human capital domains. However, these organizations have an in-depth understanding of the culture, and they gain lot of support from stakeholders in the ecosystem to mitigate these existing challenges. In contrast, findings illustrate that pro-poor institutions, in ecosystems with emergent fintech organizations (in this case EMicro, ITradie, and BusiNet), face challenges mainly in the areas of culture, finance, support, and market. They have an advantage (and opportunities) in relation to policy and human capital domains. But, as case country one demonstrates these dynamics in case country two could also change with the maturity of the ecosystem.

The findings in this chapter contribute to both financial inclusion and entrepreneurial ecosystem literature. First, the preliminary assessment of the two countries here explains how fintech organizations embed themselves in the ecosystem of the country to provide services to the poor. Hence, the chapter contributes by outlining the challenges and opportunities faced by pro-poor fintech organizations. Next, the chapter contributes to ecosystem literature by showing the differences between an ecosystem with established fintechs and an ecosystem with emergent fintechs. This comparison could be used to further develop scholarly and practical work in relation to the progression of ecosystems. Finally, the chapter also contributes by providing empirical evidence from a geographical region that is less explored.

However, this chapter is not without its limitations. First, this chapter presents only a preliminary analysis and has used primary data from only three organizations from each country. To validate these preliminary findings, additional primary data needs to be collected from fintech organizations in each country, and then tested and validated in other countries in South Asia. In addition, to develop a more comprehensive assessment of the ecosystem, data needs to be collected from other stakeholders, such as banks, regulators/legislators, and investors. Such data could provide multiple viewpoints and a more nuanced understanding of the ecosystem.

Conclusion

The preliminary ecosystem analysis in this study elaborates implications for policy and practice. The policymakers in both ecosystems with emergent and established organizations require extensive collaboration and coordination with practitioners and other stakeholders (e.g., banks, investors, incubators) to facilitate the development of the industry. Although type of activities or policy or regulatory decisions vary according to the maturity of the ecosystem, such collaborations and coordination provide an alignment between the industry needs and policy/regulation. For example, in an ecosystem with the established fintechs, there is a need for policymakers to facilitate fair competition to avoid few dominating the market, take initiatives to develop human capital, and promote innovative business models. In contrast, in an ecosystem with the emergent fintechs, there is a need for policymakers to facilitate entry of new players to promote tech-enabled solutions, promote financing and investments, and even provide visibility to emergent players without over-regulating. Such efforts facilitate the co-creation of ecosystems according to the maturity level of the industry.

In conclusion, this chapter provides a preliminary analysis of two ecosystems and outlines the opportunities and challenges in the ecosystem from a fintech organizational perspective. The findings show that country-level ecosystems, even within the same region, need to be studied separately by looking at the domains of policy, culture, human capital, market, support, and finance to get a comprehensive understanding of the factors and underlying interactions within them. Without such analysis, achieving financial inclusion could be difficult, as each ecosystem has different challenges and opportunities due to the level of maturity of the fintech industry.

References

Agwu, M. E. (2021). Can technology bridge the gap between rural development and financial inclusions? *Technology Analysis & Strategic Management, 33*(2), 123–133. https://doi.org/10.1080/09537325.2020.1795111

Alaassar, A., Mention, A. L., & Aas, T. H. (2021). Ecosystem dynamics: Exploring the interplay within fintech entrepreneurial ecosystems. *Small Business Economics, 58*, 2157–2182. https://doi.org/10.1007/s11187-021-005 05-5

Aziz, A., & Naima, U. (2021). Rethinking digital financial inclusion: Evidence from Bangladesh. *Technology in Society, 64*. https://doi.org/10.1016/j.tec hsoc.2020.101509

Deloitte. (2020). "The next wave:" Emerging digital life in South and Southeast Asia. *Inclusion Fintech Conference*. https://www2.deloitte.com/content/dam/Deloitte/cn/Documents/technology-media-telecommunications/del oitte-cn-tmt-inclusion-en-200924.pdf

Dev, S. M. (2006). Financial inclusion: Issues and challenges. *Economic and Political Weekly, 41*(41), 4310–4313. http://www.jstor.org/stable/4418799

Isenberg, D. J. (2016). Applying the ecosystem metaphor to entrepreneurship: Uses and abuses. *The Antitrust Bulletin, 61*(4), 564–573. https://doi.org/10.1177/0003603X16676162

Jones, L. (2018). Guest editorial: Poverty reduction in the FinTech age. *Enterprise Development and Microfinance, 29*(2), 99–102. https://doi.org/10.3362/1755-1986.2018.29-2.ED

Harris, J. L. (2021). Bridging the gap between 'Fin' and 'Tech': The role of accelerator networks in emerging FinTech entrepreneurial ecosystems. *Geoforum, 122*, 174–182. https://doi.org/10.1016/j.geoforum.2021.04.010

Klapper, L. (2017). How digital payments can benefit entrepreneurs. *IZA World of Labor*. Institute for the Study of Labor (IZA). https://doi.org/10.15185/izawol.396

Lagna, A., & Ravishankar, M. N. (2021). Making the world a better place with fintech research. *Information Systems Journal, 32*, 61–102. https://doi.org/10.1111/isj.12333

Liu, J., Li, X., & Wang, S. (2020). What have we learnt from 10 years of fintech research? A scientometric analysis. *Technological Forecasting and Social Change, 155*. https://doi.org/10.1016/j.techfore.2020.120022

Murthy, G., & Faz, X. (2021). Fintech and financial Inclusion: A funders' guide to greater impact. *Focus note*. CGAP. https://www.cgap.org/sites/default/files/publications/2021_06_Focus_Note_Fintech_and_Financial_Inclusion_Funders_Guide.pdf

Muthukannan, P., Tan, B., Gozman, D., & Johnson, L. (2020). The emergence of a Fintech ecosystem: A case study of the Vizag Fintech Valley in India. *Information & Management, 57*(8), 1–14. https://doi.org/10.1016/j.im.2020.103385

Ozili, P. K. (2018). Impact of digital finance on financial inclusion and stability. *Borsa Istanbul Review*, *18*(4), 329–340. https://doi.org/10.1016/j.bir.2017.12.003

Palmié, M., Wincent, J., Parida, V., & Caglar, U. (2020). The evolution of the financial technology ecosystem: An introduction and agenda for future research on disruptive innovations in ecosystems. *Technological Forecasting and Social Change*, *151*, 1–10. https://doi.org/10.1016/j.techfore.2019.119779

Roundy, P. T., Bradshaw, M., & Brockman, B. K. (2018). The emergence of entrepreneurial ecosystems: A complex adaptive systems approach. *Journal of Business Research*, *86*, 1–10. https://doi.org/10.1016/j.jbusres.2018.01.032

Sohns, F., & W'ojcik, D. (2020). The impact of Brexit on London's entrepreneurial ecosystem: The case of the FinTech industry. *Economy and Space*, *52*(8), 1539–1559. https://doi.org/10.1177/0308518X20925820

Spigel, B. (2017). The relational organization of entrepreneurial ecosystems. *Entrepreneurship Theory and Practice*, *41*(1), 49–72. https://doi.org/10.1111/etap.12167

The World Bank. (2021). *Databank: World development indicators*. https://databank.worldbank.org/reports.aspx?source=2&series=IT.NET.SECR.P6&country=SAS

The World Bank. (2020). *Poverty and shared prosperity 2020: Reversals of fortune*. https://www.worldbank.org/en/publication/poverty-and-shared-prosperity

Investigating Variables that Increase the Desire and Loyalty to Utilize Fintech After the COVID-19 Lockdown: A New Normal Behavior

Minh T. H. Le

INTRODUCTION

Financial technology (fintech) is an emerging innovation in the financial industry, driven in part by the era of Industry 4.0.[1] The availability of the internet and widespread use of mobile communication have become indispensable to modern life and have made the US a huge market for digital financial services. Fintech's possible actions include checking bank balances, making payments, and performing account transactions (Tiwari,

---

[1] Industry 4.0 is revolutionizing the way companies manufacture, improve, and distribute their products.

M. T. H. Le (✉)
University of Economics Ho Chi Minh City (UEH), Ho Chi Minh, Vietnam
e-mail: minhlth@ueh.edu.vn

© The Author(s), under exclusive license to Springer Nature
Switzerland AG 2023
T. Walker et al. (eds.), *The Fintech Disruption*, Palgrave Studies
in Financial Services Technology,
https://doi.org/10.1007/978-3-031-23069-1_11

267

2019). In 2018, the US fintech market was $18 billion, and fintech start-ups have recently boomed (Kauflin, 2020). According to Forbes, consumer utilization of finance apps grew 71% in 2019 (see Fig. 11.1) (Salz, 2020). Internet financial service users are going mobile, and most banks and other financial services are competing for users (Fisher, 2001; Lee et al., 2012). During the COVID-19 lockdown, shops and borders have closed and fintech has accelerated at a rapid speed (Talwar et al., 2020). These events have created significant opportunities for fintech firms.

Previous research has examined how consumers adopt fintech, with a focus on its perceived risks, the security of its data (Fernando & Touriano, 2018; Lim et al., 2019), its perceived ease of use and usefulness (Chuang et al., 2016; Das, 2019; Fu & Mishra, 2020a; Kauflin, 2020; Salz, 2020; Wang & Chang, 2018), and perspectives on interaction via technological platforms (Gimpel et al., 2018). Consumers have recognized fintech's benefits, such as its low-cost transaction fees and highly effective solutions to customers (Saksonova & Kuzmina-Merlino, 2017). These benefits encourage consumers to continue to use technology-based financial services (Chuang et al., 2016; Lim et al., 2019; Ryu, 2018). Fintech increases the self-efficacy of both financial organizations and consumers by reducing time wasted on travel and paperwork (Ashta & Biot-Paquerot, 2018; Das, 2019), and saves costs by reducing physical transactions (Lootsma, 2017). However, the COVID-19 pandemic has

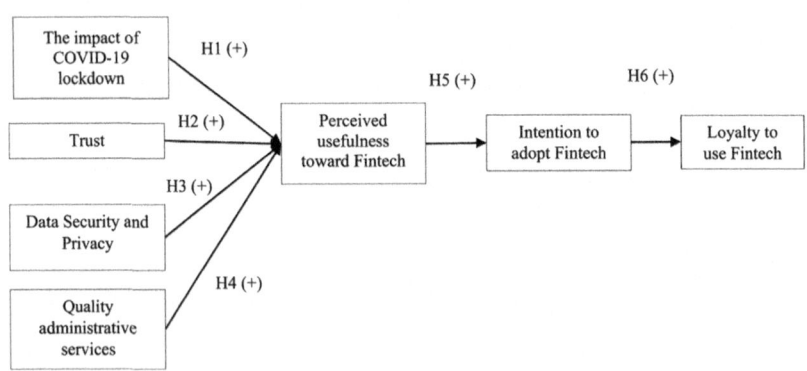

Fig. 11.1   The research model

significantly changed consumers' day-to-day lives. Under normal circumstances, consumers prefer to shop in person rather than online, and to use face-to-face financial services (Scarpi et al., 2014). During lockdowns, all transactions need to be transferred online. Fintech services have thus become a key tool in maintaining frictionless transactions. Therefore, previous studies have not assessed how the COVID-19 lockdown has changed the behavior of users and consumers.

Furthermore, in a lockdown state that has been ongoing for a year, users realize how useful fintech services are in maintaining a normal life. Users may therefore become familiar with the convenience of this service and continue to use it post-COVID-19. Fintech services are competing with one another to maintain existing customers and attract new ones. It is essential to determine which characteristics affect fintech's perceived usefulness and can thus predict a user's intention to adopt fintech, as well as increase a service's competitive advantage. Thus, this study identifies which critical factors impact the perceived usefulness of fintech services during the COVID-19 lockdown. These factors indirectly influence the intention of users to use the service during and after the pandemic.

In addition, the consequences of using fintech services have not yet been determined. If consumers feel satisfied with the service, they tend to keep using it for a long time, that is, they become loyal customers (Kumar et al., 2018). This study assesses the loyalty of users as a result of having good financial service experiences during a forced situation, that is, the COVID-19 lockdown. The findings may shed light on users' positive behaviors toward the use of fintech services. In addition, this study assesses the impact of users' computer literacy on their adoption of financial technology services. The future tendency to use fintech during and after COVID-19 is also assessed.

THE TECHNOLOGY ACCEPTANCE MODEL

The theory of reasoned action (TRA) (Ajzen & Fishbein, 1980; Fishbein, 1980; Vance et al., 2008) suggests that people form intentions to adopt a behavior or technology based on their beliefs about the consequences of adoption. TRA has been used to understand the adoption of behaviors, technologies, or advice. Building on TRA, Davis et al. (1989a) developed the technology acceptance model (TAM). TAM attempts to explain why individuals choose to adopt a particular technology when performing a task (Davis et al., 1989a). The TAM explains the relationship between behavioral intention that predicts a user's acceptance of information technology (Chuang et al., 2016). TAM posits that if a technology or innovation enhances a person's performance, it is considered useful, and the person will be more likely to adopt the technology, service, or behavior. The results of numerous studies have supported the validity and reliability of the perceived usefulness and perceived ease of use variables in the TAM (Wallace & Sheetz, 2014). These two theories are valuable for assessing the usefulness of technology (Davis et al., 1989b).

Fintech refers to companies which use technology to make financial services more efficient (Puschmann, 2017). This study applied TAM and TRA to explain users' behavior toward fintech during lockdown, when its convenience has been particularly beneficial. It furthermore explores the fintech experiences of users during a lockdown. The COVID-19 lockdown has forced most people to purchase products and services through financial technology. Users tend to be familiar and interested in a service with trust, privacy, and administration services. Perceived usefulness refers to the degree to which an individual believes that using a particular technology enhances performance (Davis, 1989). With positive feedback and experience, users may become loyal to fintech services.

HYPOTHESES

The Impact of the COVID-19 Lockdown, Trust, Data Security and Privacy, QAS, and Perceived Usefulness Toward Fintech

The ongoing COVID-19 pandemic has already impacted almost everyone across the globe as everyone needs to stay at home and shops have closed due to government policy. Despite these measures, individuals need to purchase products and use services (Fu & Mishra, 2020) for work and entertainment (Wójcik & Ioannou, 2020). The growing field of fintech and the different financial paradigms and technologies will be boosted by COVID-19 (Das, 2019). The spread of COVID-19 and related government lockdowns has led to a 24–32% increase in the relative rate of daily downloads of fintech service applications. Furthermore, as users are required to use digital financial services during the COVID-19 lockdown, they gradually recognize the usefulness of fintech in their daily lives (Fu & Mishra, 2020). We therefore formulate the following hypothesis:

H1: The COVID-19 lockdown has positively impacted the perceived usefulness of fintech.

Trust refers to the belief in the services or reputation of a business (Lewis & Weigert, 1985). Trust in digital financial services includes confidentiality, availability, and transaction security (Hansen et al., 2018; Siau & Shen, 2003; Vance et al., 2008). It plays a vital role in shaping the adoption of fintech services (Gefen, 2000; Joubert & Van Belle, 2013; Malaquias & Hwang, 2016; Wu et al., 2016) and in enhancing customer attitudes in the context of mobile applications (Mahatanankoon et al., 2005). Customers recognize perceived usefulness when they trust the data security, privacy, and quality of service. The importance of consumer trust and technological tools of fintech services is a widely studied TAM belief (Chuang et al., 2016; Vance et al., 2008). When consumers receive useful assistance, it can increase their trust in the quality of the system (Similarly, Wang et al., 2019). Specifically, fintech indicates transactions occur online without human connection (Singh & Sinha, 2020). Thus, in the context of fintech service adoption, trust is one of the first concerns in customers' minds. We therefore formulate the following hypothesis:

H2: Trust has a positive impact on the perceived usefulness of fintech.

The second factor to consider is the security of data that needs to be ensured through the organization's IT system. The trust is not only based on service quality, but also on the security of information. Data security and privacy are key elements to encourage consumers to adopt a digital financial service (Chang et al., 2016). By downloading and installing apps, smartphone users increase their risk of falling prey to design flaws, malware attacks, and data theft. Users are concerned that their personal and bank account information will be leaked or stolen (Noor et al., 2019), as large amounts of money have been stolen due to information leakage or financial systems' lack of protection (Byrnes, 2020; Yang et al., 2018). Despite the apprehension many users express, the number of mobile app downloads worldwide increases continuously. Nonetheless, users require fintech to be more transparent about collecting data on their online behavior. A service's success in protecting its users' data is indirectly part of its reputation and increases its competitive advantage. Higher levels of data security protection, security control mechanisms, and/or security procedures allow fintech services to be provided stably, and in compliance with users' expectations. If customers feel their confidential information is protected, this will increase their desire to continue using the service

(Hu et al., 2019; Stewart & Jürjens, 2018). Thus, fintech services with highly secure data security and privacy systems definitely attract the trust of users and retain customers in the long term. We therefore formulate the following hypothesis:

H3: Data security and privacy have a positive impact on the perceived usefulness of fintech.

The quality of administrative services (QAS) refers to services pertaining to contract management, subcontract management, online transactions, and other similar services (Gomber et al., 2018). While most online transactions are based on technology systems, the quality of administrative services (QAS) is a human-connected method. Therefore, QAS represents bank credibility or brand image (Chuang et al., 2016). When there are issues with online transactions such as fraud, transferring incorrect amounts, and so on, users would need to stop their transactions as soon as possible. If users face difficulty or have bad experiences with QAS services, they will become disappointed and seek alternative financial services (Hu et al., 2019; Razzaque et al., 2020). E-admin services include both artificial intelligence and staff services. Using an online chat conversation via text or text-to-speech to answer customer questions during 24/7 service allows companies to respond to consumer enquires quickly (Belanche et al., 2019). E-admin services such as chatbots, call-to-action on apps or websites, or online chat services should be available (Jang et al., 2021). In addition, online customer staff should be continuously trained to have advanced knowledge and expertise, enabling them to provide quick, high-quality services to the clients (Chuang et al., 2016). In return, consumers perceive the usefulness of fintech services and are increasingly likely to use fintech in the future (Kim et al., 2016). Therefore, QAS can enhance the usefulness of fintech. We therefore formulate the following hypothesis:

H4: Quality administrative services have a positive impact on the perceived usefulness of fintech.

The operational definition of perceived usefulness is the belief in the degree of helpfulness of using a fintech service (Davis, 1989). The attributes of perceived usefulness used in this study were selected from the scale developed by Davis (1989). Fintech services bring benefits to everyone by, for example, increasing completion of work tasks, reducing travel time, and reducing excess paperwork (Chuang et al., 2016; Lee et al., 2019). Recognizing the usefulness of fintech, especially during the

COVID-19 lockdown, will help users to realize the importance of such services (Billore & Billore, 2020). Usefulness includes many factors, such as usability, the ability to secure the information, and satisfaction with the quality of service. The COVID-19 is an opportunity for people to use fintech services without having to promote many marketing activities. Users stay at home, but can still perform online financial transactions effectively, quickly, easily, and safely (Jiwasiddi et al., 2019; Tat Huei et al., 2018), and are sure to recognize the potential usefulness of fintech beyond the COVID-19 pandemic (Revathy & Balaji, 2020). The usefulness of fintech encourages users to have an intention to adopt it. We therefore formulate the following hypothesis:

H5: Fintech's perceived usefulness positively impacts users' intention to adopt it.

Customer loyalty now extends to online services, and online loyalty extends the traditional concept of brand loyalty to consumers' online behavior (Corstjens & Lal, 2000). E-loyalty refers to customers' repeated visits to the same online store, the repurchasing of products and future reusing of services (Anderson & Srinivasan, 2003; Larsson, 2018). Within the context of this study, user loyalty refers to the ways in which fintech customers who have a positive experience using apps or online services are more likely to intend to repeatedly use the same services and promote such services to others. In terms of intentional loyalty, the determinants of online customer loyalty include product quality (Aisyah, 2018), interactivity and service quality (Gefen, 2000; Larsson & Viitaoja, 2017; Toufaily et al., 2013; Yen & Lu, 2008), and trust in services (Ponnavolu, 2000; Shin, 2010). The data security of online services can increase the loyalty to fintech (Tarafdar & Zhang, 2008; Yun & Good, 2007). Fintech experiences can affect customer loyalty toward fintech service providers (Anderson et al., 2014; Wang & Chang, 2018). We therefore formulate the following hypothesis:

H6: Intention to adopt fintech positively influences loyalty to use fintech.

The Impact of Technology Literacy Skills in Multi-Groups on the Intention to Adopt Fintech

The perceived usefulness of fintech depends upon users' computer literacy skills (Rauniar et al., 2014; Ryu, 2018; Talwar et al., 2020). If consumers

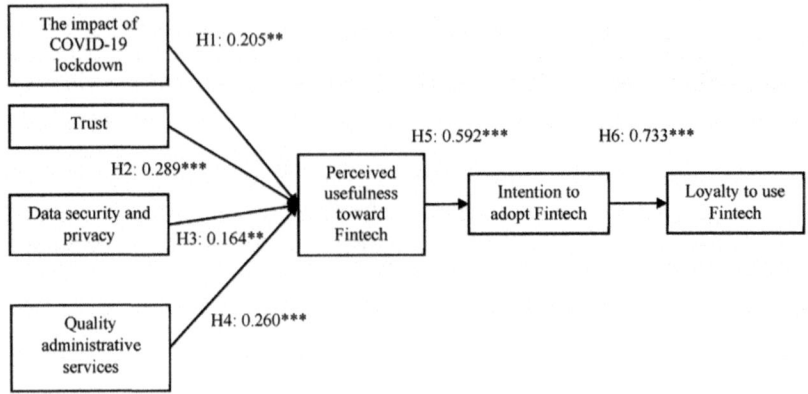

Fig. 11.2 The results of the research model

are comfortable with technology, it will be easier for them to adopt new technological services, and they may even be enthusiastic about using high-tech tools (Fain & Roberts, 1997). Meanwhile, consumers who struggle with technology tend to resist using high-tech services, and instead prefer cash transactions (Tapia, 2004). The current study explores the different influences of computer literacy on the adoption of fintech among different groups. In addition, this study measures the difference in intention to use fintech after the COVID-19 lockdown by comparing it with how customers behave during and after lockdown related to using fintech services. The research model is illustrated in Fig. 11.2, where the control variable is computer literacy.

Research Methodology

Data Collection

We developed an open-ended survey via Google Forms and administered it on Amazon Mechanical Turk (MTurk) in June 2020. Subjects were over 18, resided in the US, and used fintech daily. They use financial transactions conveniently and quickly through apps or websites. The US is one of the countries facing a severe situation during the COVID-19 pandemic, and citizens have been forced to remain inside their homes. Sample characteristics and data screening were assessed to ensure the quality of the data. Participants were asked to answer two screening questions about whether they use fintech and whether they have been making purchases online during the COVID-19 lockdown. If they answered "Yes," they would move to the next section. The participants answered all questions in approximately one to three minutes.

Data from 247 respondents was used to test the proposed model, with a rate of effectiveness of 94.4%. Of these, two respondents were eliminated as they used the wrong MTurk ID. This study has six latent independent variables pointing to one latent dependent variable. Following the 10 times rule, the minimum sample size for PLS-SEM should be 60. There should be at least 10 cases per measured variable for (1) the number of indicators in the largest latent factor block, or (2) the largest number of incoming causal arrows for any latent variable in the model (Hair Jr et al., 2016). The demographic features of the respondents are reported in Table 11.1. The data includes more women (69.5%) than men (30.5%), most participants of either gender (61.94%) were under 35, and the majority had a higher level of education (65.8%). In terms of occupation, professionals (48.2%) accounted for the highest proportion, followed by white-collar workers (19.8%). The overall frequency of fintech use was 39.8%, followed by "often" (31.7%). Frequency of using fintech was determined by asking participants about their intention to use the service during and post-COVID-19 lockdown. The comparison between the two points confirms the potential market for fintech firms.

Procedure Development

The construct items use those from previous research on fintech services. The scale items are measured on a five-point Likert scale (1 = strongly disagree to 5 = strongly agree) (see Table 11.2).

Trust is evaluated using five items adapted from Stewart and Jürjens (2018). The alpha coefficient for trust is 0.780.

Data privacy and security are evaluated using four items adapted from Stewart and Jürjens (2018). The alpha coefficient for data privacy and data security is 0.752 (see Table 11.2).

QAS is evaluated using six items adapted from Russell-Bennett et al. (2007). The coefficient alpha is 0.728.

The impact of the COVID-19 lockdown is evaluated using five items adapted from Baker et al. (2020). The coefficient alpha is 0.827.

Table 11.1 Descriptive statistics for user groups

		N = 247	%
Gender	Male	76	30.50
	Female	173	69.50
Age	<35	153	61.94
	153	80	32.38
	61.94%	16	6.48
Education	Primary school	0	0
	High school	19	7.60
	Undergraduate	164	65.9
	Postgraduate	66	26.5
Occupation	Students	3	1.20
	Service industry proprietors	38	15.40
	Professionals	119	48.20
	White collars	49	19.80
	Homemakers	11	4.50
	Unemployment	3	1.20
	Others	24	9.70
fintech Usage Frequency	Frequently	79	31.70
	Often	99	39.80
	Sometimes	67	26.90
	Rarely	4	1.60
Computer literacy skills	Basic	7	2.80
	Intermediate	50	20.24
	Advanced	130	52.63
	Expert	60	24.29

The perceived usefulness of fintech is evaluated using four items adopted from Davis et al. (1989a). The alpha coefficient is 0.768.

The intention to adopt fintech is evaluated using five items adapted from Chuang et al. (2016). The alpha coefficient is 0.792.

Loyalty to use fintech is evaluated by four items adapted from Anderson and Srinivasan (2003). The alpha coefficient is 0.743 (see Table 11.2).

ANALYSIS AND RESULTS

Measurement Model

Data collected from the same source may lead to a potential common method variance. We used Harman's single-factor tests to examine this

Table 11.2 Measurement model resulting from confirmation factor analysis

Constructs and variables	Standardized factor loadings	Cronbach alpha	AVE
Trust		**0.780**	**0.780**
This fintech service is trustworthy		0.652	
This fintech service is reputable		0.688	
This fintech service makes honest claims		0.566	
This fintech service has a long-lasting nature		0.579	
Wherever I go, this fintech service is present		0.572	
Data security and privacy		**0.752**	**0.759**
I trust in the technology of fintech service that is being used	0.730		
I trust in the ability of fintech service to protect my privacy	0.662		
I trust the fintech service as a bank	0.745		
Using a fintech service is financially secure	0.734		
I am not worried about the security of a fintech service	0.664		
When a fintech service promises to do something by a certain time, it does so	0.730		
I trust in the ability of a fintech service to protect my privacy			
Quality administrative services		**0.728**	**0.732**
Administrators of fintech services show the confidence in customers	0.795		
I feel safe in my transactions with fintech services	0.741		
Administrators of fintech services are consistently courteous with me	0.671		
Administrators of fintech services have the knowledge to answer my questions	0.760		

(continued)

Table 11.2 (continued)

Constructs and variables	Standardized factor loadings	Cronbach alpha	AVE
The impact of COVID-19 lockdown		0.827	0.830
I need to purchase online due to COVID-19 lockdown			
I use fintech service to purchase online during COVID-19 lockdown			
I use e-commerce platforms to buy things I need due to COVID-19 lockdown			
I use original products website to buy things I need due to COVID-19 lockdown			
I need to use fintech service when using online purchasing platforms during COVID-19 lockdown			
Perceived usefulness toward fintech		0.768	0.773
Using fintech service helps me online purchasing more quickly	0.759		
Using fintech service enhances my online purchasing effectively	0.756		
Using fintech service makes it easier to do my online purchasing	0.736		
Overall, using fintech service is useful	0.818		
Intention to adopt fintech		0.792	0.794
I intend to use fintech services	0.788		
I predict I will use fintech services	0.719		
I plan to use fintech services	0.714		
I will strongly recommend others to use fintech services	0.754		
If I have access to fintech services, I want to use it as much as possible	0.715		

(continued)

Table 11.2 (continued)

Constructs and variables	Standardized factor loadings	Cronbach alpha	AVE
Loyalty to use fintech		0.743	0.746
I will say positive word-of-mouth about fintech service	0.791		
I will recommend fintech service to others	0.743		
I will encourage others to use fintech service	0.740		
Fintech service is the first choice to pay for future	0.733		

Notes AVE: Average variance extracted

type of bias (Podsakoff et al., 2003). The results indicate five factors with eigenvalues larger than one, and the first factor accounts for 35.790% of the total variance. The results suggest that common method bias is not of concern with regard to the data used in this study.

Next, to assess convergent validity, three items with low factor loadings (below 0.50) were dropped from further analysis (Gerbing & Anderson, 1992). The fit statistic is 653.558 with 356 degrees of freedom ($\chi2/df = 1482$) ($p<0.001$). The root mean square error of approximation (RMSEA) is $0.044 < 0.08$, the comparative fit index (CFI) is $0.926 > 0.800$, the normed fit index (NFI) is $0.805 > 0.800$, and the Tucker-Lewis coefficient TLI (rho2) is $0.917 > 0.800$.

Discriminant validity was checked for the correlation of each construct with other factors (Fornell & Larcker, 1981). QAS and data security and privacy have a high correlation ($\Phi = 0.733$, $\Phi^2 = 0.533$), and the variance extracted estimates are 0.566 and 0.533, respectively, suggesting adequate discriminant validity (see Table 11.3).

Structural Model

The maximum likelihood is used to assess the fit parameters. The model shows good fit with the data ($\chi2/df = 2.147$, CFI $= 0.818$, TLI $= 0.804$, RMSEA $= 0.068$, $p<0.01$) (Hair et al., 2014). The index shows a goodness-of-fit index (GFI) of 0.90, and the Bentler and Bonett (1980) normed fit index (NFI) shows a goodness-of-fit index (GFI) of 0.90. The

Table 11.3   Correlation of the research variables

	CR	CI	IAF	LUF	PU	SP	QAS	TR
CI	0.878	0.768						
IAF	0.857	0.534	0.739					
LUF	0.839	0.508	0.733	0.752				
PU	0.852	0.509	0.592	0.610	0.768			
SP	0.834	0.413	0.606	0.536	0.589	0.708		
QAS	0.831	0.446	0.530	0.571	0.610	0.648	0.743	
TR	0.850	0.415	0.577	0.569	0.608	0.594	0.527	0.730

Notes CR: Composite reliability; QAS: Quality Administrative Services; CI: The impact of COVID-19 lockdown; IAF: Intention to adopt fintech; LUF: Loyalty to use fintech; PU: Perceived usefulness toward fintech; SP: Data security and Privacy; TR: Trust

impact of the COVID-19 lockdown, trust, data security, privacy, and QAS have high-squared multiple correlations with the perceived usefulness of fintech. The standardized parameter estimates were presented in Table 11.4.

H1–H4 show the structural relationships among the impact of the COVID-19 lockdown, trust, data security and privacy, and QAS in terms of perceived usefulness. In detail, the impact of these factors has had a positive effect on the perceived usefulness of fintech ($\beta_{Covid-19} = 0.205$, t-value$_{covid-19} = 2.883$; $\beta_{trust} = 0.289$, t-value$_{trust} = 3.493$; $\beta_{SP} = 0.205$, t-value$_{SP} = 2.883$; $\beta_{ASQ} = 0.205$, t-value$_{ASQ} = 2.883$), and all are statistically significant at the $p<0.001$ level, supporting H1, H2, H3, and H4 (see Table 11.4).

As expected, perceived usefulness toward fintech significantly affects the intention to adopt fintech ($\beta = 0.592$, t-value $= 11.977$, $p<0.001$), supporting H5. Intention to adopt fintech has a considerable positive influence on loyalty to use fintech ($\beta = 0.733$, t-value $= 21.546$) and is statistically significant at the $p<0.001$ level, supporting H6.

Multi-Group Test of Computer Literacy Skills

To assess whether users' level of computer skills impacts their ability to use fintech services, a multi-group analysis was conducted to find out the differences (if any) between each groups with technology skills (Justwan et al., 2018). The differences between high and low literacy can be observed in Table 11.6 through the comparison of each PLS model for

Table 11.4 Analysis of competing structural models

Hypotheses	Path	Path coefficient sample estimates	T-statistics (C.R)	p-value	Results
H1	The impact of COVID-19 lockdown → Perceived usefulness toward fintech	0.205	2.882	0.004	Approved
H2	Trust → Perceived usefulness toward fintech	0.289	3.493	0.000	Approved
H3	Data security and privacy → Perceived usefulness toward fintech	0.164	2.155	0.0031	Approved
H4	Quality Administrative Services → Perceived usefulness toward fintech	0.260	3.888	0.0000	Approved
H5	Perceived usefulness toward fintech → Intention to adopt fintech	0.592	11.977	0.000	Approved
H6	Intention to adopt fintech → Loyalty to use fintech	0.733	21.546	0.000	Approved
	R^2				
	Perceived usefulness toward fintech 0.527 (52.7%)				
	Intention to adopt fintech 0.348 (34.8%)				
	Loyalty to use fintech 0.537 (53.7%)				

each category. Regarding the intention to use fintech, there was no difference between computer literacy levels (see Table 11.5). As such, there is no clear difference in technology skills affecting users' ability to use fintech.

Intention to Adopt Fintech During and Post-COVID-19 Lockdown

In terms of the impact of the COVID-19 lockdown on users' intentions to adopt as well as continue using fintech, a dependent t-test was used to check the difference between two points and to predict the tendency to using fintech during the COVID-19 epidemic and later (Hair et al., 2014). Respondents were asked about their intention to adopt fintech

Table 11.5   Path coefficient and p-values of multi-group analysis between High computer literacy and Low computer literacy

	β-diff (|Advanced Expert |)	p-Value (Advanced vs Expert)	β-diff (|Advanced Interme- diate|)	p-Value (Advanced vs Interme- diate)	β-diff (|Expert Interme- diate|)	p-Value (Expert vs Interme- diate)
CI → PU	0.135	0.218	0.138	0.194	0.003	0.465
IAF → LUF	0.089	0.930	0.093	0.195	0.182	0.033
PU → IAF	0.036	0.646	0.071	0.308	0.107	0.226
SP → PU	0.118	0.769	0.165	0.775	0.047	0.565
QAS → PU	0.220	0.098	0.033	0.446	0.187	0.802
TR → PU	0.266	0.901	0.028	0.568	0.238	0.137

Notes QAS: Quality Administrative Services; CI: The impact of COVID-19 lockdown; IAF: Intention to adopt fintech; LUF: Loyalty to use fintech; PU: Perceived usefulness toward fintech; SP: Data security and privacy; TR: Trust

Table 11.6   Paired samples statistics of using fintech during and post-COVID-19 lockdown

	Paired differences		t	Df	Sig. (2-tailed)
	Mean	Std.D			
During COVID-19 lockdown - Post-COVID-19 lockdown	− 0.558	1.145	−7.690	248	0.000

during and post-COVID-19 lockdowns. The paired-mean differences between these two answers were computed to predict user behavior. The dependent t-test between intention to adopt fintech during and post lockdown was $t(248) = -7.690$, $p<0.0005$. We can therefore conclude that there was a significant increase in the use of fintech services 1.98 to 2.54 ($p<0.0005$); and an improvement of 0.56 (see Table 11.6) from before to during the lockdowns.

DISCUSSION

Focusing on TAM theory and the adoption of fintech, this study examines how fintech might be used post-COVID-19 lockdown by looking at the impact of the lockdown in combination with user's loyalty to fintech services. While previous research focused on the ways in which the assurance of privacy and the quality of administrative services influence the perceived usefulness of fintech, our study sheds light on the fact that users who have positive experiences using fintech during lockdown are significantly more likely to want to continue using these services post-lockdown. The factors which most impact a user's enjoyment of fintech are the service's perceived usefulness, safety, security, and the quality of its administrative services. Users' trust in the security, reliability, and ease of use of a service is the factor which most heavily influences the likelihood of their continuing to use that service during and after the pandemic ($\beta = 0.289$). It is followed by the quality of administrative services ($\beta = 0.260$), the impact of COVID-19 lockdown ($\beta = 0.205$), and the ability of a service to provide security and privacy with regard to user data ($\beta = 0.164$). Scholars and managers alike are anticipating the continued use of fintech services after the pandemic and are thus developing suitable strategies (Gnan & Masciandaro, 2016).

Theoretical Implication

Supporting the findings of previous research on the TAM model (Chuang et al., 2016; Kang, 2018; Stewart & Jürjens, 2018), our research confirms that privacy and QAS have significant effects on fintech's perceived usefulness. We also find that the COVID-19 pandemic has increased the perceived usefulness of fintech, as it is convenient and allows users to minimize in-person interactions (Chuang et al., 2016; Davis et al., 1989b; Ryu, 2018; Saksonova & Kuzmina-Merlino, 2017; Stewart & Jürjens, 2018). Our results indicate that the ability to protect users' data, users' trust in the service will positively affect the acceptance and continued use of fintech by consumers. The present research examines the impact of the COVID-19 lockdown on consumers' use of fintech services and predicts the potential future of fintech firms.

In addition, this study finds that the quality of a service's administrative staff plays a vital role in ensuring the loyalty of users to a service. This study emphasizes how crucial it is to have humans in administrative positions, even in high-technology areas, as opposed to AI. Furthermore, we demonstrate that the fact of having humans in administrative positions indirectly enhances the intention service, that is, the degree of customers' loyalty. Specifically, the findings add to the knowledge on how technology services can build up and nurture current consumers to be loyal toward fintech services (Chuang et al., 2016; Davis et al., 1989b). Therefore, increasing QAS in significant organizations' systems should be paid attention.

Next, the study examines which extended factors influence the perceived usefulness of fintech and increase customers' intentions to use fintech services (Stewart & Jürjens, 2018). The theory of planned behavior was added to perceived usefulness as an antecedent in adopting fintech services. Results reveal that four factors (COVID-19 lockdown impact, security and privacy, trust, and QAS) significantly affect and contribute to perceived usefulness, increasing the intention to adopt fintech post-COVID-19 lockdown. This study added the COVID-19 lockdown as an updated factor, rather than a normal process development, which has encouraged consumers to use fintech services. In this study, we extend the impact of the COVID-19 lockdown as a situational impact but present an opportunity to increase the perceived usefulness of fintech.

Thus, the COVID-19 pandemic has helped users to realize the usefulness of fintech services, and users will become loyal to fintech services which have proven useful to them during the pandemic. That usefulness comes from factors that have been shown by this research to be reliability, service quality, and safety and security. Companies must ensure, however, that these factors are guaranteed if they want to maintain the loyalty of their customers. Our findings show that the level of computer skills does not impact the likelihood of a consumer using fintech services. That this fact is true indicates that there are more opportunities for services to attract new users.

Practical Implications

The COVID-19 lockdowns have forced consumers to bank and shop online and have proven the convenience and effectiveness of fintech services in allowing users to shop and conduct tasks in relation to finance from home. This study's findings suggest that an increasing number of users will use fintech services in coming years, and thus predicts an increasing demand for fintech post-COVID. We therefore suggest that firms prepare technological infrastructure and minimize network issues. Therefore, managers should maintain service quality and expand other transaction facilities, such as cooperation with many other brands or services to build a shopping ecosystem. Combining trust, data security and privacy, and QAS satisfies user's expectations regarding their experience of using fintech. Consumer satisfaction will engage consumers with the service and enhance their trust in it.

Managers should ensure their staff are well trained and can meet consumer's needs with regard to financial online services. In addition, they should regularly update their software to ensure that the customer database is secure and protected. When consumers feel that they can trust that their private information is being protected, and trust in the quality of the services they use, they are more likely to become loyal to that service. Managers should thus focus on advertising their services' ensured security and privacy. Previous customer relationship studies in marketing indicate that the consumers' trust in a service leads them to reuse that service, become loyal to it, and be more willing to pay a higher price for it (Larsson & Viitaoja, 2017).

Furthermore, the more satisfied customers are with their experience of using a service, the more likely they are to perceive that service positively, which in turn also leads to their loyalty to a service. Managers should thus conduct fintech service audits on the quality of services, user satisfaction, and loyalty. A short online survey with rewards is one method to quickly collect information on users' experiences. This method would provide an overview of customers' perceptions, as well as of their expectations and needs. The results of this study support managers in determining more suitable policies to enhance consumer loyalty.

Limitations and Future Research

Whereas this study was limited in terms of the subjects from which data was collected, future studies could collect data from a larger, more representative pool of people. First, data was collected only in the US, which means that it is limited to the culture and economy of the US. Future research should examine a broader range of cultures and economies (in both developing and developed countries) to enhance generalizability in consumer-brand relationships. Second, the current study that collects data has twice as many women answering the questionnaire as men, so the results of this Fintech study tend to be more female than male. Future research can collect data to ensure a balance between the sexes, from which the conclusions drawn can be applied to all genders.

Third, this is a cross-sectional study conducted at a specific point in time. The relationship between fintech services and their users, however, is a dynamic one. Future research could use longitudinal methods to investigate changes in the consumer-brand relationship over time (Kohn & Rosman, 1972) and capture updated trends in real time. Future research could also choose and compare several specific fintech services to determine which features of each service can give it a competitive advantage (Ryabova, 2015).

The world is adapting to a so-called new normal, and we need to accept the precarity of the healthcare system. In addition, many countries around the world are operating in an increasingly cashless way, especially since the COVID-19 pandemic. Fintech services have therefore had the opportunity to develop in this increasingly cashless world, and to provide positive experiences for, and acquire loyal customers. In the future, if fintech is to continue to prosper, enterprises will need to learn more about users' online activities and habits in order to adapt to their needs.

Funding   This chapter was funded by University of Economics Ho Chi Minh City (UEH), Vietnam.

References

Aisyah, M. (2018). Islamic bank service quality and its impact on Indonesian customers' satisfaction and loyalty. *Al-Iqtishad, 10*(2), 367–388. https://doi. org/10.15408/aiq.v10i2.7135

Anderson, J. C., & Gerbing, D. W. (1992). Assumptions and comparative strengths of the two-step approach: Comment on Fornell and Yi. *Sociological Methods & Research, 20*(3), 321–333. https://doi.org/10.1177/004912419 2020003002

Anderson, K. C., Knight, D. K., Pookulangara, S., & Josiam, B. (2014). Influence of hedonic and utilitarian motivations on retailer loyalty and purchase intention: A Facebook perspective. *Journal of Retailing and Consumer Services, 21*(5), 773–779. https://doi.org/10.1016/j.jretconser.2014.05.007

Anderson, R. E., & Srinivasan, S. S. (2003). E-satisfaction and e-loyalty: A contingency framework. *Psychology and Marketing, 20*(2), 123–138. https:// doi.org/10.1002/mar.10063

Ashta, A., & Biot-Paquerot, G. (2018). Fintech evolution: Strategic value management issues in a fast changing industry. *Strategic Change, 27*(4), 301–311. https://doi.org/10.1002/jsc.2203

Baker, S. R., Farrokhnia, R. A., Meyer, S., Pagel, M., & Yannelis, C. (2020). How does household spending respond to an epidemic? Consumption during the 2020 COVID-19 pandemic. *The Review of Asset Pricing Studies, 10*(4), 834–862.

Barth, S., de Jong, M. D. T., Junger, M., Hartel, P. H., & Roppelt, J. C. (2019). Putting the privacy paradox to the test: Online privacy and security behaviors among users with technical knowledge, privacy awareness, and financial resources. *Telematics and Informatics, 41*, 55–69. https://doi.org/10.1016/j.tele.2019.03.003

Belanche, D., Casaló, L. V., & Flavián, C. (2019). Artificial intelligence in fintech: Understanding robo-advisors adoption among customers. *Industrial Management and Data Systems, 119*(7), 1411–1430. https://doi.org/10.1108/IMDS-08-2018-0368

Bentler, P. M., & Bonett, D. G. (1980). Significance tests and goodness of fit in the analysis of covariance structures. *Psychological Bulletin, 88*(3), 588–606. https://doi.org/10.1037/0033-2909.88.3.588

Billore, S., & Billore, G. (2020). Consumption switch at haste: Insights from Indian low-income customers for adopting fintech services due to the pandemic. *Transnational Marketing Journal, 8*(2), 197–218. https://doi.org/10.33182/tmj.v8i2.1064

Byrnes, S. (2020). Can consumer data privacy coexist with how businesses want to use data? *Forbes.* https://www.forbes.com/sites/forbestechcouncil/2020/04/27/can-consumer-data-privacy-coexist-with-how-businesses-want-to-use-data/?sh=f6ca29928180

Chang, Y., Wong, S. F., Lee, H., & Jeong, S. P. (2016, August). *What motivates Chinese consumers to adopt fintech services: A regulatory focus theory.* https://doi.org/10.1145/2971603.2971643

Chuang, L.-M., Liu, C.-C., & Kao, H.-K. (2016). The adoption of fintech service: Tam perspective. *International Journal of Management and Administrative Sciences, 3*(7), 1–15.

Corstjens, M., & Lal, R. (2000). Building store loyalty through store brands. *Journal of Marketing Research, 37*(3), 281–291. https://doi.org/10.1509/jmkr.37.3.281.18781

Das, S. R. (2019). The future of fintech. *Financial Management, 48*(4), 981–1007. https://doi.org/10.1111/fima.12297

Davis, F. D. (1989). Perceived usefulness, perceived ease of use, and user acceptance of information technology. *MIS Quarterly, 13*(3), 319–340. https://doi.org/10.2307/249008

Davis, F. D., Bagozzi, R. P., & Warshaw, P. R. (1989a). User acceptance of computer technology. *Journal of Management Sciences, 35*(8), 982–1003. https://doi.org/10.1287/mnsc.35.8.982

Davis, F. D., Bagozzi, R. P., & Warshaw, P. R. (1989b). User acceptance of computer technology: A comparison of two theoretical models. *Management Science, 35*(8), 982–1003. https://doi.org/10.1287/mnsc.35.8.982

Eren, B. A. (2021). Determinants of customer satisfaction in chatbot use: Evidence from a banking application in turkey. *International Journal of Bank Marketing, 39*(2), 294–311. https://doi.org/10.1108/IJBM-02-2020-0056

Fain, D., & Roberts, M. L. (1997). Technology vs. consumer behavior: The battle for the financial services customer. *Journal of Direct Marketing, 11*(1), 44–54. https://doi.org/10.1002/(SICI)1522-7138(199724)11:1<44::AID-DIR5>3.0.CO;2-Z

Fernando, E., & Touriano, D. (2018). Development and validation of instruments adoption fintech services in Indonesia (perspective of trust and risk). Paper presented at the 2018 International Conference on Sustainable Information Engineering and Technology (SIET). https://ieeexplore.ieee.org/abstract/document/8693192

Fishbein, M. (1980). A theory of reasoned action: Some applications and implications. *Nebraska Symposium on Motivation, 27*, 65–116. PMID: 7242751.

Fisher, A. (2001). Winning the battle for customers. *Journal of Financial Services Marketing, 6*(1), 77–83. https://doi.org/10.1057/palgrave.fsm.4770042

Fishbein, M., Jaccard, J., Davidson, A. R., Ajzen, I., & Loken, B. (1980). Predicting and understanding family planning behaviors. In *Understanding attitudes and predicting social behavior*. Prentice Hall. https://nyuscholars.nyu.edu/en/publications/predicting-and-understanding-family-planning-behaviorsJournalname?

Fornell, C., & Larcker, D. F. (1981). Evaluating structural equation models with unobservable variables and measurement error. *Journal of Marketing Research, 18*(1), 39–50. https://doi.org/10.1177/002224378101800104

Fu, J., & Mishra, M. (2020a). The global impact of Covid-19 on fintech adoption. Journal of Financial Intermediation. *Available at SSRN 3588453.* https://doi.org/10.2139/ssrn.3588453

Gefen, D. (2000). E-commerce: The role of familiarity and trust. *Omega, 28*(6), 725–737. https://doi.org/10.1016/S0305-0483(00)00021-9

Gerbing, D. W., & Anderson, J. C. (1992). Monte Carlo evaluations of goodness of fit indices for structural equation models. *Sociological Methods & Research, 21*(2), 132–160. https://doi.org/10.1177/0049124192021002002

Gimpel, H., Rau, D., & Röglinger, M. (2018). Understanding fintech start-ups—A taxonomy of consumer-oriented service offerings. *Electronic Markets, 28*(3), 245–264. https://doi.org/10.1007/s12525-017-0275-0

Gnan, E., & Masciandaro, D. (2016). Central banking and monetary policy: What will be the post-crisis new normal? *Central Banking and Monetary Policy, 7, Conference Proceedings.*

Gomber, P., Kauffman, R. J., Parker, C., & Weber, B. W. (2018). On the fintech revolution: Interpreting the forces of innovation, disruption, and transformation in financial services. *Journal of Management Information Systems, 35*(1), 220–265. https://doi.org/10.1080/07421222.2018.1440766

Hair, J. F., Jr., Black, W. C., Babin, B. J., & Anderson, R. E. (2014). *Multivariate data analysis* (7th International ed.). Pearson Education Limited.

Hair, Jr., J. F., Hult, G. T. M., Ringle, C., & Sarstedt, M. (2016). *A primer on partial least squares structural equation modeling (PLS-SEM).* Sage.

Hansen, J. M., Saridakis, G., & Benson, V. (2018). Risk, trust, and the interaction of perceived ease of use and behavioral control in predicting consumers' use of social media for transactions. *Computers in Human Behavior, 80,* 197–206. https://doi.org/10.1016/j.chb.2017.11.010

Hu, Z., Ding, S., Li, S., Chen, L., & Yang, S. (2019). Adoption intention of fintech services for bank users: An empirical examination with an extended technology acceptance model. *Symmetry, 11*(3), 340. https://doi.org/10.3390/sym11030340

Jang, M., Jung, Y., & Kim, S. (2021). Investigating managers' understanding of Chatbots in the Korean financial industry. *Computers in Human Behavior, 120.*https://doi.org/10.1016/j.chb.2021.106747

Jiwasiddi, A., Adhikara, C., Adam, M., & Triana, I. (2019). Attitude toward using fintech among millennials. Paper presented at the The 1st Workshop on Multimedia Education, Learning, Assessment and its Implementation in Game and Gamification in conjunction with COMDEV, *2018.* https://doi.org/10.4108/eai.26-1-2019.2283199

Joubert, J., & Van Belle, J. (2013). The role of trust and risk in mobile commerce adoption within South Africa. *International Journal of Business, Humanities and Technology, 3*(2), 27–38.

Jung, J.-H., & Shin, J.-I. (2019). The effect of choice attributes of internet specialized banks on integrated loyalty: The moderating effect of gender. *Sustainability, 11*(24), 7063. https://doi.org/10.3390/su11247063

Justwan, F., Baumgaertner, B., Carlisle, J. E., Clark, A. K., & Clark, M. J. J. o. E. (2018). Social media echo chambers and satisfaction with democracy among democrats and republicans in the aftermath of the 2016 US elections. *Journal of Elections, Public Opinion and Parties, 28*(4), 424–442. https://doi.org/10.1080/17457289.2018.1434784

Kang, J. (2018). Mobile payment in fintech environment: Trends, security challenges, and services. *Human-Centric Computing and Information Sciences, 8*(1), 1–16. https://doi.org/10.1186/s13673-018-0155-4

Kauflin, J. (2020). *The 10 biggest fintech companies in America 2020*. Forbes. https://www.forbes.com/sites/jeffkauflin/2020/02/12/the-10-biggest-fintech-companies-in-america-2020/#7e7279691259

Kim, D. J. (2012). An investigation of the effect of online consumer trust on expectation, satisfaction, and post-expectation. *Information Systems and e-Business Management, 10*(2), 219–240. https://doi.org/10.1007/s10257-010-0136-2

Kim, Y., Choi, J., Park, Y.-J., & Yeon, J. (2016). The adoption of mobile payment services for "fintech". *International Journal of Applied Engineering Research, 11*(2), 1058–1061.

Kohn, M., & Rosman, B. L. (1972). A social competence scale and symptom checklist for the preschool child: Factor dimensions, their cross-instrument generality, and longitudinal persistence. *Developmental Psychology, 6*(3), 430–444. https://doi.org/10.1037/h0032583

Kumar, D. S., Purani, K., & Viswanathan, S. A. (2018). Influences of 'appscape' on mobile app adoption and m-loyalty. *Journal of Retailing and Consumer Services, 45*, 132–141. https://doi.org/10.1016/j.jretconser.2018.08.012

Larsson, A. (2018). *A study of Swedish bank managers' perceptions of fintech's effects on digitalization and customer e-loyalty*. The Rise and Development of fintech: Accounts of Disruption from Sweden and Beyond, 130.

Larsson, A., & Viitaoja, Y. (2017). Building customer loyalty in digital banking. *International Journal of Bank Marketing, 35*(6), 858–877. https://doi.org/10.1108/IJBM-08-2016-0112

Lee, J., Ryu, M. H., & Lee, D. (2019). A study on the reciprocal relationship between user perception and retailer perception on platform-based mobile payment service. *Journal of Retailing and Consumer Services, 48*, 7–15. https://doi.org/10.1016/j.jretconser.2019.01.007

Lee, Y.-K., Park, J.-H., Chung, N., & Blakeney, A. (2012). A unified perspective on the factors influencing usage intention toward mobile financial services. *Journal of Business Research, 65*(11), 1590–1599. https://doi.org/10.1016/j.jbusres.2011.02.044

Lewis, J. D., & Weigert, A. (1985). Trust as a social reality. *Social Forces, 63*(4), 967–985. https://doi.org/10.2307/2578601

Lim, S. H., Kim, D. J., Hur, Y., & Park, K. (2019). An empirical study of the impacts of perceived security and knowledge on continuous intention to use mobile fintech payment services. *International Journal of Human-Computer Interaction, 35*(10), 886–898. https://doi.org/10.1080/10447318.2018.1507132

Lootsma, Y. V. O. N. N. E. (2017). *From fintech to regtech: The possible use of blockchain for KYC*. Fintech To Regtech Using Block Chain.

Mahatanankoon, P., Wen, H. J., & Lim, B. (2005). Consumer-based m-commerce: Exploring consumer perception of mobile applications. *Computer*

Standards and Interfaces, 27(4), 347–357. https://doi.org/10.1016/j.csi. 2004.10.003

Malaquias, F. F., & Hwang, Y. (2016). Trust in mobile banking under conditions of information asymmetry: Empirical evidence from Brazil. *Information Development, 32*(5), 1600–1612. https://doi.org/10.1177/026666691561 6164

Moon, J.-W., & Kim, Y.-G. (2001). Extending the tam for a World-Wide-Web context. *Information and Management, 38*(4), 217–230. https://doi.org/ 10.1016/S0378-7206(00)00061-6

Noor, U., Anwar, Z., Amjad, T., & Choo, K.-K.R. (2019). A machine learning-based fintech cyber threat attribution framework using high-level indicators of compromise. *Future Generation Computer Systems, 96*, 227–242. https://doi.org/10.1016/j.future.2019.02.013

Podsakoff, N. P. (2003). Common method biases in behavioral research: A critical review of the literature and recommended remedies. *Journal of Applied Psychology, 885*(879), 10–1037. https://doi.org/10.1037/0021-9010.88.5.879

Ponnavolu, K. (2000). *Customer loyalty in interactive media: An exploration of its antcedents and consequences.* Drexel University.

Puschmann, T. (2017). fintech. *Business and Information Systems Engineering, 59*(1), 69–76. https://doi.org/10.1007/s12599-017-0464-6

Rauniar, R., Rawski, G., Yang, J., & Johnson, B. (2014). Technology acceptance model (TAM) and social media usage: An empirical study on Facebook. *Journal of Enterprise Information Management, 27*(1), 6–30. https://doi. org/10.1108/JEIM-04-2012-0011

Razzaque, A., Cummings, R. T., Karolak, M., & Hamdan, A. (2020). The propensity to use fintech: Input from bankers in the kingdom of Bahrain. *Journal of Information and Knowledge Management, 19*(1), 2040025. https://doi.org/10.1142/S0219649220400250

Revathy, C., & Balaji, P. (2020). Determinants of behavioural intention on e-wallet usage: An empirical examination in amid of covid-19 lockdown period. *International Journal of Management (IJM), 11*(6), 92–104. https://doi. org/10.34218/IJM.11.6.2020.008

Russell-Bennett, R., McColl-Kennedy, J. R., & Coote, L. V. (2007). Involvement, satisfaction, and brand loyalty in a small business services setting. *Journal of Business Research, 60*(12), 1253–1260. https://doi.org/10.1016/ j.jbusres.2007.05.001

Ryabova, A. (2015). Emerging fintech market: Types and features of new financial technologies. *Journal of Economics and Social Sciences, 7*, 4.

Ryu, H.-S. (2018). What makes users willing or hesitant to use fintech? The moderating effect of user type. *Industrial Management and Data Systems, 118*(3), 541–569. https://doi.org/10.1108/IMDS-07-2017-0325

Saksonova, S., & Kuzmina-Merlino, I. (2017). Fintech as financial innovation—The possibilities and problems of implementation. *European Research Studies Journal, XX*(3A), 961–973. https://doi.org/10.35808/ersj/757

Salz, P. A. (2020). Mobile marketing experts show how fintech apps will emerge fighting fit from the Covid-19 crisis. *Forbes.* https://www.forbes.com/sites/peggyannesalz/2020/05/04/mobile-marketing-experts-show-how-fintech-apps-will-emerge-fighting-fit-from-the-covid-19-crisis/#4136976c4d50

Scarpi, D., Pizzi, G., & Visentin, M. (2014). Shopping for fun or shopping to buy: Is it different online and offline? *Journal of Retailing and Consumer Services, 21*(3), 258–267. https://doi.org/10.1016/j.jretconser.2014.02.007

Shin, D.-H. (2010). The effects of trust, security and privacy in social networking: A security-based approach to understand the pattern of adoption. *Interacting with Computers, 22*(5), 428–438. https://doi.org/10.1016/j.intcom.2010.05.001

Siau, K., & Shen, Z. (2003). Building customer trust in mobile commerce. *Communications of the ACM, 46*(4), 91–94. https://doi.org/10.1145/641205.641211

Singh, N., & Sinha, N. (2020). How perceived trust mediates merchant's intention to use a mobile wallet technology. *Journal of Retailing and Consumer Services, 52,* 101894.

Statista. (2019). *Number of mobile phone users worldwide from 2015 to 2020.* https://www.statista.com/statistics/274774/forecast-of-mobile-phone-users-worldwide/

Stewart, H., & Jürjens, J. (2018). Data security and consumer trust in fintech innovation in Germany. *Information and Computer Security, 26*(1), 109–128. https://doi.org/10.1108/ICS-06-2017-0039

Talwar, S., Dhir, A., Khalil, A., Mohan, G., & Islam, A. K. M. N. (2020). Point of adoption and beyond. Initial trust and mobile-payment continuation intention. *Journal of Retailing and Consumer Services, 55,* 102086. https://doi.org/10.1016/j.jretconser.2020.102086

Tapia, A. H. (2004). Resistance or deviance? A high-tech workplace during the bursting of the dot-com bubble. In *Information systems research* (pp. 577–596). Springer.

Tarafdar, M., & Zhang, J. (2008). Determinants of reach and loyalty—A study of website performance and implications for website design. *Journal of Computer Information Systems, 48*(2), 16–24. https://doi.org/10.1080/08874417.2008.11646005

Tat Huei, C., Suet Cheng, L., Chee Seong, L., Aye Khin, A., & Ling Leh Bin, R. (2018). Preliminary study on consumer attitude towards fintech products and services in Malaysia. *International Journal of Engineering and Technology, 7*(2), 166–169. https://doi.org/10.14419/ijet.v7i2.29.13310

Tiwari, P., & Kartika. (2019). Impact of digitalization on empowerment and transformation of society. *Research Journal of Humanities and Social Sciences, 10*(2), 305–310. https://doi.org/10.5958/2321-5828.2019.00054.8

Toufaily, E., Ricard, L., & Perrien, J. (2013). Customer loyalty to a commercial website: Descriptive meta-analysis of the empirical literature and proposal of an integrative model. *Journal of Business Research, 66*(9), 1436–1447. https://doi.org/10.1016/j.jbusres.2012.05.011

Vance, A., Elie-dit-Cosaque, C., & Straub, D. W. (2008). Examining trust in information technology artifacts: The effects of system quality and culture. *Journal of Management Information Systems, 24*(4), 73–100. https://doi.org/10.2753/MIS0742-1222240403

Venkatesh, V., & Davis, F. D. (2000). A theoretical extension of the technology acceptance model: Four longitudinal field studies. *Management Science, 46*(2), 186–204. https://doi.org/10.1287/mnsc.46.2.186.11926

Wallace, L. G., & Sheetz, S. D. (2014). The adoption of software measures: A technology acceptance model (TAM) perspective. *Information and Management, 51*(2), 249–259. https://doi.org/10.1016/j.im.2013.12.003

Wang, M., & Chang, Y. (2018). *Technology leadership, brand equity, and customer loyalty towards fintech service providers in China.*

Wang, Z., GUAN, Z.(G)., Hou, F., Li, B. & Zhou, W. (2019). What determines customers' continuance intention of FinTech? Evidence from YuEbao. *Industrial Management & Data Systems, 119*(8), 1625–1637. https://doi.org/10.1108/IMDS-01-2019-0011

Wójcik, D., & Ioannou, S. (2020). Covid-19 and finance: Market developments so far and potential impacts on the financial sector and centres. *Tijdschrift voor Economische en Sociale Geografie, 111*(3), 387–400. https://doi.org/10.1111/tesg.12434

Wu, J., Liu, L., & Huang, L. (2016). *Exploring user acceptance of innovative mobile payment service in emerging market: the moderating effect of diffusion stages of WeChat payment in China.*

Yang, A., Xu, J., Weng, J., Zhou, J., & Wong, D. S. (2018). Lightweight and privacy-preserving delegatable proofs of storage with data dynamics in cloud storage. *IEEE Transactions on Cloud Computing, 9*(1), 212–225.

Yen, C. H., & Lu, H. P. (2008). Effects of e-service quality on loyalty intention: An empirical study in online auction. *Managing Service Quality, 18*(2), 127–146. https://doi.org/10.1108/09604520810859193

Yun, Z. S., & Good, L. K. (2007). Developing customer loyalty from e-tail store image attributes. *Managing Service Quality, 17*(1), 4–22. https://doi.org/10.1108/09604520710720647

Evidence From Around the World

CHAPTER 12

Fintech and Financial Inclusion in Developing Countries

Charles Adjasi, Calumn Hamilton, and Robert Lensink⬤

INTRODUCTION

The last two decades have seen financial inclusion becoming firmly established as the primary international objective for developing countries' financial sectors (Lensink et al., 2022). The shift in focus from financial development, which captures the overall relative *size* of the financial sector, to financial inclusion, which focuses instead on *breadth* in terms

C. Adjasi
Development Finance and Economics, University of Stellenbosch Business (USB) School, Cape Town, South Africa
e-mail: charlesa@usb.ac.za

C. Hamilton · R. Lensink (✉)
Faculty of Economics and Business, University of Groningen, Groningen, The Netherlands
e-mail: B.W.Lensink@rug.nl

C. Hamilton
e-mail: c.g.hamilton@rug.nl

of inclusivity of financial sector access and use, is perhaps one of the most notable examples of a successful move away from conventional macroeconomic aggregates to more socially nuanced indicators. The reasons for the high priority assigned to developing countries' financial inclusion by international organizations and policymakers are manyfold and will later be briefly discussed. At this stage, financial inclusion is identified as a key enabler for seven of the seventeen Sustainable Development Goals (World Bank, 2018) and has long been considered as a necessary condition for optimal population participation in social and economic life (Anderloni et al., 2008). Most importantly, there are well-established causal links between the financial inclusion of women and female economic and empowerment outcomes (Duvendack & Mader, 2020; Hansen et al., 2021; Pitt et al., 2006), which further underscore the social necessity of increasing financial inclusion, particularly with a gendered focus.

The fintech revolution of the early twenty-first century is rapidly emerging as a major influence on developing a country's financial sectors and has widespread implications for the crucial development goal of increased financial inclusion. Fintech evolves somewhat differently in developing countries than in advanced economies, but the impacts of this evolution remain highly relevant. In their discussion of the different eras and phases of fintech, Arner et al. (2015) note that while the twenty-first-century fintech revolution in the developed world has seen financial technologies becoming increasingly more advanced and complex, developing countries' financial innovations are inherently more low-fi and focus on navigating and surmounting the obstacles and infrastructural inadequacies which have acted as breaks on more traditional financial service providers and facilities. For example, rather than designing complex apps that presuppose widespread smartphone ownership and digital literacy, fintech innovators in the developing world focus on providing new financial products and services specifically in ways that circumvent the need for these preconditions. The vastly successful takeoff of *Mobile Money* services, particularly in Africa, which are purposefully designed to require only the most basic cell phones, regular 2G signal coverage, and a highly localized system of agents is the prime example of this (Allen et al., 2014; Hinson et al., 2019; Suri & Jack, 2016). What Mobile Money

---

R. Lensink
University of Stellenbosch Business (USB) School, Cape Town, South Africa

lacks in technological sophistication is more than compensated by its extraordinarily rapid adoption in many countries.

In Lensink et al. (2022), we argued that understanding the implications and impacts that different forms of fintech have both for and through financial inclusion on social and economic outcomes represents one of the most exciting and important research frontiers in the field of development finance. In this chapter, we further elaborate on this point. After briefly acquainting the reader with the relevant concepts and indicators of financial inclusion and providing an overview of the current state of fintech in the developing world along with some fintech definitions, we expand the empirical discussion of Lensink et al. (2022) into a comparison of the penetration of key fintech products and services between different developing regions. These products and services range from deliberately low-fi innovations such as Mobile Money and simple peer-to-peer platforms to frontier technologies such as crowdfunding apps, RegTechs, cryptocurrencies, and blockchain. We then review the main findings of the literature thus far regarding the impacts of fintech—and particularly, Mobile Money—on financial inclusion and development outcomes. Afterward, we discuss the risks associated with the rapid shift in the financial sector landscape that the fintech revolution implies and the accompanying regulatory implications. Finally, we conclude by proposing two alternative future scenarios for the long-term implications of fintech on developing countries' financial inclusion. The first is that, by actually being ahead of the curve in the adoption and proliferation of many new financial technologies, developing countries may find that the fintech revolution acts as an equalizer by which the constraints of physical resources and infrastructure are relieved, and populations face rapidly expanding and more inclusive financial access. The second more somber scenario is that, as fintechs in advanced countries become ever more complicated and digital infrastructure and literacy in the developing world continues to lag, the fintech revolution may only serve to create further forms of division between and within country's financial exclusion as swathes of the world population are shut out of these new innovations.

FINTECH AND FINANCIAL INCLUSION
IN THE DEVELOPING WORLD

What Is Financial Inclusion, and How Can Fintech Impact It?

A useful working definition of financial inclusion (FI) is that "[financial inclusion involves] broadening access, availability, and enhancing the usage of formal financial services by all segments of the population" (Sarma, 2008). As FI is a multifaceted concept, preferred definitions may vary, but this definition concisely captures its essence. The key elements of this definition are first and foremost that financial inclusion involves increasing the levels of financial sector access and usage for individuals. Furthermore, this should be independent of population segmentation, such that different ethnic, social, gender, geographic, age, etc., groups enjoy equal opportunities to access and make use of financial services within developing countries. Finally, we are talking about formal financial services, in that a key element of financial inclusion is supporting poorer and more marginalized individuals to move away from reliance on informal and perhaps predatory financial service arrangements.[1] Therefore, to understand the financial inclusion concept clearly, it can also be useful to turn it around: if financial exclusion is the inability of individuals in developing countries to access and use formal financial services due to a lack of available or affordable products in their area, lower levels of financial literacy, discrimination, mistrust, or some other reason, the goal of financial inclusion is to bring these individuals into the financial system by overcoming these obstacles. Therefore, financial inclusion differs from the earlier concept of financial development, where financial sectors are evaluated according to their size (Hannig & Jansen, 2010; Lensink et al., 2022), such as the relative volume of loans outstanding or deposits on

---

[1] To the extent that there are also some positive aspects of informal finance, such as the leveraging of local knowledge to reduce collateral requirements (Manig, 1990) or the social interaction gains from participating in savings clubs (Anderson & Baland, 2002), financial inclusion interventions can also seek to incorporate these into formal financial products and services so as to improve their appeal and by extension their breadth of usage.

account,[2] and instead evaluates financial sectors according to their degree of inclusivity at the individual level.

We measure levels of financial inclusion according to the shares of individuals, preferably stratified by social groups, who have access to and make use of formal financial products and services (Allen et al., 2014; Demirgüç-Kunt & Klapper, 2013; Demirgüç-Kunt et al., 2017, 2018). These latter references refer to the Global Findex Database, which since 2011 has provided triennial[3] survey-based indicators of the population share of individuals who access and use various forms of financial services and transactions and which forms the 'gold standard' of financial inclusion data (Lensink et al., 2022). As such, it will become immediately apparent that fintech revolution[4] has the potential to boost levels of financial inclusion in three different ways:

1. By utilizing technological solutions to reduce frictions in access to or use of existing financial products and services, such as reducing fixed costs, overcoming infrastructure constraints, etc., so that those who wish to become financially included but face barriers now see those barriers lowered.
2. By allowing existing financial service providers to adapt their financial products and services in order to make them more appealing to individuals who had thus far chosen not to make use of them.
3. By developing new financial products and services which act as substitutes for those already in existence but have greater scope for reaching those who remain financially excluded.

The first two points, if successful, would therefore lead to observable rises in conventional financial inclusion indicators such as the share of

---

[2] The key difference being that financial development concepts tell us nothing about the extent to which financial sector usage is concentrated. For example, small numbers of urban elites could own large deposit holdings, and access voluminous credit, in a financial sector which therefore appears large but in fact is completely closed to most people and has little impact on general living standards or poverty reduction. For a full overview of the shortcomings of the financial development concept and the academic and policy shift in focus toward financial inclusion, see Lensink et al. (2022).

[3] Until disrupted by the Global COVID-19 Pandemic in 2020–2022.

[4] Given the context of this book, we deem it superfluous to define 'fintech' or 'the fintech revolution' here, although of course we will later make clear the prevalent forms fintech takes in the developing world.

adults with a bank account or the share of adults currently holding credit. However, the latter point requires new indicators, such as the share of individuals accessing these new products and services, which will lead to debates over the degree of substitutability between the new services and the old ones. Some of these new indicators have already been incorporated into later rounds of Findex Surveys as individuals in developing countries are asked about their financial sector engagement in a manner which is then easily aggregated into national level variables.

Predominant Fintechs in Developing Countries

As indicated in our introduction, the fintech revolution can be usefully deconstructed into two components—that which is taking place in advanced economies, and that in the developing world. This broadly matches the split between Arner et al.'s (2015) 'FinTech 3.0' and '3.5'. In general, both of these represent elements of an era during which fintech has become detached from conventional banks and financial service providers, taking advantage of technological innovation in tandem with the reputational blows to the existing system caused by the Global Financial Crisis of 2008 and its aftermath in order to overcome skepticism of new service alternatives by individuals and governments (Chamley et al., 2012; Philippon, 2016). However, the two elements of this split take place in very different institutional and infrastructural landscapes.

The predominant fintech innovations which characterize the ongoing fintech revolution in the developed world are usefully surveyed by Gomber et al. (2018) and will be familiar to most readers of this book. They subdivide these innovations into four basic categories: operations management, payments and transfer innovations, lending and deposit innovations, and investment innovations. We do not discuss operations management as it does not really relate to financial inclusion, but of the latter three, there is clear relevance to developing country contexts. Payment and transfer innovations, and lending and deposit innovations clearly relate directly to established financial inclusion concepts and metrics. Nevertheless, the major examples Gomber et al. (2018) provide for each category vary in terms of relevance for developing countries at the present time. Cryptocurrency and blockchain may have a future role to play in developing countries, particularly as they relate to cross-border transactions. However, other than in outliers such as El Salvador, there is little penetration thus far. Ndemo (2022) demonstrates that cryptocurrency markets are much smaller in the developing regions of Africa, the Middle East, and Latin America than that of North America and Western Europe; although East Asian and South Asian markets are less far behind, Ndemo argues that the rate of market growth in Africa is rapid. It is difficult to imagine how investment innovations such as robo-advisory and online stock-market portfolio suites are especially relevant to developing countries' financial inclusion at the present time. However, peer-to-peer lending and crowdfunding platforms for capital investments may be, and such platforms have already made some headway in developing countries with regard to investments in agricultural equipment (Hinson et al., 2019). Nevertheless, as Cozzens and Thakur (2014) repeatedly illustrate, most of such innovations originate in and are designed for developed countries as developing countries are recipients of exogenous technology and are left to adopt and adapt them if they can.

The other aspect of the fintech revolution which relates more directly to developing countries is inherently different. Rather than the somewhat complex innovations discussed above, which place high demands both on infrastructure and human capital, some fintechs evolve for very different reasons. Traditional supply-side constraints on financial inclusion in developing countries include high fixed costs of retail nodes such as banks and ATMs (Mas, 2011; Ouma et al., 2017), shortages of educated financial sector workers (Allen et al., 2021), unreliable infrastructure (Ogawa et al., 2021), and informational constraints (Karlan & Zinman, 2009). Demand-side constraints include lack of financial literacy, lack of trust in financial institutions and contracts, and low levels of income and wealth (Lensink et al., 2022). Naturally, these constraints are equally relevant for new fintechs as for conventional financial sector services, and thus overcoming these constraints is a necessary condition for any fintech to take off in developing countries at scale. Therefore, the fintech revolution as it pertains to developing countries is largely concerned with circumnavigating these constraints. Mobile Money, which is discussed in greater depth in the next section, is the flagship innovation of developing countries' fintech thus far.

Constraints on Fintech in Developing Countries

Inadequate digital infrastructure has proven to be a major binding constraint on the international proliferation of fintech (Diniz et al., 2012).

In an econometric study of the relevance of information and communications technology (ICT) infrastructure for fintech in Nigeria, Morakinyo et al. (2019) find that the probability of adopting fintech crucially depends on the proximity to network infrastructure. In most Sub-Saharan African countries, distances to appropriate networks are vast. Moreover, the electrical and communications infrastructure provides limited and unreliable access to broadband Internet connections (Yermack, 2018). This is especially the case in rural areas where the infrastructure is not fintech-enabling. Clearly, as long as the necessary information infrastructure, including a reliable low-cost electricity grid and mobile networks, is not available, the diffusion of fintech will not take place.

To promote adequate ICT infrastructure, it seems indispensable that African policymakers create a supportive regulatory framework or ease regulatory bottlenecks at the very least. However, we know surprisingly little about the optimal regulatory framework to promote fintech. African governments have mostly taken a hands-off approach regarding fintech regulations. In Kenya and South Africa, the two most successful fintech adopting countries in Africa, a specific fintech legal framework does not exist, and governments tried to address various issues as they emerge (Didenko, 2018). Major fintech crises did not occur in these countries, which suggests that the legal framework is somehow properly used. Yet, it is unclear whether future regulatory responses will be appropriate and how other African countries will respond. Therefore, an in-depth analysis of the appropriate regulatory frameworks and legal systems which best promotes fintechs generally is of utmost importance. Importantly, Yermack (2018) finds that the adoption of fintech in African countries is much higher in countries with a common law system than in countries with a civil law system. This is probably because common law protects better against risk (i.e., better investor protection) and ensures lower costs of capital than civil law, which incentivizes risky investments in fintech. The regulatory implications of fintech for developing countries will be discussed in greater detail in section "Risks and Regulatory Implications of the Fintech Revolution in Developing Countries".

MOBILE MONEY ADOPTION: A REGIONAL COMPARISON

Consider the following stylized example: A middle-aged man named Ngugi, using his simple analog phone in Nairobi, Kenya, has just transferred money to his 80-year-old mother and his older brother in the village of Kilingili, about 237 km away. Floods in Kilingili have done considerable damage to the family farm, so the money from Ngugi's job in the city is welcomed. There is no cable-internet in Kilingili, and Ngugi's mother does not have a cellphone, but these things do not matter—she goes to collect the money from Mr Hasan at the grocery kiosk, who also earns small commissions as a Mobile Money agent using his analog phone on the side. At the same time, Delali, a 28-year-old woman in Kpoeta, Ghana, has just been notified by SMS that her Mobile Money account has reached her savings goal of 150 cedis, after she chose to deposit 10 cedis per week for the last few months. This goal, together with her credit score from Mobile Money transactions, qualifies her for an instant microloan of 300 cedis. She uses this money to buy a portable high-capacity rice-milling machine and expand her rice production business. Welcome to the world of Mobile Money.

Introduction to Mobile Money

Mobile Money is the use of the cellular network and mobile phone handsets as infrastructure for financial sector transactions. Donovan (2012) defines Mobile Money as the provision of financial services through a mobile device. Internationally, the real pioneer in the Mobile Money market was M-Pesa, which first emerged in Kenya. This innovation was initially designed by Safaricom, a mobile network operator (MNO), to allow users to deposit and transfer small amounts of money via SMS using their cellphones. M-Pesa was launched in 2007 and piggybacked on the network of MNO agents scattered all over Kenya, including in small villages and isolated areas, from which SIM-cards and airtime could be purchased or transferred in very small units. Safaricom took advantage of this wide and already well-established agent network and the wider accessibility of mobile phones to offer a faster and cheaper means of remitting money across long distances. This immediately solved the problem of the huge transfer costs associated with money transfers through banks, and the risk of theft or loss in the case of cash transfers by the poor along physical transport links. The network of mobile agents was part of the key infrastructure in delivering fast payment services at an affordable rate and is also a large part of the reason why Mobile Money achieved scale so quickly. As noted in Mas and Radcliffe (2011) and Lensink et al. (2022), Mobile Money agents act as the 'retail arm' of the Mobile Money system, and customers or Mobile Money users only need access to a cell phone and small cash float to start transacting.

Mas and Radcliffe (2011) provide a detailed overview of precisely how Mobile Money strategically overcomes the supply- and demand-side constraints on developing country fintech proliferation discussed in the previous section. First, as with M-Pesa and Safaricom, Mobile Money piggybacks on existing infrastructure. This means that it always ensures that network requirements are already in place. This includes ensuring all operations can be performed on the existing 2G cell phone network, and initially locating agents and outlets in existing consumer focal points such as village convenience stores and kiosks. The agent's system also overcomes human capital constraints as it negates the need for quali-fied financial service staff. Second, the high fixed costs of conventional banking and even microfinance retail nodes are converted into variable costs, as Mobile Money agents are employed as contractors working on commission for the transactions, they facilitate or are existing shopkeepers merely adding another product or service to the array of things they already sell. Third, the business model of Mobile Money centers around profiting from volume of transactions rather than volume of deposits. That is, profits are made more from commissions rather than lending out deposit holdings or from collecting account ownership fees. This means that even customers with no meaningful funds on deposit are still of value so long as they perform transactions, and that Mobile Money accounts themselves can be offered for free. Finally, Mobile Money focuses on the products and services for which traditionally financially excluded individuals have the most pressing need—that is, secure savings and instantaneous transfer facilities, rather than more complex insurance and savings products, although these are also offered in more recent permu-tations of Mobile Money (Hinson et al., 2019). These features serve to illustrate the adaptability of successful developing country fintech, and to indicate the approaches other innovators can take if they wish to gain footing at scale in the Global South.

Empirical Overview of Mobile Money Penetration

In Chapter 6 of Lensink et al. (2022), we provided an empirical overview of the preponderance of Mobile Money in Sub-Saharan Africa as of 2017, demonstrating that the African continent really is the world leader in terms of Mobile Money adoption and penetration, albeit with highly heterogeneous experiences across the continent. We now extend this overview to the other developing regions and a broader set of Mobile

Money indicators, also updated with the recently released 2021 data. However, the 2021 Findex data comes with a large caveat. As a result of COVID-19, fewer countries were sampled than in the 2017 round, and it appears that the omitted countries were often at the lower end of the development spectrum. Table 12.2, which shows the shares of non-high-income countries in each region which passed certain Mobile Money adoption thresholds, demonstrates the reduction in sample size in some of the regions. It may therefore be that seeming improvements in the degree of Mobile Money proliferation between 2017 and 2021 are in fact a result of some lower penetration countries dropping out of the sample, and readers may therefore prefer to focus on the 2017 data as an older but more complete overview. While so often in development economics, the discussion focuses on how Sub-Saharan Africa can 'catch-up' to other regions, in the case of Mobile Money, the story is reversed—it is Sub-Saharan Africa, or at least large swathes of it, which have set the standard for other developing regions to replicate. This again serves to illustrate how carefully designed fintechs can fundamentally uproot conventional development disparities.

When empirically analyzing financial inclusion across any dimension, decisions must be made over the selection of appropriate indicators. The difficulty is that there are several different measures of, for example, the scale of adoption of Mobile Money at the individual-user level and attempts to rank countries or regions on the basis of financial inclusion may depend heavily on the selection of indicators. Attempts have been made to construct FI indices by combining multiple variables into a single univariate index (Sarma, 2008), but while there remains no consensus over which variables should be included and how they should be weighted, it remains preferable to examine individual financial inclusion variables. In Lensink et al. (2022), we focused on the share of adult individuals with a Mobile Money account and the share of total domestic remittances received via a mobile phone. Now, however, we defer to the Mobile Money usage measures[5] of Khera et al. (2021) in a recent International Monetary Fund (IMF) report: share of adults (age 15+) with

---

[5] Khera et al. (2021) also propose some 'supply-side' access measures of Mobile Money penetration, such as number of agents per capita, however for reasons of concision, we do not focus on these as they are less relevant to the discussion of financial inclusion at the individual level.

a Mobile Money account, share of adults who receive salary via a cellphone, and share of adults who use the cellphones to pay utility bills. Via this selection of the most common regular incoming and outgoing transactions which individuals make, we gain a broader impression of how and where Mobile Money has made the greatest inroads in terms of people's daily financial lives.

Table 12.1 presents an overview of the depth of Mobile Money penetration in the major developing regions from the most recent rounds of Findex data in 2017 and 2021 along the three indiators favored by Khera et al. (2021) and listed in the above paragraph. In the case of the latter two indicators, we restrict the denominator to the shares of adults who receive some form of wages, and who pay utility bills, respectively. High-income countries are excluded according to World Bank income classifications. Most questions regarding Mobile Money usage were not included in the earlier rounds of Findex data, hence we do not have data from the 2011 and 2014 Findex reports. However, as the earliest Mobile Money services in Kenya were launched in 2007, all of this data grew from 0% in the ten or fewer years preceding 2017. The right-hand side of Table 12.1 shows the country in each region with the highest value for each indicator in each sample year. The countries with the lowest values for each indicator have shares close to 0% in all cases.

Focusing particularly on the more complete 2017 sample, the aforementioned positive gap between Sub-Saharan Africa and the other developing regions is clearly observable in the upper panel of Table 12.1, although in the usage measures of the middle and lower panels, it can be seen that East Asia and Pacific (EAP) is also an early and heavier adopter alongside SSA. This relates to the previously discussed latent demand in Sub-Saharan Africa for fast and secure methods of transfer between individuals rather than between individuals and large companies such as employers and utility providers (Mas & Radcliffe, 2011). Also note that using a mobile phone to receive wages can involve using conventional banking apps in addition to specific Mobile Money accounts, which likely explains the low Mobile Money account ownership but relatively high cellphone usage among wage recipients in EAP. Unsurprisingly, given its pioneer status, Kenya leads not only Sub-Saharan Africa, but the world across all three indicators. Iran was the lead country in the Middle East and North Africa (MENA), China and Mongolia led EAP, Bangladesh and Pakistan led South Asia (SA), and there were no consistent leaders across indicators in Europe and Central Asia (ECA) and Latin America

Table 12.1 Aggregate mobile money penetration in 2017 and 2021* in the developing world

Men and women

	2017	2021*		2017		2021*
Share of 15+ Individuals who have a Mobile Money Account						
East Asia and Pacific	1%	6%	Mongolia	22%	Thailand	60%
Europe and Central Asia	3%	17%	Turkey	16%	Russia	33%
Latin America and the Caribbean	5%	23%	Paraguay	29%	Paraguay	38%
The Middle East and North Africa	6%	6%	Iran	26%	Iran	12%
South Asia	4%	12%	Bangladesh	21%	Bangladesh	29%
Sub-Saharan Africa	21%	33%	Kenya	73%	Kenya	69%
Share of 15+ wage receiving Individuals who received salary through a cellphone						
East Asia and Pacific	24%	3%	China Mongolia	33% 33%	Mongolia	61%
Europe and Central Asia	6%	17%	Tajikistan	17%	Russia	29%
Latin America and the Caribbean	2%	18%	Venezuela	12%	Venezuela	38%
The Middle East and North Africa	2%	2%	Iran	7%	Jordan	5%
South Asia	3%	11%	Pakistan Bangladesh	4% 4%	Maldives	15%
Sub-Saharan Africa	19%	32%	Kenya	33%	Kenya	60%
Share of 15+ bill paying Individuals who pay utility bills via a cellphone						
East Asia and Pacific	19%	5%	China	25%	Mongolia	62%
Europe and Central Asia	10%	41%	Croatia	23%	Kazakhstan	68%
Latin America and the Caribbean	5%	31%	Haiti	17%	Venezuela	52%
The Middle East and North Africa	11%	16%	Iran	43%	Saudi Arabia	80%
South Asia	4%	15%	Pakistan	11%	Bangladesh	28%
Sub-Saharan Africa	23%	37%	Kenya	82%	Kenya	84%

Notes Upper Table shows the aggregate share of individuals with a Mobile Money account, Middle Table shows the aggregate share of individuals who receive wages via a mobile phone, Lower Table shows the aggregate share of individuals who pay utility bills via a mobile phone. Left-hand side shows the data for each of the developing regions of the world according to the World Bank regional classifications, Right-hand side shows the data for the highest performing country in each region for each indicator. High-income countries and individuals under 15 years old are excluded. Data comes from the World Bank Global Findex Database utilizing the regional aggregates as provided (Demirgüç-Kunt et al., 2018, 2022). *2021 data aggregates omit some countries as compared to the 2017 data as some countries were unable to be surveyed during the Covid period; as omitted countries are likely systematically lower in terms of level of development, direct comparisons between the two sample years should be treated with caution

Table 12.2   Intra-regional Intensity of Mobile Money Penetration in 2017 and 2021* in the Developing World

Countries	2017	2021*		2017	2021*
Share of **countries** *where the share of adults who* **have a Mobile Money Account** *is > 20%*					
East Asia and Pacific	10% (1/10)	50% (5/10)	The Middle East and North Africa	10% (1/10)	0% (0/10)
Europe and Central Asia	0% (0/22)	6% (1/18)	South Asia	17% (1/6)	14% (1/7)
Latin America and the Caribbean	6% (1/17)	38% (6/16)	Sub-Saharan Africa	51% (18/35)	85% (22/26)
Share of **countries** *where the share of wage earners who* **received salary through a cellphone** *is > 20%*					
East Asia and Pacific	20% (2/10)	70% (7/10)	The Middle East and North Africa	10% (1/10)	0% (0/10)
Europe and Central Asia	5% (1/22)	11% (2/18)	South Asia	0% (0/6)	0% (0/7)
Latin America and the Caribbean	0% (0/17)	13% (2/16)	Sub-Saharan Africa	51% (18/35)	81% (21/26)
Share of **countries** *where the share of bill-payers who* **pay utility bills via a cellphone** *is >20%*					
East Asia and Pacific	20% (2/10)	30% (3/10)	The Middle East and North Africa	0% (0/10)	10% (1/10)
Europe and Central Asia	0% (0/22)	61% (11/18)	South Asia	0% (0/6)	14% (1/7)
Latin America and the Caribbean	0% (0/17)	38% (6/16)	Sub-Saharan Africa	43% (15/35)	73% (19/26)

Notes Upper Table shows the share of countries in each developing region where the proportion of adults with a Mobile Money account is greater than 20%, Middle Table shows the share of countries in each developing region where the aggregate share of individuals who receive wages via a mobile phone is greater than 20%, Lower Table shows the share of countries in each developing region where the aggregate share of individuals who pay utility bills via a mobile phone is greater than 20%. Regions are according to the World Bank regional classifications. High-income countries and individuals under 15 years old are excluded. Data comes from the World Bank Global Findex Database utilizing the regional aggregates as provided (Demirgüç-Kunt et al., 2018, 2022). *2021 data aggregates omit some countries as compared to the 2017 data as some countries were unable to be surveyed during the COVID period; as omitted countries are likely systematically lower in terms of level of development, direct comparisons between the two sample years should be treated with caution and the Caribbean (LAC), likely due in part to generally low levels of Mobile Money penetration and adoption across these regions. Focusing on the reduced sample with 2021 data, rapid growth can be observed in some regions; we of course repeat the caveat that this may in part be due to some countries with lower levels of Mobile Money penetration dropping out of the sample. Nevertheless, rapid growth in Latin America across all three indicators, and to a slightly lesser extent in Europe and Central Asia, suggests that other parts of the developing world are beginning to take Mobile Money more seriously and to seek to catch-up with Sub-Saharan Africa. The very rapid growth of Mobile Money in Thailand appears to be a particularly interesting case; moving from just 8% of adults with an account in 2017 (not shown in the table) to 60% in 2021, Thailand has seen a surge almost as deep and rapid as Kenya and the other African leaders achieved a few years earlier. Explaining this rapid rise will be an interesting case study for future research; a speculative explanation might be that particularly severe COVID-19 restrictions in some East Asian countries acted as a catalyst for people to find simple digital alternatives to cash and physical transactions. Mongolia, which was already a regional leader in 2017, has also seen rapid growth in the years since then. Turning to Europe and Central Asia, the rapid rise of Mobile Money penetration in Russia cannot be ignored, although this data was collected prior to the invasion of Ukraine and the situation may therefore have changed. South Asia and the Middle East and North Africa still remain very nascent in terms of Mobile Money adoption. In summary, the 2021 data seems to suggest that Mobile Money is beginning to take off in some but not in all developing regions outside of the lead region, Sub-Saharan Africa, albeit with the caveat of a smaller sample of countries and the exogenous shock of the COVID-19 pandemic and accompanying restrictions in many parts of the world.

Looking solely at the lead countries in each region, however, gives little insight into how evenly Mobile Money penetration is dispersed within each region. Table 12.2 shows the *share of countries* in each region with values for each indicator above 20% in 2017 and 2021, and the total number of countries in each region which exceed this threshold. The changes in the denominators of these shares illustrate how many countries are missing from each region in the COVID-19 impacted 2021 survey. The 20% cut-off point is chosen arbitrarily, but is comparable to what would generally be considered a 'very low' level of financial inclusion for more conventional banking products (Lensink et al., 2022). As can be seen across all indicators, in 2017 the *share of countries* and *number of countries* with a sizable magnitude of Mobile Money penetration was very small in all regions except Sub-Saharan Africa. This discovery suggested three alternative possibilities regarding the future of Mobile Money in the non-African developing regions: either, (a) other regions lag behind Sub-Saharan Africa and can replicate the SSA experience of diffusion of Mobile Money penetration from the lead country if given more time, (b) other regions face constraints on the diffusion of Mobile Money adoption which are not present in SSA, such as cultural resistance or regulatory barriers, or (c) other regions have less need or demand for Mobile Money services than SSA, perhaps because more conventional forms of finance are more developed, and therefore could rapidly adopt Mobile Money but collectively choose not to.

The 2021 data may provide some limited indication as to which of these prognoses are more plausible, although in truth situation is likely to vary between regions and over time. The fact that two other developing regions—East Asia and Pacific and Latin America and the Caribbean—have seen a sizable increase in the share of countries with a 'larger' Mobile Money share between 2017 and 2021 is suggestive of catch-up potential at least in these regions, albeit with Sub-Saharan Africa still far out in front. Conversely, the failure of takeoff in both the Middle East and North Africa and South Asia indicates that the future of Mobile Money is by no means a settled question across the developing world. The next round of Findex should tell us more about the long-term trends in Mobile Money adoption and other digital financial services when divorced from COVID-19 distortions and the reduced sample size; meanwhile, researchers will doubtless continue to explore the reasons why Mobile Money expands with depth and speed in some countries and regions while remaining nascent in others.

Evolution and Impacts of Mobile Money

Even across its relatively short lifespan, Mobile Money has evolved from simple payment and transfer services to other more complex financial products (Hinson et al., 2019). M-Pesa, the aforementioned Mobile Money pioneer, has grown to include the whole suite of financial services from savings and deposits to credit, insurance, and investments. On the basis of past experience, where M-Pesa goes, others will follow. Mobile Money also offers other points of appeal to developing country consumers. Ndung'u[6] (2021) summarizes Mobile Money benefits in the case of Kenya. According to Ndung'u, Mobile Money has created an electronic retail payment system, enhanced financial inclusion, created new and sustainable business models, and improved government e-services and tax collection. Thankor (2020) also confirms that Mobile Money has had a positive impact on widening access to electronic payment systems.

Does Mobile Money indeed lead to enhanced financial inclusion? The answer may not be quite as obvious as it may first appear. While Mobile Money accounts function broadly as de facto bank accounts, they only have meaningful impacts on financial inclusion if they proliferate among individuals who do not already have other forms of financial access. With Mobile Money, access to financial services is often available at a lower and more affordable cost than the same services offered by alternative providers due to the lower infrastructure costs (Maurer, 2012), which can render it appealing to previously unbanked individuals. As a result of the reduced setup and transaction costs associated with Mobile Money in financial transactions, Mobile Money can increase access to credit many of the small and informal firms which characterize much of the developing country manufacturing and services sectors (McMillan & Zeufack, 2022). In a study of enterprises in East Africa, Gosvai (2018) shows that firms which have adopted Mobile Money are more likely to access credit and therefore become financially included along the credit dimension. Lensink et al. (2022), however, document a high correlation between shares of individuals with Mobile Money accounts and conventional bank accounts in SSA, but it remains unclear whether this implies that the same individuals are commonly holding both, or that there are necessary country-level preconditions for the takeoff of both which then nevertheless attract differing clientele.

In terms of the wider societal and economic impacts of Mobile Money, or to be more precise, of financial inclusion via the channel of Mobile Money, the nascent literature is already giving cause for optimism. For example, it has been argued that Mobile Money significantly reduces economic distortions due to theft and expropriation when compared with cash transactions (Donovan, 2012; Kumar & Dutta, 2015). Furthermore, Mobile Money allows for risk-sharing between families and associates across wide geographic areas. If extended family members are dispersed across different towns and regions, an emergency or exogenous shock befalling one arm of the family can easily and swiftly be mitigated by a flow of domestic remittances via Mobile Money from the other family members. Maybe some months later, those who sent money will themselves experience an emergency and become the receiving parties—this is the essence of intra-familial risk-sharing, for which swift, safe, and geographically diffuse transfers are a necessary condition.

Key studies by Jack and Suri (2011, 2014) show how Mobile Money plays a useful role in risk management by households when faced with exogenous shocks in Kenya. They find that households with Mobile Money accounts are more adept in managing idiosyncratic shocks such as unexpected job losses, harvest, or livestock failures than those without Mobile Money. The same authors in Suri and Jack (2016) demonstrate that Mobile Money access increased household consumption generally, especially among female-headed households, and reduced the incidence of extreme poverty. This is in large part due to the positive effect of Mobile Money access on the ability to smooth consumption over time. These authors demonstrate how fintechs can work through financial inclusion to have major economic impacts. Donovan (2012) reiterates this point and states that, unlike household assets which are 'lumpy' and difficult to swiftly liquidate in the face of shocks, Mobile Money balances can be withdrawn as cash almost instantaneously. Riley (2018) provides evidence that Mobile Money plays an instrumental role in inter-location risk-sharing, such that in the event of covariate shocks, households with Mobile Money do not suffer consumption losses to the extent of those without Mobile Money. Other studies with similar conclusions on risk-sharing benefits also include Blumenstock et al. (2016), Aron (2018), and Okello et al. (2018). The aforementioned study of Gosavi (2018) shows that not only do firms that have Mobile Money accounts become more financially included in terms of credit access and utilization, they also experience productivity gains.

The evidence of Mobile Money impacts on societal, as opposed to individual, welfare is more varied. Blumenstock et al. (2015), Munyegera and Matsumoto (2014), and Natile (2020) demonstrated the existence of social welfare gains from Mobile Money access via improved access to and price of health services, energy, and sanitation. However, much of this evidence is less econometrically robust than the individual-level studies in terms of dealing with endogeneity biases (Aron, 2018). Positive impacts of Mobile Money on agricultural markets and outcomes have been documented by Kirui et al. (2013) and Hinson et al. (2019), the latter of which also touches upon other agri-business fintechs. While early evidence on the impact of Mobile Money on financial inclusion, and through financial inclusion into tangible societal and economic outcomes, is positive, the recency and novelty of Mobile Money means that the body of quality empirical research into impact is lacking. In particular, much of the key research into Mobile Money impact has taken place in Kenya due to the pioneer status of this country in terms of Mobile Money proliferation. It remains to be seen whether these findings will generalize when tested in other countries and contexts.

CRYPTOCURRENCY AND BLOCKCHAIN: NEXT FRONTIER, OR A BRIDGE TOO FAR?

For many people, the first financial innovations which come to mind when speaking of 'the fintech revolution' are cryptocurrencies and blockchain. Dominant features of both the media and increasingly academic conversation around fintech, cryptocurrencies, and their accompanying facilitatory technology encapsulate everything which is exciting and revelatory about fintech in the twenty-first century for some, while others remain skeptical as to their potential, longevity, or even their inherent value.

It is difficult to decide at what length we should discuss cryptocurrencies and blockchain here. It is the case that cryptocurrencies and blockchain are considered key features of the fintech revolution in the developed world (Fernandez-Vazquez et al., 2019), are starting to play a larger role in a small number of specific developing countries such as El Salvador (Zagorsky, 2021) and Nigeria, and have been proposed as having significant potential for development through means of reduced cost remittances and fraud reduction (Kshetri & Voas, 2018), and as an alternative store of value in countries with poor inflationary records. However, these technologies remain very much in the realm of 'developed country fintechs' in Arner et al.'s (2015) classification. Additionally, as was discussed in section "Fintech and Financial Inclusion in the Developing World", penetration into developing country markets remains slight, as does cryptocurrency investment in or innovation from developing countries (Ndemo, 2022). Figure 12.1 shows the share of the total global cryptocurrency value received which flowed to each world region in the year until June 2021, adjusted for purchasing power parity (PPP). The data is from Chainanalysis, a private company which compiles blockchain analytics. We must note that the regions do not precisely match the World Bank classifications discussed earlier. From Fig. 12.1, it can be seen that, even with the PPP adjustment which adds additional weight to the less developed countries, the majority of global cryptocurrency value received flows to Europe and North America. Despite each containing the hugely populous countries of China and India respectively, the regions of East Asia, and Central and South Asia each received only 14% of the global flows of cryptocurrency flows in the most recent year. In contrast, Latin America, the Middle East, and Africa all have shares in the single digits. Additionally, there is currently very little quality empirical research into the effects of cryptocurrencies and blockchain on developing country outcomes. This includes the potential impact they have on financial inclusion. Thus, so much of what can be said about their potential impact on FI, and through FI, remains speculative.

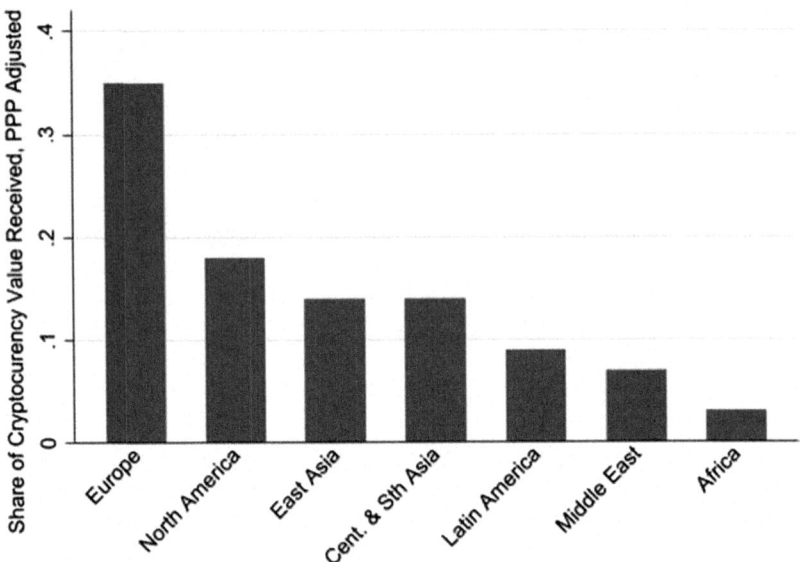

Fig. 12.1 Share of cryptocurrency global value received by world region, PPP adjusted (*Note* Figure shows the share of the total cryptocurrency value received by each developing region of the global total. Data from Chainanalysis [2021])

In order for cryptocurrencies and other innovations based on blockchain to facilitate financial inclusion, it would be necessary not only for them to take off in developing countries at scale, but also to appeal to financially excluded individuals. This could happen in one of two ways—either via a relaxation of the constraints on access which prevent those who are financially excluded from adopting other forms of financial product, or by providing such a strong incentive to the unbanked to begin using cryptocurrencies and the accompanying accounts and digital wallets to overcome these constraints for themselves. The former path seems less probable with cryptocurrencies in their current form. If anything, cryptocurrency platforms originating from developed countries are likely to be more onerous in terms of human capital requirements, more dependent on digital infrastructure, and more prone to trust concerns than conventional banking services. Nevertheless, just as Mobile Money proved a great success in many developing countries due to tailoring to their needs and constraints, there might be potential for cryptocurrency platforms originating from developing countries to do the same, if such innovations can be encouraged. The latter path, however, may prove more fruitful in the short run. If cryptocurrency becomes a major global channel for the flow of international remittances (Scott, 2016), and more developing countries' citizens may be incentivized to participate and become financially included in order to receive funds from abroad, especially if their international relatives assist them with the technical aspects. Similarly, if cryptocurrencies allow for the bypassing of foreign exchange controls, this may yield an incentive to join the financial system in countries with unstable currencies, although again this is more likely for wealthier, already banked citizens. For definitions, risks and a wider discussion of cryptocurrencies, blockchain, financial inclusion, and development, the interested reader can refer to Chapter 6 of Lensink et al. (2022). However, as the technology is nascent in developing countries, so is the empirical literature. The key research required in order to properly understand the potential for fintech to influence developing country's financial inclusion, economic, and welfare outcomes remains to be done.

RISKS AND REGULATORY IMPLICATIONS OF THE FINTECH REVOLUTION IN DEVELOPING COUNTRIES

New technologies almost always come with new risks and developing countries' fintechs are no exception. The main types of risk can be divided into two groups. The first group relates to security and privacy challenges, as well as the associated risks that fintech *users* may face. The second group relates to technical and technological risks contained within fintechs which may have an impact beyond individual users, to banks, financial institutions, and the financial system as a whole. It should be noted that both types of risk may be exacerbated in the developing countries' context where the trust levels of individuals (Mattes & Moreno, 2018) and the stability of financial systems (Montiel & Servén, 2006) may be weaker than in the developed world.

In fintech, as with all digital systems, security and data privacy are of paramount concern. For fintech applications, critical information may be stored on mobile devices that are prone to loss or theft. Security of mobile devices can also be compromised through mobile payment applications. It should be noted that citizens of developing countries may have lower levels of financial or general literacy, leading to a greater likelihood of forgetting or writing down key passwords or PINs, and an inability to follow complex security protocols. As a result, fintech companies need to develop appropriate measures to protect sensitive consumer data from unauthorized access and to help users to protect themselves. Jagtiani and Lemieux (2018) note that novel fintechs tend to use some data sources which are more prone to error and thus could potentially create further risks to consumers. Such technical and technological failure can also generate other risks for the poor, who may not be well-placed to act swiftly to report faults, follow-up technical errors, etc.

From the bank and financial system perspective, the Bank for International Settlements (BIS) (2018) identifies potential systemic risk arising from increased network-interconnectedness of Mobile Money operations, cellular networks, MNOs, and banks. Just like in the O-Ring Theory of Economic Development (Kremer, 1993), failure of the weakest part of the network can lead to failure of the entire system. As with all digital systems, there is a risk of technical failure. This is not only a burden for fintech providers but also for larger firms or institutions which connect with fintech, as they inherit the need also to manage and mitigate technical failures.

These identified risks pose substantial regulation challenges to regulatory authorities. Unlike traditional banking models, which while embracing digital technologies are often backed with physical paper records, most fintechs are entirely virtual. Furthermore, the rapid evolution of technological innovation in current fintechs means that there is a constant lag between regulation and the innovation of the industry. This gap makes it difficult for regulators to appropriately come up with regulatory policies that can cope with the rapid growth in fintech innovations. Perhaps ironically however, Arner et al. (2015) note that the instability and stunted growth of conventional financial institutions may in fact render developing country policymakers more adaptable to the regulatory challenges posed by new fintechs. While developed countries may feel the need to protect established financial sector players and restrict new technologies, developing countries may embrace the chance to try something new in the face of persistent failures of the conventional systems. This may in part explain why SSA is such a world leader in Mobile Money adoption, as detailed in the previous section.

BIS (2018) identifies 10 implications of fintech development which form a useful bedrock for thinking through appropriate regulatory frameworks. As these implications are lengthy, we will not lay them out here, but they draw attention fundamentally to the unpredictability of fintech challenges, the preponderance of new and unlicensed entrants in fintech markets, and the potential of fintechs to change the nature of existing financial sector actors. Bains et al. (2022) discuss two main approaches to regulating a financial sector with rapidly evolving innovation: the entity-based approach and the activity-based approach. Then, they propose a third hybrid approach. The entity-based approach follows a traditional focus on regulation of licensed firms engaged in regulated financial services, which is good for adapting to new innovations but somewhat rigid in terms of catering to new market entrants. The activity-based approach, by contrast, is not restricted to licensed firms but instead focuses on regulating specific activities which any firms may then conduct, provided they adhere to these rules. This is more conducive to new entrants and competition but makes regulation much more difficult to channel and enforce. For this reason, Bains, Sugimoto, and Wilson propose a hybrid model which has two layers of regulation—one based on entities and the other based on activities, which have a smoother path for new firms to become licensed entities.

Amstad (2019) takes the alternative view that fintech firms can be seen as similar to banks as they provide similar services and if classified as such, they therefore fit within existing regulation. It then follows that where fintechs do innovate entirely new services, these should be ignored and kept unregulated as the current industry and technology is still in an infantile stage of development and growth, a 'wait-and-see'-style approach. This was largely the approach taken in Kenya, the Mobile Money pioneer. Ndung'u (2021) states that in the absence of regulatory guidelines prior to the launch of M-Pesa, regulatory authorities in Kenya gave a letter of no objection to Safaricom and adopted what it called a "watch and learn" position to assess the innovation and its effects and before providing appropriate regulation. Tanzania, another successful case in Mobile Money, also adopted a similar position dubbed as "test and learn". This is further evidence of how, contrary to past experiences, developing countries are often proving to be more flexible in the case of fintech regulation than their developed world counterparts.

In lieu of these frameworks, specific regulatory models have been proposed as means to structure fintech regulation more effectively. Three main models have been outlined: innovation offices, regulatory sandboxes, and RegTechs. Innovation offices within governments have traditionally existed in most developed countries as units or divisions of conventional regulatory authorities tasked with adapting to the challenges of new innovations (UNSGSA, 2019). The quality of resources and the support provided by regulatory authorities to innovation offices is key to their success and are inputs which may prove lacking in developing country contexts.

In the second alternative, regulatory sandboxes are structured live environments which are used to roll out and test innovations as they emerge. Sandboxes can be structured as product testing sandboxes or policy testing sandboxes (UNSGSA, 2019). Product testing sandboxes exist when new products or services are piloted under official observation and at small scale before formal registration or licensing. Policy testing sandboxes use the sandbox environment to assess effectiveness of regulations with regard to innovations, thereby allowing regulators to come up with appropriate regulatory frameworks in a reactive manner. The two approaches need not be mutually exclusive since product testing sandboxes implicitly test the appropriateness of existing regulatory policies. A multi-jurisdictional sandbox has also been proposed to address cross-border regulatory issues and promote the harmonization of regulatory jurisdictions across borders (UNSGSA, 2019). This could prove particularly useful for cross-border payments and transfers using novel fintechs.

Finally, RegTechs are technology-enabled regulatory instruments which are designed to assist regulators in effective regulation of the fintech environment (Mueller & Murphy, 2018). RegTechs act algorithmically to monitor the compliance of fintechs as well as to identify potential regulatory gaps. However, these are probably of less relevance to the more 'low-fi' fintechs which form the backbone of the fintech revolution in developing countries.

Conclusion and Prognoses for Internationally Inclusive Fintech

The potential for fintechs in general and mobile financial technologies in particular to promote financial inclusion and to contribute to the UN Sustainable Development Goals seem close to undisputable. The success stories of Mobile Money services, such as M-Pesa in Kenya, has shaped the view that fintech, and especially branchless ICT innovations, will be able to raise living standards in poor rural areas in African economies and other developing countries, and help to induce a process of inclusive growth. Nevertheless, aside from Mobile Money, the diffusion of more advanced fintechs over the developing world has tended to lag behind developed regions, with these countries lacking both the digital infrastructure and the population buy-in necessary for such technologies to achieve any kind of scale. For example, in the period 2010–2014, only 0.33% of worldwide investments in fintech took place in Africa (U.S. ITA, 2016), with similarly low levels of investment occurring in several other developing regions. If developing countries have few options other than to 'catch' fintechs as they fall from the developed world, they will end up with products and services which are not tailored to the needs of their populations and the constraints of their infrastructure.

It should be noted that even if fintech does start to diffuse worldwide, it will only be successful in promoting inclusive growth if it meets the needs of broad numbers of disadvantaged groups, including smallholders, who often are first-time users of fintech and may have low literacy and numeracy skills (Demirgüç-Kunt et al., 2018). It is to be expected that richer, higher income, and more literate individuals in urban sectors of developing countries may benefit most from advanced fintech, with the concomitant risk of exacerbating internal inequality within often already unequal and elite-dominated societies. This especially holds for digital finance, as digital platforms are more likely to be used by richer households and households in urban areas (Beck & Brown, 2011). If fintechs diffuse to developing countries without much alteration from their developed country precursors, they may even negatively affect the poor. If providers decide to focus less on impoverished and uneducated communities, or discontinue provisions of specific fintech services in high-risk rural areas (Ozili, 2018), it will lead to more inequality. This could also lead to further financial exclusion of certain groups. Thus, to give fintech the best possible chance of playing a transformative role and creating possibilities for improving living standards across society, policies need to be developed to ensure that poor and rural smallholders are not shut out. The most natural starting place for policy would be encouraging and fostering local fintech development and innovation, instead of an intensive focus on how to co-opt fintechs from abroad.

On the basis of the nascent literature on fintech and financial inclusion, alongside our conclusions and our speculations, we propose that there are two potential dichotomous routes in which the relationship between fintech and FI may be expected to evolve in the developing world. First, the optimistic prognostication is that developing countries can get ahead of the curve in the adoption and proliferation of many new financial technologies which are specifically tailored to their needs, with resulting benefits not only for the financial inclusion of their citizens and higher-order economic outcomes, but also for closing the gap between their financial sectors and those of the developing world. The basis for this possibility is the observed takeoff of Mobile Money and other low-fi fintechs in Sub-Saharan Africa, whereby this poorest region of the world has most rapidly and widely embraced a new and transformative financial technology. There is also the possibility that the failure of legacy banking and financial institutions to widely include citizens and provide stable financial sectors will render developing country policymakers more open to new technologies, making them more supportive in terms of regulation. Secondly, the alternative future is more pessimistic but equally plausible. As advanced countries' fintechs become ever more complicated, if there is no concerted effort to tailor these to developing country populations or to develop locally targeted alternatives, the digital infrastructure and human capital demands of fintech could increase much more rapidly than the developing world is able to supply, resulting in large swathes of the global population being shut out of fintechs entirely, which will create new forms of intra- and international financial exclusion. Determining which of these prognostications is more likely depends strongly on whether developing countries become passive absorbers or active innovators of fintech in the forthcoming years.

REFERENCES

Allen, F., Carletti, E., Cull, R., Qian, J., Senbet, L., & Valenzuela, P. (2014). The African financial development and financial inclusion gaps. *Journal of African Economies, 23*(5), 614–642. https://doi.org/10.1093/jae/eju015

Allen, F., Carletti, E., Cull, R., Qian, J., Senbet, L., & Valenzuela, P. (2021). Improving access to banking: Evidence from Kenya. *Review of Finance, 25*(2), 403–447. https://doi.org/10.1093/rof/rfaa024

Amstad, M. (2019). *Regulating FinTech: Objectives, principles and practices* (ADBI Working Paper Series 1016). Tokyo Asian Development Bank Institute.

Anderloni, L., Bayot, B., Błędowski, P., Iwanicz-Drozdowska, M., & Kempson, E. (2008). *Financial services provision and prevention of financial exclusion.* European Commission, Directorate-General for Employment, Social Affairs and Equal Opportunities. https://www.fi-compass.eu/sites/default/files/publications/financial-services-provision-and-prevention-of-financial-exclus ion.pdf

Anderson, S., & Baland, J. (2002). The economics of roscas and intrahousehold resource allocation. *The Quarterly Journal of Economics, 117*(3), 963–995. https://doi.org/10.1162/003355302760193931

Arner, D., Barberis, J., & Buckley, R. (2015). *The evolution of FinTech: A new post-crisis paradigm* (UNSW Law Research Paper No. 2016-62). The University of New South Wales (UNSW) and the University of Hong Kong.

Aron, J. (2018). Mobile money and the economy: A review of the evidence. *World Bank Research Observer, 33*(2), 135–188. https://doi.org/10.1093/wbro/lky001

Bains, P., Sugimoto, N., & Wilson, C. (2022). *BigTech in financial services: Regulatory approaches and architecture* (FINTECH Notes 2022/002). IMF.

Beck, T., & Brown, M. (2011). *Use of banking services in emerging markets-household level evidence* (CEPR Discussion Paper 8467).

BIS. (2018, February). *Sound practices: Implications of FinTech developments for banks and bank supervisors, Basel Committee on Banking Supervision.* Bank for International Settlement (BIS).

Blumenstock, J. E., Cadamuro, G., & On, R. (2015). Predicting poverty and wealth from mobile phone metadata. *Science, 350*(6264), 1073–1076. https://doi.org/10.1126/science.aac4420

Blumenstock, J. E., Eagle, N., & Fafchamps, M. (2016). Airtime transfers and mobile communications: Evidence in the aftermath of natural disasters.

Journal of Development Economics, 120, 157–181. https://doi.org/10.1016/j.jdeveco.2016.01.003

Chainanalysis. (2021). *The 2020 geography of cryptocurrency report.* chainanalysis.com

Chamley, C., Kotlikoff, L., & Polemarchakis, H. (2012). Limited-purpose banking—Moving from "trust me" to "show me" banking. *American Economic Review, 102*(3), 113–119. https://doi.org/10.1257/aer.102.3.113

Cozzens, S., & Thakur, D. (2014). *Innovation and inequality: Emerging technologies in an unequal world* (1st ed.). Edward Elgar.

Demirgüç-Kunt, A., & Klapper, L. (2013). Measuring financial inclusion: The global Findex database. *Brookings Papers on Economic Activity* (Spring), 279–321.

Demirgüç-Kunt, A., Klapper, L., Singer, D., & Ansar, S. (2022). *The Global Findex Database 2021: Financial inclusion, digital payments, and resilience in the age of COVID-19.* World Bank.

Demirgüç-Kunt, A., Klapper, L., Singer, D., Ansar, S., & Hess, J. (2017). *The Global Findex Database: Measuring financial inclusion and the FinTech revolution.* World Bank Presentation.

Demirgüç-Kunt, A., Klapper, L., Singer, D., Ansar, S., & Hess, J. (2018). *The Global Findex Database 2017: Measuring financial inclusion and the FinTech revolution.* World Bank.

Didenko, A. (2018). *Regulating FinTech: Lessons from Africa* (Unpublished Manuscript). ssrn.com/abstract_id=3135604

Diniz, E., Birochi, R., & Pozzebon, M. (2012). Triggers and barriers to financial inclusion: The use of ICT-based branchless banking in an Amazon county. *Electronic Commerce Research and Applications, 11*(5), 484–494. https://doi.org/10.1016/j.elerap.2011.07.006

Donovan, K. (2012). Mobile money for financial inclusion. In T. Kelly, N. Friederici, M. Minges, & M. Yamamichi (Eds.), *Information and communications for development: Maximising mobile* (pp. 61–74). World Bank.

Duvendack, M., & Mader, P. (2020). Impact of financial inclusion in low-and middle income countries: A systematic review of reviews. *Journal of Economic Surveys, 34*(3), 594–629. https://doi.org/10.1111/joes.12367

Fernandez-Vazquez, S., Rosillo, R., De La Fuente, D., & Priore, P. (2019). Blockchain in FinTech: A mapping study. *Sustainability, 11*(22), 6366. https://doi.org/10.3390/su11226366

Gomber, P., Kauffman, R., Parker, C., & Weber, B. (2018). On the FinTech revolution: Interpreting the forces of innovation, disruption, and transformation in financial services. *Journal of Management Information Systems, 35*(1), 220–265. https://doi.org/10.1080/07421222.2018.1440766

Gosavi, A. (2018). Can mobile money help firms mitigate the problem of access to finance in Eastern Sub-Saharan Africa? *Journal of African Business, 19*(3), 343–360. https://doi.org/10.1080/15228916.2017.1396791

Hannig, A., & Jansen, S. (2010). Financial inclusion and financial stability: Current policy issues. *SSRN Electronic Journal.*

Hansen, N., Huis, M., & Lensink, R. (2021). Microfinance services and women's empowerment. In S. J. Leire, J. L. Retolaza, & L. Van Liedekerke (Eds.), *International handbooks in business ethics* (pp. 161–182). Springer.

Hinson, R., Lensink, R., & Mueller, A. (2019). Transforming agribusiness in developing countries: SDGs and the role of FinTech. *Current Opinion in Environmental Sustainability, 41*, 1–9. https://doi.org/10.1016/j.cosust.2019.07.002

Jack, W., & Suri, T. (2011). *Mobile money: The economics of M-PESA* (NBER Working Paper No. 16721). National Bureau of Economic Research.

Jack, W., & Suri, T. (2014). Risk sharing and transactions costs: Evidence from Kenya's mobile money revolution. *American Economic Review, 104*(1), 183–223. https://doi.org/10.1257/aer.104.1.183

Jagtiani, J. A., & Lemieux, C. M. (2018). Do FinTech lenders penetrate areas that are underserved by traditional banks? *Journal of Economics and Business, 100*, 43–54. https://doi.org/10.1016/j.jeconbus.2018.03.001

Karlan, D., & Zinman, J. (2009). Observing unobservables: Identifying information asymmetries with a consumer credit field experiment. *Econometrica, 77*(6), 1993–2008. https://doi.org/10.3982/ecta5781

Khera, P., Ng, S., Ogawa, S., & Sahay, R. (2021). *Is digital financial inclusion unlocking growth*. IMF Working Papers, (Working paper No. 2021/167).

Kirui, O. K., Okello, J. J., & Njiraini, G. W. (2013). Impact of mobile phone-based money transfer services in Agriculture: Evidence from Kenya. *Quarterly Journal of International Agriculture, 52*, 141–162. https://doi.org/10.22004/ag.econ.173644

Kremer, M. (1993). The O-Ring theory of economic development. *The Quarterly Journal of Economics, 108*(3), 551–575. https://doi.org/10.2307/2118400

Kshetri, N., & Voas, J. (2018). Blockchain in developing countries. *IEEE IT Professional, 20*(2), 11–14. https://doi.org/10.1109/MITP.2018.021921645

Kumar, L., & Dutta, S. (2015). Role of mobile money in replacing cash: A Study among migrant workers in South India. *Economic and Political Weekly, 50*(28), 39–47. https://www.jstor.org/stable/24481801

Lensink, R., Hamilton, C., & Adjasi, C. (2022). *Advanced introduction to financial inclusion* (1st ed.). Edward Elgar.

Manig, W. (1990). Formal and informal credit markets for agricultural development in developing countries—The example of Pakistan. *Journal of Rural Studies, 6*(2), 209–215. https://doi.org/10.1016/0743-0167(90)90007-U

Mas, I. (2011). Why are banks so scarce in developing countries? A regulatory and infrastructure perspective. *Critical Review, 23*(1–2), 135–145. https://doi.org/10.1080/08913811.2011.574476

Mas, I., & Radcliffe, D. (2011). Scaling mobile money. *Journal of Payments Strategy & Systems, 5*(3). Available at SSRN: https://ssrn.com/abstract=1681245

Mattes, R., & Moreno, A. (2018). Social and political trust in developing countries: Sub-Saharan Africa and Latin America. In *Oxford handbook of social and political trust* (pp. 357–382). Oxford University Press.

Maurer, B. (2012). Mobile money: Communication, consumption and change in the payments space. *Journal of Development Studies, 48*(5), 589–604. https://doi.org/10.1080/00220388.2011.621944

McMillan, M., & Zeufack, A. (2022). labor productivity growth and industrialization in Africa. *Journal of Economic Perspectives, 36*(1), 3–32. https://doi.org/10.1257/jep.36.1.3

Montiel, P., & Servén, L. (2006). Macroeconomic stability in developing countries: How much is enough? *The World Bank Research Observer, 21*(2), 151–178. https://doi.org/10.1093/wbro/lkl005

Morakinyo, O., Adetutu, L. R., Murinde, V., Odusanya, K. A., & Ogbeide, F. J. (2019). *Network infrastructure, mobile money and financial inclusion: Micro-spatial evidence from rural Nigeria* (Unpublished Manuscript). SOAS.

Mueller, J., & Murphy, D. (2018). *RegTech: Opportunities for more efficient and effective regulatory supervision and compliance*. Milken Institute.

Munyegera, G. K., & Matsumoto, T. (2014). *Mobile money, remittances and rural household welfare: Panel evidence from Uganda* (GRIPS Discussion Paper, 14–22). National Graduate Institute for Policy Studies.

Natile, S. (2020). Digital finance and the mobile money "social" enterprise: A socio-legal critique of M-Pesa in Kenya. *Historical Social Research, 45*(3), 74–94. https://doi.org/10.2307/26918405

Ndemo, B. (2022). The role of cryptocurrencies in sub-Saharan Africa. In *Foresight Africa 2022 Report*. The Brookings Institute.

Ndung'u, N. S. (2021). *A digital financial services revolution in Kenya: The M-Pesa case study* (African Economic Research Consortium Nairobi 00200).

Ogawa, S., Khera, P., Ng, S., & Sahay, R. (2021). Is digital financial inclusion unlocking growth? *SSRN Electronic Journal*. https://doi.org/10.2139/ssrn.4026364

Okello, G. C. B., Ntayi, J. M., Munene, J. C., & Malinga, C. A. (2018). Mobile money and financial inclusion in Sub-Saharan Africa: The moderating role of social networks. *Journal of African Business, 19*(3), 361–384. https://doi.org/10.1080/15228916.2017.1416214

Ouma, S., Odongo, T., & Were, M. (2017). Mobile financial services and financial inclusion: Is it a boon for savings mobilization? *Review of Development Finance, 7*(1), 29–35. https://doi.org/10.1016/j.rdf.2017.01.001

Ozili, P. K. (2018). Impact of digital finance on financial inclusion and stability. *Borsa Istanbul Review, 18*(4), 329–340. https://doi.org/10.1016/j.bir.2017.12.003

Philippon, T. (2016). *The FinTech opportunity* (National Bureau of Economic Research Working Paper 22476).

Pitt, M. M., Khandker, S. R., & Cartwright, J. (2006). Empowering women with micro finance: Evidence from Bangladesh. *Economic Development and Cultural Change, 54*(4), 891–831. https://doi.org/10.1086/503580

Riley, E. (2018). Mobile money and risk sharing against village shocks. *Journal of Development Economics, 135*, 43–58. https://doi.org/10.1016/j.jdeveco.2018.06.015. S0304387818304413.

Sarma, M. (2008, August). *Index of financial inclusion* (ICRIER Working Paper).

Scott, B. (2016). *How can cryptocurrency and blockchain technology play a role in building social and solidarity finance?* (UNRISD Working Paper No. 2016-1).

Suri, T., & Jack, W. (2016). The long-run poverty and gender impacts of mobile money. *Science, 354*(6317), 1288–1292. https://doi.org/10.1126/science.aah5309

Thankor, A. V. (2020). FinTech and banking: What do we know? *Journal of Financial Intermediation, 41*, 100833. https://econpapers.repec.org/scripts/redir.pf?u=https%3A%2F%2Fdoi.org%2F10.1016%252Fj.jfi.2019.100833;h=repec:eee:jfinin:v:41:y:2020:i:c:s104295731930049x

UNSGSA FinTech Working Group and CCAF. (2019). *Early lessons on regulatory innovations to enable inclusive FinTech: Innovation offices, regulatory sandboxes, and RegTech.* Office of the UNSGSA and CCAF.

U.S. International Trade Administration. (2016). *Top markets report: Financial technology.* U.S. Department of Commerce.

World Bank. (2012). *Information and communications for development 2012: Maximizing mobile.* World Bank.

World Bank. (2018). *UFA2020 overview: Universal financial access by 2020.* https://www.worldbank.org/en/topic/financialinclusion/brief/achieving-universal-financial-access-by-2020

World Bank and CCAF. (2019). *Regulating alternative finance: Results from a global regulator survey.*

Yermack, D. (2018). *FinTech in Sub-Saharan Africa: What has worked well, and what hasn't* (National Bureau of Economic Research, W25007).

Zagorsky, J. (2021). Bitcoin is now 'legal tender' in El Salvador—Here's what that means. *The Conversation*. https://theconversation.com/bitcoin-is-now-legal-tender-in-el-salvador-heres-what-that-means-167099

CHAPTER 13

The Cash Holdings of Fintechs and SMEs: Evidence from OECD Countries

Kaleemullah Abbasi, Ashraful Alam, Noor Ahmed Brohi, Makhmoor Fiza, Shahzad Nasim, and Imtiaz Ali Brohi

INTRODUCTION

Small Medium Enterprises (SMEs) form an important part of an economy given their contribution toward economic growth and employment (Radas & Božić, 2009). Thus, it is economically important to recognize specific mechanisms that may bolster SMEs' cash holdings, thereby

K. Abbasi (✉) · N. A. Brohi · M. Fiza · S. Nasim · I. A. Brohi
Department of Management Sciences & Technology, The Begum Nusrat
Bhutto Women University, Sukkur, Pakistan
e-mail: kaleemullah.abbasi@bnbwu.edu.pk

N. A. Brohi
e-mail: noor.brohi@bnbwu.edu.pk

M. Fiza
e-mail: makhmoor.fiza@bnbwu.edu.pk

S. Nasim
e-mail: shahzad.nasim@bnbwu.edu.pk

© The Author(s), under exclusive license to Springer Nature
Switzerland AG 2023
T. Walker et al. (eds.), *The Fintech Disruption*, Palgrave Studies
in Financial Services Technology,
https://doi.org/10.1007/978-3-031-23069-1_13

329

enhancing their chances of survival. Technological advancements have affected the traditional ways of business operations. Financial technologies (fintechs), which are recognized as a game-changer in the financial industry, offer lower operations cost, shorter turnaround period in gaining access to finance, real-time management information, and, unlike conventional banks, create a direct link between lenders and borrowers (Abbasi et al., 2021; Lee & Shin, 2018; Rosavina et al., 2019).

According to the theory of reasoned action, SMEs are expected to implement policies that are advantageous to them (Abbasi et al., 2021). Due to their smaller size, SMEs usually experience liquidity constraints (Cowling, Lee, et al., 2020). This is especially critical in the recent environment wherein COVID-19 has severely affected the SMEs' cash holdings (Cowling, Brown, et al., 2020). As a result, we contend that SMEs are likely to utilize fintechs. There are multiple arguments that suggest an impact of fintechs on cash holding of SMEs. As compared to conventional lending through banks, firms may attain loans at lower interest rates from fintech companies (Jagtiani & Lemieux, 2019). Further, by utilizing fintechs, firms may send money abroad at a lower cost (Lee & Shin, 2018). Additionally, when analyzing investment opportunities for unutilized cash, robo-advisory, in comparison to humans, may offer superior return because of the low cost of financial advisory stemming from the use of artificial intelligence (Brenner & Meyll, 2020; Lui & Lamb, 2018). Moreover, fintechs enable firms to have access to rich data on customers, which may enable a relatively more accurate analysis of the probability of customer default (Jagtiani & John, 2018). Thus, by utilizing fintechs, SMEs may be more likely to provide credit to their customers with a lower likelihood of default.

Our study contributes to the literature in two ways. We examine the association between fintechs and SME cash holdings in Organisation for Economic Co-operation and Development (OECD) member countries from 2011 to 2018 and find a positive link between fintechs and cash

I. A. Brohi
e-mail: imtiaz.brohi@bnbwu.edu.pk

K. Abbasi · A. Alam
Salford Business School, University of Salford, Salford, UK
e-mail: m.a.alam@salford.ac.uk

holdings, thereby contributing toward fintechs and finance research. Poor cash flow may suggest an inability to pay short-term operating costs, which is likely to make it difficult for SMEs to survive. Hence, analyzing the impact of fintechs on SMEs' cash holdings examines whether fintechs enhance the survival of SMEs. Second, we find that greater institutional quality strengthens the positive link between fintechs and SMEs' cash holdings. High-quality institutions in a country are likely to provide a conducive environment for entrepreneurs, which may lead to more fintech startups, thereby leading to an increase in cash holdings.

The second section of this chapter describes our theoretical framework and develops our hypotheses. The third section describes the methodology adopted for this study. The fourth section presents the results, while the fifth section concludes this study.

Theoretical Framework and Hypotheses

Theory of reasoned action contends that beliefs (which may be either positive or negative) are developed based on an individual's perception that a desired outcome could be attained through performance of a specific action (Xiao, 2020). Such beliefs, if positive, could drive individuals to perform the specific action (Morais et al., 2018; Petrescu et al., 2018). As a result, theory of reasoned action posits that firms are expected to adopt policies which they consider to be of benefit to the firm (Abbasi et al., 2021; Fishbein & Ajzen, 1975; Liu et al., 2017; Troudi & Bouyoucef, 2020; Vanyushyn, 2008). Abbasi et al. (2021) and Lee et al. (2012) find that the theory of reasoned action affects the decisions of SMEs. Therefore, as per the theory of reasoned action, it is expected that SMEs are likely to utilize fintechs to realize higher cash flows.

Due to lower interest rates, fintechs are likely to reduce the borrowing costs of SMEs, which in turn enhances cash flows of SMEs (Abbasi et al., 2021; Baber, 2019; Odinet, 2018). The following are the mechanisms which may explain the lower borrowing cost stemming from fintechs. First, fintechs operate with limited office space compared to conventional banks as fintechs mostly operate online. This ultimately benefits fintechs in terms of lower operating costs (Lee & Shin, 2018; Lu, 2018) and as a result, they are able to charge a lower interest rate. Second, fintechs provide a platform for investors to lend finance to borrowers, and thereby do not require holding significant capital reserves for credit risk protection (Anagnostopoulos, 2018; Odinet, 2018). This enhances the supply of funds, which in turn reduces interest rates (Abbasi et al., 2021).

Gaining quicker access to funds through fintechs leads SMEs to utilize funds at an opportune time, thereby enhancing revenue (Rosavina et al., 2019; Sangwan et al., 2020). Further, Fuster et al. (2019) provide evidence that loans are processed quicker in fintechs compared to other avenues. As a result, quicker processing of loans in the context of fintechs enable SMEs to experience lower search costs (Gomber et al., 2018). Moreover, fintechs enable SMEs to benefit from lower travel costs as the firms are able to make payments of operational expenses such as rent and electricity through fintechs rather than by way of visiting conventional banks (Chuen & Teo, 2015; Lee & Shin, 2018; Ozili, 2018). Additionally, by utilizing fintechs, SMEs can receive or send money abroad at lower costs (Chuen & Teo, 2015; Lee & Shin, 2018). Further, fintechs' use of robo-advisory help SMEs to attain wealth management advice at lower cost (Abbasi et al., 2021; Brenner & Meyll, 2020; Lui & Lamb, 2018). Lastly, the use of big data in fintechs allows SMEs to assess the likelihood of debtor default more accurately, which in turn enables SMEs to provide credit to those debtors who have greater chance of paying back their loans (Jagtiani & John, 2018).

Therefore, given the aforementioned arguments, we predict that fintechs are likely to increase the cash flows of SMEs. Hence, we hypothesize the following:

H1: There is a positive association between fintechs and cash holdings of SME.

Institutional theory posits that a country's institutions can have a significant impact on producing a conducive environment for investments by, for example, providing incentives, mitigating uncertainty, and establishing a stable environment (Alam et al., 2019). Institutions' quality encompass six dimensions, namely voice and accountability, regulatory quality, political stability, rule of law, government effectiveness and control of corruption (Alam et al., 2019). Innovation activities, such as fintech startups, are also influenced by the institutional quality of a country (Waarden, 2001). Pattit et al. (2012) substantiated that institutions have an influence on technological advancement in the United States. High-quality institutions promote innovative entrepreneurship by way of mitigating agency problems and reducing finance availability issues (Laeven, 2003).

Improved government effectiveness restores confidence among investors and safeguards their return from the investment (Alam et al., 2019). Jiao et al. (2015) also argue that effective government enhances entrepreneurial endeavors. When the government plays an active role, it points to the availability of greater support and subsidies and creates links between firms and individuals, thereby, fostering innovation (Alam et al., 2019; Mehmood & Rafi, 2005).

Voice and accountability are defined as "the extent to which a country's citizens are able to participate in selecting their government, as well as freedom of expression and an independent media" (Fereidouni et al., 2011, p. 803; Kaufmann et al., 2009; Panayides et al., 2015). Higher voice and accountability results in an improved innovative system (Sabry, 2019) as it creates an environment of coordination, association, and exchange of information among institutions, enterprises, and individuals, which are crucial to innovation (OECD, 1997). Free media, which is another component of voice and accountability, fosters innovation by increasing the flow of information and ideas (Dutta et al., 2011). Moreover, Varsakelis (2006) evidences a positive relation between media independency and innovation. Rule of law determines the strength of the judicial system in a country and how strictly the law is enforced (Alam et al., 2019; Wan & Hoskisson, 2003). La Porta et al. (1997) provide evidence that shows if the rule of law is strong, it helps in developing financial markets. Hence, this may help in removing barriers related to the availability of finance, resulting in higher innovative startups, such as fintechs. Jiao et al. (2015) find a positive link between a country's legal environment and its level of innovation. Similarly, Seitz and Watzinger (2017) show that, due to Germany's superior rule of law in comparison to Italy's, it has greater research and development investments. Strong legal systems are also associated with greater protection of patents and creditors' rights, which result in higher confidence among investors and lenders to provide finance for innovative startups (Acharya & Subramanian, 2009; Furukawa, 2007; Pindado et al., 2017; Seitz & Watzinger, 2017).

In relation to furthering investments, the political landscape has an impact on governmental policy (Julio & Yook, 2012). Political instability induces uncertainty as it leads to changes in already ascertained economic policies, which may act as a dissuading factor for investments in innovative endeavors such as fintechs. Masino (2015) argues that there is lower investment in innovative activities when an economy is volatile. Henisz (2002) and Allard et al. (2012) find a negative association between political instability and innovation.

Corruption is defined as using the public office for personal benefit (Rodriguez et al., 2005). Corruption negatively influences the institutional trust required for investing in innovation activities (Alam et al., 2019; Anokhin & Schulze, 2009). Further, corruption leads to payment of bribes for obtaining patents, which increases the cost of innovative startups (and thereby reduces the return on investment), reducing incentives for investors (Daude & Stein, 2007; Javorcik & Wei, 2009). Finally, this leads to a limited amount of fintech startups.

Alam et al. (2019) argues that higher regulatory quality enables firms to be up to date with developments, making it more knowledgeable to invest in innovations. Kirkpatrick et al. (2006) observe that foreign investors are not motivated to invest in innovative startups due to poor regulatory quality. Mahendra et al. (2015) find a negative association between regulatory quality and innovation.

The above arguments suggest that greater institutional quality will positively moderate the link between fintechs and cash holdings of SMEs. As a result, we predict the following:

H2: Higher institutional quality positively influences the association between fintechs and cash holdings of SMEs.

Methodology

This study focuses on SME firms in OECD countries.[1] We obtained fintech data (number of fintechs in a specific country in a given year) from Crunchbase (Abbasi et al., 2021), while financial characteristics were collected from the Osiris database. This study excludes financial firms due to their distinct regulatory structure (Gull et al., 2018). Our sample is taken from 2011, to avoid causing bias arising from the global financial crisis of 2008–2010 (Aidukaite, 2019), and ends in 2018, as it was

[1] Australia, Austria, Belgium, Denmark, Finland, France, Germany, Greece, Ireland, Israel, Italy, Japan, the Netherlands, Norway, Poland, Republic of Korea, Spain, Sweden, Switzerland, Turkey, the United Kingdom, and the United States of America.

the last year for which data is available. After the global financial crisis, fintechs became prominent and thus there was proliferation of fintech startups from 2011 (Baber, 2019; Lee & Shin, 2018; Odinet, 2018), leading us to begin our sample period from 2011. After incorporating the missing data, firm-year observations for both models (defined below) were 6559. We define a SME as a firm which employs less than 500 employees (Arend, 2006; Brooksbank, 1991; Chu, 2009; George et al., 2005). The main independent variable of this study is the log of the number of fintech in a given country in a specific year (Abbasi et al., 2021). We measure a firm's cash holdings through the proportion of cash to sales (Harford et al., 2008). Moreover, we determine the institutional quality by averaging the six institutional quality dimensions: (1) voice and accountability, (2) regulatory quality, (3) political stability, (4) rule of law, (5) government effectiveness, and (6) control of corruption as reported by Worldwide Governance Indicator[2] (Alam et al., 2020). Our control variables include firm size, leverage, and firm performance. Higher leverage suggests financial distress, leading firms to accumulate more cash reserves to reduce the chances of bankruptcy (Guney et al., 2007). Large and better performing firms are expected to be more successful, which in turn suggests higher cash holdings (Dittmar et al., 2003; Wasi-uzzaman, 2014). We also include industry, year, and country dummies to control for characteristics pertaining to specific industry, year, and country, respectively.

To test our hypotheses, we use the following models:

$$Cash\ Holdings_{i,t} = \beta1 Cash\ Holdings_{i,t-1} + \beta2 fintechs_{i,t}$$
$$+ \beta k Controls_{i,t} + Industry + Year + \varepsilon \quad (13.1)$$

$$Cash\ Holdings_{i,t} = \beta1 Cash\ Holdings_{i,t-1} + \beta2 fintechs_{i,t}$$
$$+ \beta3 fintechs_{i,t} * Institutional\ Quality$$
$$+ \beta k Controls_{i,t} + Industry + Year + \varepsilon \quad (13.2)$$

In models (13.1) and (13.2), firm and year are depicted by i and t, respectively. We adopt the Generalized Method of Moments (GMM) as our econometric technique for the following four reasons. First, it is

---

[2] Data can be accessed from http://info.worldbank.org/governance/wgi/#home.

considered to be a more robust method to address the issue of endogeneity (Gull et al., 2018). As a result, it helps to address issues stemming from omitted variable bias (correlation between explanatory variables and error term) and reverse causality (Alam et al., 2019). Second, it mitigates heteroscedasticity, which may stem from the residuals not being constant across observations due to the distinct characteristics of countries in our sample (Alam et al., 2019; David et al., 2006). Third, it tackles the issue of firm-specific heterogeneity (Abbasi et al., 2021). Fourth, given that we include lagged dependent variables in our model as current year's firm cash flows are influenced by last year's cash flows, it may be unsuitable to utilize fixed or random effects model (Alam et al., 2020; Casu & Girardone, 2009).

We implement a two-step GMM estimation rather than one-step because it is robust to heteroscedasticity and serial correlation which ensures greater efficiency of two-step estimation (Alam et al., 2020; Musolesi & Nosvelli, 2007; Zhao & Dong, 2017). However, standard errors are downwardly biased in two-step GMM estimation, therefore, we apply Windmeijer's (2005) correction (Abbasi et al., 2021; Nguyen et al., 2015). Moreover, given that difference GMM suffers from the issue of intensification of gaps due to unbalanced panels, we choose system GMM (Roodman, 2009; Uddin et al., 2017). Additionally, system GMM produces better estimations as compared to difference GMM (Asongu et al., 2018; Beyzatlar & Yetkiner, 2017).

In order to assess the appropriateness of our chosen GMM model, we conducted two tests, namely the Hansen-J test and second-order autocorrelation in the first differenced residuals (AR(2)) test (shown in Table 13.4) (Abdallah et al., 2015). In all the models, the Hansen-J test and the AR (2) test are insignificant. This suggests that our instruments are unrelated to error term and the models do not suffer from second-order autocorrelation respectively (Abbasi et al., 2021; Hillier et al., 2011; Teixeira & Queiros, 2016). Further, in relation to our interaction model, we mean center the variables fintechs and institutional quality to reduce multicollinearity concerns (Nguyen et al., 2015; Wan & Yiu, 2009).

Results

Our result in Column 1 of Table 13.3 indicates that fintechs are positively associated with cash holdings, which supports our view that fintechs lower financing costs (Baber, 2019; Odinet, 2018), limit travel costs due to online payment of bills (Chuen & Teo, 2015; Lee & Shin, 2018; Ozili, 2018), reduce the cost of international transfer of money (Chuen & Teo, 2015; Lee & Shin, 2018), offer wealth management advice cost-effectively (Brenner & Meyll, 2020; Lui & Lamb, 2018), reduce the chances of bad debts (Jagtiani & John, 2018), and enable SMEs to increase revenue (and thereby cash flow) by attaining rapid access to finance (Rosavina et al., 2019; Sangwan et al., 2020) (Tables 13.1 and 13.2).

As fintechs are positively linked with cash holdings, our findings support theory of reasoned action, as the result suggests that firms may adopt fintechs due to their belief that this would result in higher cash flows. Moreover, our findings are in line with existing literature evidencing positive impact of fintechs on firm outcomes such as firm performance and access to finance (Abbasi et al., 2020, 2021).

With regard to control variables, firm size and firm performance positively affect cash holdings as expected. This corroborates our view that

Table 13.1 Variables definition

Cash Holdings	Proportion of cash to sales
fintechs	Log of the number of fintechs in a particular country in a specific year
Institutional quality	Average of the six institutional quality dimensions reported by Worldwide Governance Indicators
Tangible assets	Proportion of fixed assets to total assets
Firm size	Log of total assets
Firm performance	Return on assets

Table 13.2 Descriptive statistics

	Mean	Std. Dev	Min	Max
Cash Holdings	0.142	0.155	0.000	0.999
fintech	3.085	1.469	0.000	7.100
Institutional quality	1.234	0.480	−0.477	1.873
Tangible assets	0.188	0.220	0.000	0.998
Firm size	10.954	1.592	4.803	16.392
Firm performance	−0.034	0.277	−8.162	3.266

firms with higher performance and large firms have higher cash flows due to their greater success (Dittmar et al., 2003; Wasiuzzaman, 2014).

Column 2 of Table 13.3 showcases that better institutional quality positively moderates the link between fintechs and cash holdings. This suggests that the greater quality of institutions motivates fintech entrepreneurs to initiate startups, which positively affects cash holdings. Our finding support Alam et al. (2020) who evidence that country-level governance affects the relation between innovation and firm-related outcomes.

As part of the robustness test, we analyzed our main result after utilizing a different method to measure our dependent variable in which we measured cash holdings as the proportion of cash to total assets (Cheung, 2016). Columns 1 and 2 of Table 13.4 suggest that our main

Table 13.3 GMM analysis

	Column 1	Column 2
Lagged Cash Holdings	0.064	0.108
	(0.350)	(0.596)
Fintechs	0.033**	0.027**
	(2.329)	(2.123)
*Institutional quality * fintechs*		0.017*
		(1.927)
Institutional quality		−0.013
		(−0.204)
Tangible assets	−0.024	0.014
	(−0.204)	(0.140)
Firm size	0.098***	0.051**
	(3.794)	(2.198)
Firm performance	0.801***	0.832***
	(3.131)	(2.902)
Constant	0	0
Observations	6559	6559
Year effects	Yes	Yes
Industry effects	Yes	Yes
Country effects	Yes	Yes
Hansen J-test	0.653	0.128
AR(2) test	0.159	0.118

All variables are defined in Table 13.1. Standard errors are clustered at firm level. t-statistics are in parentheses. ***$p < 0.01$, **$p <$ 0.05, *$p < 0.1$

Table 13.4
Robustness test (measuring cash holdings through the proportion of cash to total assets)

	Column 1	Column 2
Lagged Cash Holdings	−0.079	0.215
	(−0.626)	(1.564)
Fintechs	0.024**	0.006
	(2.040)	(0.889)
Institutional quality * fintechs		0.007*
		(1.666)
Institutional quality		−0.019
		(−0.603)
Tangible assets	0.099*	0.002
	(1.954)	(0.043)
Firm size	−0.007	−0.010
	(−0.595)	(−1.048)
Firm performance	0.315***	0.354***
	(2.853)	(2.681)
Constant	0	0.084
		(0.509)
Observations	6550	6,559
Year effects	Yes	Yes
Industry effects	Yes	Yes
Country effects	Yes	Yes
Hansen J-test	0.500	0.908
AR(2)	0.316	0.105

All variables are defined in Table 13.1. Standard errors are clustered at firm level. t-statistics are in parentheses. ***$p < 0.01$, **$p < 0.05$, *$p < 0.1$

results are robust to measuring the dependent variable through a different method.

Conclusion

Given that greater cash holdings strengthen the survival of SMEs, we examine whether fintechs are positively associated with SMEs' cash holdings. Fintechs have been associated with lower borrowing costs, relatively quicker access to loans to take advantage of potential business opportunity, providing credit to debtors with greater likelihood of repayment, and lower wealth advisory, travel, and foreign money transfer costs (Abbasi et al., 2020). This is likely to positively influence the cash flows of SMEs. By analyzing OECD countries from 2011 to 2018, we show that fintechs enhance cash holdings of SMEs. Further, better institutional quality positively affects the link between fintechs and cash holdings.

Our study has important implications for managers and policymakers. Fintechs may act as a useful tool for SMEs aiming to enhance their cash balance. Further, our study supports the continuous efforts of regulators toward greater fintech startups. For example, policymakers in Australia, France, and Switzerland have implemented policies that help entrepreneurs to successfully launch their fintech startups (Zetzsche et al., 2017). Moreover, our results indicate that legislators may improve the quality of institutions (which could be, for example, through devising policies to curtail corruption, better enforcement of laws, and having a stable political environment) for an enhanced impact of fintechs on cash holdings.

There are three limitations to this study that we must highlight here. First, although we utilize a more robust econometric method (GMM) to answer our research questions, it does have limitations. For instance, when time-variant variables are omitted, GMM produces biased estimations (Abbasi et al., 2021). Second, it does not present results through qualitative techniques (for example, interviews and surveys) to corroborate the quantitative findings. Third, it only examines institutional quality as a moderating variable, given that there may be other factors such as culture which may influence the association between Fintechs and cash flows.

Funding   This research did not receive any specific grant from funding agencies in the public, commercial, or not-for-profit sectors.

References

Abbasi, K., Alam, A., Du, M., & Huynh, T. L. D. (2020). Fintech, SME efficiency and national culture: Evidence from OECD countries. *Technological Forecasting and Social Change, 143.* https://doi.org/10.1016/j.techfore.2020.120454

Abbasi, K., Alam, A., Brohi, N. A., Brohi, I. A., & Nasim, S. (2021). P2P lending Fintechs and SMEs' access to finance. *Economics Letters, 204.* https://doi.org/10.1016/j.econlet.2021.109890

Abdallah, W., Goergen, M., & O'Sullivan, N. (2015). Endogeneity: How failure to correct for it can cause wrong inferences and some remedies. *British Journal of Management, 26*(4), 791–804. https://doi.org/10.1111/1467-8551.12113

Acharya, V. V., & Subramanian, K. V. (2009). Bankruptcy codes and innovation. *Review of Financial Studies, 22*(12), 4949–4988. https://doi.org/10.1093/rfs/hhp019

Aidukaite, J. (2019). The welfare systems of the Baltic states following the recent financial crisis of 2008–2010: Expansion or retrenchment? *Journal of Baltic Studies, 50*(1), 39–58. https://doi.org/10.1080/01629778.2019.1570957

Alam, A., Uddin, M., & Yazdifar, H. (2019). Institutional determinants of R & D investment: Evidence from emerging markets. *Technological Forecasting and Social Change, 138*, 34–44. https://doi.org/10.1016/j.techfore.2018.08.007

Alam, A., Uddin, M., Yazdifar, H., Shafique, S., & Lartey, T. (2020). R&D investment, firm performance and moderating role of system and safeguard: Evidence from emerging markets. *Journal of Business Research, 106*, 94–105. https://doi.org/10.1016/j.jbusres.2019.09.018

Allard, G., Martinez, C. A., & Williams, C. (2012). Political instability, pro-business market reforms and their impacts on national systems of innovation. *Resources Policy, 41*, 638–651. https://doi.org/10.1016/j.respol.2011.12.005

Anagnostopoulos, I. (2018). Fintech and regtech: Impact on regulators and banks. *Journal of Economics and Business, 100*, 7–25. https://doi.org/10.1016/j.jeconbus.2018.07.003

Anokhin, S., & Schulze, W. S. (2009). Entrepreneurship, innovation, and corruption. *Journal of Business Venturing, 24*(5), 465–476. https://doi.org/10.1016/j.jbusvent.2008.06.001

Arend, R. J. (2006). SME: Supplier alliance activity in manufacturing—Contingent benefits and perceptions. *Strategic Manangement Journal, 27*(8), 741–763. https://doi.org/10.1002/smj.538

Asongu, S., Nwachukwu, J., & Orim, S. (2018). Mobile phones, institutional quality and entrepreneurship in Sub-Saharan Africa. *Technological Forecasting and Social Change, 131*, 183–203. https://doi.org/10.1016/j.techfore.2017.08.007

Baber, H. (2019). Fintech, crowdfunding and customer retention in Islamic banks. *Vision: The Journal of Business Perspective, 24*(3), 260–268. https://doi.org/10.1177/0972262919869765

Beyzatlar, M., & Yetkiner, H. (2017). Convergence in transportation measures across the EU15. *Transportation, 44*(5), 927–940. https://doi.org/10.1007/s11116-016-9686-6

Brenner, L., & Meyll, T. (2020). Robo-advisors: A substitute for human financial advice? *Journal of Behavioral and Experimental Finance, 25*. https://doi.org/10.1016/j.jbef.2020.100275

Brooksbank, R. (1991). Defining the small business: A new classification of company size. *Entreprenuership & Regional Development: An International Journal, 3*(1), 17–31. https://doi.org/10.1080/08985629100000002

Casu, B., & Girardone, C. (2009). Testing the relationship between competition and efficiency in banking: A panel data analysis. *Economics Letters, 105*(1), 134–137. https://doi.org/10.1016/j.econlet.2009.06.018

Cheung, A. (2016). Corporate social responsibility and corporate cash holdings. *Journal of Corporate Finance, 37*, 412–430. https://doi.org/10.1016/j.jco rpfin.2016.01.008

Chuen, D. L. K., & Teo, E. G. S. (2015). Emergence of fintech and the LASIC Principles. *Journal of Financial Perspectives, 3*(3), 1–26. https://doi.org/10. 2139/ssrn.2668049

Chu, W. (2009). The influence of family ownership on SME performance: Evidence from public firms in Taiwan. *Small Business Economics, 33*, 353–373. https://doi.org/10.1007/s11187-009-9178-6

Cowling, M., Brown, R., & Rocha, A. (2020). Did you save some cash for a rainy COVID-19 day? The crisis and SMEs. *International Small Business Journal, 38*(7), 593–604. https://doi.org/10.1177/0266242620945102

Cowling, M., Lee, N., & Ughetto, E. (2020). The price of a disadvantaged location: Regional variation in the price and supply of short-term credit to SMEs in the UK. *Journal of Small Business Management, 58*(3), 648–668. https://doi.org/10.1080/00472778.2019.1681195

Daude, C., & Stein, E. (2007). The quality of institutions and foreign direct investment. *Economics Policy, 19*, 317–344. https://doi.org/10.1111/j.1468-0343.2007.00318.x

David, P., Yoshikawa, T., Chari, M. D. R., & Rasheed, A. A. (2006). Strategic investments in Japanese corporations: Do foreign portfolio owners foster underinvestment or appropriate investment? *Strategic Management Journal, 27*(6), 591–600. https://doi.org/10.1002/smj.523

Dittmar, A., Mahrt-Smith, J., & Servaes, H. (2003). International corporate governance and corporate cash holdings. *The Journal of Financial and Quantitative Analysis, 38*(1), 111–133. https://doi.org/10.2307/4126766

Dutta, N., Roy, S., & Sobel, R. S. (2011). Does a free press nurture entrepreneurship? *American Journal of Entrepreneurship, 4*(1), 71.

Fereidouni, H. G., Masron, T. A., & Amiri, R. E. (2011). The effects of FDI on voice and accountability in the MENA region. *International Journal of Social Economics, 38*(9), 802–815. https://doi.org/10.1108/03068291111157258

Fishbein, M., & Ajzen, I. (1975). *Belief, attitude, intention, and behaviour: An introduction to theory and research.* Addison-Wesley.

Furukawa, Y. (2007). The protection of intellectual property rights and endogenous growth: Is stronger always better? *Journal of Economic Dynamics and Control, 31*(11), 3644–3670. https://doi.org/10.1016/j.jedc.2007.01.011

Fuster, A., Plosser, M., Schnabl, P., & Vickery, J. (2019). The role of technology in mortgage lending. *Review of Financial Studies, 32*(5), 1854–1899. https://doi.org/10.1093/rfs/hhz018

George, G., Wiklund, J., & Zahra, S. (2005). Ownership and the internationalization of small firms. *Journal of Management, 31*(2), 210–233. https://doi.org/10.1177/0149206304271760

Gomber, P., Kauffman, R. J., Parker, C., & Weber, B. W. (2018). On the fintech revolution: Interpreting the forces of innovation, disruption, and transformation in financial services. *Journal of Management Information Systems, 35*(1), 220–265. https://doi.org/10.1080/07421222.2018.1440766

Gull, A. A., Nekhili, M., Nagati, H., & Chtioui, T. (2018). Beyond gender diversity: How specific attributes of female directors affect earnings management. *British Accounting Review, 50*(3), 255–274. https://doi.org/10.1016/j.bar.2017.09.001

Guney, Y., Ozkan, A., & Ozkan, N. (2007). International evidence on the non-linear impact of leverage on corporate cash holdings. *Journal of Multinational Financial Management, 17*(1), 45–60. https://doi.org/10.1016/j.mulfin.2006.03.003

Harford, J., Mansi, S. A., & Maxwell, W. F. (2008). Corporate governance and firm cash holdings in the US. *Journal of Financial Economics, 87*(3), 535–555. https://doi.org/10.1016/j.jfineco.2007.04.002

Henisz, W. (2002). The institutional environment for infrastructure investment. *Industrial and Corporate Change, 11*(2), 355–389. https://doi.org/10.1093/icc/11.2.355

Hillier, D., Pindado, J., de Queiroz, V., & de la Torre, C. (2011). The impact of country-level corporate governance on research and development. *Journal of International Business Studies, 42*(1), 76–98. https://doi.org/10.1057/jibs.2010.46

Jagtiani, J., & John, K. (2018). Fintech: The impact on consumers and regulatory responses. *Journal of Economics and Business, 100*, 1–6. https://doi.org/10.1016/j.jeconbus.2018.11.002

Jagtiani, J., & Lemieux, C. (2019). *The roles of alternative data and machine learning in fintech lending: Evidence from the LendingClub* (Fed Working Paper 18-15). https://doi.org/10.21799/frbp.wp.2018.15

Javorcik, B. S., & Wei, S.-J. (2009). Corruption and cross-border investment in emerging markets: Firm-level evidence. *Journal of International Money and Finance, 28*, 605–624. https://doi.org/10.1016/j.jimonfin.2009.01.003

Jiao, H., Koo, C. K., & Cui, Y. (2015). Legal environment, government effectiveness and firms innovation in China: Examining the moderating influence of government ownership. *Technological Forecasting and Social Change, 96*, 15–24. https://doi.org/10.1016/j.techfore.2015.01.008

Julio, B., & Yook, Y. (2012). Political uncertainty and corporate investment cycle. *Journal of Finance, 67*(1), 45–83. https://doi.org/10.1111/j.1540-6261.2011.01707.x

Kaufmann, D., Kraay, A. & Mastruzzi, M. (2009). *Governance matters VIII: Aggregate and individual governance indicators, 1996–2008* (World Bank Policy Research Working Paper 4978). https://doi.org/10.1596/1813-9450-4978

Kirkpatrick, C., Parker D., & Zhang, Y-F. (2006). Foreign direct investment in infrastructure in developing countries: Does regulation make a difference. *Transnational Corporations, 15*(1),143–71.

Laeven, L. (2003). Does financial liberalisation reduce financing constraints? *Financial Management, 32*(1), 5–34. https://doi.org/10.2307/3666202

La Porta, R., Lopez-de-Silanes, F., Shleifer, A., & Vishny, R. (1997). Legal determinants of external finance. *Journal of Finance, 52*(3), 1131–1150. https://doi.org/10.2307/2329518

Lee, I., & Shin, Y. J. (2018). Fintech: Ecosystem, business models, investment decisions, and challenges. *Business Horizons, 61*(1), 35–46. https://doi.org/10.1016/j.bushor.2017.09.003

Lee, M. H., Mak, A. K., & Pang, A. (2012). Bridging the gap: An exploratory study of corporate social responsibility among SMEs in Singapore. *Journal of Public Relation Research, 24*(4), 299–317. https://doi.org/10.1080/1062726X.2012.689898

Liu, Y., Segev, S., & Villar, M. E. (2017). Comparing two mechanisms for green consumption: Cognitive-affect behavior vs theory of reasoned action. *Journal of Consumer Marketing, 34*(5), 442–454. https://doi.org/10.1108/JCM-01-2016-1688

Lui, A., & Lamb, G. W. (2018). Artificial intelligence and augmented intelligence collaboration: Regaining trust and confidence in the financial sector. *Information & Communications Technology Law, 27*(3), 267–283. https://doi.org/10.1080/13600834.2018.1488659

Lu, L. (2018). Promoting SME finance in the context of the fintech revolution: A case study of the UK's practice and regulation. *Banking & Finance Law Review, 33*(3), 317–343.

Mahendra, E., Zuhdi, U., & Muyanto, R. (2015). Determinants of firm innovation in Indonesia: The role of institutions and access to finance. *Economics and Finance in Indonesia, 61*(3), 149–179. https://doi.org/10.47291/efi.v61i3.512

Mahmood, I. P., & Rufin, C. (2005). Governments dilemma: The role of government in imitation and innovation. *Academy of Management Review, 30*(2), 338–360.

Masino, S. (2015). Macroeconomic volatility, institutional instability and incentive to innovate. *Review of Development Economics, 19*(1), 116–131. https://doi.org/10.1111/rode.12127

Morais, M., Borges, J. A. R., & Binotto, E. (2018). Using the reasoned action approach to understand Brazilian successors' intention to take over the farm. *Land Use Policy, 71,* 445–452. https://doi.org/10.1016/j.landusepol.2017.11.002

Musolesi, A., & Nosvelli, M. (2007). Dynamics of residential water consumption in a panel of Italian municipalities. *Applied Economics Letters, 14*(6), 441–444. https://doi.org/10.1080/13504850500425642

Nguyen, T., Locke, S., & Reddy, K. (2015). Ownership concentration and corporate performance from a dynamic perspective: Does national governance quality matter? *International Review of Financial Analysis, 41,* 148–161. https://doi.org/10.1016/j.irfa.2015.06.005

OECD. (1997). *National innovation systems.* OECD Publishing.

Odinet, C. K. (2018). Consumer Bitcredit and fintech lending. *Alabama Law Review, 69*(4), 781–858.

Ozili, P. K. (2018). Impact of digital finance on financial inclusion and stability. *Borsa Istanbul Review, 18*(4), 329–340. https://doi.org/10.1016/j.bir.2017.12.003

Panayides, P. M., Parola, F., & Lam, J. S. L. (2015). The effect of institutional factors on public-private partnership success in ports. *Transportation Research Part A: Policy and Practice, 71,* 110–127. https://doi.org/10.1016/j.tra.2014.11.006

Pattit, J. M., Raj, S. P., & Wilemon, D. (2012). An institutional theory investigation of US technology development trends since the mid-19th century. *Resources Policy, 41,* 306–318. https://doi.org/10.1016/j.respol.2011.10.008

Petrescu, M., Gironda, J. T., & Korgaonkar, P. K. (2018). Online piracy in the context of routine activities and subjective norms. *Journal of Marketing Management, 34*(3–4), 314–346. https://doi.org/10.1080/0267257X.2018.1452278

Pindado, J., Requejo, I., & Rivera, J. C. (2017). Economic forecast and corporate leverage choices: The role of institutional environment. *International Review of Economics and Finance, 51,* 121–144. https://doi.org/10.1016/j.iref.2017.05.006

Radas, S., & Božić, L. (2009). The antecedents of SME innovativeness in an emerging transition economy. *Technovation, 29*(6–7), 438–450. https://doi.org/10.1016/j.technovation.2008.12.002

Rodriguez, P., Uhlenbruck, K., & Eden, L. (2005). Government corruption and the entry strategies of multinationals. *Academy of Management Review, 30*(2), 383–396. https://doi.org/10.5465/amr.2005.16387894

Roodman, D. (2009). A note on the theme of too many instruments. *Oxford Bulletin of Economics and Statistics, 71*, 135–158. https://doi.org/10.1111/j.1468-0084.2008.00542.x

Rosavina, M., Rahadi, R. A., Kitri, M. L., Nuraeni, S., & Mayangsari, L. (2019). P2P lending adoption by SMEs in Indonesia. *Qualitative Research in Financial Markets, 11*(2), 260–279. https://doi.org/10.1108/QRFM-09-2018-0103

Sabry, M. I. (2019). Fostering innovation under institutional deficiencies: Formal state–business consultation or cronyism? *Economia Politica, 36*(1), 79–110. https://doi.org/10.1007/s40888-018-00137-1

Sangwan, V., Harshita, N., Prakash, P., & Singh, S. (2020). Financial technology: A review of extant literature. *Studies in Economics and Finance, 37*(1), 71–88. https://doi.org/10.1108/SEF-07-2019-0270

Seitz, M., & Watzinger, M. (2017). Contract enforcement and R&D investment. *Resources Policy, 46*(1), 182–195. https://doi.org/10.1016/j.respol.2016.09.015

Teixeira, A. A. C., & Queiros, A. S. S. (2016). Economic growth, human capital and structural change: A dynamic panel data analysis. *Resources Policy, 45*(8), 1636–1648. https://doi.org/10.1016/j.respol.2016.04.006

Troudi, H., & Bouyoucef, D. (2020). Predicting purchasing behavior of green food in Algerian context. *European Journal Business, 15*(1), 1–21. https://doi.org/10.1108/EMJB-03-2019-0046

Uddin, M. A., Ali, M. H., & Masih, M. (2017). Political stability and growth: An application of dynamic GMM and quantile regression. *Economic Modelling, 64*, 610–625. https://doi.org/10.1016/j.econmod.2017.04.028

Vanyushyn, V. (2008). The dual effect of resellers on electronic business adoption by SMEs. *International Journal of Entrepreneurial Innovation, 9*(1), 43–49. https://doi.org/10.5367/000000008783563019

Varsakelis, N. C. (2006). Education, political institutions and innovative activity: A cross-country empirical investigation. *Research Policy, 35*(7), 1083–1090. https://doi.org/10.1016/j.respol.2006.06.002

Waarden, F. V. (2001). Institutions and innovation: The legal environment of innovating firm. *Organization Studies, 22*(5), 765–795. https://doi.org/10.1177/0170840601225002

Wan, W. P., & Hoskisson, R. E. (2003). Home country environments, corporate diversification strategies, and firm performance. *Academy of Management Journal, 46*(1), 27–45. https://doi.org/10.2307/30040674

Wan, Y. P., & Yiu, D. W. (2009). From crisis to opportunity: Environmental jolt, corporate acquisitions, and firm performance. *Strategic Management Journal, 30*(7), 791–801. https://doi.org/10.1002/smj.744

Wasiuzzaman, S. (2014). Analysis of corporate cash holdings of firms in Malaysia. *Journal of Asia Business Studies, 8*(2), 118–135. https://doi.org/10.1108/JABS-10-2012-0048

Windmeijer, F. (2005). A finite sample correction for the variance of linear efficient two-step GMM estimators. *Journal of Econometrics, 126*(1), 25–51. https://doi.org/10.1016/j.jeconom.2004.02.005

Xiao, M. (2020). Factors influencing eSports viewership: An approach based on the theory of reasoned action. *Communication & Sport, 8*(1), 92–122. https://doi.org/10.1177/2167479518819482

Zetzsche, D., Buckley, R., Barberis, J., & Arner, D. (2017). Regulating a revolution: From regulatory sandboxes to smart regulation. *Fordham Journal of Corporate & Financial Law, 23*(1), 31–103. https://doi.org/10.2139/ssrn.3018534

Zhao, L., & Dong, Y. (2017). Tourism agglomeration and urbanization: Empirical evidence from China Tourism. *Asian Pacific Journal of Tourism Research, 22*(5), 512–523. https://doi.org/10.1080/10941665.2016.1277545

Fintech Companies in Brazil: Assessing Their Effects on Competition in the Brazilian Financial System from 2018 to 2020

Norberto Montani Martins[iD]*, Paula Marina Sarno,*
Luiz Macahyba, and Dalton Boechat Filho

Introduction

Economic literature on fintechs often emphasize the disruptive potential the entrance of new firms that adopt technology-enabled innovations have (Bofondi & Gobbi, 2017; International Organization of Securities Commissions, 2017; Navaretti et al., 2017; Philippon, 2016; Restoy, 2021; US Treasury, 2018; Zetzsche & Dewi, 2018). As highlighted by

N. Montani Martins (✉) · L. Macahyba · D. B. Filho
The Federal University of Rio de Janeiro (UFRJ), Rio de Janeiro, Brazil
e-mail: norberto.martins@ie.ufrj.br

P. M. Sarno
Fluminense Federal University (UFF), Niterói, Brazil

© The Author(s), under exclusive license to Springer Nature
Switzerland AG 2023
T. Walker et al. (eds.), *The Fintech Disruption*, Palgrave Studies
in Financial Services Technology,
https://doi.org/10.1007/978-3-031-23069-1_14

349

the Financial Stability Board (FSB) (2019), new entrants into the financial services space can change market structures and affect the degree of concentration and contestability in financial services, promoting greater competition and diversity.

However, the actual impacts of fintechs on competition in the real world is less clear as the lack of data and dedicated studies on this topic are still an issue. A branch of the literature resorted to private surveys to fill informational gaps. The World Economic Forum (2017, p. 12), for instance, after engaging with over 150 experts, concludes that 'fintechs have materially changed the basis of competition in financial services, but have not yet materially changed the competitive landscape.' Other branch of the literature focus on case studies with actual data, such as the discussion on the competition for deposits between fintechs and banks in China (Zhu & Lu, 2022) or the impact of fintech in financial institutions' profitability in India (Singh et al., 2021).

This chapter develops a first approximation to the study of fintechs and competition in Brazil, combining an overview of regulatory and market structure aspects with an analysis of real-world data. It analyzes the competitive impacts of fintechs in the Brazilian financial industry, focusing on payment institutions, as regulated by the Central Bank of Brazil (BCB), and assessing how, and through which channels these firms are affecting the profit rate of incumbent banks. We use data from the balance sheets of Brazil's larger universal banks[1] and larger payment fintechs[2] to build indicators to assess which traditional banking revenues would potentially be under threat from such fintechs.

The first part of this chapter explores the regulatory definitions of what constitutes a Brazilian fintech. From the perspective of the BCB, who is responsible for ensuring the stability of the financial system, fintechs are regulated entities that are subject to a set of objective obligations and supervision. In the current regulatory framework, they correspond to Direct Credit Societies (DCSs) and Peer-to-Peer Loan Companies (P2PLCs). To these, we also add Payment Institutions (PIs) due to their very nature, as will be discussed below.

In the media in general, different types of fintechs are commonly called 'digital banks.' In Brazilian regulations, there are no special licensing

---

[1] Itaú Unibanco, Banco do Brasil, Bradesco, Caixa Econômica Federal, and Santander.

[2] Cielo, Getnet, PagSeguro, Redecard, and Stone.

requirements regarding digital banking. As such, these 'digital banks' do not formally exist—they are digital arms of commercial or universal banks or of financial conglomerates that involve different types of non-banking financial institutions. Due to this, we separate in our analysis actual new competitors from digital arms of traditional banks.

The second part of the chapter identifies the possible impacts that the activities of fintechs have already had on revenues of Brazilian banks. In particular, we examine the revenues of specific activities in which new entrants operate. It is important to anticipate here that the available information and its levels of disaggregation make it difficult to identify the portion of bank revenues that would be pressured by the new entrants. In other words, a better delimitation of the relevant markets that are under competitive pressure would require the disclosure of more granular and standardized data for a better comparison between fintechs and established banks.

In our research, we use as reference the data from income statements and balance sheets of Brazil's main universal banks and the most representative fintechs with a special focus on PIs. Based on data available in the financial statements, we build indicators to assess the weight of fintechs in the Brazilian financial industry and more specifically which revenue segments are potentially under competitive threat from these new entrants.

This work is one of the first research efforts to explore this topic in Brazil. For this reason, it has some limits chiefly imposed by the lack of data. Since this study only encompasses two years and the number of fintechs authorized by the BCB is relatively small, econometric methods were ruled out, providing room for descriptive analysis and statistics.

FINTECHS AND COMPETITION: AN OVERVIEW

The term fintechs has been used to identify financial firms that adopt 'new' technologies with the purpose of changing how financial products and services are provided. The speed with which so many modalities, areas, and even products emerge in the wake of this innovative revolution makes the effort to build a taxonomy capable of encompassing such a diversity of business models a Herculean task.

One criterion for the classification of these firms separates the 'fins' from the 'techs.' 'Fins' offer services and products originally provided by traditional bank conglomerates. They are active in areas such as payments, investment advice, and loans. They compete for banks' clients through lower prices or tailor-made products, all of which are adjusted to the profile of each individual consumer. Typically, they engage in Business-to-Client (B2C) relationships.

'Techs,' on the other hand, are firms that supply technological inputs that can be acquired by financial service providers, changing the production function of these players. Segments such as cloud computing, cryptography, and information management are the focus of these firms, which have business models characterized by Business-to-Business (B2B) relationships. In this case, 'techs' cooperate or engage in partnerships with incumbent financial institutions. Thus, they are not a source of competitive pressure.

Such classification has clear limits as 'techs,' especially BigTechs,[3] are increasingly engaging in financial activities themselves, adopting some kind of vertical integration in the provision of financial products and services (Crisanto, Ehrentraud & Fabian, 2021). Moreover, new financial firms can also partner with 'old' incumbents or derive from them, such as in the case of neobanks that are 'digital' arms of traditional banking. An example of this is the case of Next, a digital bank owned by Bradesco, one of Brazil's largest banking institutions (e.g., Caciatori Jr., 2020).

Efforts to create a taxonomy are directly linked to one of the main controversies about fintechs, namely their ability to pressure the competitive environment in which incumbents operate. For instance, in Brazil, Martins et al. (2022, pp. 25–26) show that the real growth of banks' revenues with service fees and tariffs slowed in recent years and a large part of the literature associates this result with the entry of fintechs in the Brazilian financial system. In reality, this is much more complex since the interaction between incumbent banks and fintechs, as well as the very effect of these firms on the market and its competitive dynamics, has multiple implications. For example, Itaú's and Bradesco's Chief Executive Officers (CEO) from the main private banks in Brazil, showed different opinions on the issue.

Cândido Bracher, then the Itaú' CEO suggests that:

---

[3] Large firms with established technology platforms, such as Alibaba, Amazon, Google, Meta.

The emergence of fintechs that compete for banks' customers is bringing more efficiency to segments and products in which banks do not offer good services today. Because of this, these firms draw attention to the quality of bank services, which increases the appetite of regulators for more regulation. (Moreira, 2019; authors' translation)

On the other hand, d, Octavio Lazari Jr., the Bradesco's CEO, states:

Bradesco must prepare itself to face the advance of the so-called Big Techs, such as Google, Apple, and Amazon, in financial services. This is the great risk we run and that we have to run after. It is not fintech. Fintechs are partners. (Ragazzi, 2018; authors' translation)

Different views are also present in academic literature. The key point of the discussion about the effects of fintechs revolves around the effects that these institutions will bring in terms of the competitive dynamics in the financial system. The predominance of large banks as central players in the provision of financial services is characteristic of several jurisdictions. In the Brazilian case, universal banks concentrated 84.6% of the total assets of the financial system in 2021, according to the BCB's IF.Data database. 80.3% of those assets are owned by twelve banks of greatest systemic relevance. In this context:

The crucial question is whether and how far fintechs are replacing banks and other incumbent financial institutions. And whether, in doing so, they will induce a healthy competitive process, enhancing efficiency in a market with high entry barriers, or rather cause disruption and financial instability. (Navaretti et al., 2017, p. 9)

Bofondi and Gobbi (2017) argue that fintechs pose a major threat to the traditional business model of banks. Zetzsche and Dewi (2018), meanwhile, propose that fintechs enter credit markets and promote competition to reduce lending rates as an alternative to imposing caps on interest rates. Thakor (2020) suggests that peer-to-peer (P2P) lending may take some market share away from banks, although a replacement for conventional credit cannot be envisioned. Chu and Wei (2021) develop a spatial model in which tougher competition from fintechs erodes banks' profits and may even affect the credit market and welfare diversely.

Notably, Restoy (2021) argues that the disruptions created by technological progress in the financial services market stem from three distinct elements: (i) the expansion of the products/services offered to consumers; (ii) the diversification of the processes and distribution channels of these products/services; and (iii) the entry of new providers. The author recognizes that:

> These developments are bound to generate profound changes in the market structure, as non-bank fintech players are now becoming very active in offering services that in the past were predominantly offered by banks. Their presence in the payment service area is already quite significant. However, they are also gaining weight in the provision of wealth management services, the sale of insurance products, and loan underwriting. (Restoy, 2021, p. 1)

Less optimistic views regarding the competitive impact of fintechs on banks highlight the potential effects of new entrants on financial stability. A balanced view is provided by the FSB (2019), which proposes that the increased competition brought by fintechs may engender a more efficient and resilient financial system, even though increased competition may put pressure on the profitability of financial institutions and lead to the assumption of new risks for these firms to be able to maintain their margins and profit rates. Studies such as that by the FSB emphasize the goal of ensuring a level playing field between entrants and incumbents, and of preventing the eventual intensification of competition from pressuring traditional banks to relax their mechanisms for risk assessment, potentially increasing the financial fragility of their balance sheets.

But there is a clear concern by transnational regulators to preserve the innovative movement without compromising the health of the financial system, as well as to prevent regulatory asymmetries from benefiting entry groups to the detriment of incumbents. In this sense, some recent studies suggest that these asymmetries be corrected by focusing regulation on the type of activity developed by the firm (activity-based regulation) and not on the type of institution that provides the service (entity-based regulation). Such an approach would help to level the competitive playing field (Stulz, 2019).

For authors such as Restoy (2021), there will remain a need to consider whether a stricter entity-focused regulation would not be necessary for the case of BigTechs, since incidents on platforms could result in events of systemic character. He also points out that entity-focused regulation aimed at curbing anticompetitive practices may also be necessary in the case of these institutions, since these practices may go beyond the frameworks of a specific activity, such as the application of product cross-subsidization.

This article is not intended to exhaust any of these debates. Its main objective is to point out how the discussions about these themes are evolving in Brazil. More specifically, it seeks to establish an analytical framework based on the regulatory definition of fintech and to evaluate, based on this approach, how and through which channels these companies may affect the profit rate of incumbent banks.

FINTECHS IN BRAZIL: AN OVERVIEW

The realm of fintechs' operations is as large as their capacity for innovation. According to the yearbook of FintechLab (2020), a hub for connecting and fostering the national fintech ecosystem in Brazil, 689 fintechs were operating domestically in August 2020, the most recent point of data. The innovations that have been introduced by these firms have brought the need for changes and adaptations in the structuring, performance, and focus of traditional institutions in the financial sector.

As in the rest of the world, the emergence of fintechs has opened an intense debate about the possibility that these new entrants may increase competitive pressures in some market niches currently occupied by incumbents. This is, for example, the view of the BCB itself, which expects fintechs to increase competition in the system by expanding the supply of products and services due to the use of more advanced and specialized technological resources, and to encourage traditional institutions to improve their operating processes. The BCB also expects that eventual partnerships and sharing of activities and costs with traditional institutions will bring gains to society (BCB, 2020).

Although the variety and number of fintechs is growing in Brazil, the BCB has officially regulated only two modalities of them which we have mentioned above: Direct Credit Societies (DCS) and Peer-to-Peer Loan Companies (P2PLC). We can add Payment Institutions (PI) to this list, which are not officially labeled as fintechs by BCB, but in practice represent one of the most relevant market segments for such firms.

A Payment Institution (PI) is defined as a legal entity that provides cash-in and cash-out services of the funds held on payment accounts, performs, or facilitates payment instructions, manages payment accounts or issues, and/or acquires payment instruments, among other functions

(Brasil, 2013). The same PI may adopt several payment arrangements in its customer relationships and may operate solely in the domestic market or also have cross-border operations. These institutions may also offer prepaid, postpaid, and deposit payment accounts and may have the role of e-money issuer, postpaid instrument issuer, merchant acquirer of payment instruments, and, finally, settlor of payment transactions. PIs are not allowed to conduct activities restricted to financial institutions, such as providing loans, but a financial institution can join a payment scheme, which is a set of rules and procedures that regulates the provision of certain payment service to the public.

Institutions that provide payment services represented the majority of fintechs created by August 2020, accounting for 28% of the total or 190 institutions, according to a survey conducted by FintechLab (2020). However, this number does not correspond to the set of firms formally authorized to operate in Brazil. In the case of the BCB, there were 37 PIs authorized to operate by December 2021 (see Fig. 14.1). On the same date, 26 Payment Schemes were registered with the BCB, of which eight referred to deposit accounts, nine to prepaid payment accounts, and nine to postpaid payment accounts. Twenty schemes cover the domestic market and six refer to cross-border operations, with Visa and Mastercard, followed by Elo Serviços, being the payment institutions with the largest number of authorized arrangements—eight, eight, and five, respectively.

It is also worth mentioning that, in the next few years, the registration of PIs is expected to gain momentum with the alteration in the operating authorization requirements. In a schedule ending at the end of 2023, the new requirements will include PIs that issue electronic money regardless of the financial volumes they handle.

In the nomenclature used by the BCB, fintechs are differentiated from PIs. DCSs are financial institutions that carry out operations of loan, financing, and acquisition of credit rights exclusively through an electronic platform. Their own capital is the sole source of resources to conduct DCS operations and the only authorized way to raise funds from the public consists in the issuance of shares. Such institutions must have a minimum of BRL 1.0 million in assets and can sell their loans to other financial institutions, securitization companies, and receivables investment funds. Besides the revenue from interest on these operations using their own resources, they also earn revenues from the sale and transfer of credit assets, as well as from fees on credit analysis services for third parties. They

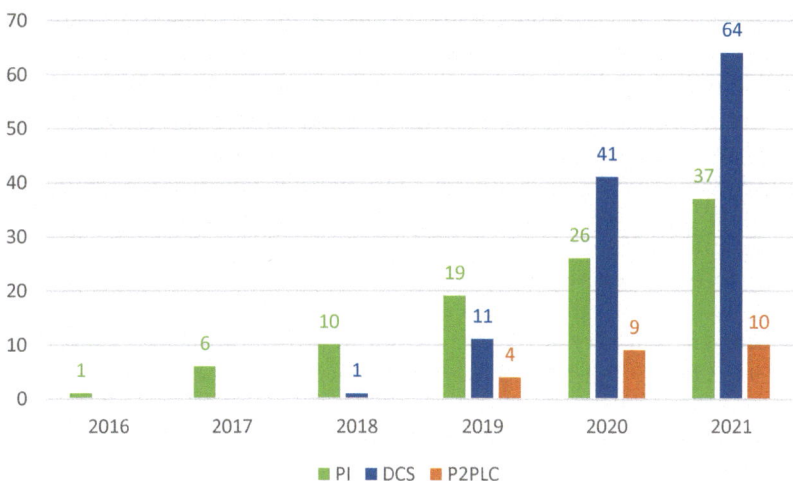

Fig. 14.1 Fintechs authorized by the Central Bank of Brazil—2016–2021 (*Source* Data on the evolution of the National Financial System, Central Bank of Brazil)

can also issue e-money, increasing operational efficiency, and the supply of products.

P2PLCs are also considered financial institutions and act as intermediaries without directly providing a loan. They are simply P2P electronic platforms performing P2P loans and financing operations. There is a maximum loan value of BRL 15,000 to be provided by the same creditor, except for creditors classified as a 'qualified investors' (institutional investors, or natural or legal persons which have a minimum of BRL 1.0 million in financial investments).

The expansion of fintechs that provide payment services was accompanied by growth in the number of DCSs, a trend which was not observed in the case of P2PLCs, as can be seen in Fig. 14.1. In the case of DCSs, many institutions that already operated in a similar way, but with less independence and scope, preferred to remain as correspondents of an incumbent financial institution, which assumes the costs of compliance and responsibility before the regulator for the controls and risk management of operations. Nevertheless, the creation of these entities maintains a higher growth rate than IPs in 2021, with large retail merchants having their own credit companies in the wake of the e-commerce explosion during the COVID-19 pandemic.

The two modalities of credit fintechs described above were regulated by the National Monetary Council (CMN) in 2018. The regulation establishes that loans must be made based on consistent, verifiable, and transparent criteria. Such criteria must include relevant aspects of the borrower's financial capacity such as the level of indebtedness and ability to generate cash flows, among others.

Table 14.1 presents a portrait of fintechs authorized to operate by the BCB, according to the IF.Data database. The numbers show that credit fintechs are still very small when compared to the rest of the financial system. On the other hand, payment fintechs show significant growth, both in the number of institutions and in the stock of assets they hold, but this figure is still very low when compared to the assets of traditional banks.

Furthermore, DCSs play a marginal role in structuring credit operations in the country, totaling BRL 107.2 million in September 2021 against BRL 4.1 trillion by traditional banks. Since P2PLCs act only as intermediary platforms, it is not possible to see the volume of loans intermediated through them. In addition, despite regulatory restrictions, some payment institutions appear with a credit portfolio classified in BCB's

Table 14.1 Statistics on fintechs and traditional banks (BCB IF.Data Database)

Type of institution	Number*				Assets (BRL billion)			
	2018	2019	2020	2021**	2018	2019	2020	2021**
Payment Institutions	10	19	26	33	216.5	242.6	302.4	346.0
Direct Credit Societies	0	5	25	35	–	0.03	0.34	1.13
P2P Loan Companies	0	2	5	6	–	0.01	0.01	0.03
Commercial and Universal Banks	95	96	98	99	7,534.3	7,895.4	9,600.2	10,290.0

Source BCB, IF.Data. *Number of institutions refers only to institutions that have balance sheet data available in the IF.Data database. **As of September 2021

IF.Data when we consider the financial conglomerate—i.e., when we consolidate other financial institutions such as consumer finance companies, as in the case of Nubank. Financial conglomerates involving PIs have a loan outstanding of BRL 23.8 billion in September 2021 (see Fig. 14.2).

Finally, as a marketing strategy, the term 'digital bank' is being used by a number of established banks and by new banking and non-banking institutions in the national financial system. This occurs despite the lack of any regulatory standards that define or license this 'new' type of institution. According to a study released by BCB (2021; authors' translation):

> the common point among the institutions that present themselves in this way is the exclusively remote and differentiated relationship with clients, usually linked to advantages and better experiences in terms of service costs, facilitation of access, and integration with other conveniences and demands of the public.

The study further opines that the 'digital banking' attribute refers to a measure of degree rather than type, given that to a lesser or

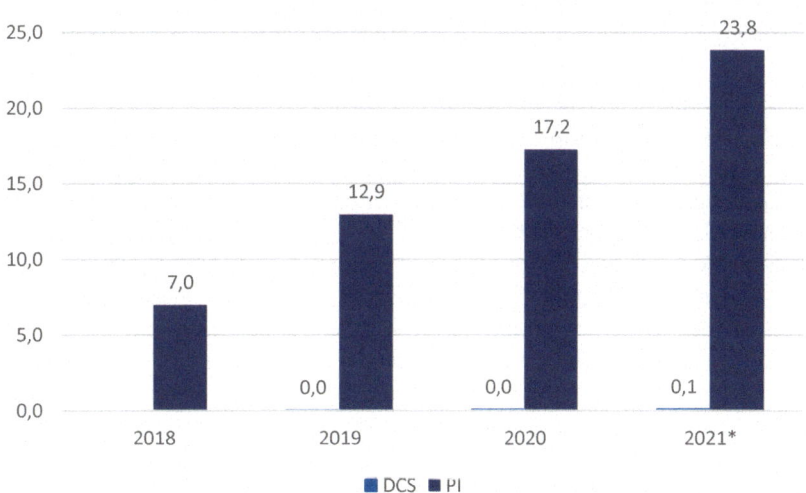

Fig. 14.2 Direct Credit Societies and Payments Institutions Loans Outstanding (BRL billion)—2018–2021* (*Source* BCB, IF.Data. * As of September 2021)

greater degree, financial institutions increasingly incorporate technological advances and digital processes:

> Thus, in the event of the establishment of a digital bank, depending on the business model one wishes to implement, one must obtain authorization to operate as a banking institution, that is, as a commercial or investment bank or, further, as an universal bank, authorized to operate with at least two operational portfolios, at least one of which must be a commercial or investment portfolio. (BCB, 2021)

In this sense, the proliferation of non-banking institutions that call themselves 'digital banks,' despite being registered in the BCB as a PI, DCS, among others, even without separate registration as a financial institution because they are part of an incumbent bank, is of concern. The 'danger' is that customers are induced to open 'digital' accounts at these institutions believing they have the legal guarantees required of banking institutions for a deposit account, such as coverage by the Credit Guarantee Fund (FGC), when in reality it may be 'only' a payment account and is therefore not covered by the FGC. The regulation was designed to protect payment accounts by requiring them to separate client's assets from the PI's assets, and establishing the mandatory allocation of these funds in an account at the BCB or in federal government bonds. However, market risks on these payment accounts prevail, since there may be price oscillations of the bonds that back such funds.

Thus, it is very important that the regulatory authorities discipline this misuse of the term 'digital bank' to respect communication, transparency, and the very safety of the huge flow of customers who are attracted by the appeals of the digital world. In fact, some jurisdictions, such as Hong Kong and Singapore, have already adopted digital banking licensing regimes (Zamil & Lawson, 2022). This is especially important given the fact that the denomination of a differentiated category of digital bank becomes less and less clear given the evolution of the banking digitalization phenomenon, widely adopted by established institutions.

Many analysts associate digital banking with the rule that deposit accounts must be opened and closed exclusively by electronic means. However, the regulations governing specific types of deposit accounts have been repealed, allowing these accounts to be opened and closed based on a request submitted by the customer through any channel made available by financial institutions for this purpose.

Despite the challenge in terms of cost, culture, and transformations in their infrastructures, established institutions have long included a strategy of operating closer to the digital world. These incumbent institutions have been investing for years in the development of their digital environments and have encouraged the migration of customers to this service channel. They created their own digital arms or presented themselves as a digital/digitized bank.

Assessing the Impacts of Fintechs on Brazilian Banks from 2018 to 2020

To assess the impact of fintechs on Brazilian banks, we asked whether or not the operations of fintechs and their business models have caused any changes in the financial results of traditional banks in Brazil? As previously discussed, there are many analyses that state that fintechs have the potential to cause significant impacts on banks' revenues, whether related to the provision of services such as bank fees or on intermediation revenues. For example, payment fintechs compete directly with banks offering accounts with no overdraft fees. Another example is the increasing number of DCS licenses, including those that are part of conglomerates led by PIs that are already established or created by important retail companies, could affect revenues related to intermediation.

The increasing number of clients that have been attracted to those new financial firms is usually highlighted as the main threat posed by fintechs. Table 14.2 shows the expressive growth in the number of fintech clients since 2018 in Brazil, with Nubank, Mercado Crédito, and PagBank (PagSeguro) rivaling large banks, leaving behind traditional institutions such as Votorantim and BMG. 'Digital banks' such as Original, Inter, and C6 also showed a very positive result.

These numbers only give insight into part of the story. It is important to ask to what extent the performance of fintechs has already impacted the competitive environment in Brazil and what impact this has had on the incumbents' revenues. The following section of this chapter will answer this question by focusing on PIs due to their greater representation in the fintech segment. We also take into account the growth of revenues from services and fees, from 2018 to 2020, of the five largest Brazilian universal banks: Banco do Brasil, Bradesco, Caixa, Itaú, and Santander. We use data disclosed in their respective balance sheets to compare these

Table 14.2 Number of clients by financial conglomerate (Million)*—2018–2021

Conglomerate	2018		2019		2020		2021	
	CCS	SCR	CCS	SCR	CCS	SCR	CCS	SCR
Established banks								
Caixa	88.1	17.6	92.5	20.0	142.4	22.8	143.6	23.8
Bradesco	84.3	41.2	87.3	47.2	90.4	43.8	91.3	44.1
Itaú	58.8	42.9	62.0	50.6	65.2	49.2	71.6	52.7
Banco do Brasil	59.8	23.2	62.9	28.2	65.3	29.8	66.1	33.1
Santander	36.2	17.6	39.3	23.3	42.5	24.9	49.7	25.8
Votorantim	0.9	4.0	3.5	4.1	9.5	4.4	17.0	5.3
BTG Pactual/PAN	0.1	0.0	0.2	0.1	0.5	0.1	11.7	9.6
Fintechs and 'Digital Banks'								
Nubank	–	–	–	0.0	10.1	–	47.9	23.5
Original	0.7	0.2	2.3	0.4	3.4	0.6	35.7	2.8
Mercado Crédito	–	–	–	–	–	–	27.5	1.8
PagBank	–	–	–	–	1.8	0.0	21.9	0.3
Inter	1.3	0.4	3.8	0.9	7.9	1.3	15.1	2.5
C6	–	–	0.7	0.1	3.7	1.2	12.2	4.4
BMG	0.1	3.9	0.7	4.6	2.1	5.1	5.7	5.2
Midway (Riachuelo)	0.0	7.6	0.0	11.4	0.0	10.8	1.1	10.5

Source Central Bank of Brazil. CCS accounts for Customers' Registration of the National Financial System. SCR accounts for the Credit Information System. *Brazilian population was 213 million in 2020, according to the estimations from the Brazilian Institute of Geography and Statistics

values to the statements of the five largest payment fintechs under the BCB umbrella: Cielo, Getnet, PagSeguro, Redecard, and Stone.

In our study, we assume that the sample is representative of the population, given that the selected entities represent more than 80% of the combined revenues in the respective segments in the analysis period. We analyzed data between 2018 and 2020 because 2018 is when most of the relevant PIs obtained registration with BCB, and 2020 is the last year for which there exists a full year of data available. At the time of our analysis, data from 2021 only covers three quarters of the year, making comparison with previous years problematic.

In addition, our choice to work with the data on revenues from the provision of services, fees, and tariffs in an open manner assumes that the scope of activity of these institutions is often broader than the one allowed to PI, given the regulations in force. In doing so, we attempt to identify the sources of similar revenues and estimate the real competitive space in operational terms that could be affected by the entrants—i.e., the relevant market—in the current state of the legislation that regulates the segment.

From the total volume of banking revenues under analysis, we estimate the revenue share from services that would be not impacted by the competition of PIs—such as management fees earned by the investment of third-party resources—and the one that would be subject to the effects of competition—such as overdraft fees. For payment fintechs, as the openness of the available data is limited, the estimate considered the total reported income from the provision of services, fees, and tariffs, which represents a significant part of the operational results of these institutions.

The lack of standardization of the information disclosed in the balance sheets of the sample banks made it necessary to consolidate the data into two main groups that would represent sources of funds similar to those obtained by PIs: those derived from credit and debit card incomes and those from service packages, such as expenditures associated with the maintenance of deposit accounts.

Starting from this simplification, our analysis shows that the effort of banks to obtain alternative sources of revenue within the provision of services in the last few years was not uniform among the largest institutions (see Fig. 14.3). Private banks such as Itaú, Bradesco, and Santander are more reliant on revenues from cards and deposit accounts, while public banks such as Banco do Brasil and Caixa are more dependent on fund management fees. All banks earn a lot of money from the maintenance of deposit accounts, therefore products such as 'free tariff and fee packages' have the potential to put a part of the revenues of traditional banks in jeopardy.

The revenues of the five largest banks most likely to be impacted—cards, deposit accounts and services—and those least likely—fund management, brokerage, and others—by PIs fintech competition did not show a clear tendency of decrease between 2018 and 2020. The values of both aggregates rose in 2019 but fell again in 2020 (see Fig. 14.4).

To assess the susceptibility of banks to competition from PIs, we built a simple indicator that consists of the volume of revenues of banks whose origin is outside the activities and services under direct competition from IP over bank revenues that will be subject to competitive pressures. The higher the indicator, the less exposed are banks to this threat, since the smaller is the share of revenues that compete with the activities of these fintechs vis-à-vis the others. Segmenting this result by shareholder

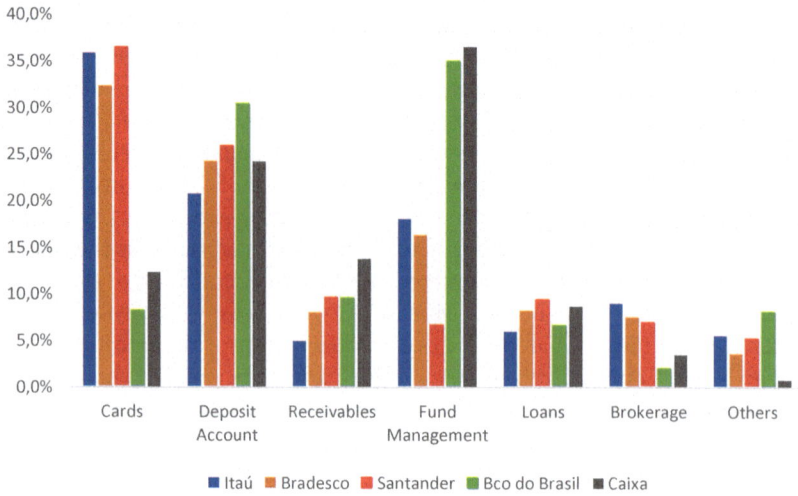

Fig. 14.3 Distribution of main revenues with fees and the provision of services from the 5 largest Brazilian banks (%)—2020 (*Source* Authors' elaboration based on banks' financial statements)

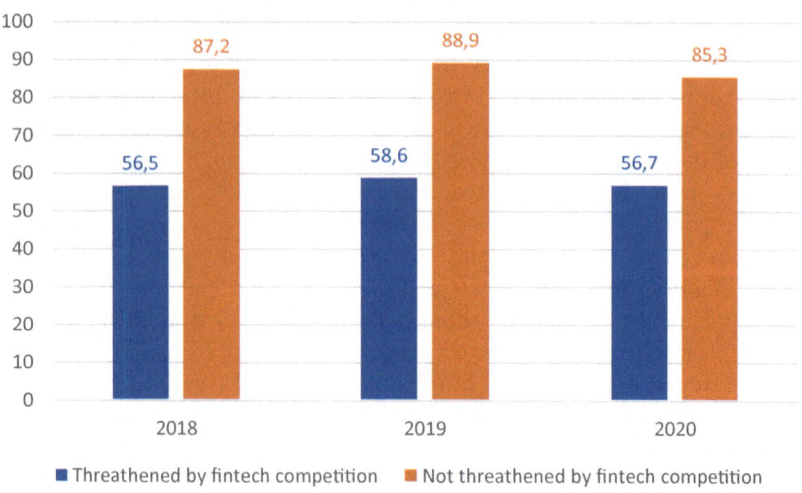

Fig. 14.4 Revenues from the provision of services and fees from the 5 major Brazilian banks (BRL Billion)—2018–2020 (*Source* Authors' elaboration based on banks' financial statements)

control, we observe that private banks kept less than half of their revenues outside this scope (47% on average) and public banks were less susceptible to the impact of fintechs (106% on average) until **2020** (Fig. 14.5).

In fact, the biggest source of revenue for public banks in Brazil comes from investment funds management. In the case of Caixa Econômica Federal, most of its funds come from social/governmental origins and are not subject to competition of fintechs or even their banking peers. As for the three largest private institutions in the country, the revenues obtained from cards (credit and debit) are the most relevant and suffer direct competition from PIs.

It is worth noting, however, that among the five largest payment fintechs, three of them are part of the holding company of these banks: Cielo is controlled by Bradesco and Banco do Brasil, Redecard by Itaú, and GetNet by Santander. Moreover, part of the competition might come from digital banks owned by the very same major institutions in their

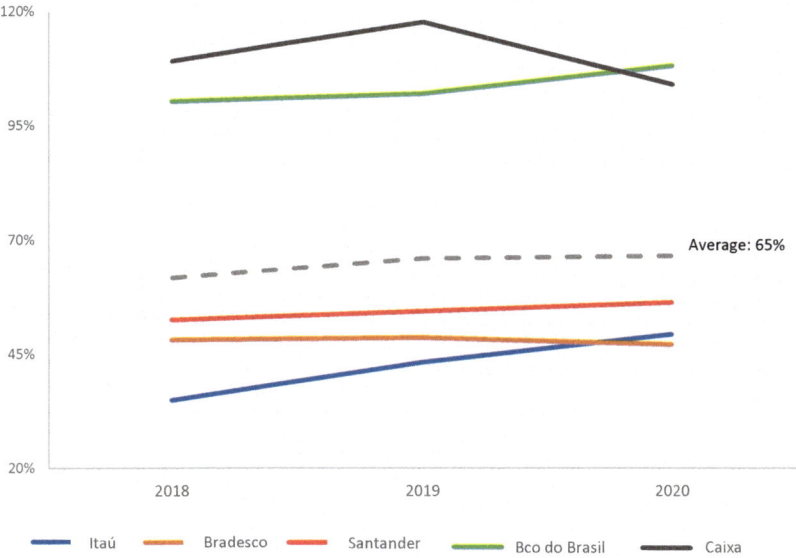

Fig. 14.5 Ratio between Revenues threatened and not threatened by payment fintechs (%)—2018–2020 (*Source* Authors' elaboration based on banks' financial statements)

conglomerates, such as *iti* in the case of Itaú and *Next* in the case of Bradesco.

When analyzing the revenues of the five largest PIs in the period, we find the figures of the industry leaders are very small vis-à-vis the equivalent revenues of the largest banks (see Table 14.3). Independent PIs reached only 3.7% on average, but it has been growing over the period, increasing from 3.3% in 2018 to 4.1% in 2020. Moreover, as shown in Fig. 14.6, the average share of payment fintechs' revenues over the share of revenues within competition with banks stood at 27.9% of the total.

When analyzed from the standpoint of market-share gain, analyses that highlight the threat that payment fintechs can have on the revenues from services and fees do not seem to find empirical support in the numbers. Despite a growing number of fintech clients, they still have a long road to travel regarding revenues and profitability. Even if the three largest IP owned by banks were considered as competitors, almost 70% of competitive revenues would still be unaffected by fintechs. At first glance, this may seem promising in terms of revenue growth for this segment, but it is also doubtful, given the regulatory limitations of the playing field and the challenges to the payments market that lie ahead.

Many of the trends that have affected the behavior of revenues from these services for traditional banking institutions—debit and credit cards' charges, competition narrowing operational margins, and the increase in

Table 14.3 Revenues from fees and the provision of services (BRL Million)

Payment Institution	2018	2019	2020
Controlled by banks	13,701	11,582	10,063
Cielo	6450	5301	5206
Redecard	5164	4259	2957
GetNet	2087	2022	1900
Independent	4701	5313	5780
Stone	973	1471	1772
PagSeguro	3728	3842	4008
5 largest PIs	18,402	16,895	15,843
5 largest banks	140,972	147,533	141,972
% share 5 largest PIs	13.1%	11.5%	11.2%
% share independent PIs	3.3%	3.6%	4.1%

Source Authors' elaboration based on the financial statements of payment institutions

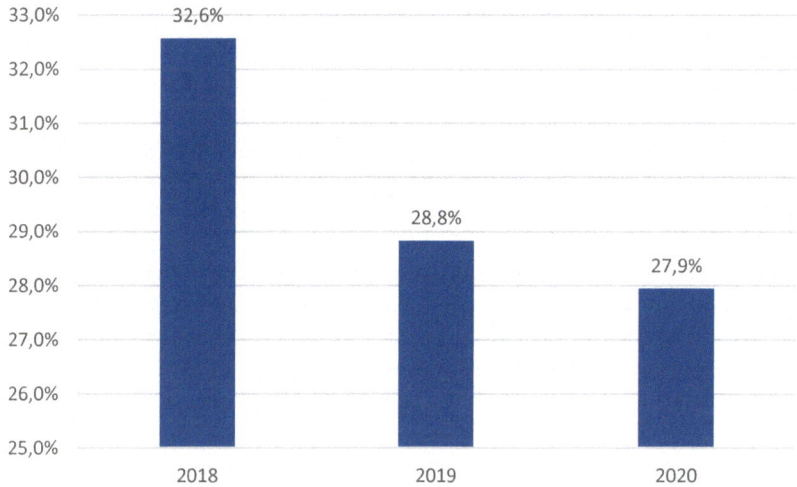

Fig. 14.6 Revenues of the 5 largest Payment Institutions (% revenues threatening traditional banks)—2018–2020 (*Source* Authors' elaboration based on banks' financial statements)

the number and in the reach of digital banks—can also affect the revenues of payment institutions.

These results, which show an absolute and relative drop in revenues, raise doubts as to the success of the investment strategies of large international investors, as well as the strong movement of mergers, acquisitions, and partnerships that have been occurring in recent years in the fintech sector, as frequently reported in the press. But it is possible that the greater interest of these investors may be related to the operationalization of open banking—or open finance—by the BCB.

Nevertheless, it is unreasonable to ignore that every evolution created by new fintechs in recent years has resulted in an acceleration in investments in the digital agenda by the traditional banking industry for catching up (Febraban, 2021). The impact of these adjustments on the established banks' spending is not small, though it is difficult to quantify that, and will still require significant efforts to adapt these institutions to the new IT ecosystem.

There is also a new challenge for traditional banks, but in this case, it is also a challenge for fintechs: the consolidation of Pix—the fast (nearly instantaneous) free retail payments system. It will require a lot of skills for institutions to recover the revenue lost by the free nature of most Pix transactions. The balance sheets published for the first quarter of 2021 of the largest banks already highlight its effects as revenues from fees charged for payments transfers are shrinking and can impact similar revenues of fintechs in the same fashion.

Finally, over the next few years, open banking will be operational, with 'the possibility for customers of financial products and services to allow the sharing of their information between different institutions authorized by the Central Bank and the movement of their bank accounts from different platforms and not only through the application or website of the bank' (BCB, 2021). This sharing, once authorized by the customer, will be accessed via application programming interfaces (API) that the institutions interested and authorized by the BCB must create to enable communication between their platforms.

Open Banking strengthens the power of the customer by giving him the possibility of having a larger base of comparison of products and services to be offered in the open system. At the same time, it creates a large market for institutions authorized to operate by the BCB to offer not only a specific financial service, as most fintechs do today in the country, but a set of products on a single platform that is easily accessible by customers.

The first experience of open banking in the world started in 2018 in the British financial sector. Open banking in the United Kingdom has represented a new interest among local fintechs in carrying out the so-called rebundling. This initiative is a regrouping by fintechs of specific niches of activity on which these institutions have tried to gain market share from traditional banks (a movement known as unbundling).

The customers' allowance of sharing their information stimulates the competition not only in payment, credit, or management sectors, but in the provision of a set of products and services. One can expect an increase in competition due to open banking if fintechs offer more favorable terms for products and services that are now offered by traditional banks. New opportunities may arise for fintechs in Brazil, but it is still too early to predict their success, their effect on incumbent institutions, and the ability of entering firms to compete in this new environment.

FINAL REMARKS

This chapter characterizes fintechs within the Brazilian regulatory framework and provides a preliminary assessment of the potential impacts and competitive pressures arising from the introduction of fintechs in Brazil on the revenues of traditional banks from 2018 to 2020.

It was shown that, according to the regulations of the National Monetary Council and the Central Bank of Brazil, fintechs, notably payment institutions (PIs), direct credit societies (DCSs), and peer-to-peer loan companies (P2Ps). The so-called 'digital banks' are not properly treated in Brazilian regulation and licensing requirements, being often a mere adaptation of existing structures (e.g., traditional banking licenses or financial conglomerates of payment institutions and consumer credit societies) and marketing strategies of incumbent banks.

With the available data, we conclude that significant changes in the results reported by Brazilian banks in recent years due to increased competition from fintechs have not yet been noticed. Although there is some anecdotal evidence to suggest that payment institutions are already putting pressure on the service revenues of the major private banks—especially in the credit card segment—the effects are not yet significant enough to confirm that this is an unequivocal trend. Defining the relevant objects of competition is of paramount importance. Though fintechs are attracting new clients, this has not jeopardized the revenues of traditional banks yet.

This is especially because the largest financial institutions in the Brazilian banking sector have moved to introduce innovations, such as digital accounts and the digitalization of their processes, data, and systems, reducing eventual gaps that have been occupied by fintechs in the period—hence the diffusion of 'digital banking.' Another strategy adopted by incumbents has been the acquisition or creation of fintechs, as in the case of three major payment institutions owned by Banco do Brasil, Bradesco, Itaú, and Santander.

In this sense, the analysis presented here offers elements confirming the argument made by Navaretti et al. (2017, p. 19; emphasis added), who stated that:

> Fintechs enhance competition in financial markets, provide services that traditional financial institutions do less efficiently or do not do at all, and widen the pool of users of such services. But *they will not replace banks*

in most of their key functions. In most cases, fintechs provide a more efficient way to do the same old things. Yet *banks are well placed to adopt technological innovations, and do the old things in the new way themselves.*

In practice, the impacts of fintechs may occur mainly on incumbents' expenses, requiring high expenditures to adapt these institutions to the new ecosystem, either through investments in R&D—for instance to adapt legacy systems—or through mergers and acquisitions. The operationalization of open banking can also generate competitive impacts with the possibility of entering firms expanding their portfolio and capturing customers in a more consolidated way, offering a wider range of services and products on platforms that allow users to choose alternatives that are closer to their needs and at lower costs. Thus, the future of competition between fintechs and established financial institutions in Brazil may see an increase with the even more intense diffusion of technological innovations and the deepening of regulatory changes that facilitate the entry of new players in the industry.

References

BCB. (2020). Fintechs de crédito e bancos digitais. [Credit fintechs and digital banks]. *Estudo Especial* 89. Available at: https://www.bcb.gov.br/conteudo/relatorioinflacao/EstudosEspeciais/EE089_Fintechs_de_credito_e_bancos_digitais.pdf

BCB. (2021). Instituições de Pagamento. [Payment Institutions]. Available at: https://www.bcb.gov.br/estabilidadefinanceira/instituicaopagamento

Bofondi, M., & Gobbi, G. (2017). The big promise of fintech. *European Economy—Banks, Regulation, and the Real Sector, 17*(2), 107–20.

Brasil. (2013). Law No. 12,865, of October 9, 2013, which regulates the payment schemes and payment institutions that hereby become part of the Brazilian Payments System.

Caciatori Jr., I. (2020). *Competitiveness of incumbent, digitalized, and digital banks: A comparative study of financial innovation in Brazil* [Doctoral dissertation, Universidade Federal do Paraná]. Repositório Institucional da Universidade Federal do Paraná.

Crisanto, J. C., Ehrentraud, J., & Fabian, M. (2021). Big techs in finance: regulatory approaches and policy options. *Financial Stability Institute Briefs* 12.

Chu, Y., & Wei, J. (2021). Fintech entry and credit market competition. *Mimeo.* https://doi.org/10.2139/ssrn.3827598

Febraban. (2021). Pesquisa FEBRABAN de Tecnologia Bancária 2021. Febraban. https://febraban.org.br/pagina/3106/48/pt-br/pesquisa
Fintechlab. (2020). *Radar FintechLab 2020.* São Paulo: FintechLab. https://fin techlab.com.br/index.php/2020/08/25/edicao-2020-do-radar-fintechlab-detecta-270-novas-fintechs-em-um-ano/
Financial Stability Board. (2019). FinTech and market structure in financial services: Market developments and potential financial stability implications. Financial Stability Board.
International Organization of Securities Commissions. (2017). IOSCO Research Report on Financial Technologies (Fintech). https://www.iosco.org/library/pubdocs/pdf/IOSCOPD554.pdf
Martins, N. M., Sarno, P. M., Boechat, D., & Macahyba, L. (2022). Taxa de lucro dos bancos no Brasil: evolução e características no período 2015–2020. *Análise Econômica,* to be published.
Moreira, T. (2019, March 27). Banco Digital é caminho para compensar queda de taxas, diz Bradesco. [Digital bank is a way to compensate the decrease in interest rates, says Bradesco]. Valor Econômico. https://www.valor.com.br/financas/6183121/banco-digital-e-caminho-para-compensar-queda-de-taxas-diz-bradesco
Navaretti, G. B., Calzolari, G., & Pozzolo, A. F. (2017). Fintech and banking. Friends or foes? *European Economy—Banks, Regulation, and the Real Sector, 17*(2), 9–30.
Philippon, T. (2016). The fintech opportunity. NBER Working Paper 22476. https://doi.org/10.3386/w22476
Ragazzi, A. P. (2018, September 12). Não vamos criar um novo banco 100% digital, diz presidente do Itaú. [We will not create a new 100% digital bank, says Itaú's CEO]. Folha de São Paulo. https://www1.folha.uol.com.br/mercado/2018/09/nao-vamos-criar-um-novo-banco-100-digital-diz-presidente-do-itau.shtml
Restoy, F. (2021). Fintech regulation: how to achieve a level playing field. *Financial Stability Institute Occasional Paper 17.*
Singh, R., Malik, G., & Jain, V. (2021). FinTech effect: Measuring impact of FinTech adoption on banks' profitability. *International Journal of Management Practice, 14*(4), 411–427. https://doi.org/10.1504/IJMP.2021.116587
Stulz, R. (2019). FinTech, BigTech, and the Future of Banks. NBER Working Paper 26312. https://doi.org/10.3386/w26312
Thakor, A. V. (2020). Fintech and banking: What do we know? *Journal of Financial Intermediation, 41,* 100833. https://doi.org/10.1016/j.jfi.2019.100833

US Treasury. (2018). A financial system that creates economic opportunities: Nonbank financials, fintech, and innovation. https://home.treasury.gov/sites/default/files/2018-08/A-Financial-System-that-Creates-Economic-Opportunities---Nonbank-Financials-Fintech-and-Innovation.pdf

World Economic Forum. (2017). Beyond fintech: A pragmatic assessment of disruptive potential in financial services. https://www3.weforum.org/docs/Beyond_Fintech_-_A_Pragmatic_Assessment_of_Disruptive_Potential_in_Financial_Services.pdf

Zamil, R., & Lawson, A. (2022). Gatekeeping the gatekeepers: when big techs and fintechs own banks—Benefits, risks and policy options. *Financial Stability Institute Insights*, *39*.

Zetzsche, D. A., & Dewi, T. R. (2018). The paradoxical case against interest rate caps for microfinance—And: How FinTech and RegTech resolve the dilemma. University of Luxembourg Law Working 2018-003. https://doi.org/10.2139/ssrn.3159202

Zhu, Y., & Lu, J. (2022). FinTech and Bank Intermediation—Evidence from the Deposit Market in China. https://doi.org/10.2139/ssrn.4030108

Index

© The Editor(s) (if applicable) and The Author(s), under exclusive
license to Springer Nature Switzerland AG 2023
T. Walker et al. (eds.), *The Fintech Disruption*, Palgrave Studies
in Financial Services Technology,
https://Doi.org/10.1007/978-3-031-23069-1

373

Printed by Printforce, United Kingdom